Nissan Murano Automotive Repair Manual

by Tim Imhoff
and John H Haynes
Member of the Guild of Motoring Writers

Models covered:

All Nissan Murano models - 2003 through 2010

(72025 - 7R1)

ABCDE
FGHIJ
KLMNO
PQR

Haynes Publishing Group
Sparkford Nr Yeovil
Somerset BA22 7JJ England

Haynes North America, Inc
861 Lawrence Drive
Newbury Park
California 91320 USA

Acknowledgements

Wiring diagrams originated exclusively for Haynes North America, Inc. by Valley Forge Technical Information Services.

© **Haynes North America, Inc. 2011**

With permission from J.H. Haynes & Co. Ltd.

A book in the Haynes Automotive Repair Manual Series

Printed in the U.S.A.

ISBN-13: 978-1-56392-921-2
ISBN-10: 1-56392-921-X

Library of Congress Control Number 2011930175

While every attempt is made to ensure that the information in this manual is correct, no liability can be accepted by the authors or publishers for loss, damage or injury caused by any errors in, or omissions from, the information given.

Contents

22

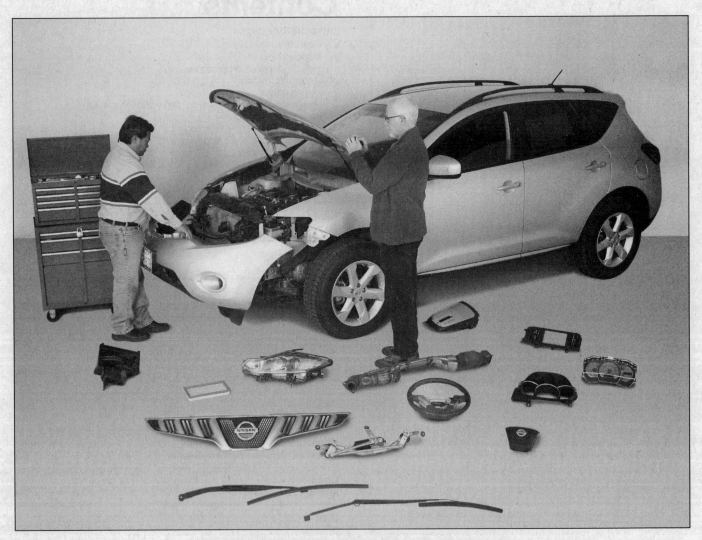

Haynes photographer and mechanic with a 2009 Nissan Murano

About this manual

Its purpose

The purpose of this manual is to help you get the best value from your vehicle. It can do so in several ways. It can help you decide what work must be done, even if you choose to have it done by a dealer service department or a repair shop; it provides information and procedures for routine maintenance and servicing; and it offers diagnostic and repair procedures to follow when trouble occurs.

We hope you use the manual to tackle the work yourself. For many simpler jobs, doing it yourself may be quicker than arranging an appointment to get the vehicle into a shop and making the trips to leave it and pick it up. More importantly, a lot of money can be saved by avoiding the expense the shop must pass on to you to cover its labor and overhead costs. An added benefit is the sense of satisfaction and accomplishment that you feel after doing the job yourself.

Using the manual

The manual is divided into Chapters. Each Chapter is divided into numbered Sections, which are headed in bold type between horizontal lines. Each Section consists of consecutively numbered paragraphs.

At the beginning of each numbered Section you will be referred to any illustrations which apply to the procedures in that Section. The reference numbers used in illustration captions pinpoint the pertinent Section and the Step within that Section. That is, illustration 3.2 means the illustration refers to Section 3 and Step (or paragraph) 2 within that Section.

Procedures, once described in the text, are not normally repeated. When it's necessary to refer to another Chapter, the reference will be given as Chapter and Section number. Cross references given without use of the word "Chapter" apply to Sections and/or paragraphs in the same Chapter. For example, "see Section 8" means in the same Chapter.

References to the left or right side of the vehicle assume you are sitting in the driver's seat, facing forward.

Even though we have prepared this manual with extreme care, neither the publisher nor the author can accept responsibility for any errors in, or omissions from, the information given.

NOTE

A **Note** provides information necessary to properly complete a procedure or information which will make the procedure easier to understand.

CAUTION

A **Caution** provides a special procedure or special steps which must be taken while completing the procedure where the Caution is found. Not heeding a Caution can result in damage to the assembly being worked on.

WARNING

A **Warning** provides a special procedure or special steps which must be taken while completing the procedure where the Warning is found. Not heeding a Warning can result in personal injury.

Introduction to the Nissan Murano

The transversely-mounted 3.5L V6 engine used in these models is equipped with a sequential multi-port electronic fuel injection system.

The engine transmits power to the front wheels through a continuously variable automatic transaxle (CVT) via independent driveaxles.

On AWD models, the rear wheels are also propelled by way of a transfer case, driveshaft, rear differential and two rear driveaxles.

The Murano has a steel uni-body and four-wheel independent suspension. The rack-and-pinion steering unit is mounted behind the engine. It has power assist as standard equipment.

All models are equipped with power assisted front and rear disc brakes. An anti-lock braking system is standard equipment on all models.

Vehicle identification numbers

Modifications are a continuing and unpublicized process in vehicle manufacturing. Since spare parts manuals and lists are compiled on a numerical basis, the individual vehicle numbers are essential to correctly identify the component required.

Vehicle Identification Number (VIN)

This very important identification number is located on a plate attached to the dashboard inside the windshield on the driver's side of the vehicle (see illustration). The VIN also appears on the Vehicle Certificate of Title and Registration. It contains information such as where and when the vehicle was manufactured, the model year and the body style.

VIN engine and model year codes

Two particularly important pieces of information found in the VIN are the engine code and the model year code. Counting from the left, the engine code letter designation is the 4th character and the model year code designation is the 10th character.

On the models covered by this manual the engine code is:

A .... VQ35DE 3.5L DOHC V6

On the models covered by this manual the model year codes are:

3 2003
4 2004
5 2005
6 2006
7 2007
8 2008
9 2009
A 2010

The Vehicle Identification Number (VIN) is visible through the driver's side of the windshield

The Manufacturer's Certification label is affixed to the drivers side door post

The Engine Identification Number is stamped on the left end (driver's side) of the engine block, near the transaxle (2.4L engine shown)

The transaxle ID number is located on top of the transaxle bellhousing, near the shift cable bracket

Manufacturer's Certification Regulation label

The manufacturer's Certification Regulation label is attached to the driver's side door post **(see illustration)**. The label contains the name of the manufacturer, the month and year of production, the Gross Vehicle Weight Rating (GVWR), the Gross Axle Weight Rating (GAWR) and the certification statement.

Engine identification number

The engine code number is located at the left end (driver's side) of the engine, just above the transaxle bellhousing **(see illustration)**.

Transaxle identification number

The transaxle identification number is stamped on top of the bellhousing **(see illustration)**.

Vehicle Emissions Control Information (VECI) label

The emissions control information label is found on the bottom side of the hood. This label contains information on the emissions control equipment installed on the vehicle **(see illustration)**.

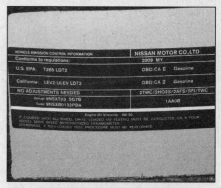

The Vehicle Emissions Control Information (VECI) label is located on the bottom side of the hood

Recall information

Vehicle recalls are carried out by the manufacturer in the rare event of a possible safety-related defect. The vehicle's registered owner is contacted at the address on file at the Department of Motor Vehicles and given the details of the recall. Remedial work is carried out free of charge at a dealer service department.

If you are the new owner of a used vehicle which was subject to a recall and you want to be sure that the work has been carried out, it's best to contact a dealer service department and ask about your individual vehicle - you'll need to furnish them your Vehicle Identification Number (VIN).

The table below is based on information provided by the National Highway Traffic Safety Administration (NHTSA), the body which oversees vehicle recalls in the United States. The recall database is updated constantly. For the latest information on vehicle recalls, check the NHTSA website at www.nhtsa.gov, or call the NHTSA hotline at 1-888-327-4236.

Recall date	Recall campaign number	Model(s) affected	Concern
MAR 24, 2003	03V123000	2003 Murano	On some models, the nut that attaches the transmission gear selector shaft to the control valve lever in the transmission may not be adequately tightened. This could result in the transmission not actually being in the gear indicated by the gear selector lever. In addition, the transmission position display in the instrument panel may not be on or may be incorrect. If the gear displayed is different from the gear engaged, this could result in unexpected vehicle movement and a crash.
NOV 04, 2003	03V455000	2003 Murano	On some models, the circuit board for the crank position sensor or cam position sensor may have an improper solder joint due to solder deformation caused by heat stress accelerated by the existence of flux residue during the soldering process. This could cause the "Service Engine Soon" warning light to come on, create a no start condition, cause reduced engine power, or cause the engine to stop running without warning during vehicle operation, which could result in a crash.
JUL 12, 2005	05V319000	2003, 2004, 2005 Murano	On some models, there is a possibility that a wire breaking inside the alternator could stop the battery from charging. If this happens, the charger warning and brake warning lamps will immediately come on and the battery will begin to discharge. After a short time, the engine will go into a "fail safe" condition which will limit vehicle speed. The engine will stop running which could result in a crash.

Recall date	Recall campaign number	Model(s) affected	Concern
JAN 09, 2006	06V003000	2003, 2004, 2005, 2006 Murano	On some models, due to the location of the forward edge of the fuel tank, in the event that a vehicle front tire runs over a small, sharp object in the road, catches it and propels it towards the rear of the vehicle, it may strike and puncture the fuel tank. A punctured tank could increase the risk of a fire.
FEB 09, 2006	06V048000	2003, 2004, 2005, 2006 Murano	On some models, in certain high speed frontal crashes, the webbing of a rear outboard seat belt may contact the rear seat back hinge where it can be cut by the sharp edge of the metal portion of the hinge. If the webbing is completely separated, it can increase the risk of injury to an occupant in a crash.
FEB 14, 2006	06V054000	2005 Murano	On some models, a fitting for vapor recirculation, which is welded on the fuel tank, may come off the fuel tank because incorrect material was used. This could result in the malfunction indicator light in the instrument panel coming on and may result in some fuel leakage. Fuel leakage, in the presence of an ignition source, could result in a fire.
OCT 18, 2006	06V401000	2005, 2006 Murano	Some models fail to conform to the requirements of Federal Motor Vehicle Safety Standard no. 114, "theft protection." During an inspection of some vehicles at the assembly plant, it was found that the steering wheel was locked with the ignition knob in the "off" position but the vehicle transmission not being in the "Park" position. If the key is turned to the "off" position without the transmission being in the "Park" position, it is possible that the steering wheel can lock when turned to the right.
FEB 12, 2008	08V066000	2009 Murano	On some models, due to incorrect software programming, the Airbag Control Unit (ACU) may cause the passenger airbag not to operate as designed if the vehicle battery becomes significantly discharged. This could result in the passenger airbag not inflating in a crash in which it was designed to do so, and increasing the risk of injury.
OCT 02, 2008	08V521000	2007, 2008, 2009 Murano	On some models equipped with Continental Automotive Systems' Occupant Classification System (OCS) control units, a varistor in the OCS control unit located in the passenger seat cushion may have been manufactured out of specification. Under certain conditions, this could cause an interruption of signal between the OCS and the Airbag Control Unit (ACU). This could result in the passenger airbag being suppressed which could fail to provide adequate protection in the event of a crash.

Recall date	Recall campaign number	Model(s) affected	Concern
MAY 14, 2009	09V169000	2003 to 2007 Murano	On some models, the intake air ducts, which are connected to the intermediate resonator in the air intake system of the engine, may separate from the resonator with engine movement. This separation occurs due to the premature aging of the material used in the intake air ducts which causes excessive shrinking. The engine may stall, increasing the risk of a crash.
OCT 01, 2009	09V393000	2008, 2009, 2010 Murano	On some models originally sold in or currently registered in the states of Connecticut, Delaware, Iowa, Illinois, Indiana, Massachusetts, Maine, Maryland, Michigan, Minnesota, Missouri, New Hampshire, New Jersey, New York, Ohio, Pennsylvania, Rhode Island, Vermont, Washington D.C., West Virginia and Wisconsin, the material in the nut used to secure the sensor-transmitter of the Tire Pressure Monitoring System (TPMS) may corrode and potentially crack in areas with heavy concentrations of road salt. If this occurs, the nut may come out of the sensor-transmitter and the TPMS lamp will illuminate. If the TPMS lamp is disregarded and the vehicle continues to be driven in this condition, the tire will quickly lose air pressure at a consistent rate, resulting in a flat tire, increasing the risk of a crash.

Buying parts

Replacement parts are available from many sources, which generally fall into one of two categories - authorized dealer parts departments and independent retail auto parts stores. Our advice concerning these parts is as follows:

Retail auto parts stores: Good auto parts stores will stock frequently needed components which wear out relatively fast, such as clutch components, exhaust systems, brake parts, tune-up parts, etc. These stores often supply new or reconditioned parts on an exchange basis, which can save a considerable amount of money. Discount auto parts stores are often very good places to buy materials and parts needed for general vehicle maintenance such as oil, grease, filters, spark plugs, belts, touch-up paint, bulbs, etc. They also usually sell tools and general accessories, have convenient hours, charge lower prices and can often be found not far from home.

Authorized dealer parts department: This is the best source for parts which are unique to the vehicle and not generally available elsewhere (such as major engine parts, transmission parts, trim pieces, etc.).

Warranty information: If the vehicle is still covered under warranty, be sure that any replacement parts purchased - regardless of the source - do not invalidate the warranty!

To be sure of obtaining the correct parts, have engine and chassis numbers available and, if possible, take the old parts along for positive identification.

Maintenance techniques, tools and working facilities

Maintenance techniques

There are a number of techniques involved in maintenance and repair that will be referred to throughout this manual. Application of these techniques will enable the home mechanic to be more efficient, better organized and capable of performing the various tasks properly, which will ensure that the repair job is thorough and complete.

Fasteners

Fasteners are nuts, bolts, studs and screws used to hold two or more parts together. There are a few things to keep in mind when working with fasteners. Almost all of them use a locking device of some type, either a lockwasher, locknut, locking tab or thread adhesive. All threaded fasteners should be clean and straight, with undamaged threads and undamaged corners on the hex head where the wrench fits. Develop the habit of replacing all damaged nuts and bolts with new ones. Special locknuts with nylon or fiber inserts can only be used once. If they are removed, they lose their locking ability and must be replaced with new ones.

Rusted nuts and bolts should be treated with a penetrating fluid to ease removal and prevent breakage. Some mechanics use turpentine in a spout-type oil can, which works quite well. After applying the rust penetrant, let it work for a few minutes before trying to loosen the nut or bolt. Badly rusted fasteners may have to be chiseled or sawed off or removed with a special nut breaker, available at tool stores.

If a bolt or stud breaks off in an assembly, it can be drilled and removed with a special tool commonly available for this purpose. Most automotive machine shops can perform this task, as well as other repair procedures, such as the repair of threaded holes that have been stripped out.

Flat washers and lockwashers, when removed from an assembly, should always be replaced exactly as removed. Replace any damaged washers with new ones. Never use a lockwasher on any soft metal surface (such as aluminum), thin sheet metal or plastic.

Fastener sizes

For a number of reasons, automobile manufacturers are making wider and wider use of metric fasteners. Therefore, it is important to be able to tell the difference between standard (sometimes called U.S. or SAE) and metric hardware, since they cannot be interchanged.

All bolts, whether standard or metric, are sized according to diameter, thread pitch and length. For example, a standard 1/2 - 13 x 1 bolt is 1/2 inch in diameter, has 13 threads per inch and is 1 inch long. An M12 - 1.75 x 25 metric bolt is 12 mm in diameter, has a thread pitch of 1.75 mm (the distance between threads) and is 25 mm long. The two bolts are nearly identical, and easily confused, but they are not interchangeable.

In addition to the differences in diameter, thread pitch and length, metric and standard bolts can also be distinguished by examining the bolt heads. To begin with, the distance across the flats on a standard bolt head is measured in inches, while the same dimension on a metric bolt is sized in millimeters (the same is true for nuts). As a result, a standard wrench should not be used on a metric bolt and a metric wrench should not be used on a standard bolt. Also, most standard bolts have slashes radiating out from the center of the head to denote the grade or strength of the bolt, which is an indication of the amount of torque that can be applied to it. The greater the number of slashes, the greater the strength of the bolt. Grades 0 through 5 are commonly used on automobiles. Metric bolts have a property class (grade) number, rather than a slash, molded into their heads to indicate bolt strength. In this case, the higher the number, the stronger the bolt. Property class numbers 8.8, 9.8 and 10.9 are commonly used on automobiles.

Strength markings can also be used to distinguish standard hex nuts from metric hex nuts. Many standard nuts have dots stamped into one side, while metric nuts are marked with a number. The greater the number of

dots, or the higher the number, the greater the strength of the nut.

Metric studs are also marked on their ends according to property class (grade). Larger studs are numbered (the same as metric bolts), while smaller studs carry a geometric code to denote grade.

It should be noted that many fasteners, especially Grades 0 through 2, have no distinguishing marks on them. When such is the case, the only way to determine whether it is standard or metric is to measure the thread pitch or compare it to a known fastener of the same size.

Standard fasteners are often referred to as SAE, as opposed to metric. However, it should be noted that SAE technically refers to a non-metric fine thread fastener only. Coarse thread non-metric fasteners are referred to as USS sizes.

Since fasteners of the same size (both standard and metric) may have different

strength ratings, be sure to reinstall any bolts, studs or nuts removed from your vehicle in their original locations. Also, when replacing a fastener with a new one, make sure that the new one has a strength rating equal to or greater than the original.

Tightening sequences and procedures

Most threaded fasteners should be tightened to a specific torque value (torque is the twisting force applied to a threaded component such as a nut or bolt). Overtightening the fastener can weaken it and cause it to break, while undertightening can cause it to eventually come loose. Bolts, screws and studs, depending on the material they are made of and their thread diameters, have specific torque values, many of which are noted in the Specifications at the beginning of each Chapter. Be sure to follow the torque recommendations closely. For fasteners not assigned a

Grade 1 or 2   Grade 5   Grade 8

Bolt strength marking (standard/SAE/USS; bottom - metric)

Grade	Identification	Grade	Identification
Hex Nut Grade 5	3 Dots	Hex Nut Property Class 9	Arabic 9
Hex Nut Grade 8	6 Dots	Hex Nut Property Class 10	Arabic 10

Standard hex nut strength markings

Metric hex nut strength markings

Class 10.9   Class 9.8   Class 8.8

Metric stud strength markings

specific torque, a general torque value chart is presented here as a guide. These torque values are for dry (unlubricated) fasteners threaded into steel or cast iron (not aluminum). As was previously mentioned, the size and grade of a fastener determine the amount of torque that can safely be applied to it. The figures listed here are approximate for Grade 2 and Grade 3 fasteners. Higher grades can tolerate higher torque values.

Fasteners laid out in a pattern, such as cylinder head bolts, oil pan bolts, differential cover bolts, etc., must be loosened or tightened in sequence to avoid warping the component. This sequence will normally be shown in the appropriate Chapter. If a specific pattern is not given, the following procedures can be used to prevent warping.

Initially, the bolts or nuts should be assembled finger-tight only. Next, they should be tightened one full turn each, in a crisscross or diagonal pattern. After each one has been tightened one full turn, return to the first one and tighten them all one-half turn, following the same pattern. Finally, tighten each of them one-quarter turn at a time until each fastener has been tightened to the proper torque. To loosen and remove the fasteners, the procedure would be reversed.

Component disassembly

Component disassembly should be done with care and purpose to help ensure that

Metric thread sizes	Ft-lbs	Nm
M-6	6 to 9	9 to 12
M-8	14 to 21	19 to 28
M-10	28 to 40	38 to 54
M-12	50 to 71	68 to 96
M-14	80 to 140	109 to 154
Pipe thread sizes		
1/8	5 to 8	7 to 10
1/4	12 to 18	17 to 24
3/8	22 to 33	30 to 44
1/2	25 to 35	34 to 47
U.S. thread sizes		
1/4 - 20	6 to 9	9 to 12
5/16 - 18	12 to 18	17 to 24
5/16 - 24	14 to 20	19 to 27
3/8 - 16	22 to 32	30 to 43
3/8 - 24	27 to 38	37 to 51
7/16 - 14	40 to 55	55 to 74
7/16 - 20	40 to 60	55 to 81
1/2 - 13	55 to 80	75 to 108

00-2 HAYNES

Standard (SAE and USS) bolt dimensions/grade marks

G   Grade marks (bolt strength)
L   Length (in inches)
T   Thread pitch (number of threads per inch)
D   Nominal diameter (in inches)

Metric bolt dimensions/grade marks

P   Property class (bolt strength)
L   Length (in millimeters)
T   Thread pitch (distance between threads in millimeters)
D   Diameter

Micrometer set

Dial indicator set

the parts go back together properly. Always keep track of the sequence in which parts are removed. Make note of special characteristics or marks on parts that can be installed more than one way, such as a grooved thrust washer on a shaft. It is a good idea to lay the disassembled parts out on a clean surface in the order that they were removed. It may also be helpful to make sketches or take instant photos of components before removal.

When removing fasteners from a component, keep track of their locations. Sometimes threading a bolt back in a part, or putting the washers and nut back on a stud, can prevent mix-ups later. If nuts and bolts cannot be returned to their original locations, they should be kept in a compartmented box or a series of small boxes. A cupcake or muffin tin is ideal for this purpose, since each cavity can hold the bolts and nuts from a particular area (i.e. oil pan bolts, valve cover bolts, engine mount bolts, etc.). A pan of this type is especially helpful when working on assemblies with very small parts, such as the carburetor, alternator, valve train or interior dash and trim pieces. The cavities can be marked with paint or tape to identify the contents.

Whenever wiring looms, harnesses or connectors are separated, it is a good idea to identify the two halves with numbered pieces of masking tape so they can be easily reconnected.

Gasket sealing surfaces

Throughout any vehicle, gaskets are used to seal the mating surfaces between two parts and keep lubricants, fluids, vacuum or pressure contained in an assembly.

Many times these gaskets are coated with a liquid or paste-type gasket sealing compound before assembly. Age, heat and pressure can sometimes cause the two parts to stick together so tightly that they are very difficult to separate. Often, the assembly can be loosened by striking it with a soft-face hammer near the mating surfaces. A regular hammer can be used if a block of wood is placed between the hammer and the part. Do

not hammer on cast parts or parts that could be easily damaged. With any particularly stubborn part, always recheck to make sure that every fastener has been removed.

Avoid using a screwdriver or bar to pry apart an assembly, as they can easily mar the gasket sealing surfaces of the parts, which must remain smooth. If prying is absolutely necessary, use an old broom handle, but keep in mind that extra clean up will be necessary if the wood splinters.

After the parts are separated, the old gasket must be carefully scraped off and the gasket surfaces cleaned. Stubborn gasket material can be soaked with rust penetrant or treated with a special chemical to soften it so it can be easily scraped off. **Caution:** *Never use gasket removal solutions or caustic chemicals on plastic or other composite components.* A scraper can be fashioned from a piece of copper tubing by flattening and sharpening one end. Copper is recommended because it is usually softer than the surfaces to be scraped, which reduces the chance of gouging the part. Some gaskets can be removed with a wire brush, but regardless of the method used, the mating surfaces must be left clean and smooth. If for some reason the gasket surface is gouged, then a gasket sealer thick enough to fill scratches will have to be used during reassembly of the components. For most applications, a non-drying (or semi-drying) gasket sealer should be used.

Hose removal tips

Warning: *If the vehicle is equipped with air conditioning, do not disconnect any of the A/C hoses without first having the system depressurized by a dealer service department or a service station.*

Hose removal precautions closely parallel gasket removal precautions. Avoid scratching or gouging the surface that the hose mates against or the connection may leak. This is especially true for radiator hoses. Because of various chemical reactions, the rubber in hoses can bond itself to the metal spigot that the hose fits over. To remove

a hose, first loosen the hose clamps that secure it to the spigot. Then, with slip-joint pliers, grab the hose at the clamp and rotate it around the spigot. Work it back and forth until it is completely free, then pull it off. Silicone or other lubricants will ease removal if they can be applied between the hose and the outside of the spigot. Apply the same lubricant to the inside of the hose and the outside of the spigot to simplify installation.

As a last resort (and if the hose is to be replaced with a new one anyway), the rubber can be slit with a knife and the hose peeled from the spigot. If this must be done, be careful that the metal connection is not damaged.

If a hose clamp is broken or damaged, do not reuse it. Wire-type clamps usually weaken with age, so it is a good idea to replace them with screw-type clamps whenever a hose is removed.

Tools

A selection of good tools is a basic requirement for anyone who plans to maintain and repair his or her own vehicle. For the owner who has few tools, the initial investment might seem high, but when compared to the spiraling costs of professional auto maintenance and repair, it is a wise one.

To help the owner decide which tools are needed to perform the tasks detailed in this manual, the following tool lists are offered: *Maintenance and minor repair, Repair/overhaul* and *Special*.

The newcomer to practical mechanics should start off with the *maintenance and minor repair* tool kit, which is adequate for the simpler jobs performed on a vehicle. Then, as confidence and experience grow, the owner can tackle more difficult tasks, buying additional tools as they are needed. Eventually the basic kit will be expanded into the *repair and overhaul* tool set. Over a period of time, the experienced do-it-yourselfer will assemble a tool set complete enough for most repair and overhaul procedures and will add tools from the special category when it is felt that the expense is justified by the frequency of use.

Dial caliper

Hand-operated vacuum pump

Fuel pressure gauge set

Compression gauge with spark plug hole adapter

Damper/steering wheel puller

General purpose puller

Hydraulic lifter removal tool

Valve spring compressor

Valve spring compressor

Ridge reamer

Piston ring groove cleaning tool

Ring removal/installation tool

Ring compressor

Cylinder hone

Brake hold-down spring tool

Torque angle gauge

Clutch plate alignment tool

Tap and die set

Maintenance and minor repair tool kit

The tools in this list should be considered the minimum required for performance of routine maintenance, servicing and minor repair work. We recommend the purchase of combination wrenches (box-end and open-end combined in one wrench). While more expensive than open end wrenches, they offer the advantages of both types of wrench.

> *Combination wrench set (1/4-inch to 1 inch or 6 mm to 19 mm)*
> *Adjustable wrench, 8 inch*
> *Spark plug wrench with rubber insert*
> *Spark plug gap adjusting tool*
> *Feeler gauge set*
> *Brake bleeder wrench*
> *Standard screwdriver (5/16-inch x 6 inch)*
> *Phillips screwdriver (No. 2 x 6 inch)*
> *Combination pliers - 6 inch*
> *Hacksaw and assortment of blades*
> *Tire pressure gauge*
> *Grease gun*
> *Oil can*
> *Fine emery cloth*
> *Wire brush*
> *Battery post and cable cleaning tool*
> *Oil filter wrench*
> *Funnel (medium size)*
> *Safety goggles*
> *Jackstands (2)*
> *Drain pan*

Note: *If basic tune-ups are going to be part of routine maintenance, it will be necessary to purchase a good quality stroboscopic timing light and combination tachometer/dwell meter. Although they are included in the list of special tools, it is mentioned here because they are absolutely necessary for tuning most vehicles properly.*

Repair and overhaul tool set

These tools are essential for anyone who plans to perform major repairs and are in addition to those in the maintenance and minor repair tool kit. Included is a comprehensive set of sockets which, though expensive, are invaluable because of their versatility, especially when various extensions and drives are available. We recommend the 1/2-inch drive over the 3/8-inch drive. Although the larger drive is bulky and more expensive, it has the capacity of accepting a very wide range of large sockets. Ideally, however, the mechanic should have a 3/8-inch drive set and a 1/2-inch drive set.

> *Socket set(s)*
> *Reversible ratchet*
> *Extension - 10 inch*
> *Universal joint*
> *Torque wrench (same size drive as sockets)*
> *Ball peen hammer - 8 ounce*
> *Soft-face hammer (plastic/rubber)*
> *Standard screwdriver (1/4-inch x 6 inch)*

> *Standard screwdriver (stubby - 5/16-inch)*
> *Phillips screwdriver (No. 3 x 8 inch)*
> *Phillips screwdriver (stubby - No. 2)*
> *Pliers - vise grip*
> *Pliers - lineman's*
> *Pliers - needle nose*
> *Pliers - snap-ring (internal and external)*
> *Cold chisel - 1/2-inch*
> *Scribe*
> *Scraper (made from flattened copper tubing)*
> *Centerpunch*
> *Pin punches (1/16, 1/8, 3/16-inch)*
> *Steel rule/straightedge - 12 inch*
> *Allen wrench set (1/8 to 3/8-inch or 4 mm to 10 mm)*
> *A selection of files*
> *Wire brush (large)*
> *Jackstands (second set)*
> *Jack (scissor or hydraulic type)*

Note: *Another tool which is often useful is an electric drill with a chuck capacity of 3/8-inch and a set of good quality drill bits.*

Special tools

The tools in this list include those which are not used regularly, are expensive to buy, or which need to be used in accordance with their manufacturer's instructions. Unless these tools will be used frequently, it is not very economical to purchase many of them. A consideration would be to split the cost and use between yourself and a friend or friends. In addition, most of these tools can be obtained from a tool rental shop on a temporary basis.

This list primarily contains only those tools and instruments widely available to the public, and not those special tools produced by the vehicle manufacturer for distribution to dealer service departments. Occasionally, references to the manufacturer's special tools are included in the text of this manual. Generally, an alternative method of doing the job without the special tool is offered. However, sometimes there is no alternative to their use. Where this is the case, and the tool cannot be purchased or borrowed, the work should be turned over to the dealer service department or an automotive repair shop.

> *Valve spring compressor*
> *Piston ring groove cleaning tool*
> *Piston ring compressor*
> *Piston ring installation tool*
> *Cylinder compression gauge*
> *Cylinder ridge reamer*
> *Cylinder surfacing hone*
> *Cylinder bore gauge*
> *Micrometers and/or dial calipers*
> *Hydraulic lifter removal tool*
> *Balljoint separator*
> *Universal-type puller*
> *Impact screwdriver*
> *Dial indicator set*
> *Stroboscopic timing light (inductive pick-up)*
> *Hand operated vacuum/pressure pump*
> *Tachometer/dwell meter*
> *Universal electrical multimeter*
> *Cable hoist*
> *Brake spring removal and installation tools*
> *Floor jack*

Buying tools

For the do-it-yourselfer who is just starting to get involved in vehicle maintenance and repair, there are a number of options available when purchasing tools. If maintenance and minor repair is the extent of the work to be done, the purchase of individual tools is satisfactory. If, on the other hand, extensive work is planned, it would be a good idea to purchase a modest tool set from one of the large retail chain stores. A set can usually be bought at a substantial savings over the individual tool prices, and they often come with a tool box. As additional tools are needed, add-on sets, individual tools and a larger tool box can be purchased to expand the tool selection. Building a tool set gradually allows the cost of the tools to be spread over a longer period of time and gives the mechanic the freedom to choose only those tools that will actually be used.

Tool stores will often be the only source of some of the special tools that are needed, but regardless of where tools are bought, try to avoid cheap ones, especially when buying screwdrivers and sockets, because they won't last very long. The expense involved in replacing cheap tools will eventually be greater than the initial cost of quality tools.

Care and maintenance of tools

Good tools are expensive, so it makes sense to treat them with respect. Keep them clean and in usable condition and store them properly when not in use. Always wipe off any dirt, grease or metal chips before putting them away. Never leave tools lying around in the work area. Upon completion of a job, always check closely under the hood for tools that may have been left there so they won't get lost during a test drive.

Some tools, such as screwdrivers, pliers, wrenches and sockets, can be hung on a panel mounted on the garage or workshop wall, while others should be kept in a tool box or tray. Measuring instruments, gauges, meters, etc. must be carefully stored where they cannot be damaged by weather or impact from other tools.

When tools are used with care and stored properly, they will last a very long time. Even with the best of care, though, tools will wear out if used frequently. When a tool is damaged or worn out, replace it. Subsequent jobs will be safer and more enjoyable if you do.

How to repair damaged threads

Sometimes, the internal threads of a nut or bolt hole can become stripped, usually from overtightening. Stripping threads is an all-too-common occurrence, especially when working with aluminum parts, because aluminum is so soft that it easily strips out.

Usually, external or internal threads are only partially stripped. After they've been cleaned up with a tap or die, they'll still work. Sometimes, however, threads are badly damaged. When this happens, you've got three choices:

1) *Drill and tap the hole to the next suitable oversize and install a larger diameter bolt, screw or stud.*
2) *Drill and tap the hole to accept a threaded plug, then drill and tap the plug to the original screw size. You can also buy a plug already threaded to the original size. Then you simply drill a hole to the specified size, then run the threaded plug into the hole with a bolt and jam nut. Once the plug is fully seated, remove the jam nut and bolt.*
3) *The third method uses a patented thread repair kit like Heli-Coil or Slimsert. These easy-to-use kits are designed to repair damaged threads in straight-through holes and blind holes. Both are available as kits which can handle a variety of sizes and thread patterns. Drill the hole, then tap it with the special included tap. Install the Heli-Coil and the hole is back to its original diameter and thread pitch.*

Regardless of which method you use, be sure to proceed calmly and carefully. A little impatience or carelessness during one of these relatively simple procedures can ruin your whole day's work and cost you a bundle if you wreck an expensive part.

Working facilities

Not to be overlooked when discussing tools is the workshop. If anything more than routine maintenance is to be carried out, some sort of suitable work area is essential.

It is understood, and appreciated, that many home mechanics do not have a good workshop or garage available, and end up removing an engine or doing major repairs outside. It is recommended, however, that the overhaul or repair be completed under the cover of a roof.

A clean, flat workbench or table of comfortable working height is an absolute necessity. The workbench should be equipped with a vise that has a jaw opening of at least four inches.

As mentioned previously, some clean, dry storage space is also required for tools, as well as the lubricants, fluids, cleaning solvents, etc. which soon become necessary.

Sometimes waste oil and fluids, drained from the engine or cooling system during normal maintenance or repairs, present a disposal problem. To avoid pouring them on the ground or into a sewage system, pour the used fluids into large containers, seal them with caps and take them to an authorized disposal site or recycling center. Plastic jugs, such as old antifreeze containers, are ideal for this purpose.

Always keep a supply of old newspapers and clean rags available. Old towels are excellent for mopping up spills. Many mechanics use rolls of paper towels for most work because they are readily available and disposable. To help keep the area under the vehicle clean, a large cardboard box can be cut open and flattened to protect the garage or shop floor.

Whenever working over a painted surface, such as when leaning over a fender to service something under the hood, always cover it with an old blanket or bedspread to protect the finish. Vinyl covered pads, made especially for this purpose, are available at auto parts stores.

Jacking and towing

Jacking

Warning: *The jack supplied with the vehicle should only be used for changing a tire or placing jackstands under the frame. Never work under the vehicle or start the engine while this jack is being used as the only means of support.*

The vehicle should be on level ground. Place the shift lever in Park. Block the wheel diagonally opposite the wheel being changed. Set the parking brake.

Remove the spare tire and jack from stowage. Remove the wheel cover and trim ring (if so equipped) with the tapered end of the lug nut wrench by inserting and twisting the handle and then prying against the back of the wheel cover. Loosen the wheel lug nuts about 1/4-to-1/2 turn each.

Place the scissors-type jack under the side of the vehicle and adjust the jack height until it fits in the notch in the vertical rocker panel flange nearest the wheel to be changed. There is a front and rear jacking point on each side of the vehicle **(see illustration)**.

Turn the jack handle clockwise until the tire clears the ground. Remove the lug nuts and pull the wheel off. Replace it with the spare.

Install the lug nuts with the beveled edges facing in. Tighten them snugly. Don't attempt to tighten them completely until the vehicle is lowered or it could slip off the jack. Turn the jack handle counterclockwise to lower the vehicle. Remove the jack and

tighten the lug nuts in a diagonal pattern.

Install the cover (and trim ring, if used) and be sure it's snapped into place all the way around.

Stow the tire, jack and wrench. Unblock the wheels.

Towing

Two-wheel drive models should be towed with the front (drive) wheels off the ground. If they can't be raised, place them on a dolly. The intelligent key must be in its slot in the instrument panel and the starter button display must be in the ACC position to unlock the steering column lock.

All-wheel drive models must be towed with all four wheels off the ground. A sling-type tow truck cannot be used, as body damage will result. The best way to tow the vehicle is with a flat-bed car carrier.

Equipment specifically designed for towing should be used. It should be attached to the main structural members of the vehicle, not the bumpers or brackets.

Safety is a major consideration when towing and all applicable state and local laws must be obeyed. A safety chain system must be used at all times.

The jack fits over the rocker panel flange (there are two jacking points on each side of the vehicle, indicated by a notch in the rocker panel flange)

Booster battery (jump) starting

Observe the following precautions when using a booster battery to start a vehicle:

a) Before connecting the booster battery, make sure the ignition switch is in the Off position.
b) Turn off the lights, heater and other electrical loads.
c) Your eyes should be shielded. Safety goggles are a good idea.
d) Make sure the booster battery is the same voltage as the dead one in the vehicle.
e) The two vehicles MUST NOT TOUCH each other.
f) Make sure the transmission is in Neutral (manual) or Park (automatic).
g) If the booster battery is not a maintenance-free type, remove the vent caps and lay a cloth over the vent holes.

Connect the red jumper cable to the positive (+) terminals of each battery.

Connect one end of the black cable to the negative (-) terminal of the booster battery. The other end of this cable should be connected to a good ground on the engine block (see illustration). Make sure the cable will not come into contact with the fan, drivebelts or other moving parts of the engine.

Start the engine using the booster battery, then, with the engine running at idle speed, disconnect the jumper cables in the reverse order of connection.

Make the booster battery cable connections in the numerical order shown (note that the negative cable of the booster battery is NOT attached to the negative terminal of the dead battery)

Automotive chemicals and lubricants

A number of automotive chemicals and lubricants are available for use during vehicle maintenance and repair. They include a wide variety of products ranging from cleaning solvents and degreasers to lubricants and protective sprays for rubber, plastic and vinyl.

Cleaners

Carburetor cleaner and choke cleaner is a strong solvent for gum, varnish and carbon. Most carburetor cleaners leave a dry-type lubricant film which will not harden or gum up. Because of this film it is not recommended for use on electrical components.

Brake system cleaner is used to remove brake dust, grease and brake fluid from the brake system, where clean surfaces are absolutely necessary. It leaves no residue and often eliminates brake squeal caused by contaminants.

Electrical cleaner removes oxidation, corrosion and carbon deposits from electrical contacts, restoring full current flow. It can also be used to clean spark plugs, carburetor jets, voltage regulators and other parts where an oil-free surface is desired.

Demoisturants remove water and moisture from electrical components such as alternators, voltage regulators, electrical connectors and fuse blocks. They are non-conductive and non-corrosive.

Degreasers are heavy-duty solvents used to remove grease from the outside of the engine and from chassis components. They can be sprayed or brushed on and, depending on the type, are rinsed off either with water or solvent.

Lubricants

Motor oil is the lubricant formulated for use in engines. It normally contains a wide variety of additives to prevent corrosion and reduce foaming and wear. Motor oil comes in various weights (viscosity ratings) from 0 to 50. The recommended weight of the oil depends on the season, temperature and the demands on the engine. Light oil is used in cold climates and under light load conditions. Heavy oil is used in hot climates and where high loads are encountered. Multi-viscosity oils are designed to have characteristics of both light and heavy oils and are available in a number of weights from 0W-20 to 20W-50.

Gear oil is designed to be used in differentials, manual transmissions and other areas where high-temperature lubrication is required.

Chassis and wheel bearing grease is a heavy grease used where increased loads and friction are encountered, such as for wheel bearings, balljoints, tie-rod ends and universal joints.

High-temperature wheel bearing grease is designed to withstand the extreme temperatures encountered by wheel bearings in disc brake equipped vehicles. It usually contains molybdenum disulfide (moly), which is a dry-type lubricant.

White grease is a heavy grease for metal-to-metal applications where water is a problem. White grease stays soft under both low and high temperatures (usually from -100 to +190-degrees F), and will not wash off or dilute in the presence of water.

Assembly lube is a special extreme pressure lubricant, usually containing moly, used to lubricate high-load parts (such as main and rod bearings and cam lobes) for initial start-up of a new engine. The assembly lube lubricates the parts without being squeezed out or washed away until the engine oiling system begins to function.

Silicone lubricants are used to protect rubber, plastic, vinyl and nylon parts.

Graphite lubricants are used where oils cannot be used due to contamination problems, such as in locks. The dry graphite will lubricate metal parts while remaining uncontaminated by dirt, water, oil or acids. It is electrically conductive and will not foul electrical contacts in locks such as the ignition switch.

Moly penetrants loosen and lubricate frozen, rusted and corroded fasteners and prevent future rusting or freezing.

Heat-sink grease is a special electrically non-conductive grease that is used for mounting electronic ignition modules where it is essential that heat is transferred away from the module.

Sealants

RTV sealant is one of the most widely used gasket compounds. Made from silicone, RTV is air curing, it seals, bonds, waterproofs, fills surface irregularities, remains flexible, doesn't shrink, is relatively easy to remove, and is used as a supplementary sealer with almost all low and medium temperature gaskets.

Anaerobic sealant is much like RTV in that it can be used either to seal gaskets or to form gaskets by itself. It remains flexible, is solvent resistant and fills surface imperfections. The difference between an anaerobic sealant and an RTV-type sealant is in the curing. RTV cures when exposed to air, while an anaerobic sealant cures only in the absence of air. This means that an anaerobic sealant cures only after the assembly of parts, sealing them together.

Thread and pipe sealant is used for sealing hydraulic and pneumatic fittings and vacuum lines. It is usually made from a Teflon compound, and comes in a spray, a paint-on liquid and as a wrap-around tape.

Chemicals

Anti-seize compound prevents seizing, galling, cold welding, rust and corrosion in fasteners. High-temperature ant-seize, usually made with copper and graphite lubricants, is used for exhaust system and exhaust manifold bolts.

Anaerobic locking compounds are used to keep fasteners from vibrating or working loose and cure only after installation, in the absence of air. Medium strength locking compound is used for small nuts, bolts and screws that may be removed later. High-strength locking compound is for large nuts, bolts and studs which aren't removed on a regular basis.

Oil additives range from viscosity index improvers to chemical treatments that claim to reduce internal engine friction. It should be noted that most oil manufacturers caution against using additives with their oils.

Gas additives perform several functions, depending on their chemical makeup. They usually contain solvents that help dissolve gum and varnish that build up on carburetor, fuel injection and intake parts. They also serve to break down carbon deposits that form on the inside surfaces of the combustion chambers. Some additives contain upper cylinder lubricants for valves and piston rings, and others contain chemicals to remove condensation from the gas tank.

Miscellaneous

Brake fluid is specially formulated hydraulic fluid that can withstand the heat and pressure encountered in brake systems. Care must be taken so this fluid does not come in contact with painted surfaces or plastics. An opened container should always be resealed to prevent contamination by water or dirt.

Weatherstrip adhesive is used to bond weatherstripping around doors, windows and trunk lids. It is sometimes used to attach trim pieces.

Undercoating is a petroleum-based, tar-like substance that is designed to protect metal surfaces on the underside of the vehicle from corrosion. It also acts as a sound-deadening agent by insulating the bottom of the vehicle.

Waxes and polishes are used to help protect painted and plated surfaces from the weather. Different types of paint may require the use of different types of wax and polish. Some polishes utilize a chemical or abrasive cleaner to help remove the top layer of oxidized (dull) paint on older vehicles. In recent years many non-wax polishes that contain a wide variety of chemicals such as polymers and silicones have been introduced. These non-wax polishes are usually easier to apply and last longer than conventional waxes and polishes.

Conversion factors

Length (distance)

Inches (in)	X	25.4	= Millimeters (mm)	X 0.0394	= Inches (in)
Feet (ft)	X	0.305	= Meters (m)	X 3.281	= Feet (ft)
Miles	X	1.609	= Kilometers (km)	X 0.621	= Miles

Volume (capacity)

Cubic inches (cu in; in^3)	X	16.387	= Cubic centimeters (cc; cm^3)	X 0.061	= Cubic inches (cu in; in^3)
Imperial pints (Imp pt)	X	0.568	= Liters (l)	X 1.76	= Imperial pints (Imp pt)
Imperial quarts (Imp qt)	X	1.137	= Liters (l)	X 0.88	= Imperial quarts (Imp qt)
Imperial quarts (Imp qt)	X	1.201	= US quarts (US qt)	X 0.833	= Imperial quarts (Imp qt)
US quarts (US qt)	X	0.946	= Liters (l)	X 1.057	= US quarts (US qt)
Imperial gallons (Imp gal)	X	4.546	= Liters (l)	X 0.22	= Imperial gallons (Imp gal)
Imperial gallons (Imp gal)	X	1.201	= US gallons (US gal)	X 0.833	= Imperial gallons (Imp gal)
US gallons (US gal)	X	3.785	= Liters (l)	X 0.264	= US gallons (US gal)

Mass (weight)

Ounces (oz)	X	28.35	= Grams (g)	X 0.035	= Ounces (oz)
Pounds (lb)	X	0.454	= Kilograms (kg)	X 2.205	= Pounds (lb)

Force

Ounces-force (ozf; oz)	X	0.278	= Newtons (N)	X 3.6	= Ounces-force (ozf; oz)
Pounds-force (lbf; lb)	X	4.448	= Newtons (N)	X 0.225	= Pounds-force (lbf; lb)
Newtons (N)	X	0.1	= Kilograms-force (kgf; kg)	X 9.81	= Newtons (N)

Pressure

Pounds-force per square inch (psi; lbf/in^2; lb/in^2)	X	0.070	= Kilograms-force per square centimeter (kgf/cm^2; kg/cm^2)	X 14.223	= Pounds-force per square inch (psi; lbf/in^2; lb/in^2)
Pounds-force per square inch (psi; lbf/in^2; lb/in^2)	X	0.068	= Atmospheres (atm)	X 14.696	= Pounds-force per square inch (psi; lbf/in^2; lb/in^2)
Pounds-force per square inch (psi; lbf/in^2; lb/in^2)	X	0.069	= Bars	X 14.5	= Pounds-force per square inch (psi; lbf/in^2; lb/in^2)
Pounds-force per square inch (psi; lbf/in^2; lb/in^2)	X	6.895	= Kilopascals (kPa)	X 0.145	= Pounds-force per square inch (psi; lbf/in^2; lb/in^2)
Kilopascals (kPa)	X	0.01	= Kilograms-force per square centimeter (kgf/cm^2; kg/cm^2)	X 98.1	= Kilopascals (kPa)

Torque (moment of force)

Pounds-force inches (lbf in; lb in)	X	1.152	= Kilograms-force centimeter (kgf cm; kg cm)	X 0.868	= Pounds-force inches (lbf in; lb in)
Pounds-force inches (lbf in; lb in)	X	0.113	= Newton meters (Nm)	X 8.85	= Pounds-force inches (lbf in; lb in)
Pounds-force inches (lbf in; lb in)	X	0.083	= Pounds-force feet (lbf ft; lb ft)	X 12	= Pounds-force inches (lbf in; lb in)
Pounds-force feet (lbf ft; lb ft)	X	0.138	= Kilograms-force meters (kgf m; kg m)	X 7.233	= Pounds-force feet (lbf ft; lb ft)
Pounds-force feet (lbf ft; lb ft)	X	1.356	= Newton meters (Nm)	X 0.738	= Pounds-force feet (lbf ft; lb ft)
Newton meters (Nm)	X	0.102	= Kilograms-force meters (kgf m; kg m)	X 9.804	= Newton meters (Nm)

Vacuum

Inches mercury (in. Hg)	X	3.377	= Kilopascals (kPa)	X 0.2961	= Inches mercury
Inches mercury (in. Hg)	X	25.4	= Millimeters mercury (mm Hg)	X 0.0394	= Inches mercury

Power

Horsepower (hp)	X	745.7	= Watts (W)	X 0.0013	= Horsepower (hp)

Velocity (speed)

Miles per hour (miles/hr; mph)	X	1.609	= Kilometers per hour (km/hr; kph)	X 0.621	= Miles per hour (miles/hr; mph)

Fuel consumption*

Miles per gallon, Imperial (mpg)	X	0.354	= Kilometers per liter (km/l)	X 2.825	= Miles per gallon, Imperial (mpg)
Miles per gallon, US (mpg)	X	0.425	= Kilometers per liter (km/l)	X 2.352	= Miles per gallon, US (mpg)

Temperature

Degrees Fahrenheit = (°C x 1.8) + 32   Degrees Celsius (Degrees Centigrade; °C) = (°F - 32) x 0.56

*It is common practice to convert from miles per gallon (mpg) to liters/100 kilometers (l/100km), where mpg (Imperial) x l/100 km = 282 and mpg (US) x l/100 km = 235

DECIMALS to MILLIMETERS

Decimal	mm	Decimal	mm
0.001	0.0254	0.500	12.7000
0.002	0.0508	0.510	12.9540
0.003	0.0762	0.520	13.2080
0.004	0.1016	0.530	13.4620
0.005	0.1270	0.540	13.7160
0.006	0.1524	0.550	13.9700
0.007	0.1778	0.560	14.2240
0.008	0.2032	0.570	14.4780
0.009	0.2286	0.580	14.7320
		0.590	14.9860
0.010	0.2540		
0.020	0.5080		
0.030	0.7620		
0.040	1.0160	0.600	15.2400
0.050	1.2700	0.610	15.4940
0.060	1.5240	0.620	15.7480
0.070	1.7780	0.630	16.0020
0.080	2.0320	0.640	16.2560
0.090	2.2860	0.650	16.5100
		0.660	16.7640
0.100	2.5400	0.670	17.0180
0.110	2.7940	0.680	17.2720
0.120	3.0480	0.690	17.5260
0.130	3.3020		
0.140	3.5560		
0.150	3.8100		
0.160	4.0640	0.700	17.7800
0.170	4.3180	0.710	18.0340
0.180	4.5720	0.720	18.2880
0.190	4.8260	0.730	18.5420
		0.740	18.7960
0.200	5.0800	0.750	19.0500
0.210	5.3340	0.760	19.3040
0.220	5.5880	0.770	19.5580
0.230	5.8420	0.780	19.8120
0.240	6.0960	0.790	20.0660
0.250	6.3500		
0.260	6.6040		
0.270	6.8580	0.800	20.3200
0.280	7.1120	0.810	20.5740
0.290	7.3660	0.820	21.8280
		0.830	21.0820
0.300	7.6200	0.840	21.3360
0.310	7.8740	0.850	21.5900
0.320	8.1280	0.860	21.8440
0.330	8.3820	0.870	22.0980
0.340	8.6360	0.880	22.3520
0.350	8.8900	0.890	22.6060
0.360	9.1440		
0.370	9.3980		
0.380	9.6520		
0.390	9.9060		
		0.900	22.8600
0.400	10.1600	0.910	23.1140
0.410	10.4140	0.920	23.3680
0.420	10.6680	0.930	23.6220
0.430	10.9220	0.940	23.8760
0.440	11.1760	0.950	24.1300
0.450	11.4300	0.960	24.3840
0.460	11.6840	0.970	24.6380
0.470	11.9380	0.980	24.8920
0.480	12.1920	0.990	25.1460
0.490	12.4460	1.000	25.4000

FRACTIONS to DECIMALS to MILLIMETERS

Fraction	Decimal	mm	Fraction	Decimal	mm
1/64	0.0156	0.3969	33/64	0.5156	13.0969
1/32	0.0312	0.7938	17/32	0.5312	13.4938
3/64	0.0469	1.1906	35/64	0.5469	13.8906
1/16	0.0625	1.5875	9/16	0.5625	14.2875
5/64	0.0781	1.9844	37/64	0.5781	14.6844
3/32	0.0938	2.3812	19/32	0.5938	15.0812
7/64	0.1094	2.7781	39/64	0.6094	15.4781
1/8	0.1250	3.1750	5/8	0.6250	15.8750
9/64	0.1406	3.5719	41/64	0.6406	16.2719
5/32	0.1562	3.9688	21/32	0.6562	16.6688
11/64	0.1719	4.3656	43/64	0.6719	17.0656
3/16	0.1875	4.7625	11/16	0.6875	17.4625
13/64	0.2031	5.1594	45/64	0.7031	17.8594
7/32	0.2188	5.5562	23/32	0.7188	18.2562
15/64	0.2344	5.9531	47/64	0.7344	18.6531
1/4	0.2500	6.3500	3/4	0.7500	19.0500
17/64	0.2656	6.7469	49/64	0.7656	19.4469
9/32	0.2812	7.1438	25/32	0.7812	19.8438
19/64	0.2969	7.5406	51/64	0.7969	20.2406
5/16	0.3125	7.9375	13/16	0.8125	20.6375
21/64	0.3281	8.3344	53/64	0.8281	21.0344
11/32	0.3438	8.7312	27/32	0.8438	21.4312
23/64	0.3594	9.1281	55/64	0.8594	21.8281
3/8	0.3750	9.5250	7/8	0.8750	22.2250
25/64	0.3906	9.9219	57/64	0.8906	22.6219
13/32	0.4062	10.3188	29/32	0.9062	23.0188
27/64	0.4219	10.7156	59/64	0.9219	23.4156
7/16	0.4375	11.1125	15/16	0.9375	23.8125
29/64	0.4531	11.5094	61/64	0.9531	24.2094
15/32	0.4688	11.9062	31/32	0.9688	24.6062
31/64	0.4844	12.3031	63/64	0.9844	25.0031
1/2	0.5000	12.7000	1	1.0000	25.4000

Safety first!

Regardless of how enthusiastic you may be about getting on with the job at hand, take the time to ensure that your safety is not jeopardized. A moment's lack of attention can result in an accident, as can failure to observe certain simple safety precautions. The possibility of an accident will always exist, and the following points should not be considered a comprehensive list of all dangers. Rather, they are intended to make you aware of the risks and to encourage a safety conscious approach to all work you carry out on your vehicle.

Essential DOs and DON'Ts

DON'T rely on a jack when working under the vehicle. Always use approved jackstands to support the weight of the vehicle and place them under the recommended lift or support points.

DON'T attempt to loosen extremely tight fasteners (i.e. wheel lug nuts) while the vehicle is on a jack - it may fall.

DON'T start the engine without first making sure that the transmission is in Neutral (or Park where applicable) and the parking brake is set.

DON'T remove the radiator cap from a hot cooling system - let it cool or cover it with a cloth and release the pressure gradually.

DON'T attempt to drain the engine oil until you are sure it has cooled to the point that it will not burn you.

DON'T touch any part of the engine or exhaust system until it has cooled sufficiently to avoid burns.

DON'T siphon toxic liquids such as gasoline, antifreeze and brake fluid by mouth, or allow them to remain on your skin.

DON'T inhale brake lining dust - it is potentially hazardous (see *Asbestos* below).

DON'T allow spilled oil or grease to remain on the floor - wipe it up before someone slips on it.

DON'T use loose fitting wrenches or other tools which may slip and cause injury.

DON'T push on wrenches when loosening or tightening nuts or bolts. Always try to pull the wrench toward you. If the situation calls for pushing the wrench away, push with an open hand to avoid scraped knuckles if the wrench should slip.

DON'T attempt to lift a heavy component alone - get someone to help you.

DON'T *rush or take unsafe shortcuts to finish a job.*

DON'T allow children or animals in or around the vehicle while you are working on it.

DO wear eye protection when using power tools such as a drill, sander, bench grinder, etc. and when working under a vehicle.

DO keep loose clothing and long hair well out of the way of moving parts.

DO make sure that any hoist used has a safe working load rating adequate for the job.

DO get someone to check on you periodically when working alone on a vehicle.

DO carry out work in a logical sequence and make sure that everything is correctly assembled and tightened.

DO keep chemicals and fluids tightly capped and out of the reach of children and pets.

DO remember that your vehicle's safety affects that of yourself and others. If in doubt on any point, get professional advice.

Steering, suspension and brakes

These systems are essential to driving safety, so make sure you have a qualified shop or individual check your work. Also, compressed suspension springs can cause injury if released suddenly - be sure to use a spring compressor.

Airbags

Airbags are explosive devices that can **CAUSE** injury if they deploy while you're working on the vehicle. Follow the manufacturer's instructions to disable the airbag whenever you're working in the vicinity of airbag components.

Asbestos

Certain friction, insulating, sealing, and other products - such as brake linings, brake bands, clutch linings, torque converters, gaskets, etc. - may contain asbestos or other hazardous friction material. Extreme care must be taken to avoid inhalation of dust from such products, since it is hazardous to health. If in doubt, assume that they do contain asbestos.

Fire

Remember at all times that gasoline is highly flammable. Never smoke or have any kind of open flame around when working on a vehicle. But the risk does not end there. A spark caused by an electrical short circuit, by two metal surfaces contacting each other, or even by static electricity built up in your body under certain conditions, can ignite gasoline vapors, which in a confined space are highly explosive. Do not, under any circumstances, use gasoline for cleaning parts. Use an approved safety solvent.

Always disconnect the battery ground (-) cable at the battery before working on any part of the fuel system or electrical system. Never risk spilling fuel on a hot engine or exhaust component. It is strongly recommended that a fire extinguisher suitable for use on fuel and electrical fires be kept handy in the garage or workshop at all times. Never try to extinguish a fuel or electrical fire with water.

Fumes

Certain fumes are highly toxic and can quickly cause unconsciousness and even death if inhaled to any extent. Gasoline vapor falls into this category, as do the vapors from some cleaning solvents. Any draining or pouring of such volatile fluids should be done in a well ventilated area.

When using cleaning fluids and solvents, read the instructions on the container carefully. Never use materials from unmarked containers.

Never run the engine in an enclosed space, such as a garage. Exhaust fumes contain carbon monoxide, which is extremely poisonous. If you need to run the engine, always do so in the open air, or at least have the rear of the vehicle outside the work area.

The battery

Never create a spark or allow a bare light bulb near a battery. They normally give off a certain amount of hydrogen gas, which is highly explosive.

Always disconnect the battery ground (-) cable at the battery before working on the fuel or electrical systems.

If possible, loosen the filler caps or cover when charging the battery from an external source (this does not apply to sealed or maintenance-free batteries). Do not charge at an excessive rate or the battery may burst.

Take care when adding water to a non maintenance-free battery and when carrying a battery. The electrolyte, even when diluted, is very corrosive and should not be allowed to contact clothing or skin.

Always wear eye protection when cleaning the battery to prevent the caustic deposits from entering your eyes.

Household current

When using an electric power tool, inspection light, etc., which operates on household current, always make sure that the tool is correctly connected to its plug and that, where necessary, it is properly grounded. Do not use such items in damp conditions and, again, do not create a spark or apply excessive heat in the vicinity of fuel or fuel vapor.

Secondary ignition system voltage

A severe electric shock can result from touching certain parts of the ignition system (such as the spark plug wires) when the engine is running or being cranked, particularly if components are damp or the insulation is defective. In the case of an electronic ignition system, the secondary system voltage is much higher and could prove fatal.

Hydrofluoric acid

This extremely corrosive acid is formed when certain types of synthetic rubber, found in some O-rings, oil seals, fuel hoses, etc. are exposed to temperatures above 750-degrees F (400-degrees C). The rubber changes into a charred or sticky substance containing the acid. *Once formed, the acid remains dangerous for years. If it gets onto the skin, it may be necessary to amputate the limb concerned.*

When dealing with a vehicle which has suffered a fire, or with components salvaged from such a vehicle, wear protective gloves and discard them after use.

Troubleshooting

Contents

This section provides an easy reference guide to the more common problems which may occur during the operation of your vehicle. Various symptoms and their possible causes are grouped under headings denoting components or systems, such as Engine, Cooling system, etc. They also refer to the Chapter and/or Section that deals with the problem.

Remember that successful troubleshooting isn't a mysterious art practiced only by professional mechanics. It's simply the result of knowledge combined with an intelligent, systematic approach to a problem. Always use a process of elimination, starting with the simplest solution and working through to the most complex - and never overlook the obvious. Anyone can run the gas tank dry or leave the lights on overnight, so don't assume that you're exempt from such oversights.

Finally, always establish a clear idea why a problem has occurred and take steps to ensure that it doesn't happen again. If the electrical system fails because of a poor connection, check all other connections in the system to make sure they don't fail as well. If a particular fuse continues to blow, find out why - don't just go on replacing fuses. Remember, failure of a small component can often be indicative of potential failure or incorrect functioning of a more important component or system.

Engine and performance

1 Engine will not rotate when attempting to start

1 Battery terminal connections loose or corroded (Chapter 1).
2 Battery discharged or faulty (Chapter 1).
3 Automatic transaxle not completely engaged in Park (Chapter 7).
4 Broken, loose or disconnected wiring in the starting circuit (Chapters 5 and 12).
5 Starter motor pinion jammed in driveplate ring gear (Chapter 5).
6 Starter solenoid faulty (Chapter 5).
7 Starter motor faulty (Chapter 5).
8 Ignition switch faulty (Chapter 12).
9 Neutral start switch faulty (Chapter 7).
10 Starter pinion or driveplate teeth worn or broken (Chapter 5).
11 Faulty Body Control Module (BCM) or Intelligent Power Distribution Module (IPDM) (see Chapter 12).

2 Engine rotates but will not start

1 Fuel tank empty.
2 Battery discharged (engine rotates slowly) (Chapter 5).
3 Battery terminal connections loose or corroded (Chapter 1).
4 Leaking fuel injector(s), fuel pump, pressure regulator, etc. (Chapter 4).

5 Fuel not reaching fuel injection system (Chapter 4).
6 Ignition system problem (Chapter 5).
7 Worn, faulty or incorrectly gapped spark plugs (Chapter 1).

3 Engine hard to start when cold

1 Battery discharged or low (Chapter 1).
2 Fuel system malfunctioning (Chapter 4).
3 Emissions or engine control system malfunctioning (Chapter 6).

4 Engine hard to start when hot

1 Air filter clogged (Chapter 1).
2 Fuel not reaching the fuel injection system (Chapter 4).
3 Corroded battery connections, especially ground (Chapter 1).
4 Emissions or engine control system malfunctioning (Chapter 6).

5 Starter motor noisy or excessively rough in engagement

1 Pinion or driveplate gear teeth worn or broken (Chapter 5).
2 Starter motor mounting bolts loose (Chapter 5).

6 Engine starts but stops immediately

1 Insufficient fuel reaching the fuel injectors (Chapter 4).
2 Vacuum leak at the gasket between the intake manifold/plenum and throttle body (Chapters 1 and 4).
3 Restricted exhaust system (most likely the catalytic converter) (Chapters 4 and 6).

7 Oil puddle under engine

1 Oil pan gasket and/or oil pan drain bolt seal leaking (Chapters 1 and 2).
2 Oil pressure sending unit leaking (Chapter 2).
3 Valve cover gaskets leaking (Chapter 2).
4 Engine oil seals leaking (Chapter 2).

8 Engine lopes while idling or idles erratically

1 Vacuum leakage (Chapter 4).
2 Plugged PCV valve (Chapter 6).
3 Air filter clogged (Chapter 1).
4 Fuel pump not delivering sufficient fuel to the fuel injection system (Chapter 4).
5 Leaking head gasket (Chapter 2).
6 Camshaft lobes worn (Chapter 2).

9 Engine misses at idle speed

1 Spark plugs worn or not gapped properly (Chapter 1).
2 Faulty ignition coil(s) (Chapter 5).
3 Vacuum leaks (Chapters 1 and 4).
4 Uneven or low compression (Chapter 2B).
5 Problem with the fuel injection system (Chapter 4).

10 Engine misses throughout driving speed range

1 Fuel filter clogged and/or impurities in the fuel system (Chapters 1 and 4).
2 Low fuel pressure (Chapter 4).
3 Faulty or incorrectly gapped spark plugs (Chapter 1).
4 Faulty emission system components (Chapter 6).
5 Low or uneven cylinder compression pressures (Chapter 2B).
6 Weak or faulty ignition coil(s) (Chapter 5).
7 Vacuum leak in fuel injection system, intake manifold or vacuum hoses (Chapter 4).

11 Engine stumbles on acceleration

1 Spark plugs fouled (Chapter 1).
2 Problem with the fuel injection system (Chapter 4).
3 Fuel filter clogged (Chapter 1).
4 Intake manifold air leak (Chapter 4).

12 Engine surges while holding accelerator steady

1 Intake air leak (Chapter 4).
2 Fuel pump faulty (Chapter 4).
3 Loose fuel injector harness connections (Chapter 4).
4 Defective PCM (Chapter 6).

13 Engine stalls

1 Fuel filter clogged and/or water and impurities in the fuel system (Chapters 1 and 4).
2 Faulty emissions system or engine control system components (Chapter 6).
3 Faulty or incorrectly gapped spark plugs (Chapter 1).
4 Vacuum leak in the intake manifold or vacuum hoses (Chapter 4).

14 Engine lacks power

1 Faulty or incorrectly gapped spark plugs (Chapter 1).
2 Restricted exhaust system (most likely the catalytic converter) (Chapters 4 and 6).

3   Fuel injection system malfunctioning (Chapter 4).
4   Faulty coil(s) (Chapter 5).
5   Brakes binding (Chapter 1).
6   Automatic transaxle fluid level incorrect (Chapter 1).
7   Fuel filter clogged and/or impurities in the fuel system (Chapter 1).
8   Emission control system not functioning properly (Chapter 6).
9   Low or uneven cylinder compression pressures (Chapter 2B).

15   Engine backfires

1   Emissions system not functioning properly (Chapter 6).
2   Fuel injection system malfunctioning (Chapter 4).
3   Vacuum leak at fuel injectors, intake manifold or vacuum hoses (Chapter 4).
4   Valves sticking (Chapter 2).

16   Pinging or knocking engine sounds during acceleration or uphill

1   Incorrect grade of fuel.
2   Fuel injection system malfunctioning Chapter 4).
3   Improper or damaged spark plugs or wires (Chapter 1).
4   Worn or damaged ignition components (Chapter 5).
5   Faulty emissions system (Chapter 6).
6   Vacuum leak (Chapter 4).

17   Engine runs with oil pressure light on

1   Low oil level (Chapter 1).
2   Short in wiring circuit (Chapter 12).
3   Faulty oil pressure sender (Chapter 2B).
4   Oil viscosity too low or oil diluted.
5   Worn engine bearings and/or oil pump (Chapter 2).

18   Engine continues to run after switching off

Faulty ignition switch (Chapter 12), Powertrain Control Module (PCM) (Chapter 6), or Body Control Module (BCM).

Engine electrical system

19   Battery will not hold a charge

1   Drivebelt worn or tensioner defective (Chapter 1).
2   Battery terminals loose or corroded (Chapter 1).

3   Alternator not charging properly (Chapter 5).
4   Loose, broken or faulty wiring in the charging circuit (Chapter 5).
5   Short in vehicle wiring (Chapters 5 and 12).
6   Internally defective battery (Chapters 1 and 5).

20   Voltage warning light fails to go out

1   Faulty alternator or charging circuit (Chapter 5).
2   Drivebelt worn or tensioner defective (Chapter 1).
3   Alternator voltage regulator inoperative (Chapter 5).

21   Voltage warning light fails to come on when key is turned on

1   Warning light bulb defective (Chapter 12).
2   Fault in the printed circuit, dash wiring or bulb holder (Chapter 12).

Fuel system

22   Excessive fuel consumption

1   Dirty or clogged air filter element (Chapter 1).
2   Emissions system not functioning properly (Chapter 6).
3   Fuel injection system malfunctioning (Chapter 4).
4   Low tire pressure or incorrect tire size (Chapter 1).

23   Fuel leakage and/or fuel odor

1   Leak in a fuel feed or vent line (Chapter 4).
2   Tank overfilled.
3   Evaporative emissions control canister defective (Chapters 1 and 6).
4   Fuel injector seals faulty (Chapter 4).

Cooling system

24   Overheating

1   Insufficient coolant in system (Chapter 1).
2   Drivebelt worn or tensioner defective (Chapter 1).
3   Radiator core blocked or grille restricted (Chapter 3).
4   Thermostat faulty (Chapter 3).
5   Electric cooling fan blades broken or cracked (Chapter 3).
6   Radiator cap not maintaining proper pressure (Chapter 3).

25   Overcooling

Incorrect (opening temperature too low) or faulty thermostat (Chapter 3).

26   External coolant leakage

1   Deteriorated/damaged hoses or loose clamps (Chapters 1 and 3).
2   Water pump seal defective (Chapters 1 and 3).
3   Leakage from radiator core (Chapter 3).
4   Engine drain or water jacket core plugs leaking.

27   Internal coolant leakage

1   Leaking cylinder head gasket (Chapter 2).
2   Cracked cylinder bore or cylinder head (Chapter 2).

28   Coolant loss

1   Too much coolant in system (Chapter 1).
2   Coolant boiling away because of overheating (Chapter 3).
3   Internal or external leakage (Chapter 3).
4   Faulty radiator cap (Chapter 3).

29   Poor coolant circulation

1   Inoperative water pump (Chapter 3).
2   Restriction in cooling system (Chapters 1 and 3).
3   Drivebelt worn or tensioner defective (Chapter 1).
4   Thermostat sticking (Chapter 3).

Automatic transaxle

Note: *Due to the complexity of the automatic transaxle, it's difficult for the home mechanic to properly diagnose and service this component. For problems other than the following, the vehicle should be taken to a dealer service department or a transmission shop.*

30   Fluid leakage

1   Automatic transmission fluid is a deep red color. Fluid leaks should not be confused with engine oil, which can easily be blown by airflow to the transaxle.
2   To pinpoint a leak, first remove all built-up dirt and grime from the transaxle housing with degreasing agents and/or steam cleaning. Drive the vehicle at low speeds so air flow will

not blow the leak far from its source. Raise the vehicle and determine where the leak is coming from. Common areas of leakage are:

a) *Fluid pan*
b) *Fill plug*
c) *Fluid cooler lines*
d) *Transmission Speed Sensor(s) (Chapter 6)*

31 Transaxle fluid brown or has a burned smell

Transaxle overheated. Change fluid (Chapter 1).

32 General shift mechanism problems

Chapter 7 deals with checking and adjusting the shift cable on automatic transaxles. Common problems which may be attributed to a poorly adjusted cable are:

a) *Engine starting in gears other than Park or Neutral.*
b) *Indicator on shifter pointing to a gear other than the one actually being used.*
c) *Vehicle moves when in Park.*

33 Engine will start in gears other than Park or Neutral

Transmission range switch malfunctioning (Chapter 6).

34 Transaxle slips, is noisy or has no drive in forward or reverse gears

There are many probable causes for the above problems, but the home mechanic should be concerned with only one possibility - fluid level. Before taking the vehicle to a repair shop, check the level and condition of the fluid as described in Chapter 1.

Correct the fluid level as necessary or change the fluid and filter if needed. If the problem persists, have a professional diagnose the probable cause.

Driveaxles

35 Clicking noise in turns

Worn or damaged outer CV joint. Check for cut or damaged boots (Chapter 1). Repair as necessary (Chapter 8).

36 Knock or clunk when accelerating after coasting

Worn or damaged CV joint. Check for cut or damaged boots (Chapter 1). Repair as necessary (Chapter 8).

37 Shudder or vibration during acceleration

Worn or damaged CV joints. Repair or replace as necessary (Chapter 8).

Driveshaft

Note: *Refer to Chapter 8, unless otherwise specified, for service information.*

38 Leaks at front of driveshaft

Defective transfer case seal.

39 Knock or clunk when transmission is under initial load (just after transmission is put into gear)

1   Loose or disconnected rear suspension components. Check all mounting bolts and bushings (Chapter 10).
2   Loose driveshaft bolts. Inspect all bolts and nuts and tighten them securely.
3   Worn or damaged universal joint bearings.
4   Worn sleeve yoke and mainshaft spline.

40 Metallic grating sound consistent with vehicle speed

1   Pronounced wear in the universal joint bearings. Replace driveshaft.
2   Worn center support bearing. Replace driveshaft.

41 Vibration

Note: *Before blaming the driveshaft, make sure the tires are perfectly balanced and perform the following test.*
1   Install a tachometer inside the vehicle to monitor engine speed as the vehicle is driven. Drive the vehicle and note the engine speed at which the vibration (roughness) is most pronounced. Now shift the transmission to a different gear and bring the engine speed to the same point.

2   If the vibration occurs at the same engine speed (rpm) regardless of which gear the transmission is in, the driveshaft is NOT at fault since the driveshaft speed varies.
3   If the vibration decreases or is eliminated when the transmission is in a different gear at the same engine speed, refer to the following probable causes:

a) *Bent or dented driveshaft. Inspect and replace as necessary.*
b) *Undercoating or built-up dirt, etc. on the driveshaft. Clean the shaft thoroughly.*
c) *Worn universal joint bearings. Replace the driveshaft.*
d) *Driveshaft and/or companion flange out of balance. Check for missing weights on the shaft. Remove driveshaft and reinstall 180-degrees from original position, then recheck. Have the driveshaft balanced if problem persists.*
e) *Loose driveshaft mounting bolts/nuts.*
f) *Worn center support bearing. Replace the driveshaft.*
g) *Worn transfer case rear bushing.*

42 Scraping noise

Make sure there is nothing, such as an exhaust heat shield or safety loop, rubbing on the driveshaft.

Rear differential

Note: *For differential servicing information, refer to Chapter 8, unless otherwise specified.*

43 Noise - same when in drive as when vehicle is coasting

1   Road noise. No corrective action available.
2   Tire noise. Inspect tires and check tire pressures (Chapter 1).
3   Hub bearings worn or damaged (Chapter 10).
4   Insufficient differential oil (Chapter 1).
5   Defective differential.

44 Knocking sound when starting or shifting gears

Worn differential.

45 Noise when turning

Worn differential.

46 Vibration

See probable causes under *Driveshaft*. Proceed under the guidelines listed for the driveshaft. If the problem persists, check the rear hub bearings by raising the rear of the vehicle and spinning the wheels by hand. Listen for evidence of rough (noisy) bearings. Remove and inspect.

47 Oil leaks

1   Pinion oil seal damaged.
2   Driveaxle oil seals damaged.
3   Loose filler or drain plug on differential (Chapter 1).
4   Clogged or damaged breather on differential.

Brakes

Note: *Before assuming that a brake problem exists, make sure . . .*

a) *The tires are in good condition and properly inflated (Chapter 1).*
b) *The front end alignment is correct (Chapter 10).*
c) *The vehicle isn't loaded with weight in an unequal manner.*

48 Vehicle pulls to one side during braking

1   Incorrect tire pressures (Chapter 1).
2   Front end out of alignment (have the front end aligned).
3   Unmatched tires on same axle.
4   Restricted brake lines or hoses (Chapter 9).
5   Sticking caliper piston (Chapter 9).
6   Loose suspension parts (Chapter 10).
7   Contaminated brake pad material (Chapter 9).
8   Excessive wear of brake pad material or disc on one side.

49 Noise (grinding or high-pitched squeal) when the brakes are applied

Disc brake pads worn out. Replace pads with new ones immediately (Chapter 9).

50 Brake roughness or chatter (pedal pulsates)

1   Excessive brake disc lateral runout (Chapter 9).
2   Parallelism of disc not within specifications (Chapter 9).
3   Uneven pad wear caused by caliper not sliding due to improper clearance or dirt (Chapter 9).
4   Defective brake disc (Chapter 9).

51 Excessive pedal effort required to stop vehicle

1   Malfunctioning power brake booster (Chapter 9).
2   Partial system failure (Chapter 9).
3   Excessively worn pads (Chapter 9).
4   One or more caliper pistons seized or sticking (Chapter 9).
5   Brake pads contaminated with oil or grease (Chapter 9).
6   New pads installed and not yet seated. It will take a while for the new material to seat.

52 Excessive brake pedal travel

1   Partial brake system failure (Chapter 9).
2   Insufficient fluid in master cylinder (Chapters 1 and 9).
3   Air trapped in system (Chapter 9).
4   Faulty master cylinder (Chapter 9).

53 Dragging brakes

1   Master cylinder pistons not returning correctly (Chapter 9).
2   Restricted brake lines or hoses (Chapters 1 and 9).
3   Incorrect parking brake adjustment (Chapter 9).
4   Defective brake calipers (Chapter 9).

54 Grabbing or uneven braking action

1   Malfunction of proportioning valve (Chapter 9).
2   Contaminated brake linings (Chapter 9).

55 Brake pedal feels spongy when depressed

1   Air in hydraulic lines (Chapter 9).
2   Master cylinder mounting bolts loose (Chapter 9).
3   Master cylinder defective (Chapter 9).

56 Brake pedal travels to the floor with little resistance

Little or no fluid in the master cylinder reservoir caused by leaking caliper, or loose, damaged or disconnected brake lines (Chapter 9).

57 Parking brake does not hold

Parking brake improperly adjusted (Chapter 9).

Suspension and steering systems

Note: *Before attempting to diagnose the suspension and steering systems, perform the following preliminary checks:*

a) *Check the tire pressures and look for uneven wear.*
b) *Check the steering universal joints or coupling from the column to the steering gear for loose fasteners and wear.*
c) *Check the front and rear suspension and the steering gear assembly for loose and damaged parts.*
d) *Look for out-of-round or out-of-balance tires, bent rims and loose and/or rough wheel bearings.*

58 Vehicle pulls to one side

1   Mismatched or uneven tires.
2   Broken or sagging springs (Chapter 10).
3   Wheel alignment incorrect.
4   Front brake dragging (Chapter 9).

59 Abnormal or excessive tire wear

1   Wheel alignment incorrect.
2   Sagging or broken springs (Chapter 10).
3   Tire out-of-balance.
4   Worn strut or shock absorber (Chapter 10).
5   Overloaded vehicle.
6   Tires not rotated regularly.

60 Wheel makes a "thumping" noise

1   Blister or bump on tire.
2   Improper strut or shock absorber action (Chapter 10).

61 Shimmy, shake or vibration

1   Tire or wheel out-of-balance or out-of-round.
2   Worn wheel bearings (Chapter 10).
3   Worn tie-rod ends (Chapter 10).
4   Worn balljoints (Chapter 10).
5   Excessive wheel runout.
6   Blister or bump on tire.

62 Hard steering

1   Worn balljoints or tie-rod ends (Chapter 10).
2   Front wheel alignment incorrect (Chapter 10).
3   Low tire pressure(s) (Chapter 1).

63 Steering wheel does not return to center position correctly

1   Worn balljoints or tie-rod ends (Chapter 10).
2   Binding in steering column (Chapter 10).
3   Defective steering gear assembly (Chapter 10).
4   Front wheel alignment problem.

64 Abnormal noise at the front end

1   Worn balljoints or tie-rod ends (Chapter 1).
2   Loose upper strut mount (Chapter 10).
3   Worn tie-rod ends (Chapter 10).
4   Loose stabilizer bar (Chapter 10).
5   Loose wheel lug nuts (Chapter 1).
6   Loose suspension bolts (Chapter 10).

65 Wander or poor steering stability

1   Mismatched or uneven tires.
2   Worn balljoints or tie-rod ends.
3   Worn struts or shock absorbers (Chapter 10).
4   Loose stabilizer bar (Chapter 10).
5   Broken or sagging springs (Chapter 10).
6   Front wheel alignment incorrect.

66 Erratic steering when braking

1   Wheel bearings worn (Chapter 10).
2   Broken or sagging springs (Chapter 10).
3   Leaking brake caliper (Chapter 9).
4   Warped brake discs (Chapter 9).
5   Wheel alignment incorrect.

67 Excessive pitching and/or rolling around corners or during braking

1   Loose stabilizer bar (Chapter 10).
2   Worn struts/shock absorbers or mounts (Chapter 10).
3   Broken or sagging springs (Chapter 10).
4   Overloaded vehicle.

68 Suspension bottoms

1   Overloaded vehicle.
2   Worn struts or shock absorbers (Chapter 10).
3   Sagging springs (Chapter 10).

69 Cupped tires

1   Wheel alignment incorrect (Chapter 10).
2   Worn struts or shock absorbers (Chapter 10).
3   Hub bearings worn (Chapter 10).
4   Excessive tire or wheel runout.
5   Worn balljoints (Chapter 10).

70 Excessive tire wear on outside edge

1   Inflation pressures incorrect (Chapter 1).
2   Excessive speed in turns.
3   Wheel alignment incorrect (excessive toe-in or positive camber). Have professionally aligned.
4   Suspension arm bent (Chapter 10).

71 Excessive tire wear on inside edge

1   Inflation pressures incorrect (Chapter 1).
2   Wheel alignment incorrect (toe-out or excessive negative camber). Have professionally aligned.
3   Loose or damaged steering components (Chapter 10).

72 Tire tread worn in one place

1   Tires out-of-balance.
2   Damaged wheel. Inspect and replace if necessary.
3   Defective tire (Chapter 1).

73 Excessive play or looseness in steering system

1   Hub bearings worn (Chapter 10).
2   Tie-rod end loose or worn (Chapter 10).
3   Steering gear loose (Chapter 10).

74 Rattling or clicking noise in steering gear

1   Steering gear mounting bolts loose (Chapter 10).
2   Steering gear defective (Chapter 10).

Notes

Chapter 1
Tune-up and routine maintenance

Contents

Specifications

Recommended lubricants and fluids

Note: *Listed here are manufacturer recommendations at the time this manual was written. Manufacturers occasionally upgrade their fluid and lubricant specifications, so check with your local auto parts store for current recommendations.*

Engine oil	
Type	API "certified for gasoline engines"
Viscosity	SAE 5W-30
Engine coolant	50/50 mixture of ethylene glycol-based antifreeze and distilled or demineralized water
Fuel	Unleaded gasoline, minimum 91 RON octane
Automatic transaxle fluid	Nissan CVT fluid NS-2*
Brake fluid	DOT 3 brake fluid
Power steering fluid	Nissan PSF or DEXRON VI automatic transmission fluid
Rear differential lubricant (AWD models)	API GL-5 SAE 80W-90 hypoid gear lubricant
Transfer case lubricant (AWD models)	API GL-5 SAE 80W-90 hypoid gear lubricant

*Use of conventional transmission fluid will damage the transaxle and void the warranty according to manufacturer

Capacities*

Engine oil (including filter)
    2007 and earlier models.. 4-1/4 quarts
    2009 and later models.. 4-7/8 quarts
Coolant (including reservoir tank).. 10 quarts
Automatic transaxle**
    2007 and earlier models.. 10-3/4 quarts
    2009 and later models.. 10-1/4 quarts

*All capacities approximate. Add as necessary to bring up to appropriate level.
**The best way to determine the amount of fluid to add during a routine fluid change is to measure the amount drained. Additionally, on 2007 and earlier models, the fluid changing procedure will require 30 to 50-percent more fluid than what is listed here (refer to Section 27).

Ignition system

Spark plugs
    2007 and earlier models
      Type... NGK PLFR5A-11
      Gap... 0.043 inch
    2009 and later models
      Type... Denso FXE22HR-11
      Gap... 0.043 inch
Firing order 1-2-3-4-5-6

Valve clearance (engine cold)

Intake valves.. 0.010 to 0.013 inch
Exhaust valves .... 0.011 to 0.015 inch

Cooling system

Thermostat starts to open.. 177 to 182 degrees F

Brakes

Disc brake pad lining thickness (minimum) .... 3/32 inch
Brake pedal height and freeplay... See Chapter 9
Parking brake adjustment... See Chapter 9

Suspension and steering

Steering wheel freeplay limit.. 0 to 1.38 inches
Balljoint allowable movement 0

FRONT

Cylinder locations

Torque specifications

Ft-lbs (unless otherwise indicated)

Note: One foot-pound (ft-lb) of torque is equivalent to 12 inch-pounds (in-lbs) of torque. Torque values below approximately 15 foot-pounds are expressed in inch-pounds, because most foot-pound torque wrenches are not accurate at these smaller values.

Engine oil drain plug.. 25
Automatic transaxle drain plug (2009 and later models) 15
Drivebelt tensioner (2008 and later models)
    Tensioner pulley mounting bolt.. 18
    Tensioner bracket mounting bolts 18
    Idler pulley mounting bolts 22
    Idler pulley bracket bolts .... 80 in-lbs
Idler pulley bolt (2003 through 2007 models) 26
Rear differential drain and fill plugs 26
Spark plugs... 168 in-lbs
Transfer case drain and fill plugs... 132 in-lbs
Wheel lug nuts.. 80

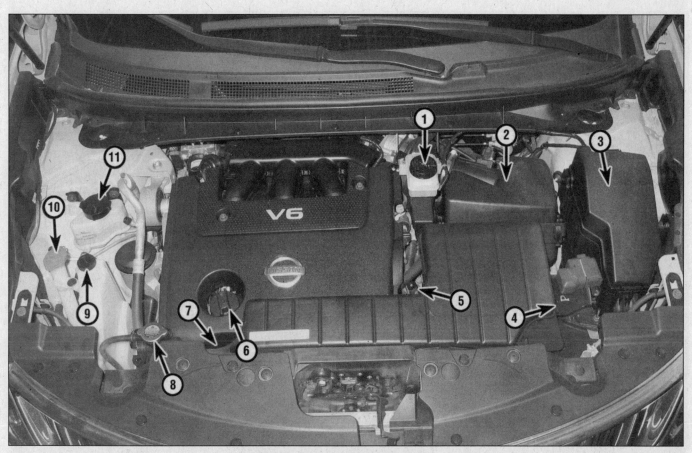

Engine compartment components

1	Brake fluid reservoir	5	Transaxle fluid dipstick	9	Engine coolant reservoir
2	Air filter housing	6	Engine oil filler cap	10	Windshield washer fluid reservoir
3	Underhood fuse/relay block	7	Engine oil dipstick	11	Power steering fluid reservoir
4	Battery	8	Radiator cap		

Engine compartment underside components

1	Lower radiator hose	4	Outer driveaxle boot	6	Tie-rod end
2	Engine oil drain plug	5	Brake caliper	7	Balljoint
3	Transaxle drain plug				

Rear underside components

| 1 | Muffler | 3 | EVAP system canister | 5 | Shock absorber |
| 2 | Exhaust system hangar | 4 | Coil spring | 6 | Fuel tank |

1 Nissan Murano maintenance schedule

The maintenance intervals in this manual are provided with the assumption that you, not the dealer, will be doing the work. These are the minimum maintenance intervals recommended by the factory for vehicles that are driven daily. If you wish to keep your vehicle in peak condition at all times, you may wish to perform some of these procedures even more often. Because frequent maintenance enhances the efficiency, performance and resale value of your car, we encourage you to do so. If you drive in dusty areas, tow a trailer, idle or drive at low speeds for extended periods or drive for short distances (less than four miles) in below freezing temperatures, shorter intervals are also recommended.

When your vehicle is new, it should be serviced by a factory authorized dealer service department to protect the factory warranty. In many cases, the initial maintenance check is done at no cost to the owner.

Every 250 miles or weekly, whichever comes first

Check the engine oil level (Section 4)
Check the engine coolant level (Section 4)
Check the windshield washer fluid level (Section 4)
Check the battery electrolyte (Section 4)
Check the brake fluid level (Section 4)
Check the tires and tire pressures (Section 5)

Every 3000 miles or 3 months, whichever comes first

All items listed above plus:
Check the power steering fluid level (Section 6)
Check the automatic transaxle fluid level (Section 7)
Change the engine oil and oil filter (Section 8)

Every 7500 miles or 6 months, whichever comes first

Inspect and replace if necessary the windshield wiper blades (Section 9)
Check and service the battery (Section 10)
Check the engine drivebelt (Section 11)
Inspect and replace if necessary all underhood hoses (Section 12)
Check the cooling system (Section 13)
Rotate the tires (Section 14)

Every 15,000 miles or 12 months, whichever comes first

All items listed above plus:
Check the differential lubricant level (Section 15)
Check the transfer case lubricant (Section 16)

Inspect the brake system (Section 17)*
Replace the cabin air filter (Section 18)
Check the air filter element (Section 19)
Inspect the fuel system (Section 20)
Inspect the suspension and steering components (Section 21)
Inspect the exhaust system (Section 22)
Check the driveaxle boots (Section 23)

Every 30,000 miles or 24 months, whichever comes first

All items listed above plus:
Replace the air filter (Section 19)
Service the cooling system (drain, flush and refill) (Section 25)
Inspect the evaporative emissions control system (Section 26)
Check and replace if necessary the PCV valve (Section 28)

Every 60,000 miles or 48 months, whichever comes first

Change the automatic transaxle fluid (Section 27)**
Change the differential lubricant (Section 29)
Change the transfer case lubricant (Section 30)
Check (and adjust if noisy) the valve clearance (Section 31)

Every 105,000 miles or 72 months, whichever comes first

Replace the spark plugs (Section 24)
* *This item is affected by "severe" operating conditions as described below. If your vehicle is operated under "severe" conditions, perform all maintenance indicated with an asterisk (*) at half the indicated intervals. Severe conditions are indicated if you mainly operate your vehicle under one or more of the following conditions:*
Operating in dusty areas
Towing a trailer
Idling for extended periods and/or low speed operation
Operating when outside temperatures remain below freezing and when most trips are less than 4 miles
** *If operated under one or more of the following conditions, change the automatic transmission fluid and differential lubricant every 30,000 miles:*
In heavy city traffic where the outside temperature regularly reaches 90-degrees F (32-degrees C) or higher
In hilly or mountainous terrain
Frequent trailer pulling

4.2 Engine oil dipstick (A) and oil filler cap (B) locations

4.4 The oil level should be at or near the H mark - if it isn't, add enough oil to bring the level to near the H mark

2   Introduction

This Chapter is designed to help the home mechanic maintain the Nissan Murano for peak performance, economy, safety and long life.

Included in this Chapter is a master maintenance schedule, followed by Sections dealing specifically with each item on the schedule. Visual checks, adjustments, component replacement and other helpful items are included. Refer to the accompanying illustrations of the engine compartment and the underside of the vehicle for the location of various components.

Servicing your Murano in accordance with the mileage/time maintenance schedule and the following Sections will provide it with a planned maintenance program that should result in a long and reliable service life. This is a comprehensive plan, so maintaining some items but not others at the specified service intervals will not produce the same results.

As you service your Murano, you will discover that many of the procedures can, and should, be grouped together because of the nature of the particular procedure you're performing or because of the close proximity of two otherwise unrelated components to one another.

For example, if the vehicle is raised for any reason, you should inspect the exhaust, suspension, steering and fuel systems while you're under the vehicle. When you're rotating the tires, it makes good sense to check the brakes and wheel bearings since the wheels are already removed.

Finally, let's suppose you have to borrow or rent a torque wrench. Even if you only need to tighten the spark plugs, you might as well check the torque of as many critical fasteners as time allows.

The first step of this maintenance program is to prepare yourself before the actual work begins. Read through all Sections pertinent to the procedures you're planning to do, then make a list of and gather together all the parts and tools you will need to do the job. If it looks as if you might run into problems during a particular segment of some procedure, seek advice from your local auto parts stores or dealer service department.

3   Tune-up general information

The term tune-up is used in this manual to represent a combination of individual operations rather than one specific procedure.

If, from the time the vehicle is new, the routine maintenance schedule is followed closely and frequent checks are made of fluid levels and high wear items, as suggested throughout this manual, the engine will be kept in relatively good running condition and the need for additional work will be minimized.

More likely than not, however, there will be times when the engine is running poorly due to lack of regular maintenance. This is even more likely if a used vehicle, which has not received regular and frequent maintenance checks, is purchased. In such cases, an engine tune-up will be needed outside of the regular routine maintenance intervals.

The first step in any tune-up or engine diagnosis to help correct a poor running engine would be a cylinder compression check. A check of the engine compression (see Chapter 2B) will give valuable information regarding the overall performance of many internal components and should be used as a basis for tune-up and repair procedures. If, for instance, a compression check indicates serious internal engine wear, a conventional tune-up will not help the running condition of the engine and would be a waste of time and money.

The following series of operations are those most often needed to bring a generally poor running engine back into a proper state of tune.

Minor tune-up

Check all engine related fluids (Section 4)
Clean, inspect and test the battery
(Section 10)
Check the drivebelts (Section 11)
Check all underhood hoses (Section 12)
Check the cooling system (Section 13)
Check the air filter (Section 19)
Replace the spark plugs (Section 24)

Major tune-up

All items listed under Minor tune-up, plus . . .
Replace the air filter (Section 19)
Check the fuel system (Section 20)
Check the charging system (Chapter 5)
Check the ignition system (Chapter 5)

4   Fluid level checks (every 250 miles or weekly)

1   Fluids are an essential part of the lubrication, cooling, brake, clutch and other systems. Because these fluids gradually become depleted and/or contaminated during normal operation of the vehicle, they must be periodically replenished. See *Recommended lubricants and fluids* and *Capacities* in this Chapter's Specifications before adding fluid to any of the following components. **Note:** *The vehicle must be on level ground before fluid levels can be checked.*

Engine oil

Refer to illustrations 4.2 and 4.4

2   The engine oil level is checked with a dipstick located at the front of the engine **(see illustration)**.
3   The oil level should be checked before the vehicle has been driven, or about 5 minutes after the engine has been shut off. If the oil is checked immediately after driving the vehicle, some of the oil will remain in the upper engine components, producing an inaccurate reading on the dipstick.
4   Pull the dipstick out and wipe all the oil from the end with a clean rag or paper towel. Insert the clean dipstick all the way back in and pull it out again. Observe the oil at the end of the dipstick; the level should be between the L and H marks **(see illustration)**.
5   It takes about one quart of oil to raise the level from the L mark to the H mark on the dipstick. Do not allow the level to drop below the L

4.8 Don't confuse the engine coolant reservoir (A) with the windshield washer fluid reservoir (B)

4.15 Remove the cell caps to check the water level in the battery - if the level is low, add distilled water only

4.17 The brake fluid level should be kept between the MIN and MAX marks on the translucent plastic reservoir

mark or oil starvation may cause engine damage. On the other hand, overfilling the engine (adding oil above the H mark) may cause oil fouled spark plugs, oil leaks or oil seal failures.

6   Wipe the area around the filler cap, then remove the cap from the valve cover to add oil. Use a funnel to prevent spills. After adding the oil, install the filler cap hand tight. Start the engine and look carefully for any small leaks around the oil filter or drain plug. Stop the engine and check the oil level again after it has had sufficient time to drain from the upper block and cylinder head galleys.

7   Checking the oil level is an important preventive maintenance step. A continually dropping oil level indicates oil leakage through damaged seals, from loose connections, or past worn rings or valve guides. If the oil looks milky in color or has water droplets in it, a cylinder head gasket may be leaking. The cylinder head should be checked immediately. The condition of the oil should also be checked. Each time you check the oil level, slide your thumb and index finger up the dipstick before wiping off the oil. If you see small dirt or metal particles clinging to the dipstick, the oil should be changed (see Section 8).

Engine coolant

Refer to illustration 4.8

Warning: *Do not allow antifreeze to come in contact with your skin or painted surfaces of the vehicle. Flush contaminated areas immediately with plenty of water. Don't store new coolant or leave old coolant lying around where it's accessible to children or pets - they're attracted by its sweet smell and may drink it. Ingestion of even a small amount of coolant can be fatal! Wipe up garage floor and drip pan spills immediately. Keep antifreeze containers covered and repair cooling system leaks as soon as they're noticed.*

8   All vehicles covered by this manual are equipped with a pressurized coolant recovery system. A white coolant reservoir, located in the right front corner of the engine compartment, is connected by a hose to the base of

the coolant filler cap **(see illustration)**. If the coolant gets too hot during engine operation, coolant can escape through the relief valve in the filler cap, then through a connecting hose into the reservoir. As the engine cools, the coolant is automatically drawn back into the cooling system to maintain the correct level.

9   The coolant level should be checked regularly. It must be between the MAX and MIN lines on the tank. The level will vary with the temperature of the engine. When the engine is cold, the coolant level should be at or slightly above the MIN mark on the tank. Once the engine has warmed up, the level should be at or near the MAX mark. If it isn't, allow the fluid in the tank to cool, then remove the cap from the reservoir and add coolant to bring the level up to the MAX line. Use only ethylene/glycol type coolant and water in the mixture ratio recommended by your owner's manual. Do not use supplemental inhibitor additives. If only a small amount of coolant is required to bring the system up to the proper level, water can be used. However, repeated additions of water will dilute the recommended antifreeze and water solution. In order to maintain the proper ratio of antifreeze and water, it is advisable to top up the coolant level with the correct mixture. Refer to your owner's manual for the recommended ratio.

10   If the coolant level drops within a short time after replenishment, there may be a leak in the system. Inspect the radiator, hoses, engine coolant filler cap, drain plugs, air bleeder plugs and water pump. If no leak is evident, have the radiator cap pressure tested by your dealer.

Warning: *Never remove the radiator cap or the coolant reservoir cap when the engine is running or has just been shut down, because the cooling system is hot. Escaping steam and scalding liquid could cause serious injury.*

11   If it is necessary to open the radiator cap, wait until the system has cooled completely, then wrap a thick cloth around the cap and turn it to the first stop. If any steam escapes, wait until the system has cooled further, then remove the cap.

12   When checking the coolant level, always note its condition. It should be relatively clear.

If it is brown or rust colored, the system should be drained, flushed and refilled. Even if the coolant appears to be normal, the corrosion inhibitors wear out with use, so it must be replaced at the specified intervals.

13   Do not allow antifreeze to come in contact with your skin or painted surfaces of the vehicle. Flush contacted areas immediately with plenty of water.

Windshield washer fluid

14   Fluid for the windshield washer system is stored in a plastic reservoir which is located on the right side of the engine compartment, adjacent to the coolant reservoir **(see illustration 4.8)**. In milder climates, plain water can be used to top up the reservoir, but the reservoir should be kept no more than two-thirds full to allow for expansion should the water freeze. In colder climates, the use of a specially designed windshield washer fluid, available at your dealer and any auto parts store, will help lower the freezing point of the fluid. Mix the solution with water in accordance with the manufacturer's directions on the container. Do not use regular antifreeze, it will damage the vehicle's paint.

Battery electrolyte

Refer to illustration 4.15

15   On models not equipped with a sealed battery, check the electrolyte level **(see illustration)** of all six battery cells. It must be between the upper and lower levels. If the level is low, remove the filler/vent cap and add distilled water. Install and securely re-tighten the cap. **Caution:** *Overfilling the cells may cause electrolyte to spill over during periods of heavy charging, causing corrosion or damage.*

Brake fluid

Refer to illustration 4.17

16   The brake master cylinder is mounted on the front of the power booster unit in the engine compartment. The fluid reservoir for the master cylinder is mounted on a bracket, inboard of the air filter housing.

17   To check the fluid level of the brake master cylinder, simply look at the marks on the reservoir **(see illustration)**. The level should be between the MIN and MAX marks.
18   If the level is low, wipe the top of the reservoir cover with a clean rag to prevent contamination of the brake system before lifting the cover.
19   Add only the specified brake fluid to the brake reservoir (refer to *Recommended lubricants and fluids* in this Chapter's Specifications or your owner's manual). Mixing different types of brake fluid can damage the system. Fill the brake master cylinder reservoir only to the MAX line. **Warning:** *Use caution when filling the reservoir - brake fluid can harm your eyes and damage painted surfaces. Do not use brake fluid that has been opened for more than one year or has been left open. Brake fluid absorbs moisture from the air. Excess moisture can cause a dangerous loss of braking.*
20   While the reservoir cap is removed, inspect the master cylinder reservoir for contamination. If deposits, dirt particles or water droplets are present, the system should be drained and refilled.
21   After filling the reservoir to the proper level, make sure the lid is properly seated to prevent fluid leakage and/or system pressure loss.
22   The fluid in the brake master cylinder

will drop slightly as the brake pads at each wheel wear down during normal operation. If the master cylinder requires repeated replenishing to keep it at the proper level, this is an indication of leakage in the brake system, which should be corrected immediately. If the brake system shows an indication of leakage check all brake lines and connections, along with the calipers and booster (see Section 17 for more information).
23   If, upon checking the brake cylinder fluid level, you discover it empty or nearly empty, the systems should be bled (see Chapter 9).

5   Tire and tire pressure checks (every 250 miles or weekly)

Refer to illustrations 5.2, 5.3, 5.4a, 5.4b and 5.8

1   Periodic inspection of the tires may spare you from the inconvenience of being stranded with a flat tire. It can also provide you with vital information regarding possible problems in the steering and suspension systems before major damage occurs.
2   Normal tread wear can be monitored with a simple, inexpensive device known as a

5.2 A tire tread depth indicator should be used to monitor tire wear - they are available at auto parts stores and service stations and cost very little

tread depth indicator **(see illustration)**. When the tread depth reaches the specified minimum, replace the tire(s).
3   Note any abnormal tread wear **(see illustration)**. Tread pattern irregularities such as cupping, flat spots and more wear on one side than the other are indications of front end

UNDERINFLATION

CUPPING

Cupping may be caused by:
• Underinflation and/or mechanical irregularities such as out-of-balance condition of wheel and/or tire, and bent or damaged wheel.
• Loose or worn steering tie-rod or steering idler arm.
• Loose, damaged or worn front suspension parts.

OVERINFLATION

INCORRECT TOE-IN OR EXTREME CAMBER

FEATHERING DUE TO MISALIGNMENT

5.3 This chart will help you determine the condition of your tires, the probable cause(s) of abnormal wear and the corrective action necessary

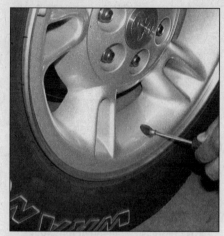

5.4a If a tire loses air on a steady basis, check the valve core first to make sure it's snug (special inexpensive wrenches are commonly available at auto parts stores)

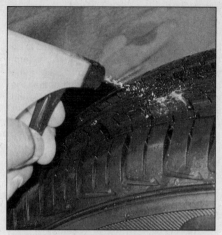

5.4b If the valve core is tight, raise the corner of the vehicle with the low tire and spray a soapy water solution onto the tread as the tire is turned slowly - slow leaks will cause small bubbles to appear

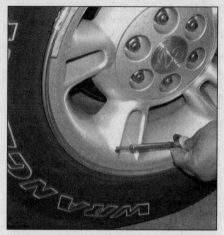

5.8 To extend the life of your tires, check the air pressure at least once a week with an accurate gauge (don't forget the spare!)

6.1 The power steering fluid reservoir is mounted at the rear of the engine compartment on the passenger's side

alignment and/or balance problems. If any of these conditions are noted, take the vehicle to a tire shop or service station to correct the problem.

4   Look closely for cuts, punctures and embedded nails or tacks. Sometimes a tire will hold its air pressure for a short time or leak down very slowly even after a nail has embedded itself into the tread. If a slow leak persists, check the valve stem core to make sure it is tight **(see illustration)**. Examine the tread for an object that may have embedded itself into the tire or for a plug that may have begun to leak (radial tire punctures are repaired with a plug that is installed in a puncture). If a puncture is suspected, it can be easily verified by spraying a solution of soapy water onto the puncture area **(see illustration)**. The soapy solution will bubble if there is a leak. Unless the puncture is inordinately large, a tire shop or gas station can usually repair the punctured tire.

5   Carefully inspect the inner sidewall of each tire for evidence of brake fluid leakage. If you see any, inspect the brakes immediately.

6   Correct tire air pressure adds miles to the lifespan of the tires, improves mileage and enhances overall ride quality. Tire pressure cannot be accurately estimated by looking at a tire, particularly if it is a radial. A tire pressure gauge is therefore essential. Keep an accurate gauge in the glove box. The pressure gauges fitted to the nozzles of air hoses at gas stations are often inaccurate.

7   Always check tire pressure when the tires are cold. "Cold" in this case, means the vehicle has not been driven over a mile in the three hours preceding a tire pressure check. A pressure rise of four to eight pounds is not uncommon once the tires are warm.

8   Unscrew the valve cap protruding from the wheel or hubcap and push the gauge firmly onto the valve **(see illustration)**. Note the reading on the gauge and compare this figure to the recommended tire pressure shown on the tire placard on the left door. Be sure to reinstall the valve cap to keep dirt and moisture out of the valve stem mechanism. Check all four tires and, if necessary, add enough air to bring them up to the recommended pressure levels.

9   Don't forget to keep the spare tire inflated to the specified pressure (consult your owner's manual). Note that the air pressure specified for the compact spare is significantly higher than the pressure of the regular tires.

---

6   Power steering fluid level check (every 3000 miles or 3 months)

Refer to illustration 6.1

1   To check the fluid level in the reservoir, simply look at the MIN and MAX on the side of the reservoir **(see illustration)**. The level should be within the specified distance from

the maximum fill line. Use the HOT range at fluid temperatures of 122 to 176 degrees F. Use the COLD range at fluid temperatures of 32 to 86 degrees F. At no time should the fluid level drop below the minimum mark on the reservoir.

2   If additional fluid is required, use a clean rag to wipe off the reservoir cap and area around the cap. This will prevent any foreign matter from entering the reservoir during the check.

3   Unscrew the top cap and pour the specified type directly into the reservoir, using a funnel to prevent spills. Install the cap and tighten securely.

4   If the reservoir requires frequent fluid additions, all power steering hoses, hose connections, the power steering pump and the rack and pinion assembly should be carefully checked for leaks

---

7   Automatic transaxle fluid level check (every 3000 miles or 3 months)

Refer to illustrations 7.4a and 7.4b

1   The level of the automatic transaxle fluid should be carefully maintained. Low fluid level can lead to slipping or loss of drive, while overfilling can cause foaming, loss of fluid and transaxle damage.

2   The transaxle fluid level should only be checked when the transaxle is hot (at its normal operating temperature). If the vehicle has just been driven over 10 miles (15 miles in a frigid climate), and the fluid temperature is 160 to 175-degrees F, the transaxle is hot. **Caution:** *If the vehicle has just been driven for a long time at high speed or in city traffic in hot weather, or if it has been pulling a trailer, an accurate fluid level reading cannot be obtained. Allow the fluid to cool down for about 30 minutes.*

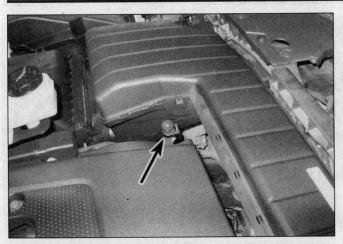

7.4a The automatic transaxle dipstick is located in a tube that is connected to the transaxle case - press the tab on the dipstick to release the lock

7.4b Check the automatic transaxle fluid with the engine idling at operating temperature and the gear selector in Park; add fluid, if necessary, to bring the level near the upper notch

3   If the vehicle has not been driven, park the vehicle on level ground, set the parking brake, then start the engine and bring it to operating temperature. While the engine is idling, depress the brake pedal and move the selector lever through all the gear ranges, beginning and ending in Park.

4   With the engine still idling, remove the dipstick from its tube **(see illustration)**. Check the level of the fluid on the dipstick **(see illustration)** and note its condition.

5   Wipe the fluid from the dipstick with a clean rag and reinsert it back into the filler tube until the cap seats. **Note:** *When inserting the dipstick, rotate it 1/2-turn so the tab on the cap doesn't lock into place when the dipstick is fully inserted.*

6   Pull the dipstick out again and note the fluid level. If the level is at the low side of the range, add the specified automatic transaxle fluid through the dipstick tube with a funnel. **Caution:** *This vehicle uses a special fluid designed specifically for the Nissan CVT transaxle. Don't use another fluid or damage may occur and the warranty may be voided. See this Chapter's Specifications for the proper fluid type.*

7   Add just enough of the recommended fluid to fill the transaxle to the proper level. It takes about one pint to raise the level from the low mark to the high mark when the fluid is hot, so add the fluid a little at a time and keep checking the level until it is correct. Once the fluid level is correct, reinstall the dipstick with the locking tab oriented correctly, making sure it locks into place.

8   The condition of the fluid should also be checked along with the level. If the fluid at the end of the dipstick is black or a dark reddish brown color, or if it emits a burned smell, the fluid should be changed (see Section 27). If you are in doubt about the condition of the fluid, purchase some new fluid and compare the two for color and smell.

8   Engine oil and oil filter change (every 3000 miles or 3 months)

Refer to illustrations 8.2, 8.5, 8.10 and 8.12

1   Frequent oil changes are the best pre-

ventive maintenance the home mechanic can give the engine, because aging oil becomes diluted and contaminated, which leads to premature engine wear.

2   Make sure that you have all the necessary tools before you begin this procedure **(see illustration)**. You should also have plenty of rags or newspapers handy for mopping up any spills.

3   Park the vehicle on a level spot. Start the engine and allow it to reach its normal operating temperature. Warm oil and contaminates will flow out more easily. Turn off the engine when it's warmed up. Remove the filler cap from the valve cover.

4   Raise the vehicle and support it securely on jackstands. **Warning:** *To avoid personal injury, never get beneath the vehicle when it is supported by only by a jack. The jack provided with your vehicle is designed solely for raising the vehicle to remove and replace the wheels. Always use jackstands to support the vehicle when it becomes necessary to place your body underneath the vehicle.*

5   Being careful not to touch the hot

8.2 These tools are required when changing the engine oil and filter

1   *Drain pan - It should be fairly shallow in depth, but wide in order to prevent spills*

2   *Rubber gloves - When removing the drain plug and filter, it is inevitable that you will get oil on your hands (the gloves will prevent burns)*

3   *Breaker bar - Sometimes the oil drain plug is pretty tight and a long breaker bar is needed to loosen it*

4   *Socket - To be used with the breaker bar or a ratchet (must be the correct size to fit the drain plug)*

5   *Filter wrench - This is a metal band-type wrench, which requires clearance around the filter to be effective*

6   *Filter wrench - This type fits on the bottom of the filter and can be turned with a ratchet or breaker bar (different size wrenches are available for different types of filters)*

8.5 Use the proper size box-end wrench or socket to remove the oil drain plug and avoid rounding it off

8.10 The oil filter is located on the right end of the engine. Use an oil filter wrench for removal; DO NOT use the wrench to tighten the new filter

8.12 Lubricate the oil filter gasket with clean engine oil before installing the filter

exhaust components, place the drain pan under the drain plug in the bottom of the pan and remove the plug **(see illustration)**. You may want to wear gloves while unscrewing the plug the final few turns if the engine is really hot.

6   Allow the old oil to drain into the pan. It may be necessary to move the pan farther under the engine as the oil flow slows to a trickle. Inspect the old oil for the presence of metal shavings and chips.

7   After all the oil has drained, wipe off the drain plug with a clean rag. Even minute metal particles clinging to the plug would immediately contaminate the new oil.

8   Clean the area around the drain plug opening, reinstall the plug and tighten it to the torque listed in this Chapter's Specifications.

9   Move the drain pan into position under the oil filter.

10   Loosen the oil filter by turning it counterclockwise with the filter wrench **(see illustration)**. Any standard filter wrench should work. Once the filter is loose, use your hands to unscrew it from the oil cooler. Just as the filter is detached from the block, immediately tilt the open end up to prevent the oil inside the filter from spilling out. **Warning:** The engine exhaust manifold may still be hot, so be careful.

11   With a clean rag, wipe off the oil filter mounting surface. Make sure that none of the old gasket remains stuck to the mounting surface. It can be removed with a scraper if necessary.

12   Compare the old filter with the new one to make sure they are the same type. Smear some engine oil on the rubber gasket of the new filter and screw it into place **(see illustration)**. Because over-tightening the filter will damage the gasket, do not use a filter wrench to tighten the filter. Most filter manufacturers recommend tightening the filter by hand only. Normally they should be tightened 2/3-turn after the gasket contacts the filter adapter/oil cooler, but be sure to follow the directions on the filter or container.

13   Remove all tools, rags, etc. from under the vehicle, being careful not to spill the oil in the drain pan, then lower the vehicle.

14   Remove the filler cap and add new oil to the engine. Use a spout or funnel to prevent oil from spilling onto the top of the engine. Pour four quarts of fresh oil into the engine. Wait a few minutes to allow the oil to drain into the pan, then check the level on the oil dipstick (see Section 4 if necessary). If the oil level is at or near the H mark, install the filler cap hand tight, start the engine and allow the new oil to circulate.

15   Allow the engine to run for about a minute. While the engine is running, look under the vehicle and check for leaks at the oil pan drain plug and around the oil filter. If either is leaking, stop the engine and tighten the plug or filter slightly.

16   Wait a few minutes to allow the oil to trickle down into the pan, then recheck the level on the dipstick and, if necessary, add enough oil to bring the level to the H mark.

17   During the first few trips after an oil change, make it a point to check frequently for leaks and proper oil level.

18   The old oil drained from the engine cannot be reused in its present state and should be disposed of. Check with your local auto parts store, disposal facility or environmental agency to see if they will accept the oil for recycling. After the oil has cooled it can be drained into a container (capped plastic jugs, topped bottles, milk cartons, etc.) for transport to one of these disposal sites. Don't dispose of the oil by pouring it on the ground or down a drain!

9 Windshield wiper blade inspection and replacement (every 7500 miles or 6 months)

Refer to illustrations 9.3, 9.5 and 9.6

1   The windshield wiper and blade assembly should be inspected periodically for damage, loose components and cracked or worn blade elements.

2   Road film can build up on the wiper blades and affect their efficiency, so they should be washed regularly with a mild detergent solution.

3   The action of the wiping mechanism can loosen bolts, nuts and fasteners, so they should be checked and tightened, as necessary **(see illustration)**, at the same time the wiper blades are checked.

4   If the wiper blade elements are cracked, worn or warped, or no longer clean adequately, they should be replaced with new ones.

5   Lift the arm assembly away from the glass for clearance, press on the release lever, then slide the wiper blade assembly out of the hook in the end of the arm **(see illustration)**.

6   Use needle-nose pliers to compress the blade element, then slide the element out of the frame and discard it **(see illustration)**.

7   Installation is the reverse of removal.

10 Battery check, maintenance and charging (every 7500 miles or 6 months)

Refer to illustrations 10.1, 10.6a, 10.6b, 10.7a and 10.7b

Warning: Certain precautions must be followed when checking and servicing the battery. Hydrogen gas, which is highly flammable, is always present in the battery cells, so keep lighted tobacco and all other open flames and sparks away from the battery. The electrolyte inside the battery is actually dilute sulfuric acid, which will cause injury if splashed on your skin or in your eyes. It will also ruin clothes and painted surfaces. When removing the battery cables, always detach the negative cable first and hook it up last!

1   A routine preventive maintenance program for the battery in your vehicle is the only way to ensure quick and reliable starts. But before performing any battery maintenance, make sure that you have the proper equipment necessary to work safely around the battery **(see illustration)**.

2   There are also several precautions that should be taken whenever battery maintenance is performed. Before servicing the battery, always turn the engine and all accessories off and disconnect the cable from the negative terminal of the battery.

9.3 Remove the trim caps and check the tightness of the wiper arm retaining nuts

9.5 Press on the release tab and push the blade assembly down out of the hook in the arm

9.6 Use needle-nose pliers to compress the rubber element, then slide the element out. Slide the new element in and lock the blade assembly fingers into the notches of the wiper element

10.1 Tools and materials required for battery maintenance

1   *Face shield/safety goggles* - *When removing corrosion with a brush, the acidic particles can easily fly up into your eyes*
2   *Rubber gloves* - *Another safety item to consider when servicing the battery; remember that's acid inside the battery*
3   *Battery post/cable cleaner* - *This wire brush cleaning tool will remove all traces of corrosion from the battery posts and cable clamps*
4   *Treated felt washers* - *Placing one of these on each post, directly under the cable clamps, will help prevent corrosion*
5   *Baking soda* - *A solution of baking soda and water can be used to neutralize corrosion*
6   *Petroleum jelly* - *A layer of this on the battery posts will help prevent corrosion*

3   The battery produces hydrogen gas, which is both flammable and explosive. Never create a spark, smoke or light a match around the battery. Always charge the battery in a ventilated area.

4   Electrolyte contains poisonous and corrosive sulfuric acid. Do not allow it to get in your eyes, on your skin or on your clothes. Never ingest it. Wear protective safety glasses when working near the battery. Keep children away from the battery.

5   Note the external condition of the battery. If the positive terminal and cable clamp on your vehicle's battery is equipped with a rubber protector, make sure it isn't torn or damaged. It should completely cover the terminal. Look for any corroded or loose connections, cracks in the case or cover or loose hold-down clamps. Also check the entire length of each cable for cracks and frayed conductors.

6   If corrosion, which looks like white, fluffy deposits (see illustration) is evident, particularly around the terminals, the battery should be removed for cleaning. Loosen the cable

10.6a Battery terminal corrosion usually appears as light, fluffy powder

10.6b Removing a cable from the battery post with a wrench - sometimes special battery pliers are required for this procedure if corrosion has caused deterioration of the nut hex (always remove the ground cable first and hook it up last!)

clamp bolts with a wrench, being careful to remove the ground cable first, and slide them off the terminals (see illustration). Then dis-

10.7a When cleaning the cable clamps, all corrosion must be removed

10.7b Regardless of the type of tool used to clean the battery posts, a clean, shiny surface should be the result

connect the hold-down clamp bolt and nut, remove the clamp and lift the battery from the engine compartment.

7   Clean the cable clamps thoroughly with a battery brush or a terminal cleaner and a solution of warm water and baking soda **(see illustration)**. Wash the terminals and the top of the battery case with the same solution but make sure that the solution doesn't get into the battery. When cleaning the cables, terminals and battery top, wear safety goggles and rubber gloves to prevent any solution from coming in contact with your eyes or hands. Wear old clothes too - even diluted, sulfuric acid splashed onto clothes will burn holes in them. If the terminals have been extensively corroded, clean them up with a terminal cleaner **(see illustration)**. Thoroughly wash all cleaned areas with plain water.

8   Make sure the battery tray is in good condition and the hold-down clamp bolt or nut is tight. If the battery is removed from the tray, make sure no parts remain in the bottom of the tray when the battery is reinstalled. When reinstalling the hold-down clamp bolt or nut, do not over-tighten it.

9   Information on removing and installing the battery can be found in Chapter 5. Information on jump starting can be found at the front of this manual. For more detailed battery checking procedures, refer to the *Haynes Automotive Electrical Manual*.

Cleaning

10   Corrosion on the hold-down components, battery case and surrounding areas can be removed with a solution of water and baking soda. Thoroughly rinse all cleaned areas with plain water.

11   Any metal parts of the vehicle damaged by corrosion should be covered with a zinc-based primer, then painted.

Charging

Warning: *When batteries are being charged, hydrogen gas, which is very explosive and flammable, is produced. Do not smoke or allow open flames near a charging or a recently charged*

battery. *Wear eye protection when near the battery during charging. Also, make sure the charger is unplugged before connecting or disconnecting the battery from the charger.*

12   Slow-rate charging is the best way to restore a battery that's discharged to the point where it will not start the engine. It's also a good way to maintain the battery charge in a vehicle that's only driven a few miles between starts. Maintaining the battery charge is particularly important in the winter when the battery must work harder to start the engine and electrical accessories that drain the battery are in greater use.

13   It's best to use a one or two-amp battery charger (sometimes called a "trickle" charger). They are the safest and put the least strain on the battery. They are also the least expensive. For a faster charge, you can use a higher amperage charger, but don't use one rated more than 1/10th the amp/hour rating of the battery. Rapid boost charges that claim to restore the power of the battery in one to two hours are hardest on the battery and can damage batteries not in good condition. This type of charging should only be used in emergency situations.

14   The average time necessary to charge a battery should be listed in the instructions that come with the charger. As a general rule, a trickle charger will charge a battery in 12 to 16 hours.

11   Drivebelt check (every 7500 miles or 6 months) and replacement

Check

Refer to illustrations 11.3 and 11.4

1   These models are equipped with two different types of drivebelt systems: 2003 through 2007 models use two drivebelts with adjusters, while 2008 and later models use a serpentine drivebelt with an automatic tensioner. Because of their composition and the high stresses to which they are subjected, drivebelts stretch and deteriorate as they get older. They must therefore be periodically inspected.

2   2007 and earlier models are equipped with a power steering pump belt and an alternator/air conditioning compressor belt. On 2008 and later engines, the serpentine drivebelt transmits power to all the accessories.

3   With the engine off, open the hood and locate the drivebelts. With a flashlight, check each belt for separation of the adhesive rubber on both sides of the core, core separation from the belt side, a severed core, separation of the ribs from the adhesive rubber, cracking or separation of the ribs, and torn or worn ribs or cracks in the inner ridges of the ribs **(see illustration)**. Also check for fraying and glazing, which gives the belt a shiny appearance. Both sides of the belt should be inspected, which means you will have to twist the belt to check the underside. Use your fingers to feel the belt where you can't see it. If any of the above conditions are evident, replace the belt (see Steps 7 through 11 or 12 through 14).

ACCEPTABLE

Cracks Running Across "V" Portions of Belt

1/2"   Missing Two or More Adjacent Ribs 1/2" or longer

UNACCEPTABLE

11.3 Here are some of the more common problems associated with drivebelts (check the belt very carefully to prevent an untimely breakdown)

Cracks Running Parallel to "V" Portions of Belt

11.4 If the indicator notch (A) on the moveable part of the tensioner passes the stationary mark (B) on the tensioner body, the drivebelt has stretched beyond its limit and should be replaced

4   Check the drivebelt tension or adjustment:

a) *On 2003 through 2007 models, check the belt tension by pushing firmly on the belt with your thumb at a distance half-way between the pulleys. Note how far the belt can be pushed (deflected), and measure this deflection with a ruler. The belt should deflect 1/4-inch if the distance from pulley center to pulley center is between 7 and 11 inches; the belt should deflect 1/2-inch if the distance from pulley center to pulley center is between 12 and 16 inches.*

b) *On 2008 and later models, check the drivebelt indicator for excessive stretch* **(see illustration)**. *If the drivebelt indicator is out of limit, replace the drivebelt.*

Adjustment - 2003 through 2007 models

Refer to illustration 11.6

5   Raise the vehicle and support it securely on jackstands. Remove the engine splash shields (see Chapter 11).

11.12 Release the tension using a wrench, then insert a drill or rod to lock the tensioner in place

11.6 Typical drivebelt routing diagram for 2003 through 2007 models

72025-1-11.6 HAYNES

6   Belt tension for the alternator and A/C compressor belt is adjusted by moving the idler pulley. To adjust the alternator belt, loosen the bolt on the idler pulley and turn the idler pulley adjusting bolt **(see illustration)**. To adjust the tension on the power steering pump belt, loosen the power steering bracket pivot bolt and the adjuster lock bolt, then turn the power steering pump adjuster bolt. Measure the belt tension (see Step 4a). Repeat this Step until the drivebelt is adjusted properly.

Drivebelt replacement
2003 through 2007 models

7   Raise the vehicle and support it securely on jackstands. Remove the engine splash shields (see Chapter 11).

8   To replace a belt, loosen the drivebelt adjustment bolt (see Step 6), slip the belt off the crankshaft pulley and remove it. If you are replacing the power steering pump belt, you'll have to remove the alternator/air conditioning compressor belt first because of the way they are arranged on the crankshaft pulley. Because of this, and because belts tend to wear out more or less together, it is a good idea to replace both belts at the same time. Mark each belt and its appropriate pulley groove so the replacement belts can be installed in their proper positions.

9   Take the old belts to the parts store in order to make a direct comparison for length, width and design.

10   After replacing a ribbed drivebelt, make

sure that it fits properly in the grooves in the pulleys. It is essential that the belt be properly centered.

11   Adjust the belt(s) (see Step 6).

2008 and later models

Refer to illustrations 11.12 and 11.14

12   Rotate the belt tensioner to release tension on the drivebelt **(see illustration)**.

13   Remove the drivebelt from the tensioner and all accessories.

14   Install the drivebelt and make sure the ribs of the drivebelt fit properly in the grooves in the pulleys **(see illustration)**. Installation is the reverse of removal.

Adjuster pulley/tensioner replacement
2003 through 2007 models

15   Remove the drivebelt (see Steps 7 and 8).

16   Remove the idler pulley lockbolt. Remove the idler pulley bolts from the bracket and separate the assembly from the engine.

17   Installation is the reverse of removal. Tighten the fasteners securely.

2008 and later models

19   Remove the drivebelt (see Steps 12 and 13).

20   Remove the drivebelt tensioner mounting bolts and remove the tensioner.

21   Installation is the reverse of removal. Tighten the tensioner mounting fasteners to the torque listed in this Chapter's Specifications.

11.14 Drivebelt routing diagram - 2008 and later models

1   *Power steering pump*
2   *Idler pulley*
3   *Alternator*
4   *Air conditioning compressor*
5   *Idler pulley*
6   *Crankshaft pulley*
7   *Tensioner pulley*

72016-1-11.9b HAYNES

Check for a chafed area that could fail prematurely.

Check for a soft area indicating the hose has deteriorated inside.

Overtightening the clamp on a hardened hose will damage the hose and cause a leak.

Check each hose for swelling and oil-soaked ends. Cracks and breaks can be located by squeezing the hose.

13.4 Hoses, like drivebelts, have a habit of failing at the worst possible time - to prevent the inconvenience of a blown radiator or heater hose, inspect them carefully as shown here

12   Underhood hose check and replacement (every 7500 miles or 6 months)

Caution: *Replacement of air conditioning hoses must be left to a dealer service department or air conditioning shop that has the equipment to depressurize the system safely. Never remove air conditioning components or hoses until the system has been depressurized.*

General

1   High temperatures in the engine compartment can cause the deterioration of the rubber and plastic hoses used for engine, accessory and emission systems operation. Periodic inspection should be made for cracks, loose clamps, material hardening and leaks.

2   Information specific to the cooling system hoses can be found in Section 13.

3   Some, but not all, hoses are secured to the fittings with clamps. Where clamps are used, check to be sure they haven't lost their tension, allowing the hose to leak. If clamps aren't used, make sure the hose has not expanded and/or hardened where it slips over the fitting, allowing it to leak.

Vacuum hoses

4   It's quite common for vacuum hoses, especially those in the emissions system, to be color coded or identified by colored stripes molded into them. Various systems require hoses with different wall thickness, collapse resistance and temperature resistance. When replacing hoses, be sure the new ones are made of the same material.

5   Often the only effective way to check a hose is to remove it completely from the vehicle. If more than one hose is removed, be sure to label the hoses and fittings to ensure correct installation.

6   When checking vacuum hoses, be sure to include any plastic T-fittings in the check. Inspect the fittings for cracks and the hose where it fits over the fitting for distortion, which could cause leakage.

7   A small piece of vacuum hose (1/4-inch inside diameter) can be used as a stethoscope to detect vacuum leaks. Hold one end of the hose to your ear and probe around vacuum hoses and fittings, listening for the hissing sound characteristic of a vacuum leak. **Warning:** *When probing with the vacuum hose stethoscope, be very careful not to come into contact with moving engine components such as the drivebelts, cooling fan, etc.*

Fuel hose

Warning: *Gasoline is flammable, so take extra precautions when you work on any part of the fuel system. Don't smoke or allow open flames or bare light bulbs near the work area, and don't work in a garage where a gas-type appliance (such as a water heater or clothes dryer) is present. Since fuel is carcinogenic, wear fuel-resistant gloves when there's a possibility of being exposed to fuel, and, if you spill any fuel on your skin, rinse it off immediately with soap and water. Mop up any spills immediately and do not store fuel-soaked rags where they could ignite. The fuel system is under constant pressure, so, if any fuel lines are to be disconnected, the fuel pressure in the system must be relieved first (see Chapter 4 for more information). When you perform any kind of work on the fuel system, wear safety glasses and have a Class B type fire extinguisher on hand.*

8   Check all flexible fuel lines for deterioration and chafing. Check especially for cracks in areas where the hose bends and just before fittings, such as where the fuel line attaches to the fuel rail.

9   If any fuel lines are to be disconnected, be prepared to catch spilled fuel. **Warning:** *Your vehicle is equipped with fuel injection*

and you must relieve the fuel system pressure before servicing the fuel lines. Refer to Chapter 4 for the fuel system pressure relief procedure.

10   When replacing a hose, use only hose that is specifically designed for your fuel injection system.

11   Some fuel lines use quick-connect fittings, which require a special tool to disconnect. See Chapter 4 for more information on these types of fittings.

Metal lines

12   Sections of metal line are often used for fuel line between the fuel pump and carburetor or fuel injection unit. Check carefully to be sure the line has not been bent or crimped and that cracks have not started in the line.

13   If a section of metal fuel line must be replaced, only seamless steel tubing should be used, since copper and aluminum tubing don't have the strength necessary to withstand normal engine vibration.

14   Check the metal brake lines where they enter the master cylinder and brake proportioning unit (if used) for cracks in the lines or loose fittings. Any sign of brake fluid leakage calls for an immediate thorough inspection of the brake system.

13   Cooling system check (every 7500 miles or 6 months)

Refer to illustration 13.4

1   Many major engine failures can be attributed to a faulty cooling system. If the vehicle is equipped with an automatic transaxle, the cooling system also cools the transaxle fluid and thus plays an important role in prolonging transaxle life.

2   The cooling system should be checked with the engine cold. Do this before the vehicle is driven for the day or after the engine has been shut off for at least three hours.

3   Remove the radiator cap by turning it to the left until it reaches a stop. If you hear a hissing sound (indicating there is still pressure in the system), wait until it stops. Press down on the cap with the palm of your hand and continue turning to the left until the cap can be removed. Thoroughly clean the cap, inside and out, with clean water. Also clean the filler neck on the radiator. All traces of corrosion should be removed. The coolant inside the radiator should be relatively transparent. If it's rust colored, the system should be drained and refilled (see Section 25). If the coolant level isn't up to the top, add additional antifreeze/coolant mixture (see Section 4).

4   Carefully check the large upper and lower radiator hoses along with the smaller diameter heater hoses which run from the engine to the firewall. Inspect each hose along its entire length, replacing any hose which is cracked, swollen or shows signs of deterioration. Cracks may become more apparent if the hose is squeezed **(see illustration)**. Regard-

14.2 The recommended tire rotation pattern for these vehicles

17.7a You will find an inspection hole like this in each caliper through which you can view the thickness of remaining friction material for the inner pad

17.7b Be sure to check the thickness of the outer pad material, too

less of condition, it's a good idea to replace hoses with new ones every two years.

5   Make sure that all hose connections are tight. A leak in the cooling system will usually show up as white or rust colored deposits on the areas adjoining the leak. If wire-type clamps are used at the ends of the hoses, it may be a good idea to replace them with more secure screw-type clamps.

6   Use compressed air or a soft brush to remove bugs, leaves, etc. from the front of the radiator or air conditioning condenser. Be careful not to damage the delicate cooling fins or cut yourself on them.

7   Every other inspection, or at the first indication of cooling system problems, have the cap and system pressure tested. If you don't have a pressure tester, most gas stations and repair shops will do this for a minimal charge.

14   Tire rotation (every 7500 miles or 6 months)

Refer to illustration 14.2

1   The tires should be rotated at the specified intervals and whenever uneven wear is noticed. Since the vehicle will be raised and the tires removed anyway, check the brakes (see Section 17) at this time.

2   Radial tires must be rotated in a specific pattern (see illustration).

3   Refer to the information in *Jacking and towing* at the front of this manual for the proper procedures to follow when raising the vehicle and changing a tire. If the brakes are to be checked, do not apply the parking brake as stated. Make sure the tires are blocked to prevent the vehicle from rolling.

4   Preferably, the entire vehicle should be raised at the same time. This can be done on a hoist or by jacking up each corner and then lowering the vehicle onto jackstands placed under

the frame rails. Always use four jackstands and make sure the vehicle is firmly supported.

5   After rotation, check and adjust the tire pressures as necessary and be sure to check the lug nut tightness.

6   For further information on the wheels and tires, refer to Chapter 10.

15   Differential lubricant level check (AWD models) (every 15,000 miles or 12 months)

1   Raise the vehicle and support it securely on jackstands. The vehicle should be as level as possible to ensure an accurate check.

2   Remove the plug from the filler hole in the differential.

3   The lubricant should be up to the bottom of the filler hole. If not, use a pump or squeeze bottle to add the specified lubricant until it just starts to run out of the hole.

4   Place a new sealing washer on the fill plug. Install the plug in the filler hole and tighten it to the torque listed in this Chapter's Specifications.

16   Transfer case lubricant level check (AWD models) (every 15,000 miles or 12 months)

1   Raise the vehicle and support it securely on jackstands. The vehicle should be as level as possible to ensure an accurate check.

2   Remove the plug from the filler hole in the transfer case.

3   The lubricant should be up to the bottom of the filler hole. If not, use a pump or squeeze bottle to add the specified lubricant until it just starts to run out of the hole.

4   Place a new sealing washer on the fill plug. Install the plug in the filler hole and tighten it to the torque listed in this Chapter's Specifications.

17   Brake check (every 15,000 miles or 12 months)

Warning: *The dust created by the brake system is harmful to your health. Never blow it out with compressed air and don't inhale any of it. An approved filtering mask should be worn when working on the brakes. Do not, under any circumstances, use petroleum-based solvents to clean brake parts. Use brake system cleaner only! Try to use non-asbestos replacement parts whenever possible.*
Note: *For detailed photographs of the brake system, refer to Chapter 9.*

1   In addition to the specified intervals, the brakes should be inspected every time the wheels are removed or whenever a defect is suspected. Any of the following symptoms could indicate a potential brake system defect: The vehicle pulls to one side when the brake pedal is depressed; the brakes make squealing or dragging noises when applied; brake pedal travel is excessive; the pedal pulsates; brake fluid leaks, usually onto the inside of the tire or wheel.

2   The disc brake pads have built-in wear indicators which should make a high pitched squealing or scraping noise when they are worn to the replacement point. When you hear this noise, replace the pads immediately or expensive damage to the discs can result.

3   Loosen the wheel lug nuts.

4   Raise the vehicle and place it securely on jackstands.

5   Remove the wheels (see *Jacking and towing* at the front of this book, or your owner's manual, if necessary).

Disc brakes

Refer to illustrations 17.7a, 17.7b and 17.11

6   There is an outer brake pad and an inner pad. Both must be checked for wear.

7   Measure the thickness of the outer pad at each end of the caliper and the inner pad through the inspection hole in the caliper body (see illustrations). Compare the measure-

17.11 Check along the brake hoses and at each fitting for deterioration and cracks

19.1a Release the clips . . .

ment with the limit given in this Chapter's Specifications; if any brake pad thickness is less than specified, then all brake pads must be replaced (see Chapter 9). **Note:** *Keep in mind that the lining material is bonded to a metal backing plate and the metal portion is not included in this measurement.*

8   If it is difficult to determine the exact thickness of the remaining pad material by the above method, or if you are at all concerned about the condition of the pads, remove the caliper(s), then remove the pads from the calipers for further inspection (see Chapter 9).

9   Once the pads are removed from the calipers, clean them with brake cleaner and re-measure them with a ruler or a vernier caliper.

10 Measure the disc thickness with a micrometer to make sure that it still has service life remaining. If any disc is thinner than the specified minimum thickness, replace it (see Chapter 9). Even if the disc has service life remaining, check its condition. Look for scoring, gouging and burned spots. If these conditions exist, remove the disc and have it resurfaced (see Chapter 9).

11 Before installing the wheels, check all brake lines and hoses for damage, wear, deformation, cracks, corrosion, leakage, bends and twists, particularly in the vicinity of the rubber hoses at the calipers **(see illustration)**. Check the clamps for tightness and the connections for leakage. Make sure that all hoses and lines are clear of sharp edges, moving parts and the exhaust system. If any of the above conditions are noted, repair, reroute or replace the lines and/or fittings as necessary (see Chapter 9).

Brake booster check

12 Sit in the driver's seat and perform the following sequence of tests.

13 With the brake fully depressed, start the engine - the pedal should move down a little when the engine starts.

14 With the engine running, depress the brake pedal several times - the travel distance should not change.

15 Depress the brake, stop the engine and hold the pedal in for about 30 seconds - the pedal should neither sink nor rise.

16 Restart the engine, run it for about a minute and turn it off. Then firmly depress the brake several times - the pedal travel should decrease with each application.

17 If your brakes do not operate as described above when the preceding tests are performed, the brake booster is either in need of repair or has failed. Refer to Chapter 9 for the removal procedure.

Parking brake

18 Actuate the parking brake with a normal amount of force and count the number of clicks. The adjustment should be within the specified number of clicks listed in the Chapter 9 Specifications. If you hear more or fewer clicks, adjust the parking brake (see Chapter 9).

19 An alternative method of checking the parking brake is to park the vehicle on a steep hill with the parking brake set and the transaxle in Neutral (be sure to stay in the vehicle during this check!). If the parking brake cannot prevent the vehicle from rolling, it is in need of adjustment (see Chapter 9).

18 Cabin air filter replacement (every 15,000 miles or 12 months)

Note: *Not all models have cabin air filters from the factory, but a filter can be installed.*

1   Remove the glove box and the lower trim panel from the right side of the dashboard (see Chapter 11).

2   Remove the filter cover. **Note:** *On 2007 and earlier models, the filter is installed above the blower motor. On 2009 and later models, it is installed in the HVAC housing and is removed by sliding it out to the right.*

3   Slide the cabin air filter from the housing.

4   Installation is the reverse of removal. Be sure to note any directional arrows printed on the filter.

19.1b . . . then separate the air filter housing and remove the filter

19 Air filter check and replacement (every 30,000 miles or 24 months)

Refer to illustrations 19.1a and 19.1b

1   The air filter is located inside the air filter housing at the left (driver's) side of the engine compartment. To remove the air filter, release the spring clips that secure the two halves of the housing together, then separate the halves and remove the air filter element **(see illustrations)**.

2   Inspect the outer surface of the filter element. If it is dirty, replace it. If it is only moderately dusty, it can be reused by blowing it clean from the back to the front surface with compressed air. Because it is a pleated paper type filter, it cannot be washed or oiled. If it cannot be cleaned satisfactorily with compressed air, discard and replace it. While the cover is off, be careful not to drop anything down into the housing. **Caution:** *Never drive the vehicle with the air cleaner removed. Excessive engine wear could result and backfiring could even cause a fire under the hood.*

20.5 Inspect the fuel filler hoses for cracks and make sure the clamps are tight

20.6 Carefully inspect the fuel line clamps for loss of tension, which can result in leaking fuel lines

3   Wipe out the inside of the air filter housing.

4   Place the new filter into the housing, making sure it seats properly.

5   Reassemble the housing halves and snap the clips into place.

20   Fuel system check (every 15,000 miles or 12 months)

Refer to illustrations 20.5 and 20.6

Warning: *Gasoline is extremely flammable, so take extra precautions when you work on any part of the fuel system. Don't smoke or allow open flames or bare light bulbs near the work area, and don't work in a garage where a gas-type appliance (such as a water heater or clothes dryer) is present. Since gasoline is carcinogenic, wear fuel-resistant gloves when there's a possibility of being exposed to fuel, and, if you spill any fuel on your skin, rinse it off immediately with soap and water. Mop up any spills immediately and do not store fuel-soaked rags where they could ignite. The fuel system is under constant pressure, so, if any fuel lines are to be disconnected, the fuel pressure in the system must be relieved first (see Chapter 4 for more information). When you perform any kind of work on the fuel system, wear safety glasses and have a Class B type fire extinguisher on hand.*

1   If you smell gasoline while driving or after the vehicle has been sitting in the sun, inspect the fuel system immediately.

2   Remove the gas cap and inspect it for damage and corrosion. The gasket should have an unbroken sealing imprint. If the gasket is damaged or corroded, remove it and install a new one.

3   Inspect the fuel feed and return lines for cracks. Make sure the threaded flare nut type connectors (which secure the metal fuel lines to the fuel injection system) and the clamps

(which secure the hoses to the in-line fuel filter) are tight.

4   Since some components of the fuel system - the fuel tank and part of the fuel feed and return lines, for example - are underneath the vehicle, they can be inspected more easily with the vehicle raised on a hoist. If that's not possible, raise the vehicle and support it securely on jackstands.

5   With the vehicle raised and safely supported, inspect the gas tank and filler neck for punctures, cracks and other damage. The connection between the filler neck and the tank is particularly critical. Sometimes a rubber filler neck will leak because of loose clamps or deteriorated rubber **(see illustration)**. These are problems a home mechanic can usually rectify. **Warning:** *Do not, under any circumstances, try to repair a fuel tank (except rubber components). A welding torch or any open flame can easily cause fuel vapors inside the tank to explode.*

6   Carefully check all rubber hoses and metal lines leading away from the fuel tank **(see illustration)**. Check for loose connections, deteriorated hoses, crimped lines and

other damage. Carefully inspect the lines from the tank to the fuel injection system. Repair or replace damaged sections as necessary (see Chapter 4).

21   Steering and suspension check (every 15,000 miles or 12 months)

Note: *For detailed illustrations of the steering and suspension components, refer to Chapter 10.*

With the wheels on the ground

Refer to illustration 21.1

1   With the vehicle stopped and the front wheels pointed straight ahead, rock the steering wheel gently back and forth. If freeplay **(see illustration)** is excessive, a front wheel bearing, main shaft yoke, intermediate shaft yoke, lower arm balljoint or steering system joint is worn or the steering gear is out of adjustment or broken. Refer to Chapter 10 for the appropriate repair procedure.

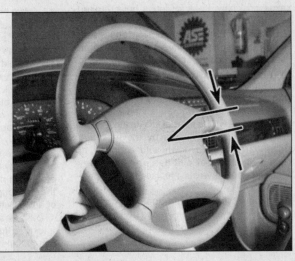

21.1 Steering wheel freeplay is the amount of travel between an initial steering input and the point at which the front wheels begin to turn (indicated by a slight resistance)

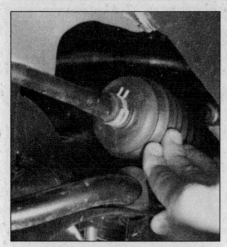

21.6a Check the steering gear boots for cracks and leaking steering fluid

21.6b Front suspension and steering components

A   Strut/coil spring assembly
B   Stabilizer bar link
C   Tie-rod end
D   Control arm balljoint
E   Control arm bushings
F   Steering gear boot

2   Other symptoms, such as excessive vehicle body movement over rough roads, swaying (leaning) around corners and binding as the steering wheel is turned, may indicate faulty steering and/or suspension components.
3   Check the shock absorbers by pushing down and releasing the vehicle several times at each corner. If the vehicle does not come back to a level position within one or two bounces, the shocks/struts are worn and must be replaced. When bouncing the vehicle up and down, listen for squeaks and noises from the suspension components.

Under the vehicle

Refer to illustrations 21.6a and 21.6b

4   Raise the vehicle with a floor jack and support it securely on jackstands.
5   Check the tires for irregular wear patterns and proper inflation. See Section 5 for information regarding tire wear.
6   Inspect the universal joint between the steering shaft and the steering gear housing. Check the steering gear housing for fluid leakage. Make sure that the boots are not damaged and that the boot clamps are not loose **(see illustration)**. Check the tie-rod ends for excessive play. Look for loose bolts, broken or disconnected parts and deteriorated rubber bushings on all suspension and steering components **(see illustration)**. While an assistant turns the steering wheel from side to side, check the steering components for free movement, chafing and binding. If the steering components do not seem to be reacting with the movement of the steering wheel, try to determine where the slack is located.
7   Check the balljoints by moving each lower arm up and down with a prybar to ensure that its balljoint has no play. If any balljoint does have play, replace it (see Chapter 10).
8   Inspect the balljoint boots for damage and leaking grease. Replace the balljoints with new ones if they are damaged (see Chapter 10).

22.2 Check the flange connections (A) for exhaust leaks and check that the retaining nuts are securely tightened; the hangers (B) must be properly connected and undamaged

22   Exhaust system check (every 15,000 miles or 12 months)

Refer to illustration 22.2

1   With the engine cold (at least three hours after the vehicle has been driven), check the complete exhaust system from its starting point at the engine to the end of the tailpipe. This should be done on a hoist where unrestricted access is available.
2   Check the pipes and connections for evidence of leaks **(see illustration)**, severe corrosion or damage. Make sure that all brackets and hangers are in good condition and tight.
3   At the same time, inspect the underside of the body for holes, corrosion, open seams, etc. which may allow exhaust gases to enter the passenger compartment. Seal all body openings with silicone or body putty.
4   Rattles and other noises can often be traced to the exhaust system, especially the mounts and hangers. Try to move the pipes,

23.2 Check the driveaxle boots for cracks or leaking grease

muffler and catalytic converter. If the components can come in contact with the body or suspension parts, secure the exhaust system with new mounts.
5   Check the running condition of the engine by inspecting inside the end of the tailpipe. The exhaust deposits here are an indication of engine state-of-tune. If the pipe is black and sooty or coated with white deposits, the engine is in need of a tune-up, including a thorough fuel system inspection.

23   Driveaxle boot check (every 15,000 miles or 12 months)

Refer to illustration 23.2

1   The driveaxle boots are very important because they prevent dirt, water and foreign material from entering and damaging the constant velocity (CV) joints.
2   Inspect the boots for tears and cracks as well as loose clamps **(see illustration)**. If there is any evidence of cracks or leaking lubricant, they must be replaced as described in Chapter 8.

24.1 Tools required for changing spark plugs

1 **Spark plug socket** - *This will have special padding inside to protect the spark plug porcelain insulator*
2 **Torque wrench** - *Although not mandatory, use of this tool is the best way to ensure that the plugs are tightened properly*
3 **Ratchet** - *Standard hand tool to fit the plug socket*
4 **Extension** - *Depending on model and accessories, you may need special extensions and universal joints to reach one or more of the plugs*
5 **Spark plug gap gauge** - *This gauge for checking the gap comes in a variety of styles. Make sure the gap for your engine is included*

24 Spark plug check and replacement (every 105,000 miles or 72 months)

Refer to illustrations 24.1 and 24.4

1   Spark plug replacement requires a spark plug socket and extension which fits onto a ratchet. This socket is lined with a rubber grommet to protect the porcelain insulator of the spark plug and to hold the plug while you remove it. You will also need a wire-type feeler gauge to check and adjust the spark plug gap and a torque wrench to tighten the new plugs to the specified torque **(see illustration)**.
2   If you are replacing the plugs, purchase the new plugs, adjust them to the proper gap and then replace each plug one at a time.
3   Inspect each of the new plugs for defects. If there are any signs of cracks in the porcelain insulator of a plug, don't use it.
4   Check the electrode gaps of the new plugs. Check the gap by inserting the wire gauge of the proper thickness between the electrodes at the tip of the plug **(see illustra-**

tion**). The gap between the electrodes should be identical to that listed in this Chapter's Specifications. If the gap is incorrect, the manufacturer recommends replacing the spark plug with a new one (rather than adjusting it).
5   If the side electrode is not exactly over the center electrode, use the notched adjuster to align them. **Caution:** *If the gap of a new plug must be adjusted, bend only the base of the ground electrode - do not touch the tip.*

Removal

Refer to illustrations 24.6 and 24.7

6   Remove the upper intake manifold for access to the rear bank spark plugs (see Chapter 2A). Remove the ignition coils **(see illustration)**.
7   Remove the spark plugs **(see illustration)**.
8   Whether you are replacing the plugs at this time or intend to reuse the old plugs, compare each old spark plug with the chart shown on the inside back cover of this manual to determine the overall running condition of the engine.

24.4 Spark plug manufacturers recommend using a wire-type gauge when checking the gap - if the wire does not slide between the electrodes with a slight drag, adjustment is required. Caution: *Do not force the gauge into the gap - the platinum or iridium coating could be scraped off*

24.6 Remove the ignition coils for access to the spark plugs

24.7 Use a spark plug socket with a ratchet and an extension to remove the spark plugs

24.9 Apply a coat of anti-seize compound to the spark plug threads, being careful not to get any near the lower threads

24.10 A length of snug-fitting rubber hose will save time and prevent damaged threads when installing the spark plugs

25.4 The radiator drain fitting is located at the bottom of the radiator

Installation

Refer to illustrations 24.9 and 24.10

9   Prior to installation, apply a coat of anti-seize compound to the plug threads **(see illustration)**.

10   It's often difficult to insert spark plugs into their holes without cross-threading them. To avoid this possibility, fit a short piece of snug-fitting rubber hose over the end of the spark plug **(see illustration)**. The flexible hose acts as a universal joint to help align the plug with the plug hole. Should the plug begin to cross-thread, the hose will slip on the spark plug, preventing thread damage. Tighten the plug to the torque listed in this Chapter's Specifications.

11   Follow the above procedure for the remaining spark plugs.

12   After replacing all the plugs, install the ignition coils (see Chapter 5) and replace the upper intake manifold (see Chapter 2A).

25   Cooling system servicing (draining, flushing and refilling) (every 30,000 miles or 24 months)

Warning: *Do not allow engine coolant (antifreeze) to come in contact with your skin or painted surfaces of the vehicle. Rinse off spills immediately with plenty of water. Antifreeze is highly toxic if ingested. Never leave antifreeze laying around in an open container or in puddles on the floor; children and pets are attracted by it's sweet smell and may drink it. Check with local authorities about disposing of used antifreeze. Many communities have collection centers which will see that antifreeze is disposed of safely.*

1   Periodically, the cooling system should be drained, flushed and refilled to replenish the antifreeze mixture and prevent formation of rust and corrosion, which can impair the performance of the cooling system and cause

engine damage. When the cooling system is serviced, all hoses and the radiator cap should be checked and replaced if necessary.

Draining

Refer to illustrations 25.4 and 25.5

2   Apply the parking brake and block the wheels. If the vehicle has just been driven, wait several hours to allow the engine to cool down before beginning this procedure.

3   Remove the radiator cap.

4   Move a large container under the radiator drain to catch the coolant. Using a large screwdriver, open the radiator drain plug and direct the coolant into the container **(see illustration)**.

5   After the coolant stops flowing out of the radiator, move the container under the engine block drain plug(s) **(see illustration)**. **Note:** *There are two drain plugs, one on each side of the engine block.* Remove the plug(s) and allow the coolant in the block to drain.

6   While the coolant is draining, check the condition of the radiator hoses, heater hoses and clamps (see Section 12).

7   Replace any damaged clamps or hoses (see Chapter 3).

Flushing

8   Once the system is completely drained, flush the radiator with fresh water from a garden hose until water runs clear at the drain. The flushing action of the water will remove sediments from the radiator but will not remove rust and scale from the engine and cooling tube surfaces.

9   These deposits can be removed by the chemical action of a cleaner. Follow the procedure outlined in the manufacturer's instructions. If the radiator is severely corroded, damaged or leaking, it should be removed (see Chapter 3) and taken to a radiator repair shop.

10   Remove the overflow hose from the coolant recovery reservoir. Drain the reservoir and

flush it with clean water, then reconnect the hose.

Refilling

Refer to illustration 25.13

11   Close and tighten the radiator drain. Install and tighten the engine block drain plug(s).

12   Make sure the heater temperature control is in the maximum heat position.

13   If you're working on a 2004 or later model, it is necessary to detach one of the heater hoses at the firewall to bleed the system as it is being filled:

   2004 through 2007 models *- Disconnect the heater hose closest to the right (passenger's) side of the vehicle (nearest the throttle body).*

   2009 and later models *- Disconnect the uppermost heater hose* **(see illustration)**.

14   Slowly refill the radiator with a 50/50 mixture of water and antifreeze until coolant

25.5 After draining the radiator, be sure to fully drain the cooling system by removing the engine block drain plug

25.13 On 2009 and later models, disconnect this heater hose when refilling the cooling system. When cooling begins flowing from the hose, reattach it (on 2007 and earlier models, detach the hose closest to the right side of the vehicle, near the throttle body)

27.7 Follow this hose from the left (driver's) side of the radiator to the pipe, then disconnect the hose from the pipe and direct the end of the hose into a drain pan (2007 and earlier models)

27.12 Transaxle fluid drain plug (2009 and later models)

flows from the disconnected heater hose, then reattach the hose and install the hose clamp. Continue adding coolant until the level reaches the lip on the radiator filler neck. Add coolant to the reservoir up to the lower mark.

15   Install the radiator cap and run the engine in a well-ventilated area until the thermostat opens (coolant will begin flowing through the radiator and the upper radiator hose will become hot).

16   Rev the engine to approximately 3000 rpm for ten seconds, then let it idle; do this a few times.

17   Turn the engine off and let it cool. Add more coolant mixture to bring the level back up to the lip on the radiator filler neck.

18   Squeeze the upper radiator hose to expel air, then add more coolant mixture if necessary. Replace the radiator cap.

19   Start the engine, allow it to reach normal operating temperature and check for leaks.

26   Evaporative emissions control system check (every 30,000 miles or 24 months)

1   The function of the evaporative emissions control system is to draw fuel vapors from the gas tank and fuel system, store them in a charcoal canister, then burn them during normal engine operation.

2   The most common symptom of a fault in the evaporative emissions system is a strong fuel odor in the engine compartment. If a fuel odor is detected, inspect the charcoal canister, located at the front of the engine compartment. Check the canister and all hoses for damage and deterioration.

3   The evaporative emissions control system is explained in more detail in Chapter 6.

27   Automatic transaxle fluid change (every 60,000 miles or 48 months)

Note: *Failure to use the correct fluid will damage the transaxle and void the warranty.*

1   At the specified time intervals, the automatic transaxle fluid should be drained and replaced.

2   Before beginning work, purchase the specified transaxle fluid (see *Recommended fluids and lubricants* and *Capacities* in this Chapter's Specifications).

3   Other tools necessary for this job include jackstands to support the vehicle in a raised position, a wrench, a large drain pan, newspapers and clean rags.

4   The fluid should be drained after the vehicle has been driven and brought to operating temperature. Hot fluid is more effective than cold fluid at removing built up sediment. **Warning:** *Fluid temperature can exceed 350-degrees F in a hot transaxle. Wear protective gloves.*

5   Raise the vehicle and place it on jackstands. Put the transaxle in Park and turn off the engine.

6   Move the necessary equipment under the vehicle, being careful not to touch any of the hot exhaust components.

2007 and earlier models

Refer to illustration 27.7

7   Disconnect the transaxle fluid cooler line that exits the radiator from the pipe that leads to the transaxle **(see illustration)**. Direct the hose into a drain pan.

8   Remove the dipstick and put a funnel in the tube. Open several quarts of transaxle fluid and set them nearby.

9   Start the engine and allow it to idle.

10   Observe the fluid coming out of the radiator/cooler while adding new fluid to the transaxle. When the new fluid begins flowing out of the cooler line, shut off the engine.

11   Connect the transaxle cooler line.

2009 and later models

Refer to illustration 27.12

12   Place a drain pan under the drain plug and remove the drain plug **(see illustration)**. Allow the fluid to drain. Once the fluid is drained, reinstall the drain plug and tighten it to the torque listed in this Chapter's Specifications.

All models

13   Lower the vehicle.

14   With the engine off, add new fluid to the transaxle through the dipstick tube (see Section 7). Use a funnel to prevent spills. It is best to add a little fluid at a time, checking the level with the dipstick. Allow the fluid time to drain into the pan.

15   Start the engine and shift the selector into all positions from Park through Low then shift into Park and apply the parking brake.

16   With the engine idling, check the fluid level. Add fluid, a little at a time, until it's up to the Cool level on the dipstick.

17   Drive the vehicle to warm the fluid to normal operating temperature, then re-check the fluid level.

18   2009 and later models: Make a note of the mileage and date when you changed the fluid. This information can be entered into the vehicle's memory by a Nissan technician to cancel the existing fluid deterioration date.

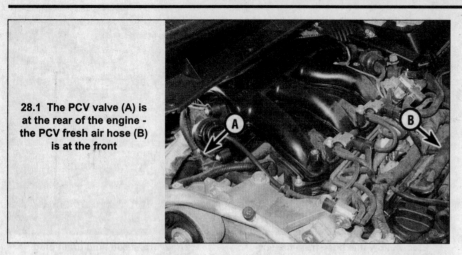

28.1 The PCV valve (A) is at the rear of the engine - the PCV fresh air hose (B) is at the front

28   Positive Crankcase Ventilation (PCV) valve check and replacement (every 30,000 miles or 24 months)

Refer to illustration 28.1

1   Remove the engine cover, then locate the PCV valve on the valve cover **(see illustration)**.

2   Disconnect the hose, then remove the PCV valve.

3   With the engine idling at normal operating temperature, place your finger over the end of the valve. If there's no vacuum at the valve, check for a plugged hose or valve.

Replace any plugged or deteriorated hoses.

4   When purchasing a replacement PCV valve, make sure it's for your particular vehicle and engine size. Compare the old valve with the new one to make sure they're the same.

5   Installation is the reverse of removal.

29   Differential lubricant change (AWD models) (every 60,000 miles or 48 months)

1   This procedure should be performed after the vehicle has been driven so the lubricant will be warm and therefore will flow out of the differential easily.

2   Raise the vehicle and support it securely on jackstands. You'll be draining the lubricant by removing the drain plug, so move a drain pan, rags, newspapers, copper plug washers and wrenches under the vehicle.

3   Remove the fill plug, then remove the drain plug and allow the fluid to drain into the pan. Clean and reinstall the drain plug. Tighten the plug to the torque listed in this Chapter's Specifications using a new copper washer.

4   Using a hand pump, syringe or squeeze bottle, fill the differential housing with the specified lubricant until it's level with the bottom of the fill-plug hole.

5   Clean and reinstall the fill plug. Tighten the plug to the torque listed in this Chapter's Specifications using a new copper washer.

6   Drive the vehicle a short distance and recheck the lubricant level.

30   Transfer case lubricant change (AWD models) (every 60,000 miles or 48 months)

1   This procedure should be performed after the vehicle has been driven so the lubricant will be warm and therefore will flow out of the transfer case easily.

2   Raise the vehicle and support it securely on jackstands. You'll be draining the lubricant by removing the drain plug, so move a drain pan, rags, newspapers, copper plug washers and wrenches under the vehicle.

3   Remove the fill plug, then remove the drain plug and allow the fluid to drain into the pan. Clean and reinstall the drain plug. Tighten the plug to the torque listed in this Chapter's Specifications using a new copper washer.

4   Using a hand pump, syringe or squeeze bottle, fill the transfer case with the specified lubricant until it's level with the bottom of the fill-plug hole.

5   Clean and reinstall the fill plug. Tighten the plug to the torque listed in this Chapter's Specifications using a new copper washer.

6   Drive the vehicle a short distance and recheck the lubricant level.

← FRONT

RIGHT CYLINDER HEAD

LEFT CYLINDER HEAD

72016-1-29.6B HAYNES

31.5a When the no. 1 piston is at TDC on the compression stroke, the valve clearance for the no. 1 and no. 6 cylinder intake valves and the no. 2 and no. 3 cylinder exhaust valves can be measured

31.5b You will feel drag as you pull the feeler gauge if the adjustment is correct

31.6 After checking the valves indicated in illustration 31.5a, turn the crankshaft 240 degrees (2/3 turn) clockwise and check the valve clearances for the no. 2 and no. 3 cylinder intake valves and the no. 4 and no. 5 cylinder exhaust valves

31.7 After checking the valves indicated in illustration 31.6, turn the crankshaft an additional 240 degrees (2/3 turn) clockwise and check the valve clearances for the no. 4 and no. 5 cylinder intake valves and the no. 1 and no. 6 cylinder exhaust valves

31 Valve clearance check and adjustment (every 60,000 miles or 48 months)

Refer to illustrations 31.5a, 31.5b, 31.6, 31.7 and 31.9

Note: *The manufacturer recommends adjusting the valve clearance at the specified interval only if the valvetrain is making excessive noise.*

1   Disconnect the cable from the negative terminal of the battery (see Chapter 5).
2   Remove the valve covers (see Chapter 2A).
3   Remove the spark plugs (see Section 24).
4   Position the number 1 piston at TDC on the compression stroke and align the timing marks (see Chapter 2A).
5   Measure the clearance of the indicated valves with a feeler gauge (**see illustrations**). Record each measurement and compare your measurements with the desired valve clearance found in this Chapter's Specifications. Note which are out of specification; this data will be used later to determine the required lifter.
6   Turn the crankshaft 240 degrees (2/3-

turn). Measure and record the clearances of the indicated valves (**see illustration**).
7   Rotate the crankshaft an additional 240 (2/3-turn) degrees and perform the same operation for the remaining valves (**see illustration**).
8   These engines don't use valve adjusting shims. If a clearance is out of specification, the lifter must be replaced with a new lifter that has a different thickness head to correct the clearance. Remove the camshafts to access the lifters (see Chapter 2A).
9   Mark the lifters that are to be replaced, and record which valve they came from. Measure the thickness of the center of the lifter with a micrometer (**see illustration**). To calculate the correct thickness of a replacement lifter that will place the valve clearance within the specified value, use the following formula:

N = T + A - V

N = *thickness of the new lifter*
T = *thickness of the old lifter*
A = *valve clearance measured*
V = *desired valve clearance (see this Chapter's Specifications)*

10   Select a lifter with a thickness as close as possible to the valve clearance calculated. Lifters are marked on the underside as to their size.

11   Mark the new lifters as to their destination, lubricate them with engine assembly lube and install them. After replacing the lifters, install the camshaft(s) (see Chapter 2A).
12   The remainder of installation is the reverse of removal. Reconnect the battery and perform the necessary re-learn procedures (see Chapter 5).

31.9 Measure the lifter thickness with a micrometer

32   Maintenance reminder indicator resetting procedure

2007 and earlier models

Note: *The maintenance reminder indicator performs two functions: It informs the driver when it's time to change the engine oil, and also when it's time to rotate the tires.*

Models with a navigation system

1   Using the joystick on the navigation unit, select either Engine Oil or Tire Rotation, then push the ENTER button.

2   Using the joystick, select Maintenance Schedule, then select the Reset key and push the ENTER button.

3   Select the Display Maintenance Notification key and press the ENTER button.

Models without a navigation system

4   Press the MAINT button on the control panel to display the item to be reset (engine oil or tire rotation).

5   Press the MAINT button or TRIP RESET button for more than two seconds.

6   Use the joystick to set the distance on the display.

2009 and later models

Note: *On these models up to four reminders can be programmed; the reset process is the same for all four.*

7   Using the multi-function controller on the display, choose the item you'd like to reset, them press the ENTER button.

8   Reset the driving distance.

9   Set the mileage interval.

10   Using the multi-function controller, select the Interval Reminder key, then push the ENTER button.

11   Press the BACK button to return to Maintenance Info.

Chapter 2 Part A
Engine

Contents

Specifications

General
Displacement	3.5L (213 cubic inches)
Designation	VQ35DE
Bore	3.760 inches
Stroke	3.205 inches
Cylinder numbers (front to rear)	
Right (rear) side	1-3-5
Left (front) side	2-4-6
Firing order	1-2-3-4-5-6

FRONT

Cylinder location diagram

Camshaft
Camshaft endplay	
Standard	0.0045 to 0.0074 inch
Limit	0.0094 inch

Camshaft (continued)

Camshaft journal diameter

No. 1 .... 1.0211 to 1.0218 inches

No. 2 through 4 .... 0.9230 to 0.9238 inch

Camshaft bearing inside diameter

No. 1 .... 1.0236 to 1.0244 inches

No. 2 through 4 .... 0.9252 to 0.9260 inch

Bearing oil clearance

No. 1.. 0.0018 to 0.0034 inch

No. 2 through 4 .... 0.0014 to 0.0030 inch

Service limit.. 0.0047 inch

Runout limit... 0.0020 inch maximum

Lobe height

Intake .... 1.7904 to 1.7978 inches

Exhaust .... 1.7907 to 1.7982 inches

Exhaust manifold

Maximum allowable warpage .... 0.012 inch

Intake manifold, lower

Maximum allowable warpage, upper surface .... 0.004 inch

Valve clearance (cold)

Intake .... 0.010 to 0.013 inch

Exhaust... 0.011 to 0.015 inch

Oil pump

Outer gear-to-body clearance.. 0.0045 to 0.0102 inch

Inner gear-to-outer gear tip clearance .... 0.0071 inch maximum

Inner gear-to-housing side clearance .... 0.0012 to 0.0028 inch

Outer gear-to-housing side clearance .... 0.0020 to 0.0043 inch

Inner rotor hub-to-housing clearance .... 0.0018 to 0.0036 inch

Torque specifications   Ft-lbs (unless otherwise indicated)

Note: *One foot-pound (ft-lb) of torque is equivalent to 12 inch-pounds (in-lbs) of torque. Torque values below approximately 15 ft-lbs are expressed in inch-pounds, since most foot-pound torque wrenches are not accurate at these smaller values.*

Camshaft sprocket bolts (1)* 76

Camshaft bearing cap bolts **(see illustration 7.15a)**

Step 1 (bolts 7 through 10).. 17 in-lbs

Step 2 (bolts 1 through 6).. 17 in-lbs

Step 3 (all bolts) .... 52 in-lbs

Step 4 (bolts 1 through 6).. 96 in-lbs

Crankshaft pulley bolt (1)*

Step 1 32

Step 2 .... Tighten an additional 90-degrees

Cylinder head bolts (in sequence; **see illustration 10.24**) (1)* (2)* (3)*

2007 and earlier models

Step 1 72

Step 2 .... Loosen completely (in reverse of tightening sequence)

Step 3 29

Step 4 .... Tighten an additional 90-degrees

Step 5 .... Tighten an additional 90-degrees

2009 and later models

Step 1 72

Step 2 .... Loosen completely (in reverse of tightening sequence)

Step 3 29

Step 4 .... Tighten an additional 103-degrees

Step 5 .... Tighten an additional 103-degrees

Valve cover bolts (2)*

Step 1 .... 17 in-lbs

Step 2 .... 74 in-lbs

Driveplate bolts (1)* 80

Exhaust manifold nuts (2)* 23

Torque specifications

Ft-lbs (unless otherwise indicated)

Note: *One foot-pound (ft-lb) of torque is equivalent to 12 inch-pounds (in-lbs) of torque. Torque values below approximately 15 foot-pounds are expressed in inch-pounds, because most foot-pound torque wrenches are not accurate at these smaller values.*

Intake manifold collector (upper intake manifold).....................................	156 to 180 in-lbs
Intake manifold (lower intake manifold) (2)*..	156 to 180 in-lbs
Oil cooler connector bolt..	34 to 40
Oil pan bolts	
Upper (aluminum) oil pan (2)*..	144 to 168 in-lbs
Lower (steel) oil pan..	82 to 94 in-lbs
Oil pan-to-transmission	37
Oil pan drain plug	22 to 29
Oil pan rear cover mounting plate	57 to 65 in-lbs
Oil pick-up tube mounting bolts	15 to 16
Oil pressure switch	108 to 144 in-lbs
Oil pump cover screws	52 to 70 in-lbs
Oil pressure relief plug...	29 to 51
Front timing chain cover bolts (2)*	
6 mm	108 to 120 in-lbs
8 mm	19 to 23
Rear timing chain cover bolts (2)*	108 to 120 in-lbs
Intake valve timing control cover bolts...	87 to 112 in-lbs
Upper timing chain guide(s) bolts	61 to 82 in-lbs
Main timing chain tensioner bolts	61 to 82 in-lbs
Main timing chain guide pivot bolt	120 to 156 in-lbs
Secondary timing chain tensioner bolts..	62 to 88 in-lbs
Rear main oil seal retainer bolts	78 in-lbs

(1)*Lubricate fastener threads and heads with clean engine oil prior to installation
(2)*Tighten fasteners in the proper sequence. See text for diagrams
(3)*Bolts must be replaced with NEW ones

1   General information

This Part of Chapter 2 is devoted to in-vehicle repair procedures for the VQ35DE 3.5L Dual Overhead Camshaft (DOHC) V6 engine. Information concerning engine removal and installation and engine overhaul can be found in Part B of this Chapter.

The following repair procedures are based on the assumption that the engine is installed in the vehicle. If the engine has been removed from the vehicle and mounted on a stand, many of the steps outlined in this Part of Chapter 2 will not apply.

2   Repair operations possible with the engine in the vehicle

Many major repair operations can be accomplished without removing the engine from the vehicle.

Clean the engine compartment and the exterior of the engine with some type of degreaser before any work is done. It will make the job easier and help keep dirt out of the internal areas of the engine.

Depending on the components involved, it may be helpful to remove the hood to improve access to the engine as repairs are performed (refer to Chapter 11 if necessary). Cover the fenders to prevent damage to the paint. Special pads are available, but an old bedspread or blanket will also work.

If vacuum, exhaust, oil or coolant leaks develop, indicating a need for gasket or seal replacement, the repairs can generally be made with the engine in the vehicle. The intake and exhaust manifold gaskets and crankshaft oil seals are accessible with the engine in place.

Some exterior engine components, such as the intake and exhaust manifolds, the lower oil pan, the water pump (see Chapter 3), the starter motor, the alternator and the fuel system components (see Chapter 4) can be removed for replacement with the engine in place.

The upper oil pan can't be removed with the engine in place on automatic transmission models. Because of this, the cylinder heads and timing chains can't be removed without first removing the engine on these vehicles.

3   Top Dead Center (TDC) for number one piston - locating

Refer to illustration 3.8

1   Top Dead Center (TDC) is the highest point in the cylinder that each piston reaches as it travels up-and-down when the crankshaft turns. Each piston reaches TDC on the compression stroke and again on the exhaust stroke, but TDC generally refers to piston position on the compression stroke.

2   Positioning the number one piston at TDC is an essential part of many procedures, such as camshaft and timing chain removal.

3.8 Align the TDC notch on the crankshaft pulley with the pointer on the timing chain cover - the TDC notch is the one farthest to the left when facing the front of the engine

1   TDC mark
2   10-degrees BTDC
3   15-degrees BTDC

3   Before beginning this procedure, be sure to place the transmission in Neutral and apply the parking brake or block the rear wheels. If method *b)* or *c)* in the next Step will be used to rotate the engine, disable the fuel system by removing the fuel pump fuse (see Chapter 4, Section 2). Remove the spark plugs (see Chapter 1).

4   In order to bring any piston to TDC, the crankshaft must be turned using one of the methods outlined below. When looking at the front of the engine (timing chain end), normal crankshaft rotation is clockwise.

a)   *The preferred method is to turn the crankshaft with a socket and ratchet attached to the bolt threaded into the front of the crankshaft.*

b)   *A remote starter switch, which may save some time, can also be used. Follow the instructions included with the switch. Once the piston is close to TDC, use a socket and ratchet as described in the previous paragraph.*

c)   *If an assistant is available to turn the ignition switch to the Start position in short bursts, you can get the piston close to TDC without a remote starter switch. Make sure your assistant is out of the vehicle, away from the ignition switch, then use a socket and ratchet as described in Paragraph a) to complete the procedure.*

5   Install a compression pressure gauge in the number one spark plug hole (see Chapter 2B). It should be a gauge with a screw-in fitting and a hose at least six inches long.

6   Loosen the right front wheel lug nuts. Raise the front of the vehicle and support it securely on jackstands. Remove the wheel and the inner fender splash shield **(see illustration 19.2** in Chapter 11**)**. Rotate the crankshaft using one of the methods described

above while observing for pressure on the compression gauge. The moment the gauge shows pressure indicates that the number one cylinder has begun the compression stroke.

7   Once the compression stroke has begun, TDC for the compression stroke is reached by bringing the piston to the top of the cylinder.

8   Continue turning the crankshaft until the TDC notch in the crankshaft damper is aligned with the pointer on the timing chain cover **(see illustration)**. At this point, the number one cylinder is at TDC on the compression stroke. If the marks are aligned but there was no compression, the piston was on the exhaust stroke. Continue rotating the crankshaft 360-degrees (1-turn). **Note:** *If a compression gauge is not available, you can simply place a blunt object (such as the end of a screwdriver handle) over the spark plug hole and listen for compression as the engine is rotated. Once compression at the No. 1 spark plug hole is noted, the remainder of the Step is the same.*

9   After the number one piston has been positioned at TDC on the compression stroke, TDC for any of the remaining cylinders can be located by turning the crankshaft 120-degrees and following the firing order (refer to the Specifications). For example, rotating the engine 120-degrees past TDC #1 will put the engine at TDC compression for cylinder #2.

4   Valve covers - removal and installation

Removal

1   Disconnect the cable from the negative terminal of the battery (see Chapter 5).
2   Remove the engine cover.
3   Remove the camshaft position sensor(s) (see Chapter 6).

Left (front) valve cover

4   Remove the front air inlet duct.
5   Remove the blow-by hose from the valve cover.

Right (rear) valve cover

6   Remove the intake manifold collector (see Section 8).

All valve covers

7   Remove the ignition coils from the cover to be removed (see Chapter 5).
8   Detach the PCV hose and any wiring which would interfere with valve cover removal.
9   Remove the valve cover bolts and washers in the reverse order of the tightening sequence **(see illustration 4.16)**.
10   Detach the valve cover. **Note:** *If the cover is stuck to the cylinder head, bump one end with a block of wood and a hammer to jar it loose. If that doesn't work, try to slip a flexible putty knife between the cylinder head and cover to break the gasket seal. Don't pry at the cover-to-cylinder head joint or damage to the sealing surfaces may occur (leading to oil leaks in the future).*

4.13 Be sure to install new spark plug tube seals into the valve cover

Installation

Refer to illustrations 4.13, 4.16a and 4.16b

11   The mating surfaces of each cylinder head and valve cover must be perfectly clean when the covers are installed. Use a gasket scraper to remove all traces of sealant and old gasket material, then clean the mating surfaces with brake system cleaner.

12   If necessary, clean the bolt threads with a wire wheel to remove any corrosion. Make sure the threaded holes in the cylinder head are clean - run a tap into them to remove corrosion and restore damaged threads.

13   Replace the spark plug tube seals **(see illustration)**.

14   Apply a thin coat of RTV sealant to the cover groove and to the corners on the front camshaft journal cap, then position the gasket inside the cover and allow the sealant to set up so the gasket adheres to the cover. If the sealant isn't allowed to set, the gasket may fall out of the cover as it's installed on the engine.

15   Carefully position the cover on the cylinder head and install the bolts.

16   Following the recommended tightening sequence, tighten the bolts, in two steps, to the torque listed in this Chapter's Specifications **(see illustrations)**.

17   The remaining installation steps are the reverse of removal.

18   Reconnect the battery and perform the necessary re-learn procedures (see Chapter 5).

5   Valve springs, retainers and seals - replacement

Refer to illustrations 5.1, 5.5, 5.7a, 5.7b, 5.13 and 5.15

Note: *Broken valve springs and defective valve stem seals can be replaced without removing the cylinder heads. Two special tools and a compressed air source are normally required to perform this operation, so read through this Section carefully. If you want to leave the head on, obtain a special on-vehicle valve spring compressor* **(see illustration 5.1)**. *Verify the availability of the correct spring compressor before beginning the job. If you can't get the special tools, then you'll have to remove the heads and use a clamp type valve spring compressor*

1   Remove the upper intake manifold (see Section 8) and the valve cover(s) (see Section 4).

2   Remove the timing chain (see Section 6) and the camshafts and lifters from both cylinder heads (see Section 7).

3   Remove the spark plugs.

4   Turn the crankshaft until the piston in the affected cylinder is at Top Dead Center (see Section 3). If you're replacing all of the valve stem seals, begin with cylinder number one and work on the valves for one cylinder at a time. Move from cylinder-to-cylinder following the firing order sequence, turning the crankshaft 120-degrees to bring the next cylinder to TDC (see this Chapter's Specifications).

5   Thread a long adapter into the spark plug hole and connect an air hose from a compressed air source to it **(see illustration)**. Most auto parts stores can supply the air hose adapter. **Note:** *Because of the length of the*

4.16a Valve cover bolt TIGHTENING sequence - 2007 and earlier models

4.16b Valve cover bolt tightening sequence - 2009 and later models

5.1 Here's an example of the special valve spring compressor that must be used to avoid having to remove the head

5.5 Thread the air hose adapter into the spark plug hole - adapters are commonly available from auto parts stores

5.7a Compress the valve spring enough to release the valve stem locks . . .

5.7b . . . and lift them out with a magnet or needle-nose pliers

spark plug tubes, it will be necessary to use a long spark plug adapter with a length of hose attached (as used on many cylinder compression gauges) utilizing a quick-disconnect fitting to hook to your air source.

6   Apply compressed air to the cylinder. **Warning:** *The piston may be forced down by the compressed air, causing the crankshaft to turn suddenly. If the wrench used when positioning the number one piston at TDC is still attached to the bolt in the crankshaft nose, it could cause damage or injury when the crankshaft moves.*

7   Stuff shop rags into the cylinder head holes around the valves to prevent parts and tools from falling into the engine, then use a valve spring compressor to compress the spring **(see illustrations)**. Remove the valve stem locks with small needle-nose pliers or a magnet. **Note:** *The valves should be held in place by the air pressure. If the valve faces or seats are in poor condition, leaks may prevent air pressure from retaining the valves. If the valves cannot hold air, the cylinder head should be removed for a valve job at a machine shop.*

8   Remove the spring retainer and valve spring, then remove the valve stem seal.

9   Wrap a rubber band or tape around the top of the valve stem so the valve won't fall into the combustion chamber, then release

the air pressure.

10   Inspect the valve stem for damage. Rotate the valve in the guide and check the end for eccentric movement, which would indicate that the valve is bent.

11   Move the valve up-and-down in the guide and make sure it doesn't bind. If the valve stem binds, either the valve is bent or the guide is damaged. In either case, the cylinder head will have to be removed for repair.

12   Reapply air pressure to the cylinder to retain the valve in the closed position, then remove the tape or rubber band from the valve stem.

13   Lubricate the valve stems with engine oil and install the new valve stem seals. Valve stem seals can be installed with a special tool, or a deep socket and hammer - tap the seal only until seated **(see illustration)**.

14   Install the valve spring in position over the valve, with the more closely-wound spring coils and the paint mark toward the cylinder head.

15   Install the valve spring retainer. Compress the valve springs and carefully position the valve stem locks in the groove. Apply a small dab of grease to the inside of each valve stem lock to hold it in place **(see illustration)**.

16   Remove the force from the spring tool and

make sure the valve stem locks are seated.

17   Disconnect the air hose and remove the adapter from the spark plug hole.

18   When all of the seals to be replaced have been replaced, position the crankshaft at TDC **(see illustration 3.8)**.

19   Install the camshafts and lifters (see Section 7), then install the timing chain (see Section 6).

20   Install the valve covers (see Section 4).

21   Install the spark plugs, ignition coils and the upper intake manifold, referring to the appropriate Sections as necessary.

22   Start and run the engine, then check for oil leaks and unusual sounds coming from the valve cover area.

---

6   Timing chain and sprockets - removal, inspection and installation

---

Warning: *The engine must be completely cool before beginning this procedure.*
Caution: *The timing system is complex. Severe engine damage will occur if you make any mistakes. Do not attempt this procedure unless you are highly experienced with this type of repair. If you are at all unsure of your abilities, consult an expert. Double-check all*

5.13 Using a deep socket and hammer, gently tap the new seals onto the valve guide only until seated

5.15 Apply a small dab of grease to each valve stem lock as shown here before installation - it will hold them in place on the valve stem as the spring is released

*your work and be sure everything is correct
before you attempt to start the engine.*

Removal

*Refer to illustrations 6.20, 6.22, 6.23, 6.24,
6.25a, 6.25b, 6.26, 6.28 and 6.29*

1   Have a qualified air conditioning shop
recover the refrigerant from the air conditioning system.

2   Relieve the fuel system pressure (see
Chapter 4), then disconnect the cable from the
negative terminal of the battery (see Chapter 5).

3   Block the rear wheels and set the parking brake. Raise the front of the vehicle and
support it securely on jackstands.

4   Drain the cooling system, the power steering fluid and the engine oil (see Chapter 1).
Remove the power steering fluid reservoir.

5   Remove the top and bottom engine covers and the right inner fender splash shield.
Remove the front air inlet duct.

6   Remove the upper intake manifold (see
Section 8).

7   Remove the valve covers (see Section 4) and the dipstick.

8   Position the number one piston at TDC
on the compression stroke (see Section 3).

9   Remove the drivebelt (see Chapter 1).

10   Remove the upper radiator hose and
disconnect the lower radiator hose from the
engine. Remove the coolant reservoir and the
cooling fan assembly (see Chapter 3).

11   Remove the starter (see Chapter 5).

12   Remove the power steering pump (see
Chapter 10).

13   Remove the air conditioning compressor
(see Chapter 3).

14   Remove the alternator and its bracket
(see Chapter 5).

15   Remove the crankshaft pulley (see Section 11). **Note:** *Don't allow the crankshaft
to rotate during removal of the pulley. If the
crankshaft moves, the number one piston will
no longer be at TDC.*

16   Remove the bolts from the engine oil

**6.20 Insert a screwdriver into the notch
at the top of the timing cover and pry the
front timing cover off the engine**

**6.22 Verify that cylinder no. 1 is at TDC on
the compression stroke by confirming that
the intake and exhaust camshaft lobes on
cylinder no. 1 are pointing upward**

cooler tube and remove its bracket.

17   Disconnect the wiring from the oil pressure switch and the valve timing control wiring harness. Label and disconnect any other
interfering wiring and hoses.

18   Remove the bolts from the IVT covers in
the reverse of the tightening sequence **(see
illustration 6.43c)**. Pull the covers straight off
so they disengage from the intake camshaft
sprocket actuator assemblies.

19   Remove the drivebelt tensioner. Remove
the air conditioning idler pulley and its
bracket.

20   Remove the bolts of the front timing
chain cover in the reverse of the tightening sequence **(see illustration 6.42b)**. Pry
the cover off using the slots at the top of the
cover **(see illustration)**. Note that various
types and sizes of bolts are used. They must
be reinstalled in their original locations. Mark
each bolt or make a sketch to help remember
where they go.

21   Remove the O-ring below each intake
camshaft sprocket.

22   Confirm that the number one piston is
still at TDC on the compression stroke by
verifying that the intake and exhaust camshaft
lobes on the number one cylinder are pointing
upward **(see illustration)**.

23   Relieve tension on the primary timing
chain. Depress the primary tensioner inward
and lock it into place by inserting a suitable
stopper pin into the hole on the front of the
tensioner **(see illustration)**. **Note:** *This engine
utilizes three timing chains. The primary timing chain runs around the crankshaft sprocket,
the water pump and around two intake camshaft sprockets. This chain synchronizes the
valve timing with the crankshaft and pistons,
while two secondary timing chains run around
the rear of the intake sprockets and separate
exhaust camshaft sprockets to synchronize
the intake and exhaust camshafts.*

24   Remove the primary timing chain
tensioner, the tensioner pivot arm/chain guide
and the upper timing chain guides from the
primary timing chain **(see illustration)**.

**6.23 An ordinary paper clip can be straightened and used to lock
the timing chain tensioner(s) in place**

**6.24 Remove the primary timing chain tensioner mounting bolts
(A), the tensioner arm/chain guide pivot bolt (B) and the upper
chain guides (C)**

6.25a   Bend two paper clips so that they're long enough to protrude out past the camshaft sprocket once they're installed . . .

6.25b   . . . then depress the secondary tensioners with a screwdriver and lock them in place by inserting a paper clip into the hole on the side of each tensioner - note that the secondary tensioner on the right bank points downward, while the secondary tensioner on the left bank points upward

6.26   Hold the lug on the camshaft with a wrench to keep it from rotating as the sprocket bolts are loosened

25   Depress the secondary timing chain tensioners and lock the tensioners in place by inserting a suitable stopper pin into the hole on the front of each tensioner (see illustrations).

26   Remove the camshaft sprocket bolts (see illustration).

27   Disengage the primary timing chain from the teeth on the chain sprockets and remove it from the engine.

28   Mark the camshaft sprockets with either an R or L to indicate the right or left side, then remove the camshaft sprockets and the secondary timing chains from the engine. Don't mix the sprockets up. They must be installed on the same camshaft from which they were removed (see illustration). Caution: *The intake camshaft sprockets are identified by the variable valve timing actuator and sensor ring which is fastened to the front of the sprocket. Be extremely careful not to damage*

or place a magnetic object of any kind near the sensor ring or a no start condition may occur after installation. Do Not disassemble the variable valve timing actuator assembly from the intake camshaft sprocket for any reason.

29   Remove the crankshaft sprocket and the lower timing chain guide (see illustration).

30   To remove the rear timing chain cover (necessary only if you're removing either cylinder head, the upper oil pan or the engine block), see Section 10.

Inspection

Refer to illustrations 6.31a and 6.31b

31   Inspect the camshaft, water pump and crankshaft sprockets for wear on the teeth and keyways. Inspect the chains for cracks or excessive wear of the rollers. Inspect the facing of the chain guides and the secondary

6.28   Note that the left intake camshaft sprocket has a sensor ring which is fastened to the front of the sprocket - be extremely careful not to damage or place a magnetic object of any kind near the sensor ring or a no start condition may occur

6.29   Remove the crankshaft sprocket (A) and the lower chain guide; make a note that the mark (B) on the chain guide must face up when reinstalling

6.31a Examine the chain guides for deep grooves and excessive wear - replace them if necessary

6.31b Secondary timing chain tensioner(s) mounting bolts (A) - make sure to replace the O-ring (B) before reinstalling the front camshaft bearing cap

timing chain tensioners for excessive wear **(see illustration)**. Note: *If the secondary timing chain tensioners need to be replaced, the front camshaft bearing cap will have to be removed from the affected cylinder head to allow access to the secondary tensioner bolts* **(see illustration)**.

Installation

Refer to illustrations 6.35, 6.37a, 6.37b, 6.41, 6.42a, 6.42b, 6.43a, 6.43b and 6.43c

Caution: *Before starting the engine, carefully rotate the crankshaft by hand through at least two full revolutions using a socket and breaker bar on the crankshaft pulley bolt. If you feel any resistance, STOP! There is something wrong - most likely, valves are hitting the pis-*

tons. You must find the problem before proceeding.

32 If you removed the rear timing chain cover, install it now (see Section 10).

33 Install the crankshaft sprocket and the lower timing chain guide with the mark facing up **(see illustration 6.29)**. If the secondary tensioners were removed, reinstall them and make sure the tensioner spring is locked in place.

34 Verify that you have the correct timing chains for your vehicle by counting the number of links each chain has and comparing the new chains with the old chains. Also compare the position of the colored links in the new chains with the position of the colored links in the old chains.

35 Make sure the camshafts are positioned

with the dowels on the exhaust camshafts in the 12 o'clock position in relation to the top of the cylinder head mating surface; the intake camshafts must be positioned with the small diameter dowel pin hole in the 12 o'clock position in relation to the top of the cylinder head mating surface. Install the secondary timing chains and sprocket assemblies on the camshafts with the timing marks aligned as shown **(see illustration)**. Install the camshaft sprocket bolts hand tight.

36 Reconfirm that the secondary camshaft sprocket timing marks are aligned correctly with the colored links on the secondary timing chains, and remove the stopper pins from the secondary chain tensioners.

37 Install the primary timing chain onto the engine by looping the chain around the crank-

6.35 Secondary timing chain alignment details

1 Rear cylinder bank exhaust camshaft sprocket: Align the two colored links with the two round marks

2 Rear cylinder bank intake camshaft sprocket: Align the single colored link with the single round mark (mark is on the backside of sprocket)

3 Front cylinder bank intake camshaft sprocket: Align the single colored link with the single oval mark (mark is on the backside of sprocket)

4 Front cylinder bank exhaust camshaft sprocket: Align the two colored links with the two oval marks

6.37a The orange colored link on the timing chain aligns with the mark on the crankshaft sprocket

6.37b Make sure the pink colored links (upper arrows) on the primary timing chain align with the marks (lower arrows) on the intake camshaft sprockets

6.41 Install new O-rings at the indicated area on the right and left side of the rear timing chain case

shaft sprocket and aligning the orange colored chain link with the mark on the crankshaft sprocket. Place the chain around the water pump sprocket and finally around the primary camshaft sprockets, making sure the pink colored links align with their respective marks on the sprockets (see illustrations). Note: It may be necessary to rotate the camshafts slightly in order to align the pink colored chain links with the marks on the intake camshaft sprockets.

38   Install the upper timing chain guides. Install the primary tensioner arm/chain guide and the timing chain tensioner assembly (see illustration 6.24). Reconfirm that the number one piston is still at TDC on the compression stroke and that the timing marks on the camshaft and crankshaft sprockets are aligned with the colored links on the chain, then

remove the stopper pin from the primary timing chain tensioner.

39   Tighten the camshaft sprocket bolts to the torque listed in this Chapter's Specifications.

40   Remove all traces of old sealant from the timing chain cover, the cover bolts and the rear cover bolt holes.

41   Install new O-rings in the variable valve timing oil control orifice of the rear timing cover (see illustration).

42   Apply a 1/8-inch bead of RTV sealant to the timing chain cover sealing surfaces (see illustration). Place the timing chain cover in position on the engine and install the bolts in their original locations. Following the recommended tightening sequence, tighten the bolts to the torque listed in this Chapter's Specifications (see illustration). Note: It will also be

6.42a Apply RTV sealant to the timing chain cover at the areas shown - be sure to wipe off any excess sealant

6.42b Front timing chain cover TIGHTENING sequence - (A) is the primary timing chain cover and (B) is the water pump cover, neither of these covers need be removed during this procedure unless they are leaking

6.43a Install new O-rings in both of the IVT orifices on the front timing chain cover

6.43b Apply a light film of engine oil to the new O-rings and install them in the groove on the IVT actuator covers, then apply a 1/8-inch bead of RTV sealant to the indicated areas

necessary to install the air conditioning compressor bracket in order to tighten the bolts in the proper sequence.

43   Install new O-rings in the IVT orifices of the front timing chain cover and on the IVT actuator covers. Then apply a 1/8-inch bead of RTV sealant to the sealing surface of the variable valve timing actuator covers (see illustrations). Place the IVT covers in position over the dowels on the front timing cover and install the bolts in their original locations. Following the recommended tightening sequence (see illustration), tighten the bolts to the torque listed in this Chapter's Specifications.

44   The remainder of the installation is the reverse of removal. Be sure to follow the sealant manufacturer's recommendations for assembly and sealant curing times. Allow all sealant to fully cure before starting the engine.

45   Fill the crankcase with oil and install a new filter (see Chapter 1). Refill the cooling system (see Chapter 1)

46   Reconnect the battery and perform the necessary re-learn procedures (see Chapter 5). Note: Timing chain noise may be apparent after performing this procedure. This noise is normal and should only last until the air has bled out of the high pressure chamber of the primary timing chain tensioner. If after several minutes the noise is still apparent, run the engine at 3,000 rpm with the transmission in Neutral or Park until the noise subsides.

7   Camshafts and lifters - removal, inspection and installation

Note: The camshafts and lifters should always be thoroughly inspected before installation, and camshaft endplay should always be checked prior to camshaft removal. Refer to Chapter 2A for the camshaft and lifter inspection procedures.

Removal

Refer to illustrations 7.4, 7.5 and 7.6

1   Remove the timing chains and the camshaft sprockets (see Section 6).

2   Remove the camshaft position sensor brackets from the driver's ends of the cylinder heads.

3   Mark each camshaft so it can be installed in the same position.

4   Mark the camshaft bearing caps from 1 to 4, and with an "I" or an "E," to indicate intake or exhaust. Also mark arrows indicating the front of the engine (see illustration). All the components must also be marked to indicate which cylinder head they came from. Loosen the camshaft bearing caps in two or three steps, in the reverse order of the tightening sequence (see illustration 7.15a). Caution: Keep the caps in order. They must go back in the same location they were removed from.

6.43c IVT cover TIGHTENING sequence

7.4 The camshaft bearing caps should be marked with a number and letter stamp or a marker to ensure correct reinstallation

7.5 The ID mark in the center of each camshaft identifies which cylinder head the camshaft belongs to; L for left (front) and R for right (rear) - paint marks between the number 1 and number 2 journals indicate that it is an intake camshaft, while paint marks between the number 3 and number 4 journals indicate that it is an exhaust camshaft

7.6 The lifters and shims can be stored in individually marked plastic bags or a divided box as shown

5   Remove the bearing caps and the camshafts. Make a note of the camshaft markings to ensure correct installation **(see illustration)**. **Note:** *The intake camshaft has a drill spot on the side of the sprocket mounting flange.*

6   Remove the lifters from the cylinder head **(see illustration)**. **Caution:** *Keep the lifters in order. They must go back in the same locations from which they were removed.*

Inspection

Refer to illustrations 7.8a, 7.8b, 7.12a, and 7.12b

7   Visually examine the camshaft lobes, journals, bearing caps and lifters. Check for score marks, pitting and evidence of overheating (blue, discolored areas). If wear is excessive or damage is evident, the component will have to be replaced.

8   Using a micrometer, measure camshaft journal diameter and lobe height **(see illustrations)**, and compare your measurements

to this Chapter's Specifications. If the lobe height is less than the minimum allowable, the camshaft is worn and must be replaced.

9   Check the camshaft runout by placing the camshaft back into the cylinder head and set up a dial indicator on the center journal. Zero the dial indicator. Turn the camshaft slowly and note the dial indicator readings. If the measured runout exceeds the specified runout, replace the camshaft.

10   Also, while the camshaft is sitting in the cylinder head, check the endplay. Install the bearing caps and tighten them securely. Mount a dial indicator with the plunger of the dial indicator in line with and touching the end of the camshaft. Gently pry the camshaft fully toward the gauge, zero the gauge, then pry the camshaft fully away from the gauge and note the gauge reading. If the measured endplay is at or beyond the specified service limit, replace the camshaft and check the endplay again. If the endplay is still excessive, replace the cylinder head.

11   Inspect each lifter for scuffing and score marks.

12   Check the oil clearance for each camshaft journal as follows:

     a) *Clean the bearing caps and the camshaft journals with brake system cleaner.*

     b) *Carefully lay the camshafts in place in the cylinder head. DON'T use any lubrication.*

     c) *Lay a strip of Plastigage on each journal.*

     d) *Install the bearing caps with the arrows pointing toward the front (timing chain end) of the engine.*

     e) *Tighten the bolts in sequence* **(see illustration 7.21a)** *to the torque listed in this Chapter's Specifications in 1/4-turn increments.* **Caution:** *Don't turn the camshaft while the Plastigage is in place.*

     f) *Remove the bolts, in the proper sequence, and detach the bearing caps.*

     g) *Compare the width of the crushed Plastigage (at it's widest point) to the scale on the Plastigage envelope* **(see illustrations)**.

     h) *If the clearance is greater than specified, replace the camshaft and/or cylinder head.*

13   Scrape off the Plastigage with your fingernail or the edge of a credit card - don't scratch or nick the journals or bearing caps.

Installation

Refer to illustrations 7.19a, 7.19b, 7.21a and 7.21b

14   Remove all old RTV sealant from the bolts and the front bearing caps.

15   Set the number one piston at TDC if it has been moved.

16   Lubricate the lifters with clean engine oil, then install the lifters into their original locations.

17   Apply moly-based engine assembly lubricant to the camshaft lobes and journals.

18   Install the exhaust camshafts in their original positions with the dowel pins facing up (12 o'clock in relation to the cylinder head mating surface) and inline with the cylinder

7.8a Measure each journal diameter with a micrometer - if any journal measures less than the specified limit, replace the camshaft

7.8b Measure the lobe heights - if any lobe height is less than the minimum listed in this Chapter's Specifications, replace the camshaft

7.12a Place a strip of Plastigage under each camshaft bearing cap and tighten the caps to Specifications

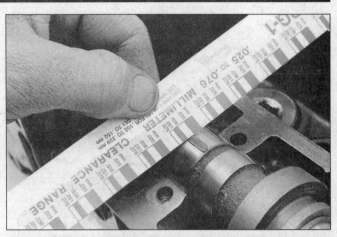

7.12b Compare the width of the crushed Plastigage to the scale on the envelope to determine the oil clearance

7.19a Apply RTV sealant to the cylinder head at the areas shown and install the secondary tensioner O-ring(s) - be sure to wipe off any excess sealant

7.19b Apply a small dab of grease to the IVT oil control orifice O-ring to hold it in place on the No. 1 bearing cap, then apply RTV sealant to the areas shown

7.21a Camshaft bearing cap TIGHTENING sequence (front cylinder head shown, rear identical)

7.21b After the camshaft bearing caps have been tightened in order, tighten the remaining bolts securing the rear timing cover to the No. 1 bearing cap(s)

bank. The small dowel hole in the end of each intake camshaft should also be facing up.

19 Apply a bead of RTV sealant to the sealing surfaces of the No. 1 bearing cap(s) and the cylinder head. Install new O-rings on the secondary timing chain tensioner(s) and the IVT oil control orifice on the No. 1 bearing cap(s) (see illustrations).

20 Install the bearing caps and bolts and tighten them hand tight. The stamp marks on the bearing caps should be in order.

21 Tighten the bearing cap bolts in three steps, to the torque listed in this Chapter's Specifications, using the proper tightening sequence (see illustrations).

8.22 Lower intake manifold bolt tightening sequence

9.2 Mounting fasteners for the front portion of the exhaust system

22   Check the protrusion of the front bearing caps in front of the cylinder head front surface. The front bearing cap should be close to 0.0055 inch behind the front face of the cylinder head. If it isn't, remove and reinstall the camshaft and caps, then check again.

23   Install the camshaft sprockets and timing chain (see Section 6). Hold the camshafts with a suitable wrench as you tighten the sprocket bolts to the specified torque.

24   The remainder of installation is the reverse of removal. If any part of the valve train was replaced, check and adjust the valve clearance (see Chapter 1).

25   Reconnect the battery and perform the necessary re-learn procedures (see Chapter 5).

8   Intake manifold - removal and installation

Warning: *The engine must be completely cool before beginning this procedure.*

Upper intake manifold

1   Disconnect the cable from the negative battery terminal (see Chapter 5).

2   Remove the engine cover and the cowl cover (see Chapter 12, Section 20).

3   Clamp-off the coolant hoses connected to the throttle body, then disconnect them from the throttle body.

4   Remove the air intake duct.

5   Disconnect the electrical connector from the throttle body and remove the throttle body (see Chapter 4).

6   Label and disconnect the following items:
   a) PCV hose (between the upper intake manifold and rear valve cover)
   b) All vacuum lines connected to the upper and lower intake manifolds

7   Detach and remove the following components:
   a) EVAP canister purge solenoid
   b) VIAS control solenoid valve and vacuum tank

   c) Power steering hose bracket
   d) Upper intake manifold support bracket

8   Loosen the upper intake manifold mounting fasteners a little at a time to prevent distortion, then remove the upper intake manifold. The upper intake manifold assembly consists of two parts: the upper intake (connects the throttle body to the plenum) and the plenum/intake manifold runners (lower part of the upper intake manifold). If you're replacing either of these parts of the upper intake manifold assembly, remove the fasteners that secure the intake to the plenum, again loosening the fasteners a little at a time to prevent distortion. If you're replacing the plenum/intake manifold runners, also remove the fasteners, a little at a time to prevent distortion, for the power valve.

9   Clean the mounting surfaces of the upper intake manifold and, if removed, the mounting surfaces of the intake and/or the power valve mounting surfaces. Be sure to carefully remove all traces of old gasket material and/or sealant.

10   Install new gaskets, reassemble (if disassembled) the upper intake manifold assembly, then install the upper intake manifold assembly and tighten the fasteners gradually and evenly, a little at a time, to the torque listed in this Chapter's Specifications. **Note:** *When tightening the upper intake manifold mounting fasteners, start with the center bolts and work your way out towards the ends.*

11   The remainder of installation is the reverse of removal. Check the coolant level, adding some if necessary (see Chapter 1).

12   Reconnect the battery and perform the necessary re-learn procedures (see Chapter 5).

Lower intake manifold

Refer to illustration 8.22

13   Relieve the fuel pressure (see Chapter 4).

14   Remove the upper intake manifold (see Steps 1 through 8).

15   Remove the fuel rail and injectors (see Chapter 4).

16   Label and detach any remaining hoses

which would interfere with the removal of the lower intake manifold.

17   Loosen the manifold bolts in the reverse of the tightening sequence **(see illustration 8.22)**.

18   Remove the manifold. The manifold will probably be stuck to the cylinder heads and force may be required to break the gasket seal. **Caution:** *Don't pry between the manifold and the heads or damage to the gasket sealing surfaces may occur, leading to vacuum leaks.*

19   Carefully use a scraper to remove all traces of old gasket material and sealant from the manifold and cylinder heads, then clean the mating surfaces with brake system cleaner.

20   Use a precision straightedge and a feeler gauge to check the flatness of the top surface of the manifold. Compare your measurement to that listed in the Specifications in this Chapter. If it's excessive, replace the manifold.

21   Install new gaskets, then position the lower manifold on the engine. Make sure the gaskets and manifolds are aligned over the studs in the cylinder heads and install the bolts.

22   Following the correct tightening sequence, tighten the nuts/bolts, in several steps, to the torque listed in this Chapter's Specifications **(see illustration)**.

23   The remainder of the installation is the reverse of the removal procedure. Refer to Steps 9 through 11 to install the upper intake manifold.

24   Reconnect the battery and perform the necessary re-learn procedures (see Chapter 5).

9   Exhaust manifold - removal, inspection and installation

Warning: *The engine must be completely cool before beginning this procedure.*
Note: *This procedure is only for vehicles with manual transmissions. The engine must be removed for removal of the exhaust manifolds on automatic transmission models.*

9.13a Exhaust manifold bolt tightening sequence (front cylinder head)

9.13b Exhaust manifold bolt tightening sequence (rear cylinder head)

Removal

Refer to illustration 9.2

1 Raise the vehicle and place it securely on jackstands.
2 Remove the front part of the exhaust pipe **(see illustration)**.
3 If you're removing the rear exhaust manifold/catalyst, support the rear part of the engine/transaxle assembly and remove the rear engine mounting bracket/insulator (see Section 18).
4 If you're removing the rear exhaust manifold/catalyst, remove the cowl cover (see Chapter 11).
5 Remove the upstream and downstream oxygen sensors (see Chapter 6).
6 Remove the exhaust manifold and catalyst heat shields.
7 Remove the catalyst-to-exhaust manifold bolts first, then remove the nut, and detach the catalyst from the manifold.
8 Remove the exhaust manifold nuts in the reverse order of the tightening sequence **(see illustrations 9.13a and 9.13b)**.
9 Remove the exhaust manifold.
10 Use a scraper to remove all traces of old gasket material and carbon deposits from the manifold and cylinder head mating surfaces.

Inspection

11 Use a precision straightedge and a feeler gauge to check the flatness of the exhaust manifold sealing surface. Compare the measurement to the maximum allowable listed in this Chapter's Specifications. Replace the manifold or have it surfaced if the warpage is excessive.

Installation

Refer to illustrations 9.13a and 9.13b

12 Position the new exhaust manifold gaskets over the studs on the cylinder head.
13 Install the manifold and thread the mounting nuts/bolts into place.
14 Tighten the nuts/bolts a little at a time **(see illustrations)** to the torque listed in this Chapter's Specifications.
15 Reinstall the remaining parts in the reverse order of removal.
16 Reconnect the battery and perform the

necessary re-learn procedures (see Chapter 5).

10 Cylinder head - removal and installation

Warning: *The engine must be completely cool before beginning this procedure*

Removal

Refer to illustration 10.12

Note: *This procedure applies to either cylinder head.*

1 Drain the coolant (see Chapter 1).
2 Remove the timing chains and timing chain sprockets (see Section 6).
3 Remove the camshafts (see Section 7).
4 Remove the intake manifold (see Section 8) and the exhaust manifold (see Section 9).
5 Remove the coolant outlet assembly (the metal pipe that carries coolant between the cylinder heads).
6 If you're removing the front cylinder head, remove the coolant hose between the radiator and the coolant inlet, then remove the coolant inlet and thermostat assembly (see Chapter 3).
7 Remove the lower and upper oil pans (see Section 13).
8 Remove the rear timing chain cover bolts in the reverse order of the tightening

sequence **(see illustration 10.26d)**. **Caution:** *If the rear cover is stuck to a cylinder head or the engine block, try to knock it loose with a dead blow hammer and a block of wood. If that doesn't work, try to break the gasket sealant by slipping a flexible putty knife between the cover and the engine. Do NOT try to just pry of the cover or you might damage the timing cover or the sealing surfaces, which will cause oil leaks.*
9 Remove the old O-rings from the front end of the cylinder heads and the engine block. **Caution:** *Even if you're only removing one head, be sure to replace all the O-rings in the front of each head.*
10 Label and remove any remaining items attached to the cylinder head, such as coolant fittings, tubes, cables, hoses, wires or brackets.
11 Using a breaker bar and the appropriate sized Allen-head socket, loosen the cylinder head bolts in 1/4-turn increments until they can be removed by hand. Loosen the bolts in the reverse order of the tightening sequence **(see illustration 10.24)** to avoid warping or cracking the head. Obtain new head bolts for installation.
12 Lift the cylinder head off the engine block. If it's stuck, very carefully pry up at a casting protrusion, beyond the gasket surface **(see illustration)**.
13 Remove all external components from the head to allow for thorough cleaning and inspection.

10.12 Pry on a casting protrusion to break the head loose

10.15 Carefully remove all traces of old gasket material from the sealing surfaces

10.24 Cylinder head bolt TIGHTENING sequence

Installation

Refer to illustrations 10.15, 10.24, 10.26a, 10.26b, 10.26c and 10.26d

14   The mating surfaces of the cylinder head and block must be perfectly clean when the head is installed.

15   Use a gasket scraper to remove all traces of carbon and old gasket material from the cylinder head and engine block, then clean the mating surfaces with brake system cleaner **(see illustration)**. If there's oil on the mating surfaces when the head is installed, the gasket may not seal correctly and leaks could develop.

16   When working on the block, stuff the cylinders with clean shop rags to keep out debris. Use a vacuum cleaner to remove material that falls into the cylinders.

17   Check the block and head mating surfaces for nicks, deep scratches and other damage. If damage is slight, it can be removed with a file; if it's excessive, machining may be the only alternative.

18   Use a tap of the correct size to chase the threads in the head bolt holes, then clean the holes with compressed air - make sure that nothing remains in the holes. **Warning:** *Wear eye protection when using compressed air!*

19   Check the cylinder head for warpage (see Chapter 2B). Check the head gasket, intake and exhaust manifold surfaces.

20   Install the components that were removed from the head.

21   Position the new cylinder head gasket over the dowel pins on the block, noting which direction on the gasket faces up.

22   Carefully set the head on the block without disturbing the gasket.

23   Before installing the head bolts, apply a small amount of clean engine oil to the threads and hardened washers (if equipped). The chamfered side of the washers must face the bolt heads.

24   Install the NEW cylinder head bolts and tighten them finger tight. Then tighten the bolts in several steps, following the proper sequence **(see illustration)**, to the torque listed in this Chapter's Specifications.

25   Remove all traces of old sealant from the rear timing chain cover and the cover bolts.

26   Apply a bead of RTV sealant to the rear timing cover sealing surfaces **(see illustration)**. Install new O-rings in the front of the engine block and in the variable valve timing oil control orifices in the cylinder head **(see illustrations)**. Place the rear timing chain cover in position over the dowels on the engine and install the bolts in their original locations. Following the recommended tightening sequence, tighten the bolts to the torque listed in this Chapter's Specifications **(see illustration)**.

27   Install the camshafts (see Section 7), then install the timing chains and sprockets (see Section 6). The remaining installation steps are the reverse of removal. If any part of the valve train was replaced, check and adjust the valve clearance (see Chapter 1).

28   Install the engine in the vehicle.

29   Refill the cooling system and engine oil, and install a new oil filter (see Chapter 1).

30   Reconnect the battery and perform the necessary re-learn procedures (see Chapter 5).

31   Start the engine and check for oil and coolant leaks.

10.26a Apply RTV sealant to the rear timing chain cover at the areas shown - be sure to wipe off any excess sealant

10.26b Install new O-rings in the front of the engine block . . .

10.26c ... and in the variable valve timing oil control orifices (arrows) in the cylinder head

10.26d Rear timing chain cover TIGHTENING sequence

11 Crankshaft pulley - removal and installation

1   Disconnect the cable from the negative terminal of the battery (see Chapter 5).
2   Block the rear wheels and set the parking brake.
3   Loosen the lug nuts of the right front wheel.
4   Raise the front of the vehicle and support it securely on jackstands. Remove the right front wheel.
5   Remove the engine splash shield.
6   Remove the drivebelt (see Chapter 1).
7   Remove the starter (see Chapter 5) and lock the driveplate using a large screwdriver.
8   Loosen the crankshaft pulley bolt.
9   Use a puller to remove the pulley from the crankshaft (see illustration). Caution: *Be sure to use the proper adapter on the end of the crankshaft to prevent damage to the threads or end of the crankshaft. Also, the jaws of the puller must bolt to the hub of the pulley or grasp the hub of the pulley, not the outer diameter.*
10   To install the crankshaft pulley, align the pulley groove with the key on the crankshaft and slide the pulley onto the crankshaft.
11   Install the crankshaft pulley retaining bolt and tighten it to the torque listed in this Chapter's Specifications.
12   The remainder of installation is the reverse of removal.
13   Reconnect the battery and perform the necessary re-learn procedures (see Chapter 5).

12 Crankshaft front oil seal - replacement

Refer to illustrations 12.2 and 12.4
1   Remove the crankshaft pulley (see Section 11).
2   Carefully pry the seal out of the cover with a seal removal tool or a large screwdriver (see illustration). Caution: *Be careful not to*
scratch, gouge or distort the area that the seal fits into or an oil leak will develop.*
3   Clean the bore to remove any old seal material and corrosion. Position the new seal in the bore with the seal lip (usually the side with the spring) facing IN (toward the engine). A small amount of oil applied to the outer edge of the new seal will make installation easier.
4   Drive the seal into the bore with a large socket and hammer (see illustration). Select a socket that's the same outside diameter as the seal and make sure the new seal is pressed into place until it's flush with the face of the case.
5   Check the surface of the damper that the oil seal rides on. If the surface has been grooved from long-time contact with the seal, the new seal will leak. Replace the crankshaft pulley.
6   Lubricate the seal lips with engine oil and reinstall the crankshaft pulley. Install the crankshaft pulley retaining bolt and tighten it to the torque listed in this Chapter's Specifications.
7   The remainder of installation is the reverse of the removal. Run the engine and check for oil leaks.

12.2 Pry the seal out very carefully with a seal removal tool or screwdriver, being careful not to nick or gouge the seal bore or the crankshaft

13 Oil pans - removal and installation

Lower oil pan
1   Raise the vehicle and support it securely on jackstands.
2   Remove the under-vehicle splash shield.
3   Refer to Chapter 1 and drain the engine oil.
4   Loosen the lower oil pan bolts in a criss-cross pattern. Remove the bolts.
5   Use a plastic-face hammer to bump the side of the oil pan to break it loose. If that doesn't work, tap a putty knife or other thin tool between the upper and lower oil pans. Remove the lower oil pan.
6   Clean all remnants of RTV sealant from the sealing surfaces. Wipe the surfaces with lacquer thinner to remove all traces of oil.
7   Check the lower steel oil pan flange for distortion, particularly around the bolt holes. If necessary, place the pan on a wood block and use a hammer to flatten and restore the gasket surface.
8   Apply a bead of RTV sealant around the steel oil pan flange and install the steel oil pan.

12.4 Use a large socket, seal driver or large-diameter pipe to drive the new seal into the cover

13.15 Insert a flathead screwdriver or small pry bar into the notch on the side of the oil pan to break it loose - be careful not to damage the sealing surfaces!

13.21 Install new O-rings in the block and the oil pump housing

9   Tighten the oil pan fasteners in several steps in a criss-cross pattern, to the torque listed in this Chapter's Specifications.

10   The remainder of installation is the reverse of removal.

Upper oil pan

Removal

Refer to illustration 13.15

Note: *The engine must be removed from the vehicle to perform this procedure.*

11   Remove the subframe (see Chapter 10).

12   Remove the rear cover from the upper oil pan.

13   Remove the four bolts that attach the upper oil pan to the transaxle.

14   Remove the upper oil pan bolts in the reverse of the tightening sequence **(see illustration 13.22).**

15   Put a prying tool into the notch in the oil pan top rail and use it to break the oil pan loose **(see illustration)**. Remove the upper oil pan.

16   Remove the two O-rings from the block and the housing of the oil pump.

17   Remove the gaskets from the front timing cover and the rear seal retainer.

Installation

Refer to illustrations 13.21 and 13.22

18   Use a scraper to remove all traces of old gasket material and sealant from the upper aluminum section of the oil pan, the lower steel pan and the engine block. Clean the mating surfaces with brake system cleaner. **Caution:** *Be careful not to scratch or gouge the gasket surface of the block or oil pan. A leak could develop after the repairs have been completed.*

19   Make sure the threaded bolt holes in the block and aluminum section of the oil pan are clean.

20   Apply a bead of RTV sealant to the ends of the timing chain cover gasket and the rear oil seal retainer gasket, then place the gaskets in position on the oil pan. Apply a bead of RTV sealant around the upper aluminum oil pan flange. **Note:** *The oil pan must be installed within 15 minutes once the sealant has been applied.*

21   Install new O-rings in the engine block and the oil pump body **(see illustration)**.

22   Carefully position the upper aluminum section of the oil pan on the engine block and install the bolts. Following the recommended sequence, tighten the fasteners in three or four steps to the torque listed in this Chapter's Specifications **(see illustration)**.

23   Install the transaxle mounting bolts.

24   The remainder of installation is the reverse of removal. Be sure to install a new oil filter (see Chapter 1) and wait at least 30 minutes after applying the silicone sealer before adding oil.

14   Oil pump - removal, inspection and installation

Removal

Refer to illustration 14.3

1   Remove the primary timing chain and the crankshaft sprocket (see Section 6). **Note:** *It is not necessary to remove the camshaft sprockets, the camshaft sprocket bolts, the secondary timing chains or the primary timing chain tensioner pivot arm/chain guide during this procedure. Simply pivot the tensioner arm/chain guide over to the left side to allow removal of the oil pump housing.*

2   Remove the oil pans (see Section 13).

3   Remove the oil strainer-to-oil pump bolts from the lower section of the oil pump. Remove the oil pump-to-engine block bolts **(see illustration)**.

4   Gently pry the oil pump housing outward enough to clear the dowel pins on the engine block and remove it from the engine.

14.3 Remove the mounting bolts (A) and detach the oil strainer from the oil pump, then remove the oil pump housing retaining bolts (B)

13.22 Upper (aluminum) oil pan TIGHTENING sequence

Engine Front

72025-2A-13.38 HAYNES

14.5 Remove the screws and lift the cover off

Inspection

Refer to illustrations 14.5, 14.7, 14.8a, 14.8b, 14.8c, 14.8d and 14.8e

5   Use a large Phillips screwdriver to remove the screws holding the front cover on the oil pump housing **(see illustration)**.
6   Clean all components with solvent, then inspect them for wear and damage.
7   Remove the oil pressure regulator cap,

14.7 Oil pressure relief valve components

1 *Plug*
2 *Washer*
3 *Outer spring*
4 *Inner spring (if equipped)*
5 *Relief valve*
6 *Oil pump housing*

washer, spring(s) and valve **(see illustration)**. Check the oil pressure regulator valve sliding surface and valve spring. If either the spring or the valve is damaged, they must be replaced as a set.
8   Check the clearance of the following oil pump components with a feeler gauge **(see illustrations)** and compare the measurements to the clearance listed in this Chapter's Specifications:

a) *Rotor tooth tip clearance*

b) *Outer rotor-to-body clearance*
c) *Cover-to-inner rotor clearance*
d) *Cover-to-outer rotor clearance*
e) *Inner rotor ridge clearance*

If any clearance is excessive, replace the entire oil pump assembly.
9   Assemble the oil pump and tighten the screws securely. **Note:** *Pack the pump with grease to prime it.* Install the oil pressure regulator valve, spring and washer, then tighten the oil pressure regulator valve cap.

14.8a Use feeler gauges to measure the rotor tooth tip clearance . . .

14.8b . . . and the outer rotor-to-body clearance

14.8c Measure the cover-to-rotor end clearance with a straightedge and feeler gauge - measure (A) above the inner rotor and (B) above the outer rotor

14.8d Use calipers to measure the diameter of the inner rotor ridge (the part of the inner rotor that rides in the pump body) . . .

14.8e . . . and subtract the inner rotor ridge diameter from the opening in the pump body where the inner rotor rides to obtain the inner rotor ridge-to-body clearance

14.10 There is a flat surface on each side of the crankshaft - align them with the flats on the inner gear

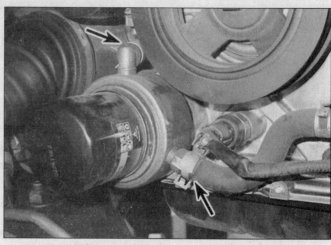

15.5 Detach the coolant hoses from the oil cooler

Installation

Refer to illustration 14.10

10   Installation is the reverse of removal. Use new gaskets (where applicable) on all disassembled parts. Align the flats on the crankshaft **(see illustration)** with the flats on the oil pump gear. Tighten all fasteners to the torque listed in this Chapter's Specifications. Note: *Before installing the oil pan, be sure to replace the O-rings on the oil pump housing and engine block* **(see illustration 13.21).**

15 Engine oil cooler and oil filter adapter - general information and replacement

General information

1   These engines are equipped with a combination oil cooler/oil filter adapter that is mounted to the right end of the oil pan. The oil cooler/oil filter adapter also incorporates an oil

pressure relief valve, which redirects oil flow to bypass the oil cooler when pressures are too high. The oil cooler has two hoses connecting the cooler to the engine.

Replacement

Refer to illustrations 15.5, 15.6 and 15.7

Warning: *The engine must be completely cool before performing this procedure.*

2   Loosen the lug nuts of the right front wheel. Raise the vehicle and support it securely on jackstands. Remove the right front wheel.

3   Remove the right front inner fender splash shield (see Chapter 11).

4   Drain the cooling system (see Chapter 1).

5   Place rags under the cooler to catch oil and coolant spillage. Detach the hose clamps and disconnect the inlet and outlet hoses from the oil cooler **(see illustration).**

6   Remove the oil filter, then remove the oil cooler connector bolt and remove the oil cooler and O-ring from the oil pan **(see illustration).**

7   Lubricate the new oil cooler O-ring with engine oil. Install the O-ring in the groove on the oil cooler **(see illustration).**

8   Position the oil cooler onto the oil pan and install the connector bolt.

9   Tighten the oil cooler connector bolt to the torque listed in this Chapter's Specifications. Do not overtighten.

10   Connect the coolant hoses to the cooler and install the clamps. Install a new oil filter, change the engine oil and refill the cooling system (see Chapter 1).

16 Driveplate - removal and installation

Refer to illustration 16.4

1   Remove the engine/transaxle assembly (see Chapter 2B), then separate the transaxle from the engine (see Chapter 7).

2   Check and replace the front pump seal/O-ring.

15.6 Remove the oil cooler connector bolt

15.7 Install a new O-ring into the groove in the oil cooler

16.4 Hold a lever against a casting protrusion on the engine block or place a screwdriver through a hole in the driveplate to hold the driveplate while the mounting bolts are removed - note the painted marks made at the crank and driveplate for alignment

3   Use paint or a center-punch to make alignment marks on the driveplate and crankshaft to ensure correct alignment during reinstallation.

4   Remove the bolts that secure the driveplate to the crankshaft **(see illustration)**. If the crankshaft turns, hold the driveplate with a pry bar or wedge a screwdriver into the ring gear teeth to jam the driveplate.

5   Remove the driveplate from the crankshaft. Since the driveplate is fairly heavy, be sure to support it while removing the last bolt.

6   Clean the driveplate to remove grease and oil. Inspect the surface for cracks, rivet grooves, burned areas and score marks. Light scoring can be removed with emery cloth. Check for cracked and broken ring gear teeth or a loose ring gear. Lay the driveplate on a flat surface and use a straightedge to check for warpage.

7   Clean and inspect the mating surfaces of the driveplate and the crankshaft. If the crankshaft rear seal is leaking, replace it before

reinstalling the driveplate.

8   Position the driveplate against the crankshaft. Be sure to align the marks made during removal. Note that some engines have an alignment dowel or staggered bolt holes to ensure correct installation. Before installing the bolts, apply thread locking compound to the threads.

9   Wedge a screwdriver into the ring gear teeth to keep the driveplate from turning as you tighten the bolts to the torque listed in this Chapter's Specifications.

10   The remainder of installation is the reverse of the removal.

17   Rear main oil seal - replacement

1   Remove the engine/transaxle assembly (see Chapter 2B), then separate the transaxle from the engine (see Chapter 7).

2   Remove the driveplate (see Section 16).

3   Remove the bolts from the rear seal retainer. Tap the retainer sideways with a plastic hammer to break the seal and remove it. Discard the seal/retainer assembly - it must be replaced with a new assembly.

4   Remove all old RTV sealant from the rear of the engine and the oil pan. Clean the surfaces with brake system cleaner.

5   Obtain special seal installation tool J-47128. It is available from automotive tool suppliers and Nissan dealerships.

6   Loosen the tool's wingnut.

7   Install the tool onto the rear of the crankshaft so it covers the sealing surface. Tighten the wingnut.

8   Apply a bead of RTV sealant to the sealing surface of the new retainer.

9   Lightly lubricate the oil seal lip with clean engine oil, then slide it over the tool and into position.

10   Loosen the wingnut and remove the tool.

11   Tighten the retainer bolts to the torque listed in this Chapter's Specifications.

12   The remaining steps are the reverse of removal.

18   Engine mounts - check and replacement

1   There are three engine mounts and one transaxle mount. The engine mounts are located on the passenger's side of the vehicle and on the front and rear side of the engine block. The transaxle mount is bolted to the left side of the transaxle.

Check

2   During the check, the engine must be raised slightly to remove the weight from the mounts.

3   Raise the vehicle and support it securely on jackstands. Support the engine/transaxle from above using a hoist or three bar support fixture.

4   Check the mounts to see if the rubber is cracked, hardened or separated from the bushing in the center of the mount.

5   Check for relative movement between the mounts and the engine or frame (use a large screwdriver or prybar to attempt to move the mounts). If movement is noted, lower the engine and tighten the mount fasteners.

Replacement

6   If you're replacing a front or rear engine mount, raise the front of the vehicle and support it securely on jackstands. Remove the splash shields from under the vehicle.

7   Attach an engine hoist to the top of the engine for lifting. **Caution:** *Do not use a jack under the oil pan to support the entire weight of the engine or the oil pump pick-up could be damaged.*

8   Remove the engine mount-to-chassis fasteners.

9   Remove the engine mount-to-engine mount bracket nut.

10   Raise the engine slightly until the engine mount can be removed from the vehicle.

11   Installation is the reverse of removal.

Notes

Chapter 2 Part B
General engine overhaul procedures

Contents

Specifications

General

Engine designation	VQ35DE
Displacement	213 cubic inches (3.5 liters)
Compression ratio	10.3:1
Cylinder compression pressure	
Standard	185 psi
Minimum	142 psi
Maximum variation between cylinders	14 psi
Oil pressure (normal, warm engine)	
Idle	14 psi
2000 rpm	43 psi

Torque specifications*

Ft-lbs (unless otherwise indicated)

Note: *One foot-pound (ft-lb) of torque is equivalent to 12 inch-pounds (in-lbs) of torque. Torque values below approximately 15 ft-lbs are expressed in inch-pounds, since most foot-pound torque wrenches are not accurate at these smaller values.*

Connecting rod cap bolts**	
Step 1	168 in-lbs
Step 2	Tighten an additional 90 degrees
Main bearing cap bolts (lower crankcase-to-block)**	
Step 1	26
Step 2	Tighten an additional 90 degrees

Refer to Part A of this Chapter for additional torque specifications.

**Replace with NEW bolts.*

1.1 An engine block being bored. An engine rebuilder will use special machinery to recondition the cylinder bores

1.2 If the cylinders are bored, the machine shop will normally hone the engine on a machine like this

1   General information - engine overhaul

Refer to illustrations 1.1, 1.2, 1.3, 1.4, 1.5 and 1.6

Included in this portion of Chapter 2 are general information and diagnostic testing procedures for determining the overall mechanical condition of your engine.

The information ranges from advice concerning preparation for an overhaul and the purchase of replacement parts and/or components to detailed, step-by-step procedures covering removal and installation.

The following Sections have been written to help you determine whether your engine needs to be overhauled and how to remove and install it once you've determined it needs to be rebuilt. For information concerning in-vehicle engine repair, see Chapter 2A.

The Specifications included in this Part are general in nature and include only those necessary for testing the oil pressure and engine compression, and bottom-end torque specifications. Refer to Chapter 2A for additional engine Specifications.

It's not always easy to determine when, or if, an engine should be completely overhauled, because a number of factors must be considered.

High mileage is not necessarily an indication that an overhaul is needed, while low mileage doesn't preclude the need for an overhaul. Frequency of servicing is probably the most important consideration. An engine that's had regular and frequent oil and filter changes, as well as other required maintenance, will most likely give many thousands of miles of reliable service. Conversely, a neglected engine may require an overhaul very early in its service life.

Excessive oil consumption is an indication that piston rings, valve seals and/or valve guides are in need of attention. Make sure that oil leaks aren't responsible before decid-

1.3 A crankshaft having a main bearing journal ground

ing that the rings and/or guides are bad. Perform a cylinder compression check to determine the extent of the work required (see Section 3). Also, check the vacuum readings under various conditions (see Section 4).

Check the oil pressure with a gauge installed in place of the oil pressure sending unit and compare it to this Chapter's Specifications (see Section 2). If it's extremely low, the bearings and/or oil pump are probably worn out.

Loss of power, rough running, knocking or metallic engine noises, excessive valve train noise and high fuel consumption rates may also point to the need for an overhaul, especially if they're all present at the same time. If a complete tune-up doesn't remedy the situation, major mechanical work is the only solution.

An engine overhaul involves restoring the internal parts to the specifications of a new engine. During an overhaul, the piston rings are replaced and the cylinder walls are reconditioned (rebored and/or honed) **(see illustrations 1.1 and 1.2)**. If a rebore is done

1.4 A machinist checks for a bent connecting rod, using specialized equipment

by an automotive machine shop, new oversize pistons will also be installed. The main bearings, connecting rod bearings and camshaft bearings are generally replaced with new ones and, if necessary, the crankshaft may be reground to restore the journals **(see illustration 1.3)**. Generally, the valves are serviced as well, since they're usually in less-than-perfect condition at this point. While the engine is being overhauled, other components, such as the distributor, starter and alternator, can be rebuilt as well. The end result should be similar to a new engine that will give many trouble free miles. **Note:** *Critical cooling system components such as the hoses, drivebelts, thermostat and water pump should be replaced with new parts when an engine is overhauled. The radiator should be checked carefully to ensure that it isn't clogged or leaking (see Chapter 3). If you purchase a rebuilt engine or short block, some rebuilders will not warranty their engines unless the radiator has been professionally flushed. Also, we don't recommend overhauling the oil pump - always* *install a new one when an engine is rebuilt.*

Overhauling the internal components on today's engines is a difficult and time-consuming task which requires a significant amount of specialty tools and is best left to a professional engine rebuilder (**see illustrations 1.4, 1.5 and 1.6**). A competent engine rebuilder will handle the inspection of your old parts and offer advice concerning the reconditioning or replacement of the original engine, never purchase parts or have machine work done on other components until the block has been thoroughly inspected by a professional machine shop. As a general rule, time is the primary cost of an overhaul, especially since the vehicle may be tied up for a minimum of two weeks or more. Be aware that some engine builders only have the capability to rebuild the engine you bring them while other rebuilders have a large inventory of rebuilt exchange engines in stock. Also be aware that many machine shops could take as much as two weeks time to completely rebuild your engine depending on shop workload. Sometimes it makes more sense to simply exchange your engine for another engine that's already rebuilt to save time.

2   Oil pressure check

Refer to illustration 2.2

1   Low engine oil pressure can be a sign of an engine in need of rebuilding. A "low oil pressure" indicator (often called an "idiot light") is not a test of the oiling system. Such indicators only come on when the oil pressure is dangerously low. Even a factory oil pressure gauge in the instrument panel is only a relative indication, although much better for driver information than a warning light. A better test is with a mechanical (not electrical) oil pressure gauge.
2   Locate the oil pressure indicator sending unit - it's low on the passenger side of the engine (**see illustration**).
3   Unscrew and remove the oil pressure

1.5 A bore gauge being used to check the main bearing bore

sending unit and then screw in the hose for your oil pressure gauge. If necessary, install an adapter fitting. Use Teflon tape or thread sealant on the threads of the adapter and/or the fitting on the end of your gauge's hose.
4   Connect an accurate tachometer to the engine, according to the tachometer manufacturer's instructions.
5   Check the oil pressure with the engine running (normal operating temperature) at the specified engine speed, and compare it to this Chapter's Specifications. If it's extremely low, the bearings and/or oil pump are probably worn out.

3   Cylinder compression check

Refer to illustration 3.6

1   A compression check will tell you what mechanical condition the upper end of your engine (pistons, rings, valves, head gaskets) is in. Specifically, it can tell you if the compression is down due to leakage caused by worn piston rings, defective valves and seats or a blown head gasket. **Note:** *The engine must be at normal operating temperature and the*

1.6 Uneven piston wear like this indicates a bent connecting rod

battery must be fully charged for this check.
2   Begin by cleaning the area around the spark plugs before you remove them (compressed air should be used, if available). The idea is to prevent dirt from getting into the cylinders as the compression check is being done.
3   Remove the ignition coil assemblies (see Chapter 5). **Note:** *If you only need to get a general idea of the condition of the engine, it's easier to test the compression only on the front bank of cylinders. This eliminates having to remove the upper intake manifold and other components for access to the rear spark plugs. If a problem is suspected after testing the front bank, perform the test on the rear cylinders as well.* Disable the fuel pump by removing the fuel pump fuse (see Chapter 4, Section 2).
4   Remove all of the spark plugs (see Chapter 1).
5   Block the throttle wide open.
6   Install a compression gauge in the spark plug hole (**see illustration**).
7   Crank the engine over at least seven compression strokes and watch the gauge. The compression should build up quickly in a

2.2 The oil pressure sending unit is located at the right end of the engine, below the crankshaft pulley

3.6 Use a compression gauge with a threaded fitting for the spark plug hole, not the type that requires hand force to maintain the seal

4.4 A simple vacuum gauge can be handy in diagnosing engine condition and performance - be sure to connect it to intake manifold vacuum (not "ported" vacuum)

STD-O-OBR HAYNES

4.6 Typical vacuum gauge readings

healthy engine. Low compression on the first stroke, followed by gradually increasing pressure on successive strokes, indicates worn piston rings. A low compression reading on the first stroke, which doesn't build up during successive strokes, indicates leaking valves or a blown head gasket (a cracked head could also be the cause). Deposits on the undersides of the valve heads can also cause low compression. Record the highest gauge reading obtained.

8   Repeat the procedure for the remaining cylinders and compare the results to this Chapter's Specifications.

9   Add some engine oil (about three squirts from a plunger-type oil can) to each cylinder, through the spark plug hole, and repeat the test.

10   If the compression increases after the oil is added, the piston rings are definitely worn. If the compression doesn't increase significantly, the leakage is occurring at the valves or head gasket. Leakage past the valves may be caused by burned valve seats and/or faces or warped, cracked or bent valves.

11   If two adjacent cylinders have equally low compression, there's a strong possibility that the head gasket between them is blown. The appearance of coolant in the combustion chambers or the crankcase would verify this condition.

12   If one cylinder is slightly lower than the others, and the engine has a slightly rough idle, a worn lobe on the camshaft could be the cause.

13   If the compression is unusually high, the combustion chambers are probably coated with carbon deposits. If that's the case, the cylinder head(s) should be removed and decarbonized.

14   If compression is way down or varies greatly between cylinders, it's a good idea to have a leak-down test performed by an automotive repair shop. This test will pinpoint exactly where the leakage is occurring and how severe it is.

4   Vacuum gauge diagnostic checks

Refer to illustrations 4.4 and 4.6

1   A vacuum gauge provides inexpensive but valuable information about what is going on in the engine. You can check for worn rings or cylinder walls, leaking head or intake manifold gaskets, incorrect carburetor adjustments, restricted exhaust, stuck or burned valves, weak valve springs, improper ignition or valve timing and ignition problems.

2   Unfortunately, vacuum gauge readings are easy to misinterpret, so they should be used in conjunction with other tests to confirm the diagnosis.

3   Both the absolute readings and the rate of needle movement are important for accurate interpretation. Most gauges measure vacuum in inches of mercury (in-Hg). The following references to vacuum assume the diagnosis is being performed at sea level. As elevation increases (or atmospheric pressure decreases), the reading will decrease. For every 1,000 foot increase in elevation above approximately 2,000 feet, the gauge readings will decrease about one inch of mercury.

4   Connect the vacuum gauge directly to the intake manifold vacuum, not to ported

(throttle body) vacuum **(see illustration)**. Some models are equipped with a vacuum fitting built into the brake booster vacuum hose grommet at the brake booster. Other models are equipped with a vacuum hose fitting on the intake manifold. Use a T-fitting to access the vacuum signal. Be sure no hoses are left disconnected during the test or false readings will result.

5   Before you begin the test, allow the engine to warm up completely. Block the wheels and set the parking brake. With the transaxle in Park, start the engine and allow it to run at normal idle speed. **Warning:** *Keep your hands and the vacuum gauge clear of the fans.*

6   Read the vacuum gauge; an average, healthy engine should normally produce about 17 to 22 in-Hg with a fairly steady needle **(see illustration)**. Refer to the following vacuum gauge readings and what they indicate about the engine's condition:

7   A low, steady reading usually indicates a leaking gasket between the intake manifold and cylinder head(s) or throttle body, a leaky vacuum hose, late ignition timing or incorrect camshaft timing. Check ignition timing with a timing light and eliminate all other possible causes, utilizing the tests provided in this Chapter before you remove the timing chain cover to check the timing marks.

6.1 After tightly wrapping water-vulnerable components, use a spray cleaner on everything, with particular concentration on the greasiest areas, usually around the valve cover and lower edges of the block. If one section dries out, apply more cleaner

6.2 Depending on how dirty the engine is, let the cleaner soak in according to the directions and then hose off the grime and cleaner. Get the rinse water down into every area you can get at; then dry important components with a hair dryer or paper towels

8   If the reading is three to eight inches below normal and it fluctuates at that low reading, suspect an intake manifold gasket leak at an intake port or a faulty fuel injector.

9   If the needle has regular drops of about two-to-four inches at a steady rate, the valves are probably leaking. Perform a compression check or leak-down test to confirm this.

10   An irregular drop or down-flick of the needle can be caused by a sticking valve or an ignition misfire. Perform a compression check or leak-down test and read the spark plugs.

11   A rapid vibration of about four in-Hg vibration at idle combined with exhaust smoke indicates worn valve guides. Perform a leak-down test to confirm this. If the rapid vibration occurs with an increase in engine speed, check for a leaking intake manifold gasket or head gasket, weak valve springs, burned valves or ignition misfire.

12   A slight fluctuation, say one inch up and down, may mean ignition problems. Check all the usual tune-up items and, if necessary, run the engine on an ignition analyzer.

13   If there is a large fluctuation, perform a compression or leak-down test to look for a weak or dead cylinder or a blown head gasket.

14   If the needle moves slowly through a wide range, check for a clogged PCV system, incorrect idle fuel mixture, throttle body or intake manifold gasket leaks.

15   Check for a slow return after revving the engine by quickly snapping the throttle open until the engine reaches about 2,500 rpm and let it shut. Normally the reading should drop to near zero, rise above normal idle reading (about 5 in-Hg over) and then return to the previous idle reading. If the vacuum returns slowly and doesn't peak when the throttle is snapped shut, the rings may be worn. If there is a long delay, look for a restricted exhaust system (often the muffler or catalytic converter). An easy way to check this is to temporarily disconnect the exhaust ahead of the suspected part and redo the test.

5   Engine rebuilding alternatives

The do-it-yourselfer is faced with a number of options when purchasing a rebuilt engine. The major considerations are cost, warranty, parts availability and the time required for the rebuilder to complete the project. The decision to replace the engine block, piston/connecting rod assemblies and crankshaft depends on the final inspection results of your engine. Only then can you make a cost effective decision whether to have your engine overhauled or simply purchase an exchange engine for your vehicle.

Some of the rebuilding alternatives include:

Individual parts - If the inspection procedures reveal that the engine block and most engine components are in reusable condition, purchasing individual parts and having a rebuilder rebuild your engine may be the most economical alternative. The block, crankshaft and piston/connecting rod assemblies should all be inspected carefully by a machine shop first.

Short block - A short block consists of an engine block with a crankshaft and piston/connecting rod assemblies already installed. All new bearings are incorporated and all clearances will be correct. The existing camshafts, valve train components, cylinder head and external parts can be bolted to the short block with little or no machine shop work necessary.

Long block - A long block consists of a short block plus an oil pump, oil pan, cylinder head, valve cover, camshaft and valve train components, timing sprockets and chain or gears and timing cover. All components are installed with new bearings, seals and gaskets incorporated throughout. The installation of manifolds and external parts is all that's necessary.

Low mileage used engines - Some companies now offer low mileage used engines which is a very cost effective way to get your vehicle up and running again. These engines often come from vehicles which have been in totaled in accidents or come from other countries which have a higher vehicle turn over rate. A low mileage used engine also usually has a similar warranty like the newly remanufactured engines.

Give careful thought to which alternative is best for you and discuss the situation with local automotive machine shops, auto parts dealers and experienced rebuilders before ordering or purchasing replacement parts.

6   Engine removal - methods and precautions

Refer to illustrations 6.1, 6.2, and 6.3

If you've decided that an engine must be removed for overhaul or major repair work, several preliminary steps should be taken. Read all removal and installation procedures carefully prior to committing to this job.

Locating a suitable place to work is extremely important. Adequate work space, along with storage space for the vehicle, will be needed. If a shop or garage isn't available, at the very least a flat, level, clean work surface made of concrete or asphalt is required.

These engines are removed by lowering the engine to the floor, along with the transaxle, then raising the vehicle sufficiently to slide the assembly out; this will require a vehicle hoist as well as an engine hoist. Make sure the hoist is rated in excess of the combined weight of the engine and transaxle. Safety is of primary importance, considering the potential hazards involved in removing the engine from the vehicle.

Cleaning the engine compartment and engine before beginning the removal procedure will help keep tools clean and organized **(see illustrations 6.1 and 6.2)**.

If you're a novice at engine removal, get at least one helper. One person cannot easily do all the things you need to do to remove a big heavy engine and transaxle assembly from the engine compartment. Also helpful is to seek advice and assistance from someone who's experienced in engine removal.

Plan the operation ahead of time. Arrange for or obtain all of the tools and equipment you'll need prior to beginning the job **(see illustration 6.3)**. Some of the equipment necessary to perform engine removal and installation safely and with relative ease are (in addition to a vehicle hoist and an engine hoist) a heavy duty floor jack (preferably fitted with a transmission jack head adapter), complete sets of wrenches and sockets as described in the front of this manual, wooden blocks, plenty of rags and cleaning solvent for mopping up spilled oil, coolant and gasoline.

Plan for the vehicle to be out of use for quite a while. A machine shop can do the work that is beyond the scope of the home mechanic. Machine shops often have a busy schedule, so before removing the engine, consult the shop for an estimate of how long it will take to rebuild or repair the components that may need work.

6.3 Get an engine stand sturdy enough to firmly support the engine while you're working on it. Stay away from three-wheeled models; they have a tendency to tip over more easily, so get a four-wheeled unit

7 Engine - removal and installation

Warning: *Gasoline is extremely flammable, so take extra precautions when you work on any part of the fuel system. Don't smoke or allow open flames or bare light bulbs near the work area, and don't work in a garage where a gas-type appliance (such as a water heater or clothes dryer) is present. Since gasoline is carcinogenic, wear fuel-resistant gloves when there's a possibility of being exposed to fuel, and, if you spill any fuel on your skin, rinse it off immediately with soap and water. Mop up any spills immediately and do not store fuel-soaked rags where they could ignite. The fuel system is under constant pressure, so, if any fuel lines are to be disconnected, the fuel pressure in the system must be relieved first (see Chapter 4 for more information). When you perform any kind of work on the fuel system, wear safety glasses and have a Class B type fire extinguisher on hand.*
Warning: *The engine must be completely cool before beginning this procedure.*
Note: *Engine removal on these vehicles is a difficult job, especially for the do-it-yourselfer working at home. The manufacturer states that the engine and transaxle have to be removed as a unit from the bottom of the vehicle, not the top. With a floor jack and jackstands, it can't be raised high enough or supported safely enough for the engine/transaxle to slide out from underneath. The manufacturer recommends that removal of the engine/transaxle only be performed with a frame-contact type hoist.*

Note: *During this procedure you'll have to adjust the height of the vehicle with the vehicle hoist to perform certain operations.*

Removal

Refer to illustration 7.34

1   Removing the hood (see Chapter 11) will make it easier to work on the vehicle but isn't necessary. Relieve the fuel pressure (see Chapter 4).
2   Park the car on a vehicle hoist, then raise the hoist arms to contact the jacking points on each side of the vehicle. Remove the front wheels.
3   Disconnect the cable from the negative terminal of the battery (see Chapter 5).
4   Drain the engine coolant (see Chapter 1) and the power steering fluid.
5   Remove the engine cover and the access panels in the wheel wells.
6   Remove the air filter housing and the air ducts (see Chapter 4).
7   Remove the battery and the battery tray (see Chapter 5).
8   Remove the drivebelt (see Chapter 1).
9   Remove the coolant reservoir tank (see Chapter 3).
10   Remove the wiper module (see Chapter 12) and the cowl top extension.
11   Drain the transaxle fluid (see Chapter 1).
12   Disconnect all of the main engine compartment wiring harnesses, including those at the Transmission Control Module (TCM) and the Engine Control Module (ECM).
13   Remove the battery support bracket along with the TCM and the ECM.
14   Unbolt the brake master cylinder reservoir bracket and secure the reservoir out of the way.
15   Disconnect both heater hoses, the EVAP hose and the fuel supply hose. Plug all open ends to prevent contamination.
16   Disconnect the shift cable from the transaxle.

17   Disconnect the brake booster vacuum hose from the engine.
18   Disconnect any ground cables or straps between the chassis and the engine or transaxle.
19   Remove the air conditioning compressor, but leave the refrigerant hoses attached. Move the compressor out of the way and secure it in place with wire.
20   Disconnect the power steering suction hoses from the reservoir and plug the end.
21   Disconnect the transaxle cooler hoses from the radiator.
22   Remove the starter (see Chapter 5).
23   Remove the front driveaxles (see Chapter 8).
24   Remove the air deflector.
25   Remove the front section of exhaust pipe.
26   On AWD models, remove the driveshaft (see Chapter 8).
27   Disconnect the steering shaft from the steering gear (see Chapter 10).
28   Disconnect the stabilizer bar links from the stabilizer bar (see Chapter 10).
29   Separate the control arms from the steering knuckles (see Chapter 10).
30   Disconnect the power steering lines from the steering gear.
31   Remove the inspection cover from the rear of the upper oil pan. Remove the bolts from the torque converter, turning the crankshaft with a wrench to access all of them (see Chapter 7).
32   Remove the transaxle bolts from the lower back side of the upper oil pan.
33   Remove the Crankshaft Position (CKP) sensor (see Chapter 6).
34   Check to be sure that there is nothing connecting the engine/transaxle and subframe to the vehicle. Label and disconnect anything remaining **(see illustration)**.
35   Support the front subframe using four jackstands. Other kinds of supports can also be used, but they must be stable and

secure enough to hold the entire engine and transaxle assembly. Slightly lower the vehicle to put some weight onto the jackstands.

36 Remove the right engine mount assembly.

37 Remove the nuts and bolts from the front subframe (see Chapter 10).

38 Slowly raise the vehicle using the hoist, making sure that nothing interferes. Continue raising it until there is enough clearance above the engine to attach an engine hoist.

39 Roll an engine hoist into position and attach it to the engine with a couple pieces of heavy-duty chain (an engine support fixture could be used instead). If the engine is equipped with lifting brackets, use them. If not, you'll have to fasten the chain to some substantial part of the engine - one that is strong enough to take the weight, but in a location that will provide good balance. If you're attaching the chain to a stud on the engine, or are using a bolt passing through the chain and into a threaded hole, place a washer between the nut or bolt head and the chain, and tighten the nut or bolt securely. Take up the slack in the chain, but don't lift the engine. **Warning:** *DO NOT place any part of your body under the engine when it's supported only by a hoist or other lifting device.*

40 Remove the power steering pump assembly including the hoses and brackets.

41 Disconnect the vacuum hoses from the engine mounts (if so equipped).

42 Lift the engine assembly slightly with the hoist. Remove the rear torque rod and its bracket. Remove the other engine mounts.

43 Lift the engine/transaxle assembly to separate it from the subframe.

44 Remove the exhaust manifolds (see Chapter 2A).

45 On vehicles with AWD, remove the transfer case (see Chapter 7B).

46 Remove the engine-to-transaxle bolts, then separate the two. Set the engine and the transaxle on wood blocks to avoid tipping and possible damage. Mount the engine on an engine stand using the hoist if necessary.

Installation

47 Installation is the reverse of removal, noting these points:

a) *Check the engine and transaxle mounts. If they're worn or damaged, replace them. Tighten all of the engine mount fasteners to the torques listed in this Chapter's Specifications.*

b) *Attach the transaxle to the engine (see Chapter 7).*

c) *Tighten the subframe mounting bolts to the torque listed in Chapter 10.*

d) *Tighten the wheel lug nuts to the torque listed in Chapter 1. Tighten the driveaxle/hub nuts to the torque listed in Chapter 8. Tighten the steering and suspension fasteners to the torque values listed in Chapter 10.*

7.34 Label both ends of each wire or vacuum connection before disconnecting them

e) *Refill the engine coolant, oil, power steering fluid and transaxle fluids (see Chapter 1).*

f) *Reconnect the battery and perform the necessary re-learn procedures (see Chapter 5). Recheck all fluid levels.*

8 Engine overhaul - disassembly sequence

1 It's much easier to remove the external components if it's mounted on a portable engine stand. A stand can often be rented quite cheaply from an equipment rental yard. Before the engine is mounted on a stand, the driveplate should be removed from the engine.

2 If a stand isn't available, it's possible to remove the external engine components with it blocked up on the floor. Be extra careful not to tip or drop the engine when working without a stand.

3 If you're going to obtain a rebuilt engine, all external components must come off first, to be transferred to the replacement engine. These components include:

Driveplate
Ignition coils and wiring harnesses
Emissions-related components
Engine mounts and mount brackets
Intake/exhaust manifolds
Fuel injection components
Oil filter and oil cooler
Spark plugs
Thermostat and housing assembly
Water pump

Note: *When removing the external components from the engine, pay close attention to details that may be helpful or important during installation. Note the installed position of gas-*

9.1 Before you try to remove the pistons, use a ridge reamer to remove the raised material (ridge) from the top of the cylinders

kets, seals, spacers, pins, brackets, washers, bolts and other small items.

4 If you're going to obtain a short block (assembled engine block, crankshaft, pistons and connecting rods), then remove the timing chain, cylinder head, oil pan, oil pump pick-up tube, oil pump and water pump from your engine so that you can turn in your old short block to the rebuilder as a core. See *Engine rebuilding alternatives* for additional information regarding the different possibilities to be considered.

9 Pistons and connecting rods - removal and installation

Removal

Refer to illustrations 9.1, 9.3 and 9.4

Note: *Prior to removing the piston/connecting rod assemblies, remove the cylinder head and oil pan (see Chapter 2A).*

1 Use your fingernail to feel if a ridge has formed at the upper limit of ring travel (about 1/4-inch down from the top of each cylinder). If carbon deposits or cylinder wear have produced ridges, they must be completely removed with a special tool (see illustration). Follow the manufacturer's instructions provided with the tool. Failure to remove the ridges before attempting to remove the piston/connecting rod assemblies may result in piston breakage.

2 After the cylinder ridges have been removed, turn the engine so the crankshaft is facing up.

3 Before the main bearing cap assembly and connecting rods are removed, check the connecting rod endplay with feeler gauges. Slide them between the first connecting rod and the crankshaft throw until the play

9.3 Checking the connecting rod endplay (side clearance)

9.4 If the connecting rods or caps are not marked, use permanent ink or paint to mark the caps to the rods by cylinder number (for example, this would be number 4 cylinder connecting rod)

is removed **(see illustration)**. Repeat this procedure for each connecting rod. The endplay is equal to the thickness of the feeler gauge(s). Check with an automotive machine shop for the endplay service limit (a typical endplay should measure between 0.005 to 0.015 inch [0.127 to 0.381 mm]). If the play exceeds the service limit, new connecting rods will be required. If new rods (or a new crankshaft) are installed, the endplay may fall under the minimum allowable. If it does, the rods will have to be machined to restore it. If necessary, consult an automotive machine shop for advice.

4   Check the connecting rods and caps for identification marks. If they aren't plainly marked, use paint or marker **(see illustration)** to clearly identify each rod and cap (1, 2, 3, etc., depending on the cylinder they're associated with). Do not interchange the rod caps. Install the exact same rod cap onto the same connecting rod. **Caution:** *Do not use a punch and hammer to mark the connecting rods or they may be damaged.*

5   Loosen each of the connecting rod cap bolts 1/2-turn at a time until they can be removed by hand. Obtain new connecting rod bolts (but save the old ones for the oil clearance check).

6   Remove the number one connecting rod cap and bearing insert. Don't drop the bearing insert out of the cap.

7   Remove the bearing insert and push the connecting rod/piston assembly out through the top of the engine. Use a wooden or plastic hammer handle to push on the upper bearing surface in the connecting rod. If resistance is felt, double-check to make sure that all of the ridge was removed from the cylinder.

8   Repeat the procedure for the remaining cylinders.

9   After removal, reassemble the connecting rod caps and bearing inserts in their respective connecting rods and install the cap bolts finger tight. Leaving the old bearing inserts in place until reassembly will help prevent the connecting rod bearing surfaces from being accidentally nicked or gouged.

10   The pistons and connecting rods are now ready for inspection and overhaul at an automotive machine shop.

Piston ring installation

Refer to illustrations 9.13, 9.14, 9.15, 9.19a, 9.19b and 9.22

11   Before installing the new piston rings, the ring end gaps must be checked. It's assumed that the piston ring side clearance has been checked and verified correct.

12   Lay out the piston/connecting rod assemblies and the new ring sets so the ring sets will be matched with the same piston and cylinder during the end gap measurement and engine assembly.

13   Insert the top (number one) ring into the first cylinder and square it up with the cylinder walls by pushing it in with the top of the piston **(see illustration)**. The ring should be near the bottom of the cylinder, at the lower limit of ring travel.

14   To measure the end gap, slip feeler gauges between the ends of the ring until a gauge equal to the gap width is found **(see illustration)**. The feeler gauge should slide between the ring ends with a slight amount of drag. A typical ring gap should fall between 0.010 and 0.020 inch (0.25 to 0.50 mm) for compression rings and up to 0.030 inch (0.76 mm) for the oil ring steel rails. If the gap is larger or smaller than specified, double-check to make sure you have the correct rings before proceeding.

15   If the gap is too small, it must be enlarged or the ring ends may come in contact with each other during engine operation, which can cause serious damage to the engine. If necessary, increase the end gaps by filing the ring ends very carefully with a fine file. Mount the file in a vise equipped with soft jaws, slip the ring over the file with the ends contacting the file face and slowly move the ring to remove material from the ends. When performing this operation, file only by pushing the

9.13 Install the piston ring into the cylinder then push it down into position using a piston so the ring will be square in the cylinder

9.14 With the ring square in the cylinder, measure the ring end gap with a feeler gauge

9.15 If the ring end gap is too small, clamp a file in a vise as shown and file the piston ring ends - be sure to remove all raised material

9.19a Installing the spacer/expander in the oil ring groove

9.19b DO NOT use a piston ring installation tool when installing the oil control side rails

ring from the outside end of the file towards the vise (see illustration).

16 Excess end gap isn't critical unless it's greater than 0.040 inch (1.01 mm). Again, double-check to make sure you have the correct ring type.

17 Repeat the procedure for each ring that will be installed in the first cylinder and for each ring in the remaining cylinders. Remember to keep rings, pistons and cylinders matched up.

18 Once the ring end gaps have been checked/corrected, the rings can be installed on the pistons.

19 The oil control ring (lowest one on the piston) is usually installed first. It's composed of three separate components. Slip the spacer/expander into the groove (see illustration). If an anti-rotation tang is used, make sure it's inserted into the drilled hole in the ring groove. Next, install the lower side rail in the same manner (see illustration). Don't use a piston ring installation tool on the oil ring side rails, as they may be damaged. Instead, place one end of the side rail into the groove between the spacer/expander and the ring land, hold it firmly in place and slide a finger around the piston while pushing the rail into the groove. Finally, install the upper side rail.

20 After the three oil ring components have been installed, check to make sure that both

the upper and lower side rails can be rotated smoothly inside the ring grooves.

21 The number two (middle) ring is installed next. It's usually stamped with a mark which must face up, toward the top of the piston. Do not mix up the top and middle rings, as they have different cross-sections. **Note:** *Always follow the instructions printed on the ring package or box - different manufacturers may require different approaches.*

22 Use a piston ring installation tool and make sure the identification mark is facing the top of the piston, then slip the ring into the middle groove on the piston (see illustration). Don't expand the ring any more than necessary to slide it over the piston. **Note:** *Be careful not to confuse the number one and number two rings.*

23 Install the number one (top) ring in the same manner.

24 Repeat the procedure for the remaining pistons and rings.

Installation

25 Before installing the piston/connecting rod assemblies, the cylinder walls must be perfectly clean, the top edge of each cylinder bore must be chamfered, and the crankshaft must be in place.

26 Remove the cap from the end of the number one connecting rod (refer to the marks made during removal). Remove the original bearing inserts and wipe the bearing surfaces of the connecting rod and cap with a clean, lint-free cloth. They must be kept spotlessly clean.

Connecting rod bearing oil clearance check

Refer to illustrations 9.30, 9.35, 9.37 and 9.41

27 Clean the back side of the new upper bearing insert, then lay it in place in the connecting rod.

28 Make sure the tab on the bearing fits into the recess in the rod. Don't hammer the bearing insert into place and be very careful not to nick or gouge the bearing face. Don't lubricate the bearing at this time.

29 Clean the back side of the other bearing insert and install it in the rod cap. Again, make sure the tab on the bearing fits into the recess in the cap, and don't apply any lubricant. It's critically important that the mating surfaces of the bearing and connecting rod are perfectly

9.22 Use a piston ring installation tool to install the compression rings - on some engines the number two compression ring has a directional mark that must face toward the top of the piston

ENGINE BEARING ANALYSIS

Debris

Babbitt bearing embedded with debris from machinings

Microscopic detail of debris

Microscopic detail of gouges

Overplated copper alloy bearing gouged by cast iron debris

Aluminum bearing embedded with glass beads

Microscopic detail of glass beads

Damaged lining caused by dirt left on the bearing back

Misassembly

Result of a lower half assembled as an upper - blocking the oil flow

Excessive oil clearance is indicated by a short contact arc

Polished and oil-stained backs are a result of a poor fit in the housing bore

Result of a wrong, reversed, or shifted cap

Overloading

Damage from excessive idling which resulted in an oil film unable to support the load imposed

Damaged upper connecting rod bearings caused by engine lugging; the lower main bearings (not shown) were similarly affected

The damage shown in these upper and lower connecting rod bearings was caused by engine operation at a higher-than-rated speed under load

Misalignment

A warped crankshaft caused this pattern of severe wear in the center, diminishing toward the ends

A poorly finished crankshaft caused the equally spaced scoring shown

A tapered housing bore caused the damage along one edge of this pair

A bent connecting rod led to the damage in the "V" pattern

Lubrication

Result of dry start: The bearings on the left, farthest from the oil pump, show more damage

Result of a low oil supply or oil starvation

Severe wear as a result of inadequate oil clearance

Corrosion

Microscopic detail of corrosion

Corrosion is an acid attack on the bearing lining generally caused by inadequate maintenance, extremely hot or cold operation, or inferior oils or fuels

Microscopic detail of cavitation

Example of cavitation - a surface erosion caused by pressure changes in the oil film

Damage from excessive thrust or insufficient axial clearance

Bearing affected by oil dilution caused by excessive blow-by or a rich mixture

9.30 Position the piston ring end gaps as shown

9.35 Use a plastic or wooden hammer handle to push the piston into the cylinder

clean and oil free when they're assembled.

30 Position the piston ring gaps at the intervals around the piston as shown **(see illustration)**.

31 Lubricate the piston and rings with clean engine oil and attach a piston ring compressor to the piston. Leave the skirt protruding about 1/4-inch to guide the piston into the cylinder. The rings must be compressed until they're flush with the piston.

32 Rotate the crankshaft until the number one connecting rod journal is at Bottom Dead Center (BDC) and apply a liberal coat of engine oil to the cylinder walls.

33 With the "front" mark (letter F or arrow) on the piston facing the front (timing chain end) of the engine, gently insert the piston/connecting rod assembly into the number one cylinder bore and rest the bottom edge of the ring compressor on the engine block. **Note:** *Some engines have a letter "F" marking on the side of the piston near the wrist pin, others have an arrow, an "F" or a dimple or groove on the top of the piston. All of these are marks that indicate the front of the piston.*

34 Tap the top edge of the ring compressor to make sure it's contacting the block around its entire circumference.

35 Gently tap on the top of the piston with the end of a wooden or plastic hammer handle **(see illustration)** while guiding the end of the connecting rod into place on the crankshaft journal. The piston rings may try to pop out of the ring compressor just before entering the cylinder bore, so keep some downward pressure on the ring compressor. Work slowly, and if any resistance is felt as the piston enters the cylinder, stop immediately. Find out what's hanging up and fix it before proceeding. Do not, for any reason, force the piston into the cylinder - you might break a ring and/or the piston.

36 Once the piston/connecting rod assembly is installed, the connecting rod bearing oil clearance must be checked before the rod cap is permanently installed.

37 Cut a piece of the appropriate size Plastigage slightly shorter than the width of the con-

9.37 Place Plastigage on each connecting rod bearing journal parallel to the crankshaft centerline

necting rod bearing and lay it in place on the number one connecting rod journal, parallel with the journal axis **(see illustration)**.

38 Clean the connecting rod cap bearing face and install the rod cap. Make sure the mating mark on the cap is on the same side as the mark on the connecting rod **(see illustration 9.4)**.

39 Install the old rod bolts at this time and tighten them to the torque listed in this Chapter's Specifications. **Note:** *Use a thin-wall socket to avoid erroneous torque readings that can result if the socket is wedged between the rod cap and the bolt or nut. If the socket tends to wedge itself between the fastener and the cap, lift up on it slightly until it no longer contacts the cap. DO NOT rotate the crankshaft at any time during this operation.*

40 Remove the fasteners and detach the rod cap, being very careful not to disturb the Plastigage. Discard the cap bolts at this time as they cannot be reused. **Note:** *You MUST use new connecting rod bolts.*

41 Compare the width of the crushed Plastigage to the scale printed on the Plastigage envelope to obtain the oil clearance **(see**

9.41 Use the scale on the Plastigage package to determine the bearing oil clearance - be sure to measure the widest part of the Plastigage and use the correct scale; it comes with both standard and metric scales

illustration). The connecting rod bearing oil clearance is usually about 0.001 to 0.002 inch. Consult an automotive machine shop for the clearance specified for the rod bearings on your engine.

42 If the clearance is not as specified, the bearing inserts may be the wrong size (which means different ones will be required). Before deciding that different inserts are needed, make sure that no dirt or oil was between the bearing inserts and the connecting rod or cap when the clearance was measured. Also, recheck the journal diameter. If the Plastigage was wider at one end than the other, the journal may be tapered. If the clearance still exceeds the limit specified, the bearing will have to be replaced with an undersize bearing. **Caution:** *When installing a new crankshaft, always use a standard size bearing.*

Final installation

43 Carefully scrape all traces of the Plasti-

10.1 Checking crankshaft endplay with a dial indicator

10.3 Checking crankshaft endplay with feeler gauges at the thrust bearing journal

gage material off the rod journal and/or bearing face. Be very careful not to scratch the bearing - use your fingernail or the edge of a plastic card.

44   Make sure the bearing faces are perfectly clean, then apply a uniform layer of clean moly-base grease or engine assembly lube to both of them. You'll have to push the piston into the cylinder to expose the face of the bearing insert in the connecting rod.

45   Slide the connecting rod back into place on the journal, install the rod cap, install the *new* bolts and tighten them to the torque listed in this Chapter's Specifications. **Note:** *You MUST install new connecting rod bolts.*

46   Repeat the entire procedure for the remaining pistons/connecting rods.

47   The important points to remember are:

a) *Keep the back sides of the bearing inserts and the insides of the connecting rods and caps perfectly clean when assembling them.*

b) *Make sure you have the correct piston/ rod assembly for each cylinder.*

c) *The mark on the piston must face the front (timing chain end) of the engine.*

d) *Lubricate the cylinder walls liberally with clean oil.*

e) *Lubricate the bearing faces when installing the rod caps after the oil clearance has been checked.*

48   After all the piston/connecting rod assemblies have been correctly installed, rotate the crankshaft a number of times by hand to check for any obvious binding.

49   As a final step, check the connecting rod endplay again. If it was correct before disassembly and the original crankshaft and rods were reinstalled, it should still be correct. If new rods or a new crankshaft were installed, the endplay may be inadequate. If so, the rods will have to be removed and taken to an automotive machine shop for machining.

10   Crankshaft - removal and installation

Removal

Refer to illustrations 10.1 and 10.3

Note: *The crankshaft can be removed only after the engine has been removed from the vehicle. It's assumed that the driveplate, crankshaft pulley, timing chain, oil pan, oil pump, oil filter and piston/connecting rod assemblies have already been removed. The rear main oil seal retainer must be unbolted and separated from the block before proceeding with crankshaft removal.*

1   Before the crankshaft is removed, measure the endplay. Mount a dial indicator with the indicator in line with the crankshaft and touching the end of the crankshaft **(see illustration)**.

2   Pry the crankshaft all the way to the rear and zero the dial indicator. Next, pry the crankshaft to the front as far as possible and check the reading on the dial indicator. The distance traveled is the endplay. A typical crankshaft endplay will fall between 0.003 to 0.010 inch (0.076 to 0.254 mm). If it is greater than that, check the crankshaft thrust washer/ bearing assembly surfaces for wear after it's removed. If no wear is evident, new main bearings should correct the endplay. Refer to Step 14 for the location of the thrust washer/ bearing assembly.

3   If a dial indicator isn't available, feeler gauges can be used. Gently pry the crankshaft all the way to the front of the engine. Slip feeler gauges between the crankshaft and the front face of the thrust bearing or washer to determine the clearance **(see illustration)**.

4   Loosen the main bearing cap/main bearing beam bolts 1/4-turn at a time each, until they can be removed by hand. Obtain new main bearing cap bolts (but save the old ones for the oil clearance check).

5   Remove the main bearing beam, noting

the arrow pointing to the front of the engine. Gently tap the main bearing caps assembly with a soft-face hammer around the perimeter of the assembly. Pull the main bearing caps straight up and off the cylinder block. Try not to drop the bearing inserts if they come out with the assembly.

6   Carefully lift the crankshaft out of the engine. It may be a good idea to have an assistant available, since the crankshaft is quite heavy and awkward to handle. With the bearing inserts in place inside the engine block and main bearing caps, reinstall the main bearing caps and main bearing beam onto the engine block and tighten the bolts finger tight. Make sure you install the main bearing main bearing beam assembly with the arrow facing the front of the engine.

Installation

7   Crankshaft installation is the first step in engine reassembly. It's assumed at this point that the engine block and crankshaft have been cleaned, inspected and repaired or reconditioned.

8   Position the engine block with the bottom facing up.

9   Remove the mounting bolts and lift off the main bearing caps.

10   If they're still in place, remove the original bearing inserts from the block and from the main bearing caps. Wipe the bearing surfaces of the block and main bearing caps with a clean, lint-free cloth. They must be kept spotlessly clean. This is critical for determining the correct bearing oil clearance.

Main bearing oil clearance check

Refer to illustrations 10.14, 10.17, 10.19 and 10.21

11   Without mixing them up, clean the back sides of the new upper main bearing inserts (with grooves and oil holes) and lay one in each main bearing saddle in the block. Each upper bearing has an oil groove and oil hole in it. **Caution:** *The oil holes in the block must*

10.14 Insert the thrust washer into the machined surface between the crankshaft and the upper bearing saddle, then rotate it down into the block until it's flush with the parting line on the main bearing saddle - make sure the oil grooves on the thrust washer face the crankshaft

10.17 Place the Plastigage onto the crankshaft bearing journal as shown

line up with the oil holes in the upper bearing inserts. Clean the back sides of the lower main bearing inserts and lay them in the corresponding location in the main bearing cap. Make sure the tab on the bearing insert fits into the recess in the block or main bearing cap. The upper bearings with the oil holes are installed into the engine block while the lower bearings without the oil holes are installed in the caps. **Caution:** *Do not hammer the bearing insert into place and don't nick or gouge the bearing faces. DO NOT apply any lubrication at this time.*

12   Clean the faces of the bearing inserts in the block and the crankshaft main bearing journals with a clean, lint-free cloth. **Note:** *The backs of all bearings and the surfaces in which they are installed must be kept clean and free of oil at all times.*

13   Check or clean the oil holes in the crankshaft, as any dirt here can go only one way - straight through the new bearings.

14   Once you're certain the crankshaft is clean, carefully lay it in position in the block, which should be oriented on the engine stand to have the bottom side Up. Lube and insert the thrust washers on each side of journal #3. The thrust washers must be installed in the correct journal. **Note:** *Install the thrust washers with the groove in the thrust washer facing the crankshaft and the smooth sides facing the main bearing saddle* **(see illustration)**. *Thrust washers are also installed along with the #3 main bearing cap.*

15   Before the crankshaft can be permanently installed, the main bearing oil clearance must be checked.

16   Cut several strips of the appropriate size of Plastigage. They must be slightly shorter than the width of the main bearing journal.

17   Place one piece on each crankshaft main bearing journal, parallel with the journal axis as shown **(see illustration)**.

18   Clean the faces of the bearing inserts in the main bearing caps. Hold the bearing inserts in place and install the assembly onto the crankshaft and cylinder block. DO NOT disturb the Plastigage. Make sure you install the main bearing cap assembly with the arrows facing the front (timing chain end) of the engine. Install the main bearing beam over the caps.

19   Apply clean engine oil to all bolt threads prior to installation, then install all bolts finger-tight. Tighten main bearing cap bolts in the sequence shown **(see illustration)** progressing in steps, to the torque listed in this Chapter's Specifications. DO NOT rotate the crankshaft at any time during this operation. **Note:** *Use the old bolts at this time (not the new ones).*

20   Remove the bolts in the reverse order of the tightening sequence and remove the main bearing beam, then carefully lift the main bearing caps straight up from the block. Do not disturb the Plastigage or rotate the crankshaft. If the main bearing caps are difficult to remove, tap gently from side-to-side with a soft-face hammer to loosen it.

21   Compare the width of the crushed Plastigage on each journal to the scale printed on the Plastigage envelope to determine the main bearing oil clearance **(see illustration)**. A typical main bearing oil clearance should fall between 0.0015 and 0.0023-inch. Check with an automotive machine shop for the clearance specified for your engine.

22   If the clearance is not as specified, the bearing inserts may be the wrong size (which means different ones will be required). Before deciding if different inserts are needed, make sure that no dirt or oil was between the bearing inserts and the cap assembly or block when the clearance was measured. If the Plastigage was wider at one end than the other, the crankshaft journal may be tapered. If the clearance still exceeds the limit specified, the bearing insert(s) will have to be

10.19 Main bearing cap/support beam bolt tightening sequence

10.21 Use the scale on the Plastigage package to determine the bearing oil clearance - be sure to measure the widest part of the Plastigage and use the correct scale; it comes with both standard and metric scales

replaced with an undersize bearing insert(s). **Caution:** *When installing a brand new crankshaft, always install a standard bearing insert set.*

23 Carefully scrape all traces of the Plastigage material off the main bearing journals and/or the bearing insert faces. Be sure to remove all residue from the oil holes. Use your fingernail or the edge of a plastic card - don't nick or scratch the bearing faces.

Final installation

24 Carefully lift the crankshaft out of the cylinder block.

25 Clean the bearing insert faces in the cylinder block, then apply a thin, uniform layer of moly-base grease or engine assembly lube to each of the bearing surfaces that contact the crankshaft. Be sure to coat the thrust faces as well as the journal face of the thrust washers.

26 Make sure the crankshaft journals are clean, then lay the crankshaft back in place in the cylinder block.

27 Clean the bearing insert faces and then apply the same lubricant to them. Clean the engine block thoroughly. The surfaces must be free of oil residue. Install the thrust washers. The grooves on the thrust washers face outward, away from the bearing.

28 Install each main bearing cap, then install the support beam. **Note:** *The arrow on the main bearing beam must point toward the front of the engine and it must be visible when looking at the bottom of the engine.*

29 Prior to installation, apply clean engine oil to the *new* bolt threads, wiping off any excess, then install all bolts finger-tight. **Note:** *The main bearing cap bolts MUST be replaced with new ones.*

30 Tighten the main bearing cap bolts to the torque listed in this Chapter's Specifications (in the proper sequence) **(see illustration 10.19).**

31 Recheck crankshaft endplay with a feeler gauge or a dial indicator. The endplay should be correct if the crankshaft thrust faces aren't worn or damaged and if new bearings have been installed.

32 Rotate the crankshaft a number of times by hand to check for any obvious binding. It should rotate with a running torque of 50 in-lbs or less. If the running torque is too high, identify and correct the problem at this time.

33 Install the new rear main oil seal and retainer (see Chapter 2A).

11 Engine overhaul - reassembly sequence

1 Before beginning engine reassembly, make sure you have all the necessary new parts, gaskets and seals as well as the following items on hand:

Common hand tools
A 1/2-inch drive torque wrench
New engine oil
Oil filter
Gasket sealant
Thread locking compound

2 If you obtained a short block it will be necessary to install the cylinder head, the oil pump and pick-up tube, the oil pan, the water pump, the timing chain and timing cover, and the valve cover (see Chapter 2A). In order to save time and avoid problems, the external components must be installed in the following general order:

Thermostat and housing cover
Water pump
Intake and exhaust manifolds
Fuel injection components
Emission control components
Spark plugs
Ignition coils
Oil filter and oil cooler
Engine mounts and mount brackets
Driveplate

12 Initial start-up and break-in after overhaul

Warning: *Have a fire extinguisher handy when starting the engine for the first time.*

1 Once the engine has been installed in the vehicle, double-check the engine oil and coolant levels.

2 With the spark plugs out of the engine and the fuel pump disabled (see Chapter 4, Section 2), crank the engine until oil pressure registers on the gauge or the light goes out.

3 Install the spark plugs and ignition coils, and reinstall the fuel pump fuse.

4 Start the engine. It may take a few moments for the fuel system to build up pressure, but the engine should start without a great deal of effort.

5 After the engine starts, it should be allowed to warm up to normal operating temperature. While the engine is warming up, make a thorough check for fuel, oil and coolant leaks.

6 Shut the engine off and recheck the engine oil and coolant levels.

7 Drive the vehicle to an area with minimum traffic, accelerate from 30 to 50 mph, then allow the vehicle to slow to 30 mph with the throttle closed. Repeat the procedure 10 or 12 times. This will load the piston rings and cause them to seat properly against the cylinder walls. Check again for oil and coolant leaks.

8 Drive the vehicle gently for the first 500 miles (no sustained high speeds) and keep a constant check on the oil level. It is not unusual for an engine to use oil during the break-in period.

9 At approximately 500 to 600 miles, change the oil and filter.

10 For the next few hundred miles, drive the vehicle normally. Do not pamper it or abuse it.

11 After 2000 miles, change the oil and filter again and consider the engine broken in.

COMMON ENGINE OVERHAUL TERMS

B

Backlash - The amount of play between two parts. Usually refers to how much one gear can be moved back and forth without moving the gear with which it's meshed.

Bearing Caps - The caps held in place by nuts or bolts which, in turn, hold the bearing surface. This space is for lubricating oil to enter.

Bearing clearance - The amount of space left between shaft and bearing surface. This space is for lubricating oil to enter.

Bearing crush - The additional height which is purposely manufactured into each bearing half to ensure complete contact of the bearing back with the housing bore when the engine is assembled.

Bearing knock - The noise created by movement of a part in a loose or worn bearing.

Blueprinting - Dismantling an engine and reassembling it to EXACT specifications.

Bore - An engine cylinder, or any cylindrical hole; also used to describe the process of enlarging or accurately refinishing a hole with a cutting tool, as to bore an engine cylinder. The bore size is the diameter of the hole.

Boring - Renewing the cylinders by cutting them out to a specified size. A boring bar is used to make the cut.

Bottom end - A term which refers collectively to the engine block, crankshaft, main bearings and the big ends of the connecting rods.

Break-in - The period of operation between installation of new or rebuilt parts and time in which parts are worn to the correct fit. Driving at reduced and varying speed for a specified mileage to permit parts to wear to the correct fit.

Bushing - A one-piece sleeve placed in a bore to serve as a bearing surface for shaft, piston pin, etc. Usually replaceable.

C

Camshaft - The shaft in the engine, on which a series of lobes are located for operating the valve mechanisms. The camshaft is driven by gears or sprockets and a timing chain. Usually referred to simply as the cam.

Carbon - Hard, or soft, black deposits found in combustion chamber, on plugs, under rings, on and under valve heads.

Cast iron - An alloy of iron and more than two percent carbon, used for engine blocks and heads because it's relatively inexpensive and easy to mold into complex shapes.

Chamfer - To bevel across (or a bevel on) the sharp edge of an object.

Chase - To repair damaged threads with a tap or die.

Combustion chamber - The space between the piston and the cylinder head, with the piston at top dead center, in which air-fuel mixture is burned.

Compression ratio - The relationship between cylinder volume (clearance volume) when the piston is at top dead center and cylinder volume when the piston is at bottom dead center.

Connecting rod - The rod that connects the crank on the crankshaft with the piston. Sometimes called a con rod.

Connecting rod cap - The part of the connecting rod assembly that attaches the rod to the crankpin.

Core plug - Soft metal plug used to plug the casting holes for the coolant passages in the block.

Crankcase - The lower part of the engine in which the crankshaft rotates; includes the lower section of the cylinder block and the oil pan.

Crank kit - A reground or reconditioned crankshaft and new main and connecting rod bearings.

Crankpin - The part of a crankshaft to which a connecting rod is attached.

Crankshaft - The main rotating member, or shaft, running the length of the crankcase, with offset throws to which the connecting rods are attached; changes the reciprocating motion of the pistons into rotating motion.

Cylinder sleeve - A replaceable sleeve, or liner, pressed into the cylinder block to form the cylinder bore.

D

Deburring - Removing the burrs (rough edges or areas) from a bearing.

Deglazer - A tool, rotated by an electric motor, used to remove glaze from cylinder walls so a new set of rings will seat.

E

Endplay - The amount of lengthwise movement between two parts. As applied to a crankshaft, the distance that the crankshaft can move forward and back in the cylinder block.

F

Face - A machinist's term that refers to removing metal from the end of a shaft or the face of a larger part, such as a flywheel.

Fatigue - A breakdown of material through a large number of loading and unloading cycles. The first signs are cracks followed shortly by breaks.

Feeler gauge - A thin strip of hardened steel, ground to an exact thickness, used to check clearances between parts.

Free height - The unloaded length or height of a spring.

Freeplay - The looseness in a linkage, or an assembly of parts, between the initial application of force and actual movement. Usually perceived as slop or slight delay.

Freeze plug - See Core plug.

G

Gallery - A large passage in the block that forms a reservoir for engine oil pressure.

Glaze - The very smooth, glassy finish that develops on cylinder walls while an engine is in service.

H

Heli-Coil - A rethreading device used when threads are worn or damaged. The device is installed in a retapped hole to reduce the thread size to the original size.

I

Installed height - The spring's measured length or height, as installed on the cylinder head. Installed height is measured from the spring seat to the underside of the spring retainer.

J

Journal - The surface of a rotating shaft which turns in a bearing.

K

Keeper - The split lock that holds the valve spring retainer in position on the valve stem.

Key - A small piece of metal inserted into matching grooves machined into two parts fitted together - such as a gear pressed onto a shaft - which prevents slippage between the two parts.

Knock - The heavy metallic engine sound, produced in the combustion chamber as a result of abnormal combustion - usually detonation. Knock is usually caused by a loose or worn bearing. Also referred to as detonation, pinging and spark knock. Connecting rod or main bearing knocks are created by too much oil clearance or insufficient lubrication.

L

Lands - The portions of metal between the piston ring grooves.

Lapping the valves - Grinding a valve face and its seat together with lapping compound.

Lash - The amount of free motion in a gear train, between gears, or in a mechanical assembly, that occurs before movement can begin. Usually refers to the lash in a valve train.

Lifter - The part that rides against the cam to transfer motion to the rest of the valve train.

M

Machining - The process of using a machine to remove metal from a metal part.

Main bearings - The plain, or babbit, bearings that support the crankshaft.

Main bearing caps - The cast iron caps, bolted to the bottom of the block, that support the main bearings.

O

O.D. - Outside diameter.

Oil gallery - A pipe or drilled passageway in the engine used to carry engine oil from one area to another.

Oil ring - The lower ring, or rings, of a piston; designed to prevent excessive amounts of oil from working up the cylinder walls and into the combustion chamber. Also called an oil-control ring.

Oil seal - A seal which keeps oil from leaking out of a compartment. Usually refers to a dynamic seal around a rotating shaft or other moving part.

O-ring - A type of sealing ring made of a special rubberlike material; in use, the O-ring is compressed into a groove to provide the sealing action.

Overhaul - To completely disassemble a unit, clean and inspect all parts, reassemble it with the original or new parts and make all adjustments necessary for proper operation.

P

Pilot bearing - A small bearing installed in the center of the flywheel (or the rear end of the crankshaft) to support the front end of the input shaft of the transmission.

Pip mark - A little dot or indentation which indicates the top side of a compression ring.

Piston - The cylindrical part, attached to the connecting rod, that moves up and down in the cylinder as the crankshaft rotates. When the fuel charge is fired, the piston transfers the force of the explosion to the connecting rod, then to the crankshaft.

Piston pin (or wrist pin) - The cylindrical and usually hollow steel pin that passes through the piston. The piston pin fastens the piston to the upper end of the connecting rod.

Piston ring - The split ring fitted to the groove in a piston. The ring contacts the sides of the ring groove and also rubs against the cylinder wall, thus sealing space between piston and wall. There are two types of rings: Compression rings seal the compression pressure in the combustion chamber; oil rings scrape excessive oil off the cylinder wall.

Piston ring groove - The slots or grooves cut in piston heads to hold piston rings in position.

Piston skirt - The portion of the piston below the rings and the piston pin hole.

Plastigage - A thin strip of plastic thread, available in different sizes, used for measuring clearances. For example, a strip of plastigage is laid across a bearing journal and mashed as parts are assembled. Then parts are disassembled and the width of the strip is measured to determine clearance between journal and bearing. Commonly used to measure crankshaft main-bearing and connecting rod bearing clearances.

Press-fit - A tight fit between two parts that requires pressure to force the parts together. Also referred to as drive, or force, fit.

Prussian blue - A blue pigment; in solution, useful in determining the area of contact between two surfaces. Prussian blue is commonly used to determine the width and location of the contact area between the valve face and the valve seat.

R

Race (bearing) - The inner or outer ring that provides a contact surface for balls or rollers in bearing.

Ream - To size, enlarge or smooth a hole by using a round cutting tool with fluted edges.

Ring job - The process of reconditioning the cylinders and installing new rings.

Runout - Wobble. The amount a shaft rotates out-of-true.

S

Saddle - The upper main bearing seat.

Scored - Scratched or grooved, as a cylinder wall may be scored by abrasive particles moved up and down by the piston rings.

Scuffing - A type of wear in which there's a transfer of material between parts moving against each other; shows up as pits or grooves in the mating surfaces.

Seat - The surface upon which another part rests or seats. For example, the valve seat is the matched surface upon which the valve face rests. Also used to refer to wearing into a good fit; for example, piston rings seat after a few miles of driving.

Short block - An engine block complete with crankshaft and piston and, usually, camshaft assemblies.

Static balance - The balance of an object while it's stationary.

Step - The wear on the lower portion of a ring land caused by excessive side and back-clearance. The height of the step indicates the ring's extra side clearance and the length of the step projecting from the back wall of the groove represents the ring's back clearance.

Stroke - The distance the piston moves when traveling from top dead center to bottom dead center, or from bottom dead center to top dead center.

Stud - A metal rod with threads on both ends.

T

Tang - A lip on the end of a plain bearing used to align the bearing during assembly.

Tap - To cut threads in a hole. Also refers to the fluted tool used to cut threads.

Taper - A gradual reduction in the width of a shaft or hole; in an engine cylinder, taper usually takes the form of uneven wear, more pronounced at the top than at the bottom.

Throws - The offset portions of the crankshaft to which the connecting rods are affixed.

Thrust bearing - The main bearing that has thrust faces to prevent excessive endplay, or forward and backward movement of the crankshaft.

Thrust washer - A bronze or hardened steel washer placed between two moving parts. The washer prevents longitudinal movement and provides a bearing surface for thrust surfaces of parts.

Tolerance - The amount of variation permitted from an exact size of measurement. Actual amount from smallest acceptable dimension to largest acceptable dimension.

U

Umbrella - An oil deflector placed near the valve tip to throw oil from the valve stem area.

Undercut - A machined groove below the normal surface.

Undersize bearings - Smaller diameter bearings used with re-ground crankshaft journals.

V

Valve grinding - Refacing a valve in a valve-refacing machine.

Valve train - The valve-operating mechanism of an engine; includes all components from the camshaft to the valve.

Vibration damper - A cylindrical weight attached to the front of the crankshaft to minimize torsional vibration (the twist-untwist actions of the crankshaft caused by the cylinder firing impulses). Also called a harmonic balancer.

W

Water jacket - The spaces around the cylinders, between the inner and outer shells of the cylinder block or head, through which coolant circulates.

Web - A supporting structure across a cavity.

Woodruff key - A key with a radiused backside (viewed from the side).

Notes

1 General information

Warning: *Do not allow antifreeze to come in contact with your skin or painted surfaces of the vehicle. Rinse off spills immediately with plenty of water. Antifreeze is highly toxic if ingested. Never leave antifreeze lying around in an open container or in puddles on the floor; children and pets are attracted by it's sweet smell and may drink it. Check with local authorities about disposing of used antifreeze. Many communities have collection centers which will see that antifreeze is disposed of safely. Never dump used antifreeze on the ground or pour it into drains.*

Engine cooling system

All modern vehicles employ a pressurized engine cooling system with thermostatically controlled coolant circulation. The cooling system consists of a radiator, an expansion tank or coolant reservoir, a pressure cap (located on the expansion tank or radiator), a thermostat, a cooling fan, and a water pump.

The water pump circulates coolant through the engine. The coolant flows around each cylinder and around the intake and exhaust ports, near the spark plug areas and in close proximity to the exhaust valve guides.

A thermostat controls engine coolant temperature. During warm up, the closed thermostat prevents coolant from circulating through the radiator. As the engine nears normal operating temperature, the thermostat opens and allows hot coolant to travel through the radiator, where it's cooled before returning to the engine.

Heating system

The heating system consists of a blower fan and heater core located in a housing under the dash, the hoses connecting the heater core to the engine cooling system and the heater/air conditioning control head on the dashboard. Hot engine coolant is circulated through the heater core. When the heater mode is activated, a flap door in the housing opens to expose the heater core to the passenger compartment through air ducts. A fan switch on the control head activates the blower motor, which forces air through the core, heating the air.

Air conditioning system

The air conditioning system consists of a condenser mounted in front of the radiator, an evaporator mounted adjacent to the heater core, a compressor mounted on the engine, a receiver-drier or accumulator and the plumbing connecting all of the above components.

A blower fan forces the warmer air of the passenger compartment through the evaporator core (sort of a radiator-in-reverse), transferring the heat from the air to the refrigerant. The liquid refrigerant boils off into low pressure vapor, taking the heat with it when it leaves the evaporator.

2 Troubleshooting

Coolant leaks

Refer to illustration 2.2

1   A coolant leak can develop anywhere in the cooling system, but the most common causes are:

   a) *A loose or weak hose clamp*
   b) *A defective hose*
   c) *A faulty pressure cap*
   d) *A damaged radiator*
   e) *A bad heater core*
   f) *A faulty water pump*
   g) *A leaking gasket at any joint that carries coolant*

2   Coolant leaks aren't always easy to find. Sometimes they can only be detected when the cooling system is under pressure. Here's where a cooling system pressure tester comes in handy. After the engine has cooled completely, the tester is attached in place of the pressure cap, then pumped up to the pressure value equal to that of the pressure cap rating **(see illustration)**. Now, leaks that only exist when the engine is fully warmed up will become apparent. The tester can be left connected to locate a nagging slow leak.

Coolant level drops, but no external leaks

Refer to illustrations 2.5a and 2.5b

3   If you find it necessary to keep adding coolant, but there are no external leaks, the probable causes include:

   a) *A blown head gasket*
   b) *A leaking intake manifold gasket (only on engines that have coolant passages in the manifold)*
   c) *A cracked cylinder head or cylinder block*

4   Any of the above problems will also usually result in contamination of the engine oil, which will cause it to take on a milkshake-like appearance. A bad head gasket or cracked head or block can also result in engine oil contaminating the cooling system.

5   Combustion leak detectors (also known as block testers) are available at most auto parts stores. These work by detecting exhaust gases in the cooling system, which indicates a compression leak from a cylinder into the coolant. The tester consists of a large bulb-type syringe and bottle of test fluid **(see illustration)**. A measured amount of the fluid is added to the syringe. The syringe is placed over the cooling system filler neck and, with the engine running, the bulb is squeezed and a sample of the gases present in the cooling system are drawn up through the test fluid **(see illustration)**. If any combustion gases are present in the sample taken, the test fluid will change color.

6   If the test indicates combustion gas is present in the cooling system, you can be sure that the engine has a blown head gasket or a crack in the cylinder head or block, and will require disassembly to repair.

Pressure cap

Refer to illustration 2.8

Warning: *Wait until the engine is completely cool before beginning this check.*

7   The cooling system is sealed by a spring-loaded cap, which raises the boiling point of the coolant. If the cap's seal or spring are worn out, the coolant can boil and escape past the cap. With the engine completely cool, remove the cap and check the seal; if it's cracked, hardened or deteriorated in any way, replace it with a new one.

8   Even if the seal is good, the spring might not be; this can be checked with a cooling system pressure tester **(see illustration)**. If the cap can't hold a pressure within approximately 1-1/2 lbs of its rated pressure (which is marked on the cap), replace it with a new one.

9   The cap is also equipped with a vacuum relief spring. When the engine cools off, a vacuum is created in the cooling system. The vacuum relief spring allows air back into the system, which will equalize the pressure and prevent damage to the radiator (the radiator tanks could collapse if the vacuum is great enough). If, after turning the engine off and

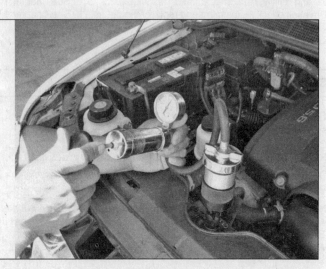

2.2 The cooling system pressure tester is connected in place of the pressure cap, then pumped up to pressurize the system

Chapter 3
Cooling, heating and air conditioning systems

Contents

Specifications

General
Radiator cap pressure rating	Refer to pressure specification on cap
Cooling system capacity...	See Chapter 1
Refrigerant type..	R-134a
Refrigerant capacity..	Refer to "Air Conditioner" label in the engine compartment

Torque specifications
Note: *One foot-pound (ft-lb) of torque is equivalent to 12 inch-pounds (in-lbs) of torque. Torque values below approximately 15 foot-pounds are expressed in inch-pounds, because most foot-pound torque wrenches are not accurate at these smaller values.*

Thermostat housing bolts	80 in-lbs
Water pump bolts	85 in-lbs

2.5a The combustion leak detector consists of a bulb, syringe and test fluid

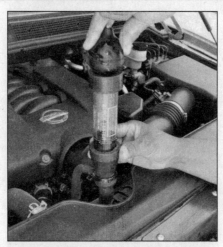

2.5b Place the tester over the cooling system filler neck and use the bulb to draw a sample into the tester

2.8 Checking the cooling system pressure cap with a cooling system pressure tester

allowing it to cool down you notice any of the cooling system hoses collapsing, replace the pressure cap with a new one.

Thermostat

Refer to illustration 2.10

10 Before assuming the thermostat **(see illustration)** is responsible for a cooling system problem, check the coolant level (see Chapter 1), drivebelt tension (see Chapter 1) and temperature gauge (or light) operation.

11 If the engine takes a long time to warm up (as indicated by the temperature gauge or heater operation), the thermostat is probably stuck open. Replace the thermostat with a new one.

12 If the engine runs hot or overheats, a thorough test of the thermostat should be performed.

13 Definitive testing of the thermostat can only be made when it is removed from the vehicle. If the thermostat is stuck in the open position at room temperature, it is faulty and must be replaced. **Caution:** *Do not drive the vehicle without a thermostat. The computer*

may stay in open loop and emissions and fuel economy will suffer.

14 To test a thermostat, suspend the (closed) thermostat on a length of string or wire in a pot of cold water.

15 Heat the water on a stove while observing thermostat. The thermostat should fully open before the water boils.

16 If the thermostat doesn't open and close as specified, or sticks in any position, replace it.

Cooling fan

Electric cooling fan

17 If the engine is overheating and the cooling fan is not coming on when the engine temperature rises to an excessive level, unplug the fan motor electrical connector(s) and connect the motor directly to the battery with fused jumper wires. If the fan motor doesn't come on, replace the motor.

18 If the radiator fan motor is okay, but it isn't coming on when the engine gets hot, the fan relay might be defective. A relay is used to control a circuit by turning it on and off in

response to a control decision by the Powertrain Control Module (PCM). These control circuits are fairly complex, and checking them should be left to a qualified automotive technician. Sometimes, the control system can be fixed by simply identifying and replacing a bad relay.

19 Locate the fan relays in the engine compartment fuse/relay box.

20 Test the relay (see Chapter 12).

21 If the relay is okay, check all wiring and connections to the fan motor. Refer to the wiring diagrams at the end of Chapter 12. If no obvious problems are found, the problem could be the Engine Coolant Temperature (ECT) sensor or the Powertrain Control Module (PCM). Have the cooling fan system and circuit diagnosed by a dealer service department or repair shop with the proper diagnostic equipment. **Note:** *These models are equipped with a cooling fan motor resistor. Have the resistor checked if the fan motor does not respond to the speed variations signaled by the PCM.*

Belt-driven cooling fan

22 Disconnect the cable from the negative terminal of the battery and rock the fan back and forth by hand to check for excessive bearing play.

23 With the engine cold (and not running), turn the fan blades by hand. The fan should turn freely.

24 Visually inspect for substantial fluid leakage from the clutch assembly. If problems are noted, replace the clutch assembly.

25 With the engine completely warmed up, turn off the ignition switch and disconnect the negative battery cable from the battery. Turn the fan by hand. Some drag should be evident. If the fan turns easily, replace the fan clutch.

Water pump

26 A failure in the water pump can cause serious engine damage due to overheating.

2.10 Typical thermostat:

1   *Flange*
2   *Piston*
3   *Jiggle valve*
4   *Main coil spring*
5   *Valve seat*
6   *Valve*
7   *Frame*
8   *Secondary coil spring*

2.28 The water pump weep hole is generally located on the underside of the pump

Drivebelt-driven water pump

Refer to illustration 2.28

27   There are two ways to check the operation of the water pump while it's installed on the engine. If the pump is found to be defective, it should be replaced with a new or rebuilt unit.

28   Water pumps are equipped with weep (or vent) holes **(see illustration)**. If a failure occurs in the pump seal, coolant will leak from the hole.

29   If the water pump shaft bearings fail, there may be a howling sound at the pump while it's running. Shaft wear can be felt with the drivebelt removed if the water pump pulley is rocked up and down (with the engine off). Don't mistake drivebelt slippage, which causes a squealing sound, for water pump bearing failure.

Timing chain or timing belt-driven water pump

30   Water pumps driven by the timing chain or timing belt are located underneath the timing chain or timing belt cover.

31   Checking the water pump is limited because of where it is located. However, some basic checks can be made before deciding to remove the water pump. If the pump is found to be defective, it should be replaced with a new or rebuilt unit.

32   One sign that the water pump may be failing is that the heater (climate control) may not work well. Warm the engine to normal operating temperature, confirm that the coolant level is correct, then run the heater and check for hot air coming from the ducts.

33   Check for noises coming from the water pump area. If the water pump impeller shaft or bearings are failing, there may be a howling sound at the pump while the engine is running. **Note:** *Be careful not to mistake drivebelt noise (squealing) for water pump bearing or shaft failure.*

34   It you suspect water pump failure due to noise, wear can be confirmed by feeling for play at the pump shaft. This can be done by rocking the drive sprocket on the pump shaft up and down. To do this you will need to remove the tension on the timing chain or belt as well as access the water pump.

All water pumps

35   In rare cases or on high-mileage vehicles, another sign of water pump failure may be the presence of coolant in the engine oil. This condition will adversely affect the engine in varying degrees. **Note:** *Finding coolant in the engine oil could indicate other serious issues besides a failed water pump, such as a blown head gasket or a cracked cylinder head or block.*

36   Even a pump that exhibits no outward signs of a problem, such as noise or leakage, can still be due for replacement. Removal for close examination is the only sure way to tell. Sometimes the fins on the back of the impeller can corrode to the point that cooling efficiency is diminished significantly.

Heater system

37   Little can go wrong with a heater. If the fan motor will run at all speeds, the electrical part of the system is okay. The three basic heater problems fall into the following general categories:

    a)   Not enough heat
    b)   Heat all the time
    c)   No heat

38   If there's not enough heat, the control valve or door is stuck in a partially open position, the coolant coming from the engine isn't hot enough, or the heater core is restricted. If the coolant isn't hot enough, the thermostat in the engine cooling system is stuck open, allowing coolant to pass through the engine so rapidly that it doesn't heat up quickly enough. If the vehicle is equipped with a temperature gauge instead of a warning light, watch to see if the engine temperature rises to the normal operating range after driving for a reasonable distance.

39   If there's heat all the time, the control valve or the door is stuck wide open.

40   If there's no heat, coolant is probably not reaching the heater core, or the heater core is plugged. The likely cause is a collapsed or plugged hose, core, or a frozen heater control valve. If the heater is the type that flows coolant all the time, the cause is a stuck door or a broken or kinked control cable.

Air conditioning system

41   If the cool air output is inadequate:

    a)   *Inspect the condenser coils and fins to make sure they're clear*
    b)   *Check the compressor clutch for slippage.*
    c)   *Check the blower motor for proper operation.*
    d)   *Inspect the blower discharge passage for obstructions.*
    e)   *Check the system air intake filter for clogging.*

42   If the system provides intermittent cooling air:

    a)   *Check the circuit breaker, blower switch and blower motor for a malfunction.*
    b)   *Make sure the compressor clutch isn't slipping.*
    c)   *Inspect the plenum door to make sure it's operating properly.*

    d)   *Inspect the evaporator to make sure it isn't clogged.*
    e)   *If the unit is icing up, it may be caused by excessive moisture in the system, incorrect super heat switch adjustment or low thermostat adjustment.*

43   If the system provides no cooling air:

    a)   *Inspect the compressor drivebelt. Make sure it's not loose or broken.*
    b)   *Make sure the compressor clutch engages. If it doesn't, check for a blown fuse.*
    c)   *Inspect the wire harness for broken or disconnected wires.*
    d)   *If the compressor clutch doesn't engage, bridge the terminals of the A/C pressure switch(es) with a jumper wire; if the clutch now engages, and the system is properly charged, the pressure switch is bad.*
    e)   *Make sure the blower motor is not disconnected or burned out.*
    f)   *Make sure the compressor isn't partially or completely seized.*
    g)   *Inspect the refrigerant lines for leaks.*
    h)   *Check the components for leaks.*
    i)   *Inspect the receiver-drier/accumulator or expansion valve/tube for clogged screens.*

44   If the system is noisy:

    a)   *Look for loose panels in the passenger compartment.*
    b)   *Inspect the compressor drivebelt. It may be loose or worn.*
    c)   *Check the compressor mounting bolts. They should be tight.*
    d)   *Listen carefully to the compressor. It may be worn out.*
    e)   *Listen to the idler pulley and bearing and the clutch. Either may be defective.*
    f)   *The winding in the compressor clutch coil or solenoid may be defective.*
    g)   *The compressor oil level may be low.*
    h)   *The blower motor fan bushing or the motor itself may be worn out.*
    i)   *If there is an excessive charge in the system, you'll hear a rumbling noise in the high pressure line, a thumping noise in the compressor, or see bubbles or cloudiness in the sight glass.*
    j)   *If there's a low charge in the system, you might hear hissing in the evaporator case at the expansion valve, or see bubbles or cloudiness in the sight glass.*

---

3   Air conditioning and heating system - check and maintenance

Air conditioning system

Refer to illustration 3.1

Warning: *The air conditioning system is under high pressure. Do not loosen any hose fittings or remove any components until after the system has been discharged. Air conditioning refrigerant should be properly discharged into an EPA-approved recovery/recycling unit at a*

3.1 The evaporator drain hose extends through the floor to allow collected condensation to run out

3.9 Insert a thermometer in the center vent, turn on the air conditioning system and wait for it to cool down; depending on the humidity, the output air should be 30 to 40 degrees cooler than the ambient air temperature

dealer service department or an automotive air conditioning repair facility. Always wear eye protection when disconnecting air conditioning system fittings.

Caution 1: *All models covered by this manual use environmentally friendly R-134a. This refrigerant (and its appropriate refrigerant oils) are not compatible with R-12 refrigerant system components and must never be mixed or the components will be damaged.*

Caution 2: *When replacing entire components, additional refrigerant oil should be added equal to the amount that is removed with the component being replaced. Be sure to read the can before adding any oil to the system, to make sure it is compatible with the R-134a system.*

1   The following maintenance checks should be performed on a regular basis to ensure that the air conditioning continues to operate at peak efficiency.

 a) *Inspect the condition of the compressor drivebelt. If it is worn or deteriorated, replace it (see Chapter 1).*

 b) *Check the drivebelt tension (see Chapter 1).*

 c) *Inspect the system hoses. Look for cracks, bubbles, hardening and deterioration. Inspect the hoses and all fittings for oil bubbles or seepage. If there is any evidence of wear, damage or leakage, replace the hose(s).*

 d) *Inspect the condenser fins for leaves, bugs and any other foreign material that may have embedded itself in the fins. Use a fin comb or compressed air to remove debris from the condenser.*

 e) *Make sure the system has the correct refrigerant charge.*

 f) *If you hear water sloshing around in the dash area or have water dripping on the carpet, check the evaporator housing drain tube* **(see illustration)** *and insert a piece of wire into the opening to check for blockage.*

2   It's a good idea to operate the system for about ten minutes at least once a month.

This is particularly important during the winter months because long term non-use can cause hardening, and subsequent failure, of the seals. Note that using the Defrost function operates the compressor.

3   If the air conditioning system is not working properly, proceed to Step 6 and perform the general checks outlined below.

4   Because of the complexity of the air conditioning system and the special equipment necessary to service it, in-depth troubleshooting and repairs beyond checking the refrigerant charge and the compressor clutch operation are not included in this manual. However, simple checks and component replacement procedures are provided in this Chapter. For more complete information on the air conditioning system, refer to the *Haynes Automotive Heating and Air Conditioning Manual.*

5   The most common cause of poor cooling is simply a low system refrigerant charge. If a noticeable drop in system cooling ability occurs, one of the following quick checks will help you determine if the refrigerant level is low.

Checking the refrigerant charge

Refer to illustration 3.9

6   Warm the engine up to normal operating temperature.

7   Place the air conditioning temperature selector at the coldest setting and put the blower at the highest setting.

8   After the system reaches operating temperature, feel the larger pipe exiting the evaporator at the firewall **(see illustration 10.5)**. The outlet pipe should be cold (the tubing that leads back to the compressor). If the evaporator outlet pipe is warm, the system probably needs a charge.

9   Insert a thermometer in the center air distribution duct **(see illustration)** while operating the air conditioning system at its maximum setting - the temperature of the output air should be 35 to 40 degrees F below the ambient air temperature (down to approximately 40 degrees F). If the ambient (outside) air temperature is very high, say 110 degrees F, the duct

air temperature may be as high as 60 degrees F, but generally the air conditioning is 30 to 40 degrees F cooler than the ambient air.

10   Further inspection or testing of the system requires special tools and techniques and is beyond the scope of the home mechanic.

Adding refrigerant

Refer to illustrations 3.11 and 3.13

Caution: *Make sure any refrigerant, refrigerant oil or replacement component you purchase is designated as compatible with R-134a systems.*

11   Purchase an R-134a automotive charging kit at an auto parts store **(see illustration)**. A charging kit includes a can of refrigerant, a tap valve and a short section of hose that can be attached between the tap valve and the system low side service valve. **Caution:** *Never add more than one can of refrigerant to the system. If more refrigerant than that is required, the system should be evacuated and leak tested.*

12   Back off the valve handle on the charging kit and screw the kit onto the refrigerant can, making sure first that the O-ring or rubber seal inside the threaded portion of the kit is in place.

3.11 R-134a automotive air conditioning charging kit

3.13 Location of the low-side charging port

4.5 Thermostat mounting bolts

Warning: *Wear protective eyewear when dealing with pressurized refrigerant cans.*

13   Remove the dust cap from the low-side charging port and attach the hose's quick-connect fitting to the port **(see illustration)**. **Warning:** *DO NOT hook the charging kit hose to the system high side! The fittings on the charging kit are designed to fit **only** on the low side of the system.*

14   Warm up the engine and turn On the air conditioning. Keep the charging kit hose away from the fan and other moving parts. **Note:** *The charging process requires the compressor to be running. If the clutch cycles off, you can put the air conditioning switch on High and leave the car doors open to keep the clutch on and compressor working. The compressor can be kept on during the charging by removing the connector from the pressure switch and bridging it with a paper clip or jumper wire during the procedure.*

15   Turn the valve handle on the kit until the stem pierces the can, then back the handle out to release the refrigerant. You should be able to hear the rush of gas. Keep the can upright at all times, but shake it occasionally. Allow stabilization time between each addition. **Note:** *The charging process will go faster if you wrap the can with a hot-water-soaked rag to keep the can from freezing up.*

16   If you have an accurate thermometer, you can place it in the center air conditioning duct inside the vehicle and keep track of the output air temperature. A charged system that is working properly should cool down to approximately 40 degrees F. If the ambient (outside) air temperature is very high, say 110 degrees F, the duct air temperature may be as high as 60 degrees F, but generally the air conditioning is 35 to 40 degrees F cooler than the ambient air.

17   When the can is empty, turn the valve handle to the closed position and release the connection from the low-side port. Reinstall the dust cap.

18   Remove the charging kit from the can and store the kit for future use with the piercing valve in the UP position, to prevent inadvertently piercing the can on the next use.

Heating systems

19   If the carpet under the heater core is damp, or if antifreeze vapor or steam is coming through the vents, the heater core is leaking. Remove it (see Section 10) and install a new unit (most radiator shops will not repair a leaking heater core).

20   If the air coming out of the heater vents isn't hot, the problem could stem from any of the following causes:

a) *The thermostat is stuck open, preventing the engine coolant from warming up enough to carry heat to the heater core. Replace the thermostat (see Section 4).*

b) *There is a blockage in the system, preventing the flow of coolant through the heater core. Feel both heater hoses at the firewall. They should be hot. If one of them is cold, there is an obstruction in one of the hoses or in the heater core, or the heater control valve is shut. Detach the hoses and back flush the heater core with a water hose. If the heater core is clear but circulation is impeded, remove the two hoses and flush them out with a water hose.*

c) *If flushing fails to remove the blockage from the heater core, the core must be replaced (see Section 10).*

Eliminating air conditioning odors

21   Unpleasant odors that often develop in air conditioning systems are caused by the growth of a fungus, usually on the surface of the evaporator core. The warm, humid environment there is a perfect breeding ground for mildew to develop.

22   The evaporator core on most vehicles is difficult to access, and factory dealerships have a lengthy, expensive process for eliminating the fungus by opening up the evaporator case and using a powerful disinfectant and rinse on the core until the fungus is gone. You can service your own system at home, but it takes something much stronger than basic household germ-killers or deodorizers.

23   Aerosol disinfectants for automotive air

conditioning systems are available in most auto parts stores, but remember when shopping for them that the most effective treatments are also the most expensive. The basic procedure for using these sprays is to start by running the system in the RECIRC mode for ten minutes with the blower on its highest speed. Use the highest heat mode to dry out the system and keep the compressor from engaging by disconnecting the wiring connector at the compressor.

24   The disinfectant can usually comes with a long spray hose. Insert the nozzle into an intake port inside the cabin, and spray according to the manufacturer's recommendations. Follow the manufacturer's recommendations for the length of spray and waiting time between applications.

25   Once the evaporator has been cleaned, the best way to prevent the mildew from coming back again is to make sure your evaporator housing drain tube is clear **(see illustration 3.1)**.

Automatic heating and air conditioning systems

26   Some vehicles are equipped with an optional automatic climate control system. This system has its own computer that receives inputs from various sensors in the heating and air conditioning system. This computer, like the PCM, has self-diagnostic capabilities to help pinpoint problems or faults within the system. Vehicles equipped with automatic heating and air conditioning systems are very complex and considered beyond the scope of the home mechanic. Vehicles equipped with automatic heating and air conditioning systems should be taken to dealer service department or other qualified facility for repair.

---

4   Thermostat - replacement

Refer to illustration 4.5

Warning: *Wait until the engine is completely cool before beginning this procedure.*

1   Drain the cooling system (see Chapter 1). If the coolant is relatively new, or is in good condition (see Section 2), save it and re-use it. **Warning:** *See **Warning** in Section 1.*

2   Unbolt the coolant reservoir and set it aside.

3   Remove the IVT solenoid valve from the front cylinder bank (see Chapter 6).

4   Disconnect the lower radiator hose from the coolant inlet. If the hose is stuck, grasp it near the end with a pair of large adjustable pliers and twist it to break the seal, then pull it off. If the hose is old or deteriorated, cut it off and install a new one.

5   Remove the thermostat housing/thermostat assembly **(see illustration)**. **Note:** *If the thermostat is defective, you'll have to replace the entire cover/thermostat assembly.*

6   Installation is the reverse of removal. Be sure to clean the gasket sealing surfaces thoroughly and always use a new gasket.

5.10 Left-side cooling fan upper mounting bolt

5.11 Fan blade mounting nut

7   Refill the cooling system (see Chapter 1).
8   Start the engine and allow it to reach normal operating temperature, then check for leaks and proper thermostat operation.

5   Engine cooling fans - replacement

Refer to illustrations 5,10, 5.11 and 5.12
Warning: *The engine must be completely cool before beginning this procedure.*
Warning: *The models covered by this manual are equipped with a Supplemental Restraint System (SRS), more commonly known as airbags. Always disarm the airbag system before working in the vicinity of any airbag system component to avoid the possibility of accidental deployment of the airbag, which could cause personal injury (see Chapter 12). Do not use a memory saving device to preserve the PCM's memory when working on or near airbag system components.*
Warning: *See the* **Warning** *in Section 1.*
Note: *The two engine cooling fans have two speeds and are controlled by the PCM (computer). The PCM receives input from the coolant temperature sensor, as well as sensors for air conditioning, vehicle speed and engine rpm. The PCM determines when the electric fan(s) should turn on, and at which speed (High or Low).*
1   Disconnect the cable from the negative terminal of the battery (see Chapter 5).
2   Remove the engine lower splash shield.
3   Drain some coolant from the radiator (to a level that's lower than the upper radiator hose) (see Chapter 1).
4   Remove the inlet air duct.
5   Remove the battery and the battery tray (see Chapter 5).
6   Remove the upper radiator hose assembly including the cap and adapter.
7   Disconnect the electrical connectors from the fans and move the wiring harness aside.
8   Disconnect the wiring from the airbag sensor and move it aside.
9   Remove the bolts from the battery tray

support bracket, then move it aside.
10   Remove the bolts at the upper corners of the fan support, then pull it upward to detach it at the bottom **(see illustration)**. Remove the fan assembly.
11   If necessary, remove the nut and detach the fan blade assembly from the motor shaft **(see illustration)**.
12   Remove the screws retaining the fan motor to the fan shroud, then detach the motor **(see illustration)**.
13   Installation is the reverse of removal. Refill the cooling system (see Chapter 1)
14   Reconnect the battery and perform the necessary re-learn procedures (see Chapter 5).

6   Radiator and coolant reservoir - removal and installation

Warning: *Wait until the engine is completely cool before beginning this procedure.*
Warning: *The models covered by this manual are equipped with a Supplemental Restraint System (SRS), more commonly known as*

airbags. Always disarm the airbag system before working in the vicinity of any airbag system component to avoid the possibility of accidental deployment of the airbag, which could cause personal injury (see Chapter 12). Do not use a memory saving device to preserve the PCM's memory when working on or near airbag system components.*
Warning: *See the* **Warning** *in Section 1.*

Radiator

Refer to illustrations 6.6 and 6.7
1   Disconnect the cable from the negative terminal of the battery (see Chapter 5). Drain the cooling system (see Chapter 1).
2   Raise the vehicle and support it securely on jackstands. Remove the lower engine splash shield, the air inlet duct and the radiator top covers.
3   Remove the grille and the hood latch assembly (see Chapter 11).
4   Remove the horn (see Chapter 12).
5   Disconnect the coolant reservoir hose from the radiator cap adapter.
6   Disconnect the transaxle cooler hoses from the radiator **(see illustration)**.

5.12 Remove the mounting screws that hold the motor to the fan shroud and remove the motor

6.6 There are two transaxle cooler hoses connected to the radiator (lower hose shown)

6.7 After disconnecting the overflow hose (A), remove the radiator cap and filler unit (B)

6.18 Remove the fastener from the windshield washer fluid reservoir neck support (A), detach the overflow hose from the radiator cap adapter (B), then remove the mounting bolts (C, other bolts not visible in this photo)

7   Remove the upper radiator hose including the cap and adapter **(see illustration)**.
8   Disconnect the lower radiator hose from the radiator.
9   Detach the upper radiator mounts by spreading the horseshoe clips to release the rubber bushings.
10   Pull the top of the radiator back and upward to lift it out.
11   With the radiator removed, it can be inspected for leaks and damage. If it needs repair, have a radiator shop or dealer service department perform the work, as special techniques are required.
12   Bugs and dirt can be removed from the radiator with a soft brush, followed by forcing water from a garden hose through the core from the engine side. Don't bend the cooling fins as this is done.
13   Installation is the reverse of the removal procedure. Be sure the radiator mounting pads are seated properly at the base of the radiator.
14   After installation, fill the cooling system with the proper mixture of antifreeze and water (see Chapter 1).

15   Reconnect the battery and perform the necessary re-learn procedures (see Chapter 5). Allow the engine to reach normal operating temperature, indicated by the upper radiator hose becoming hot. Recheck the coolant level and add more if required.
16   Check and add transmission fluid as needed (see Chapter 1).

Coolant reservoir

Refer to illustration 6.18

17   Disconnect the overflow hose from the fitting by the radiator cap.
18   Unbolt the coolant reservoir and remove it from the vehicle **(see illustration)**.
19   Pour the coolant into a container. Wash out the reservoir, using soapy water and a long brush to make the coolant level easier to read. Inspect the reservoir for cracks and chafing. Replace it if any damage is found.
20   Installation is the reverse of removal.

7   Water pump - replacement

Refer to illustrations 7.12, 7.14, 7.15 and 7.17
Warning: *Wait until the engine is completely cool before beginning this procedure.*
Warning: *See the* **Warning** *in Section 1.*
1   Disconnect the cable from the negative terminal of the battery (see Chapter 5).
2   Drain the cooling system (see Chapter 1). If the coolant is relatively new, or is in good condition, save it and re-use it.
3   Loosen the right-front wheel lug nuts. Raise the vehicle and support it securely on jackstands.
4   Remove the right front wheel and the inner fender splash shield (see Chapter 11).
5   Remove the inlet air duct and the engine lower splash shield.
6   Set the engine to TDC on the compression stroke for cylinder no. 1 (see Chapter 2A). Make sure that the pointer is aligned with the TDC mark on the crankshaft pulley and that the engine is on the compression stroke.
7   Remove the drivebelt (see Chapter 1).
8   Remove the belt idler pulley and the air conditioning idler pulley.
9   Remove the coolant reservoir (see Section 6). Unbolt the power steering fluid reservoir and set it aside with the lines attached.
10   Place a floor jack under the oil pan using a block of wood as a pad. Raise the jack to take weight off of the engine mounts.
11   Remove the right engine mount assembly and the torque rod (see Chapter 2A).
12   Remove the coolant drain plug from the water pump side of the engine block **(see illustration)**.
13   Disconnect the wiring from the front IVT control valve. Remove the front IVT control valve cover.
14   Remove the chain tensioner cover and the water pump cover from the engine front cover **(see illustration)**.
15   Push the tensioner plunger in, then lock it in the retracted position by inserting a small drill bit or similar steel rod into the hole **(see illustration)**.

7.12 Location of the water pump drain plug

7.14 Remove the timing chain tensioner cover (A) and the water pump cover (B) from the timing chain cover

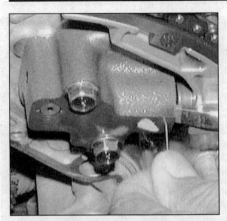

7.15 Depress the timing chain tensioner and lock it into place by inserting a paper clip into the hole on the front of the tensioner

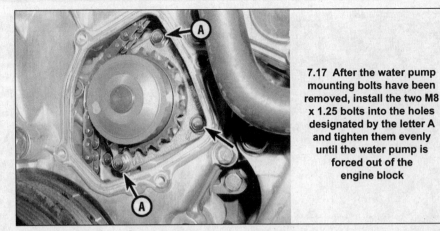

7.17 After the water pump mounting bolts have been removed, install the two M8 x 1.25 bolts into the holes designated by the letter A and tighten them evenly until the water pump is forced out of the engine block

16   Carefully rotate the crankshaft pulley clockwise until the timing chain becomes somewhat loose on the tensioner side, then remove the tensioner.

17   Remove the water pump mounting bolts **(see illustration). Caution:** *Don't allow the bolts to drop into the timing chain cover.*

18   Turn the crankshaft counterclockwise (no more than 20 degrees) until the chain becomes slack on the water pump sprocket.

19   Install two 8 mm bolts, about 2 inches long and of the proper thread pitch (1.25 mm), into the water pump bolt holes and tighten them equally until they bottom against the timing chain cover. It will be necessary to rotate the water pump slightly to allow the bolts to drive against the rear timing chain case cover instead of the bolt holes.

20   Remove the water pump.

21   Clean the sealant from the mating surface and replace the O-rings.

22   Install the O-ring with the white paint mark into the groove closest to the pump flange and the second O-ring into its groove. Apply a light amount of oil to the O-rings. Tighten the pump bolts to the torque listed in this Chapter's Specifications.

23   Installation is the reverse of removal.

24   Refill the cooling system (see Chapter 1). Reconnect the battery and perform the necessary re-learn procedures (see Chapter 5).

8   Blower motor - removal and installation

Refer to illustration 8.3

Warning: *The models covered by this manual are equipped with a Supplemental Restraint System (SRS), more commonly known as airbags. Always disarm the airbag system before working in the vicinity of any airbag system component to avoid the possibility of accidental deployment of the airbag, which could cause personal injury (see Chapter 12). Do not use a memory saving device to preserve the PCM's memory when working on or near airbag system components.*

1   Disconnect the cable from the negative terminal of the battery (see Chapter 5).

2   Remove the glove box and the lower trim panel from the instrument panel (see Chapter 11).

3   Disconnect the electrical connector from the blower motor **(see illustration)**.

4   Remove the three screws and lower the blower motor out.

5   Installation is the reverse of removal.

6   Reconnect the battery and perform the necessary re-learn procedures (see Chapter 5).

9   Heater and air conditioning control assembly - removal and installation

Refer to illustrations 9.2, 9.4a and 9.4b

Warning: *The models covered by this manual are equipped with a Supplemental Restraint System (SRS), more commonly known as airbags. Always disarm the airbag system before working in the vicinity of any airbag system component to avoid the possibility of accidental deployment of the airbag, which could cause personal injury (see Chapter 12). Do not use a memory saving device to preserve the PCM's memory when working on or near airbag system components.*

1   Disconnect the cable from the negative terminal of the battery (see Chapter 5).

2   Remove the screws from the bottoms of both side trim panels of the center instrument panel (see Chapter 11) **(see illustration)**.

8.3 Blower motor electrical connector and mounting screws

9.2 These side trim panels must be removed for access to the heater control mounting screws

9.4a Heater control unit mounting screws

9.4b Pull the unit rearward to release the clips (A), then disconnect the wiring (B)

3   Use a plastic trim tool or a screwdriver wrapped with tape to carefully pry up the trim panels and remove them.
4   Remove the mounting screws from the heater control unit, then pull it out **(see illustration)**. Disconnect the wiring from the rear of the unit **(see illustration)**.
5   Installation is the reverse of removal.
6   Reconnect the battery and perform the necessary re-learn procedures (see Chapter 5).

10 Heater core - removal and installation

Refer to illustration 10.5
Warning: *Wait until the engine is completely cool before beginning this procedure.*
Warning: *The models covered by this manual are equipped with a Supplemental Restraint System (SRS), more commonly known as*

10.5 The air conditioning refrigerant lines pass through the firewall at this point - disconnect them and seal the open ends to prevent contamination

airbags. Always disarm the airbag system before working in the vicinity of any airbag system component to avoid the possibility of accidental deployment of the airbag, which could cause personal injury (see Chapter 12). Do not use a memory saving device to preserve the PCM's memory when working on or near airbag system components.
Note: *Replacement of the heater core is a difficult procedure for the home mechanic, involving removal of the entire dashboard, console, and many wiring connectors. If you attempt it at home, keep track of the assemblies by taking notes and keeping screws and other hardware in small, marked plastic bags for reassembly.*
1   Have the air conditioning system evacuated by a properly equipped shop.
2   Disconnect the cable from the negative terminal of the battery (see Chapter 5).
3   Drain the cooling system (see Chapter 1).
4   Disconnect the heater hoses from the pipes that protrude through the firewall.
5   Disconnect the air conditioning lines from the expansion valve block at the firewall **(see illustration)**. Seal all open ends to prevent contamination.
6   Remove the entire instrument panel assembly (see Chapter 11).
7   Remove the vertical instrument panel brace from the area of the accelerator pedal.
8   Remove the four heater unit mounting bolts.
9   Remove the mounting nuts from the steering column, then disconnect the three ground wires from the instrument panel cross bar.
10   Disconnect the wiring from the heater unit.
11   Remove the three bolts from each end of the instrument panel cross bar, then remove the bar.
12   Disconnect the evaporator drain hose.
13   Remove the rear air ducts from the heater unit.

14   Remove the heater unit from the vehicle.
15   Remove the heater tubing grommet, support and cover from the heater tubes.
16   Remove the left footwell air duct.
17   Slide the heater core from the case.
18   Reinstall the heater core into the heater unit and replace the assembly in the reverse order of removal.
19   Refill the cooling system (see Chapter 1). Reconnect the battery and perform the necessary re-learn procedures (see Chapter 5). Check for leaks and proper system operation. Check the operation of all electrical components of the steering column and dash.
20   Have the air conditioning system recharged by the shop that discharged it.

11 Air conditioning compressor - removal and installation

Refer to illustrations 11.8a and 11.8b
Warning: *The air conditioning system is under high pressure. Do not loosen any fittings or remove any components until after the system has been discharged. Air conditioning refrigerant should be properly discharged into an EPA-approved container at a dealer service department or an automotive air conditioning repair facility. Always wear eye protection when disconnecting air conditioning system fittings.*
1   Have the refrigerant discharged at a dealer service department or an automotive air conditioning repair facility.
2   Disconnect the cable from the negative terminal of the battery (see Chapter 5).
3   Raise the vehicle and support it securely on jackstands. Remove the lower engine splash shield.
4   Remove the drivebelt (see Chapter 1).
5   Disconnect both refrigerant lines from the compressor and seal all openings with tape to prevent contamination.

11.8a These bolts secure the compressor at the front
of the engine

11.8b Compressor side mounting bolts

6   Disconnect the wiring from the compressor.

7   Remove the bolts from the oil cooler lines, then move them aside.

8   Remove the compressor mounting bolts and remove the compressor from the bottom of the engine compartment **(see illustrations)**. **Note:** *Keep the compressor level during handling and storage. If the compressor seized or you find metal particles in the refrigerant lines, the system must be flushed out by an air conditioning technician and the receiver-drier must be replaced (see Section 13).*

9   Prior to installation, turn the center of the clutch six times to evenly disperse any oil that has collected in the head.

10   Install the compressor in the reverse order of removal.

11   If you are installing a new compressor, the cycling clutch assembly may have to be transferred to the new compressor. **Note:** *The removal of the clutch assembly will require the use of several special tools. You may want to have the clutch assembly transferred to the new compressor by an air conditioning shop or dealer service department. Refer to the compressor manufacturer's instructions for adding refrigerant oil to the system.* **Caution:** *Use only refrigerant oil compatible with the R-134a system in your vehicle.*

12   Reconnect the battery and perform the necessary re-learn procedures (see Chapter 5).

13   Have the system evacuated, charged and leak tested by the shop that discharged it.

12 Air conditioning condenser - removal and installation

Warning: *The models covered by this manual are equipped with a Supplemental Restraint System (SRS), more commonly known as airbags. Always disarm the airbag system before working in the vicinity of any airbag system component to avoid the possibility of accidental deployment of the airbag, which could cause personal injury (see Chapter 12). Do not use a memory saving device to preserve the PCM's memory when working on or near airbag system components.*
Warning: *The air conditioning system is under high pressure. Do not loosen any fittings or remove any components until after the system has been discharged. Air conditioning refrigerant should be properly discharged into an EPA-approved container at a dealer service department or an automotive air conditioning repair facility. Always wear eye protection when disconnecting air conditioning system fittings.*

1   Have the refrigerant discharged at a dealer service department or an automotive air conditioning repair facility.

2007 and earlier models

Warning: *The engine must be completely cool before beginning this procedure.*

2   Drain the engine coolant (see Chapter 1).

3   Remove the engine cooling fans (see Section 5).

4   Remove the bolt and detach the refrigerant lines from the right (passenger's) side of the vehicle **(see illustration 12.12)**. Plug the line to prevent the entry of moisture or contaminants.

5   Remove the upper radiator mounts (see Section 6).

6   Tilt the radiator and condenser to the rear, remove the condenser mounting bolts, the lift the condenser from the engine compartment. Be careful not to damage the radiator cooling fins.

7   Installation is the reverse of removal. Be sure to use new O-rings on the refrigerant line fittings.

12.12 The air conditioning refrigerant lines attach to the condenser at this connection

8   If a new condenser is installed, add 1.2 ounces (35 cc) of refrigerant oil to it. **Caution:** *Use only refrigerant oil compatible with the R-134a system in your vehicle.*

9   Refill the cooling system (see Chapter 1).

10   Have the system evacuated, charged and leak tested by the shop that discharged it.

2009 and later models

Refer to illustrations 12.12 and 12.13

11   Remove the bumper cover (see Chapter 11) and crossmember to which the horns are mounted.

12   Remove the bolt and detach the refrigerant lines from the right (passenger's) side of the vehicle **(see illustration)**. Plug the line to prevent the entry of moisture or contaminants.

12.13 Disconnect the electrical connector from the pressure sensor (A), then release the upper retaining tabs (B)

13.4 Receiver-drier clamp bolt

13.5 Receiver-drier clamp lower mounting bolt

13   Disconnect the electrical connector from the pressure sensor, then release the retaining tab on each side and lift the condenser out **(see illustration)**.

14   Installation is the reverse of removal. Be sure to use new O-rings on the refrigerant line fittings.

15   If a new condenser is installed, add 1.2 ounces (35 cc) of refrigerant oil to it. **Caution:** *Use only refrigerant oil compatible with the R-134a system in your vehicle.*

16   Have the system evacuated, charged and leak tested by the shop that discharged it.

13   Air conditioning receiver-drier - removal and installation

Refer to illustrations 13.4 and 13.5

1   Have the refrigerant discharged at a dealer service department or an automotive air conditioning repair facility.

2   Remove the bumper cover (see Chapter 11).

3   Disconnect the electrical connector from the pressure sensor **(see illustration 12.13)**.

4   Remove the clamp bolt **(see illustration)**.

5   Remove the mounting bolt at the bottom **(see illustration)**, then pull the receiver-drier off the refrigerant lines.

6   When installing the new receiver-drier, add 0.3 ounce (10 cc) of refrigerant oil to it. **Caution:** *Use only refrigerant oil compatible with the R-134a system in your vehicle.*

7   Installation is the reverse of removal. Be sure to use new O-rings on the refrigerant line fittings.

8   Have the system evacuated, charged and leak tested by the shop that discharged it.

Chapter 4
Fuel and exhaust systems

Contents

|---|---|---|---|
Air filter housing - removal and installation	9	Fuel rail and injectors - removal and installation	11
Exhaust system servicing - general information	6	Fuel tank - removal and installation	8
Fuel lines and fittings - general information and disconnection	5	General information	1
Fuel pressure - check	4	Throttle body - removal and installation	10
Fuel pressure relief procedure	3	Troubleshooting	2
Fuel pump/fuel level sensor modules - removal and installation	7		

Specifications

Fuel system pressure (approximate) .... 51 psi

Torque specifications

Note: *One foot-pound (ft-lb) of torque is equivalent to 12 inch-pounds (in-lbs) of torque. Torque values below approximately 15 ft-lbs are expressed in inch-pounds, since most foot-pound torque wrenches are not accurate at these smaller values.*

Throttle body mounting fasteners .... 74 in-lbs

1   General information

Fuel system warnings

Gasoline is extremely flammable and repairing fuel system components can be dangerous. Consider your automotive repair knowledge and experience before attempting repairs which may be better suited for a professional mechanic.

- Don't smoke or allow open flames or bare light bulbs near the work area
- Don't work in a garage with a gas-type appliance (water heater, clothes dryer)
- Use fuel-resistant gloves. If any fuel spills on your skin, wash it off immediately with soap and water

- Clean up spills immediately
- Do not store fuel-soaked rags where they could ignite
- Prior to disconnecting any fuel line, you must relieve the fuel pressure (see Section 3)
- Wear safety glasses
- Have a proper fire extinguisher on hand

Fuel system

The fuel system consists of the fuel tank, electric fuel pump/fuel level sending unit (located in the fuel tank), fuel rail and fuel injectors. The fuel injection system is a multi-port system; multi-port fuel injection uses timed impulses to inject the fuel directly into the intake port of each cylinder. The Powertrain Control Module (PCM) controls the injectors. The PCM monitors various engine parameters and delivers the exact amount of fuel required into the intake ports.

Fuel is circulated from the fuel pump to the fuel rail through fuel lines running along the underside of the vehicle. Various sections of the fuel line are either rigid metal or nylon, or flexible fuel hose. The various sections of the fuel hose are connected either by quick-connect fittings or threaded metal fittings.

Exhaust system

The exhaust system consists of the exhaust manifold(s), catalytic converter(s), muffler(s), tailpipe and all connecting pipes, flanges and clamps. The catalytic converters are an emission control device added to the exhaust system to reduce pollutants.

2   Troubleshooting

Fuel pump

Refer to illustration 2.2

1   The fuel pump is located inside the fuel tank. Sit inside the vehicle with the windows closed, turn the ignition key to ON (not START) and listen for the sound of the fuel pump as it's briefly activated. You will only hear the sound for a second or two, but that sound tells you that the pump is working. Alternatively, have an assistant listen at the fuel filler cap.

2   If the pump does not come on, check the fuel pump fuse **(see illustration)**. If the fuse is okay, check the wiring back to the fuel pump. If the fuse and wiring are okay, the pump might be defective. Other possibilities include a faulty fuel pump relay, which is part of the Intelligent Power Distribution Module (which is part of the underhood fuse/relay box), or a faulty Powertrain Control Module (PCM). If the pump runs continuously with the ignition key in the ON position, the Powertrain Control Module (PCM) is probably defective. Have the PCM checked by a professional mechanic.

Fuel injection system

Refer to illustration 2.9

Note: *The following procedure is based on the assumption that the fuel pump is working and the fuel pressure is adequate (see Section 4).*

3   Check all electrical connectors that are related to the system. Check the ground wire connections for tightness.

4   Verify that the battery is fully charged (see Chapter 5).

5   Inspect the air filter element (see Chapter 1).

6   Check all fuses related to the fuel system (see Chapter 12).

7   Check the air induction system between the throttle body and the intake manifold for air leaks. Also inspect the condition of all vacuum hoses connected to the intake manifold and to the throttle body.

8   Remove the air intake duct from the throttle body and look for dirt, carbon, varnish, or other residue in the throttle body, particularly around the throttle plate. If it's dirty, clean it with carb cleaner, a toothbrush and a clean shop towel.

9   With the engine running, place an automotive stethoscope against each injector, one at a time, and listen for a clicking sound that indicates operation **(see illustration)**. **Warning:** *Stay clear of the drivebelt and any rotating or hot components.*

10   If you can hear the injectors operating, but the engine is misfiring, the electrical circuits are functioning correctly, but the injectors might be dirty or clogged. Try a commercial injector cleaning product (available at auto parts stores). If cleaning the injectors doesn't help, replace the injectors.

11   If an injector is not operating (it makes no sound), disconnect the injector electrical connector and measure the resistance across the injector terminals with an ohmmeter. Compare this measurement to the other injectors. If the resistance of the non-operational injector is quite different from the other injectors, replace it.

12   If the injector is not operating, but the resistance reading is within the range of resistance of the other injectors, the PCM or the circuit between the PCM and the injector might be faulty.

3   Fuel pressure relief procedure

Warning: *Gasoline is extremely flammable. See* **Fuel system warnings** *in Section 1.*
Note: *After the fuel pressure has been relieved, it's a good idea to lay a shop towel over any fuel connection to be disassembled, to absorb the residual fuel that may leak out when servicing the fuel system.*

1   Remove the fuel pump fuse from the underhood fuse/relay box **(see illustration 2.2)**.

2   Start the engine and allow it to run until it stops. This should take only a few seconds. Disconnect the cable from the negative terminal of the battery before working on the fuel system (see Chapter 5).

3   The fuel system pressure is now relieved. It is a good idea to surround any fuel line that will be disconnected using a shop rag to catch fuel that might spill out.

4   When you're finished working on the fuel system, install the fuel pump fuse back into the fuse panel, connect the negative cable to the battery and perform the necessary relearn procedures (see Chapter 5).

2.2 The fuel pump fuse is located in the engine compartment fuse box

2.9 An automotive stethoscope is used to listen to the fuel injectors in operation

4.1a The fuel line connector is under this plastic cover - pry it up, then use a special tool to disconnect it before attaching a pressure gauge tee fitting

4.1b A typical fuel pressure gauge, with hoses and fittings suitable for tee-ing into the fuel delivery system

6.1 A typical exhaust system hanger. Inspect regularly and replace at the first sign of damage or deterioration

4 Fuel pressure - check

Refer to illustrations 4.1a and 4.1b

Warning: *Gasoline is extremely flammable. See* **Fuel system warnings** *in Section 1.*

Note: *To perform the fuel pressure test, you will need to obtain a special fuel pressure gauge and adapter set (fuel line fittings).*

1   Relieve the fuel pressure (see Section 3). Disconnect the quick-connect fuel supply line fitting at the fuel rail **(see illustration)**. You must connect a special tee adapter in the line that incorporates a fuel pressure gauge. This special tee can be purchased or you can fabricate your own out of various fittings, hose and hose clamps **(see illustration)**.

2   With the gauge connected and leak-tested, start the engine and allow it to idle. Note the gauge reading as soon as it stabilizes and compare it with the pressure listed in this Chapter's Specifications.

3   If the fuel pressure is far out of specification, check the following:

a) *Check for a restriction in the fuel system (kinked fuel line, plugged fuel pump inlet strainer or clogged fuel filter). If no restrictions are found, replace the fuel pump module (see Section 7).*

b) *If the fuel pressure is higher than specified, replace the fuel pump module (see Section 7).*

4   Turn off the engine. Fuel pressure should not fall more than 8 psi over five minutes. If it does, the problem could be a leaky fuel injector, fuel line leak, or faulty fuel pump module.

5   Disconnect the fuel pressure gauge. Wipe up any spilled gasoline.

5 Fuel lines and fittings - general information and disconnection

Warning: *Gasoline is extremely flammable. See* **Fuel system warnings** *in Section 1.*

1   Relieve the fuel pressure before servicing fuel lines or fittings (see Section 3), then disconnect the cable from the negative battery terminal (see Chapter 5) before proceeding.

2   The fuel supply line connects the fuel pump in the fuel tank to the fuel rail on the engine. The Evaporative Emission (EVAP) system lines connect the fuel tank to the EVAP canister and connect the canister to the intake manifold.

3   Whenever you're working under the vehicle, be sure to inspect all fuel and evaporative emission lines for leaks, kinks, dents and other damage. Always replace a damaged fuel or EVAP line immediately.

4   If you find signs of dirt in the lines during disassembly, disconnect all lines and blow them out with compressed air. Inspect the fuel strainer on the fuel pump pick-up unit for damage and deterioration.

Steel tubing

5   It is critical that the fuel lines be replaced with lines of equivalent type and specification.

6   Some steel fuel lines have threaded fittings. When loosening these fittings, hold the stationary fitting with a wrench while turning the tube nut.

Plastic tubing

7   When replacing fuel system plastic tubing, use only original equipment replacement plastic tubing. **Caution:** *When removing or installing plastic fuel line tubing, be careful not to bend or twist it too much, which can damage it. Also, plastic fuel tubing is NOT heat resistant, so keep it away from excessive heat.*

Flexible hoses

8   When replacing fuel system flexible hoses, use only original equipment replacements.

9   Don't route fuel hoses (or metal lines) within four inches of the exhaust system or within ten inches of the catalytic converter. Make sure that no rubber hoses are installed

directly against the vehicle, particularly in places where there is any vibration. If allowed to touch some vibrating part of the vehicle, a hose can easily become chafed and it might start leaking. A good rule of thumb is to maintain a minimum of 1/4-inch clearance around a hose (or metal line) to prevent contact with the vehicle underbody.

6 Exhaust system servicing - general information

Refer to illustration 6.1

Warning: *Allow exhaust system components to cool before inspection or repair. Also, when working under the vehicle, make sure it is securely supported on jackstands.*

1   The exhaust system consists of the exhaust manifolds, catalytic converter, muffler, tailpipe and all connecting pipes, flanges and clamps. The exhaust system is isolated from the vehicle body and from chassis components by a series of rubber hangers **(see illustration)**. Periodically inspect these hangers for cracks or other signs of deterioration, replacing them as necessary.

2   Conduct regular inspections of the exhaust system to keep it safe and quiet. Look for any damaged or bent parts, open seams, holes, loose connections, excessive corrosion or other defects which could allow exhaust fumes to enter the vehicle. Do not repair deteriorated exhaust system components; replace them with new parts.

3   If the exhaust system components are extremely corroded, or rusted together, a cutting torch is the most convenient tool for removal. Consult a properly-equipped repair shop. If a cutting torch is not available, you can use a hacksaw, or if you have compressed air, there are special pneumatic cutting chisels that can also be used. Wear safety goggles to protect your eyes from metal chips and wear work gloves to protect your hands.

4   Here are some simple guidelines to follow when repairing the exhaust system:

Disconnecting Fuel Line Fittings

Two-tab type fitting; depress both tabs with your fingers, then pull the fuel line and the fitting apart

On this type of fitting, depress the two buttons on opposite sides of the fitting, then pull it off the fuel line

Threaded fuel line fitting; hold the stationary portion of the line or component (A) while loosening the tube nut (B) with a flare-nut wrench

Plastic collar-type fitting; rotate the outer part of the fitting

Metal collar quick-connect fitting; pull the end of the retainer off the fuel line and disengage the other end from the female side of the fitting . . .

. . . insert a fuel line separator tool into the female side of the fitting, push it into the fitting and pull the fuel line off the pipe

Some fittings are secured by lock tabs. Release the lock tab (A) and rotate it to the fully-opened position, squeeze the two smaller lock tabs (B) . . .

. . . then push the retainer out and pull the fuel line off the pipe

Spring-lock coupling; remove the safety cover, install a coupling release tool and close the tool around the coupling . . .

. . . push the tool into the fitting, then pull the two lines apart

Hairpin clip type fitting: push the legs of the retainer clip together, then push the clip down all the way until it stops and pull the fuel line off the pipe

7.4 Fuel pump/fuel level sensor inspection hole cover. Turn the retainers clockwise to release them

7.5 Depress the tang and disconnect the electrical connector, then detach the fuel and EVAP lines

a) *Work from the back to the front when removing exhaust system components.*
b) *Apply penetrating oil to the exhaust system component fasteners to make them easier to remove.*
c) *Use new gaskets, hangers and clamps.*
d) *Apply anti-seize compound to the threads of all exhaust system fasteners during reassembly.*
e) *Be sure to allow sufficient clearance between newly installed parts and all points on the underbody to avoid overheating the floor pan and possibly damaging the interior carpet and insulation. Pay particularly close attention to the catalytic converter and heat shield.*

7 Fuel pump/fuel level sensor modules - removal and installation

Warning: *Gasoline is extremely flammable. See* **Fuel system warnings** *in Section 1.*
Note: *The components of the module (with*

the exception of the fuel level sensor) are not replaceable individually. The entire module must be replaced if any part of it is defective.

Removal

Refer to illustrations 7.4, 7.5, 7.7, 7.8 and 7.9
Note: *This general procedure applies to both the primary (driver's side) and secondary (passenger's side) modules.*
1   Relieve the fuel pressure (see Section 3).
2   Disconnect the cable from the negative terminal of the battery (see Chapter 5).
3   Remove the rear seat cushion and recliner from the vehicle (see Chapter 11).
4   Remove the access cover for the fuel pump/fuel level sending unit assembly or the secondary fuel level sensor **(see illustration)**.
5   Disconnect the electrical connectors from the fuel pump/fuel level sending unit **(see illustration)**.
6   Disconnect the hoses and lines from the fuel level sending unit/fuel pump assembly.
7   Using a brass drift and hammer, tap the

lock ring on the assembly counterclockwise **(see illustration)**. Remove the lock ring from the assembly.
8   Lift the fuel pump module from the fuel tank. Manipulate it as you lift so you don't bend the float arm **(see illustration)**.
9   Disconnect the suction hose and the in-tank wiring that connects the secondary fuel module to the primary module **(see illustration)**.

Fuel level sensor replacement
Note: *The main fuel pump module consists of the fuel pump, a filter and the primary fuel level sensor. It's under a cover beneath the rear seat on the driver side of the vehicle. There is also a secondary fuel level sensor under a similar cover on the passenger side.*

Primary sensor
Refer to illustration 7.11
10   Remove the fuel pump module from the driver's side of the vehicle (see Steps 1 through 9). Disconnect the electrical connector.

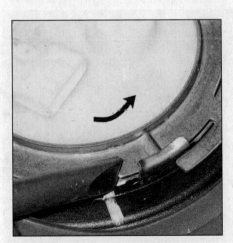

7.7 Use a brass drift and a hammer to rotate the locking ring

7.8 The fuel level float arm is easily bent, so proceed carefully when lifting the fuel pump module out

7.9 Secondary fuel module-to-primary module electrical connector (right arrow) and suction hose (left arrow)

7.11 The fuel level sensor is secured with retaining tabs; squeeze them, then slide the sensor off

7.17 Install a new O-ring seal

11   Squeeze the fuel level sensor lock tabs **(see illustration)**, then slide the sensor sideways to remove it.
12   Installation is the reverse of removal.

Secondary sensor

13   Remove the fuel level sensor module from the passenger side of the vehicle.
14   Disconnect the in-tank wiring. Use a thin tool to release the fuel level sensor lock **(see illustration 7.11)**.
15   Slide the sensor downward to remove it.
16   Installation is the reverse of removal.

Installation

Refer to illustrations 7.17 and 7.19

17   Replace the O-ring seal **(see illustration)**.
18   Carefully lower the fuel pump module or fuel level module into the fuel tank.
19   Rotate the assembly until the alignment mark is positioned facing the front of the vehicle and the two arrows are aligned **(see illustration)**.

20   Align the lock ring, then turn it clockwise to secure it in place.
21   Reconnect the hoses and electrical connector, then reinstall the access cover.
22   Reinstall the rear seat cushion and recliner.
23   Reconnect the battery and perform the necessary re-learn procedures (see Chapter 5).

8   Fuel tank - removal and installation

Refer to illustration 8.11
Warning: *Gasoline is extremely flammable. See* **Fuel system warnings** *in Section 1.*
Note: *The following procedure is much easier to perform if the fuel tank is empty. Drain the fuel into an approved fuel container using a commercially available siphoning kit (NEVER start the siphoning action by mouth), or wait until the fuel tank is nearly empty, if possible.*

1   Remove the fuel tank filler cap to relieve fuel tank pressure.
2   Relieve the fuel system pressure (see Section 3).
3   Disconnect the cable from the negative terminal of the battery (see Chapter 5).
4   Remove both fuel pump/fuel level sensor modules (see Section 7).
5   Raise the vehicle and place it securely on jackstands.
6   If there is still fuel in the tank, siphon it out. Remember - NEVER start the siphoning action by mouth! Use a siphoning kit, which can be purchased at most auto parts stores.
7   Remove the rear section of the exhaust system.
8   Remove the driveshaft on AWD models (see Chapter 8).
9   Remove the rear parking brake cables.
10   On AWD models, remove the entire rear suspension subframe assembly as one unit (see Chapter 10).
11   Remove the fuel tank shields **(see illustration)**.

7.19 The alignment mark on the fuel pump module must face the front of the vehicle and align with the other arrow

8.11 The plastic fuel tank shields and the rear portion of the exhaust system must be removed before the fuel tank can be lowered

9.4 Air filter housing cover details

A Retaining clips
B MAF sensor electrical connector
C Air intake duct clamp

9.6 The lower housing is secured by this bolt and two lower nuts (not visible in this photo)

12 Disconnect the fuel filler and vent hoses from the fuel tank.

13 Support the fuel tank with two floor jacks - one beneath each lobe of the fuel tank. Position a wood block between the jack heads and the fuel tank to protect the tank.

14 Remove the fuel tank straps.

15 Slowly lower the tank with the jacks and remove the tank from the vehicle.

16 Installation is the reverse of removal.

17 Reconnect the battery and perform the necessary re-learn procedures (see Chapter 5).

9 Air filter housing - removal and installation

Refer to illustrations 9.4 and 9.6

1 Remove the left and right radiator top covers.

2 Remove the large plastic air inlet duct.

3 Disconnect the wiring from the Mass Airflow/Intake Air Temperature (MAF/IAT) sensor (see Chapter 6). Disconnect the PCV hose (see Chapter 1).

4 Loosen the air intake duct clamp and disconnect the electrical connector from the MAF/IAT sensor **(see illustration)**.

5 Remove the lid of the air filter housing with the duct and MAF/IAT sensor attached. Remove the air filter element.

6 Remove the mounting bolt from the top of the air filter housing, then pull the housing from the grommets at the bottom **(see illustration)**.

7 Installation is the reverse of removal.

10 Throttle body - removal and installation

Refer to illustration 10.4

Warning: *The engine must be completely cool before beginning this procedure.*

1 Disconnect the cable from the negative terminal of the battery (see Chapter 5).

2 Remove the cowl cover (see Chapter 11).

Note: *It isn't absolutely necessary to remove the cowl cover, but doing so will provide more working room.*

3 Remove the air filter housing cover and the air intake duct (see Section 9).

4 Clamp-off the coolant hoses to the throttle body, then disconnect them **(see illustration)**.

5 Disconnect the wiring from the throttle body. Disconnect any remaining hoses and connectors.

6 Loosen the throttle body mounting bolts a little at a time in a criss-cross pattern to prevent distortion.

7 Remove the throttle body. **Note:** *Don't try to disassemble the throttle body. If it's faulty, it must be replaced.*

8 Installation is the reverse of removal; use a new throttle body O-ring if the old one is not in perfect condition. Tighten the bolts a little at a time in a criss-cross pattern to the torque listed in this Chapter's Specifications.

9 Check the coolant level, adding as necessary (see Chapter 1).

10 Reconnect the battery and perform the necessary re-learn procedures (see Chapter 5).

11 Fuel rail and injectors - removal and installation

Refer to illustrations 11.8a, 11.8b, 11.10 and 11.11

1 Relieve the fuel system pressure (see Section 3).

2 Disconnect the cable from the negative terminal of the battery (see Chapter 5).

3 Remove the upper intake manifold (see Chapter 2A).

4 Disconnect the fuel supply line from the fuel rail (see Section 5).

5 Disconnect the electrical connector from each fuel injector.

10.4 Throttle body details

1 Coolant hoses
2 Electrical connector
3 Mounting bolts

11.8a To free each injector from the fuel rail, pull off the retainer with a pair of pliers . . .

11.8b . . . then pull the injector straight out of its bore in the fuel rail

6   Remove the fuel rail mounting bolts, starting with the two bolts farthest away from the fuel inlet.

7   Carefully lift the fuel rail from the engine with the injectors attached.

8   Remove the injectors from the fuel rail, then remove and discard the O-rings **(see illustrations)**.

9   If necessary, remove the fuel pressure damper. Use a new O-ring on installation.

10   Replace both O-rings of each fuel injector and lubricate them with clean engine oil prior to installation **(see illustration)**.

11   Install the injector retaining clips and insert each injector into its bore in the fuel rail until the retaining clip snaps into place **(see illustration)**.

12   The remainder of installation is the reverse of removal. Tighten the fuel rail mounting bolts starting with the two closest to the fuel inlet.

13   Reconnect the battery and perform the necessary re-learn procedures (see Chapter 5).

11.10 Whether you're installing new injectors or reusing the old ones, always remove the old O-rings and replace them with new ones

11.11 To install an injector, align the slot in the clip (A) with the tab (B) on the fuel rail, then push the injector firmly into place until the clip snaps onto the ridge of the injector bore

Chapter 5
Engine electrical systems

Contents

1 General information and precautions

General information

Ignition system

The electronic ignition system consists of the Crankshaft Position (CKP) sensor, the Camshaft Position (CMP) sensor, the Knock Sensor (KS), the Powertrain Control Module (PCM), the ignition switch, the battery, the individual ignition coils or a coil pack, and the spark plugs. For more information on the CKP, CMP and KS sensors, as well as the PCM, refer to Chapter 6.

Charging system

The charging system includes the alternator (with an integral voltage regulator), the Powertrain Control Module (PCM), the Body Control Module (BCM), a charge indicator light on the dash, the battery, a fuse or fusible link and the wiring connecting all of these components. The charging system supplies electrical power for the ignition system, the lights, the radio, etc. The alternator is driven by a drivebelt.

Starting system

The starting system consists of the battery, the ignition switch, the starter relay, the Powertrain Control Module (PCM), the Body Control Module (BCM), the Transmission Range (TR) switch, the starter motor and solenoid assembly, and the wiring connecting all of the components.

Precautions

Always observe the following precautions when working on the electrical system:

a) *Be extremely careful when servicing engine electrical components. They are easily damaged if checked, connected or handled improperly.*

b) *Never leave the ignition switched on for long periods of time when the engine is not running.*

c) *Never disconnect the battery cables while the engine is running.*

d) *Maintain correct polarity when connecting battery cables from another vehicle during jump starting - see the "Booster battery (jump) starting" Section at the front of this manual.*

e) *Always disconnect the cable from the negative battery terminal before working on the electrical system, but read the battery disconnection procedure first (see Section 3).*

It's also a good idea to review the safety-related information regarding the engine electrical systems located in the *Safety first!* Section at the front of this manual before beginning any operation included in this Chapter.

2   Troubleshooting

Ignition system

1   If a malfunction occurs in the ignition system, do not immediately assume that any particular part is causing the problem. First, check the following items:

   a) *Make sure that the cable clamps at the battery terminals are clean and tight.*
   b) *Test the condition of the battery (see Steps 21 through 24). If it doesn't pass all the tests, replace it.*
   c) *Check the ignition coil or coil pack connections.*
   d) *Check any relevant fuses in the engine compartment fuse and relay box (see Chapter 12). If they're burned, determine the cause and repair the circuit.*

Check

Refer to illustration 2.3

Warning: *Because of the high voltage generated by the ignition system, use extreme care when performing a procedure involving ignition components.*

Note 1: *The ignition system components on these vehicles are difficult to diagnose. In the event of ignition system failure that you can't diagnose, have the vehicle tested at a dealer service department or other qualified auto repair facility.*

Note 2: *You'll need a spark tester for the following test. Spark testers are available at most auto supply stores.*

2   If the engine turns over but won't start, verify that there is sufficient ignition voltage to fire the spark plugs as follows.

3   On models with a coil-over-plug type ignition system, remove a coil and install the tester between the boot at the lower end of the coil and the spark plug **(see illustration)**. On models with spark plug wires, disconnect a spark plug wire from a spark plug and install the tester between the spark plug wire boot and the spark plug.

4   Crank the engine and note whether or not the tester flashes. **Caution:** *Do NOT crank the engine or allow it to run for more than five*

seconds; running the engine for more than five seconds may set a Diagnostic Trouble Code (DTC) for a cylinder misfire.

Models with a coil-over-plug type ignition system

5   If the tester flashes during cranking, the coil is delivering sufficient voltage to the spark plug to fire it. Repeat this test for each cylinder to verify that the other coils are OK.

6   If the tester doesn't flash, remove a coil from another cylinder and swap it for the one being tested. If the tester now flashes, you know that the original coil is bad. If the tester still doesn't flash, the PCM or wiring harness is probably defective. Have the PCM checked out by a dealer service department or other qualified repair shop (testing the PCM is beyond the scope of the do-it-yourselfer because it requires expensive special tools).

7   If the tester flashes during cranking but a misfire code (related to the cylinder being tested) has been stored, the spark plug could be fouled or defective.

Models with spark plug wires

8   If the tester flashes during cranking, sufficient voltage is reaching the spark plug to fire it.

9   Repeat this test on the remaining cylinders.

10   Proceed on this basis until you have verified that there's a good spark from each spark plug wire. If there is, then you have verified that the coils in the coil pack are functioning correctly and that the spark plug wires are OK.

11   If there is no spark from a spark plug wire, then either the coil is bad, the plug wire is bad or a connection at one end of the plug wire is loose. Assuming that you're using new plug wires or known good wires, then the coil is probably defective. Also inspect the coil pack electrical connector. Make sure that it's clean, tight and in good condition.

12   If all the coils are firing correctly, but the engine misfires, then one or more of the plugs might be fouled. Remove and check the spark plugs or install new ones (see Chapter 1).

13   No further testing of the ignition system is possible without special tools. If the problem persists, have the ignition system tested

by a dealer service department or other qualified repair shop.

Charging system

14   If a malfunction occurs in the charging system, do not automatically assume the alternator is causing the problem. First check the following items:

   a) *Check the drivebelt tension and condition, as described in Chapter 1. Replace it if it's worn or deteriorated.*
   b) *Make sure the alternator mounting bolts are tight.*
   c) *Inspect the alternator wiring harness and the connectors at the alternator and voltage regulator. They must be in good condition, tight and have no corrosion.*
   d) *Check the fusible link (if equipped) or main fuse in the underhood fuse/relay box. If it is burned, determine the cause, repair the circuit and replace the link or fuse (the vehicle will not start and/or the accessories will not work if the fusible link or main fuse is blown).*
   e) *Start the engine and check the alternator for abnormal noises (a shrieking or squealing sound indicates a bad bearing).*
   f) *Check the battery. Make sure it's fully charged and in good condition (one bad cell in a battery can cause overcharging by the alternator).*
   g) *Disconnect the battery cables (negative first, then positive). Inspect the battery posts and the cable clamps for corrosion. Clean them thoroughly if necessary (see Chapter 1). Reconnect the cables (positive first, negative last).*

Alternator - check

15   Use a voltmeter to check the battery voltage with the engine off. It should be at least 12.6 volts **(see illustration 2.21)**.

16   Start the engine and check the battery voltage again. It should now be approximately 13.5 to 15 volts.

17   If the voltage reading is more or less than the specified charging voltage, the voltage regulator is probably defective, which will require replacement of the alternator (the voltage regulator is not replaceable separately). Remove the alternator and have it bench tested (most auto parts stores will do this for you).

18   The charging system (battery) light on the instrument cluster lights up when the ignition key is turned to ON, but it should go out when the engine starts.

19   If the charging system light stays on after the engine has been started, there is a problem with the charging system. Before replacing the alternator, check the battery condition, alternator belt tension and electrical cable connections.

20   If replacing the alternator doesn't restore voltage to the specified range, have the charging system tested by a dealer service department or other qualified repair shop.

2.3 Spark tester

**2.21 To test the open circuit voltage of the battery, touch the
black probe of the voltmeter to the negative terminal and the
red probe to the positive terminal of the battery; a fully charged
battery should be at least 12.6 volts**

**2.23 Connect a battery load tester to the battery and check
the battery condition under load following the tool
manufacturer's instructions**

Battery - check

Refer to illustrations 2.21 and 2.23

21   Check the battery state of charge. Visually inspect the indicator eye on the top of the battery (if equipped with one); if the indicator eye is black in color, charge the battery as described in Chapter 1. Next perform an open circuit voltage test using a digital voltmeter. **Note:** *The battery's surface charge must be removed before accurate voltage measurements can be made. Turn on the high beams for ten seconds, then turn them off and let the vehicle stand for two minutes.* With the engine and all accessories Off, touch the negative probe of the voltmeter to the negative terminal of the battery and the positive probe to the positive terminal of the battery **(see illustration)**. The battery voltage should be 12.6 volts or slightly above. If the battery is less than the specified voltage, charge the battery before proceeding to the next test. Do not proceed with the battery load test unless the battery charge is correct.

22   Disconnect the negative battery cable, then the positive cable from the battery.

23   Perform a battery load test. An accurate check of the battery condition can only be performed with a load tester **(see illustration)**. This test evaluates the ability of the battery to operate the starter and other accessories during periods of high current draw. Connect the load tester to the battery terminals. Load test the battery according to the tool manufacturer's instructions. This tool increases the load demand (current draw) on the battery.

24   Maintain the load on the battery for 15 seconds and observe that the battery voltage does not drop below 9.6 volts. If the battery condition is weak or defective, the

tool will indicate this condition immediately. **Note:** *Cold temperatures will cause the minimum voltage reading to drop slightly. Follow the chart given in the manufacturer's instructions to compensate for cold climates. Minimum load voltage for freezing temperatures (32 degrees F) should be approximately 9.1 volts.*

Starting system

The starter rotates, but the engine doesn't

25   Remove the starter (see Section 8). Check the overrunning clutch and bench test the starter to make sure the drive mechanism extends fully for proper engagement with the flywheel ring gear. If it doesn't, replace the starter.

26   Check the flywheel ring gear for missing teeth and other damage. With the ignition turned off, rotate the flywheel so you can check the entire ring gear.

The starter is noisy

27   If the solenoid is making a chattering noise, first check the battery (see Steps 21 through 24). If the battery is okay, check the cables and connections.

28   If you hear a grinding, crashing metallic sound when you turn the key to Start, check for loose starter mounting bolts. If they're tight, remove the starter and inspect the teeth on the starter pinion gear and flywheel ring gear. Look for missing or damaged teeth.

29   If the starter sounds fine when you first turn the key to Start, but then stops rotating the engine and emits a zinging sound, the problem is probably a defective starter drive that's not staying engaged with the ring gear. Replace the starter.

The starter rotates slowly

30   Check the battery (see Steps 21 through 24).

31   If the battery is okay, verify all connections (at the battery, the starter solenoid and motor) are clean, corrosion-free and tight. Make sure the cables aren't frayed or damaged.

32   Check that the starter mounting bolts are tight so it grounds properly. Also check the pinion gear and flywheel ring gear for evidence of a mechanical bind (galling, deformed gear teeth or other damage).

The starter does not rotate at all

33   Check the battery (see Steps 21 through 24).

34   If the battery is okay, verify all connections (at the battery, the starter solenoid and motor) are clean, corrosion-free and tight. Make sure the cables aren't frayed or damaged.

35   Check all of the fuses in the underhood fuse/relay box.

36   Check that the starter mounting bolts are tight so it grounds properly.

37   Check for voltage at the starter solenoid "S" terminal when the ignition key is turned to the start position. If voltage is present, replace the starter/solenoid assembly. If no voltage is present, the problem could be the starter relay, the Transmission Range (TR) switch (see Chapter 6) or clutch start switch (see Chapter 8), or with an electrical connector somewhere in the circuit (see the wiring diagrams at the end of Chapter 12). Also, on many modern vehicles, the Powertrain Control Module (PCM) and the Body Control Module (BCM) control the voltage signal to the starter solenoid; on such vehicles a special scan tool is required for diagnosis.

3   Battery - disconnection and reconnection

Caution: *Always disconnect the cable from the negative battery terminal FIRST and hook it up LAST or the battery may be shorted by the tool being used to loosen the cable clamps.*

Some systems on the vehicle require battery power to be available at all times, either to maintain continuous operation (alarm system, power door locks, etc.), or to maintain control unit memory (radio station presets, Powertrain Control Module and other control units). When the battery is disconnected, the power that maintains these systems is cut. So, before you disconnect the battery, please note that on a vehicle with power door locks, it's a wise precaution to remove the key from the ignition and to keep it with you, so that it does not get locked inside if the power door locks should engage accidentally when the battery is reconnected!

Devices known as "memory-savers" can be used to avoid some of these problems. Precise details vary according to the device used. The typical memory saver is plugged into the cigarette lighter and is connected to a spare battery. Then the vehicle battery can be disconnected from the electrical system. The memory saver will provide sufficient current to maintain audio unit security codes, PCM memory, etc. and will provide power to always hot circuits such as the clock and radio memory circuits. **Warning 1:** *Some memory savers deliver a considerable amount of current in order to keep vehicle systems operational after the main battery is disconnected. If you're using a memory saver, make sure that the circuit concerned is actually open before servicing it.* **Warning 2:** *If you're going to work near any of the airbag system components, the battery MUST be disconnected and a memory saver must NOT be used. If a memory saver is used, power will be supplied to the airbag, which means that it could accidentally deploy and cause serious personal injury.*

Disconnection

1   Install a memory saver device to avoid having to reprogram several of the vehicle's systems (see above). **Warning:** *If you're working near any airbag system component, DO NOT use a memory saver.*
2   To disconnect the battery for service procedures requiring power to be cut from the vehicle, loosen the cable end bolt and disconnect the cable from the negative battery terminal. Isolate the cable end to prevent it from coming into accidental contact with the battery terminal.

Reconnection

3   Connect the positive battery cable first, followed by the negative cable.

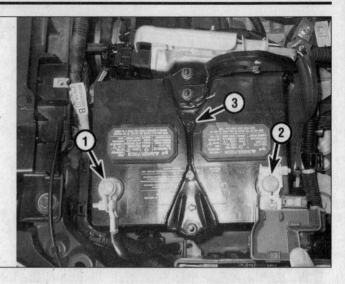

4.2 Battery details:

1   *Negative battery cable*
2   *Positive battery cable*
3   *Battery hold-down clamp*

4   After reconnecting the battery, several re-learn procedures must be performed. These include:

Accelerator pedal released position learning
Throttle valve closed position learning
Idle air volume learning
*Power window initialization and anti-pinch feature**
*Sunroof memory and anti-pinch feature**
*Radio presets**
*Navigation system adjustment**

* If a memory saver was used when the battery was disconnected, these functions won't have to be performed.

5   Refer to your owner's manual for information on resetting the radio presets and navigation system adjustment.

Accelerator pedal released position learning

6   With the accelerator pedal at rest (fully released), turn the ignition to On and wait at least two seconds.
7   Turn the ignition Off and wait at least ten seconds.
8   Turn the ignition back On again and wait at least two seconds.
9   Turn the ignition Off and wait at least ten seconds.

Throttle valve closed position learning

10   Open the hood.
11   With the accelerator pedal at rest (fully released), turn the ignition to On, then Off. Within a ten-second period, listen for the sound of the throttle body motor actuating, indicating that it has moved and found the closed position of the throttle plate.

Idle air volume learning

12   The engine and transmission must be at operating temperature for this procedure. Also make sure that the transmission is in Park.
13   The air conditioner, headlights and

defogger must be off. Point the wheels straight ahead and make sure the vehicle isn't moving. If the vehicle has daytime running lights, set the parking brake before starting the engine to turn them off.
14   Perform the accelerator pedal released position learning procedure (see Steps 6 through 9) and the throttle valve closed learning procedure (see Steps 10 and 11).
15   Start the engine and make sure it's warm and all the above conditions are satisfied.
16   Turn the engine Off and wait ten seconds or longer.
17   Ensure that the accelerator pedal is not touched. Turn the ignition On and wait three seconds.
18   Press the accelerator pedal to the floor and release it completely five times within a five second period.
19   Wait for seven seconds with the pedal fully released.
20   Press the pedal to the floor and hold it there for 20 seconds. The CHECK ENGINE light will blink during this period. When it stops blinking and stays on, release the pedal within three seconds.
21   Start the engine and let it idle for 20 seconds.

Power window initialization and anti-pinch feature check

22   Turn the ignition to the On position.
23   Open the window completely (if it already isn't open completely).
24   Pull the power window switch up to close the window, holding the switch in the Up position for at least four seconds after the glass has closed completely.
25   Open the window completely, then place a piece of wood or other object near the top of the window frame. **Warning:** *Do not use any part of your body for this check.*
26   Using the AUTO-UP feature, close the window; confirm that the window automatically reverses direction as soon as it contacts the object.

6.4 Press the tab (A) and disconnect the electrical connector, then remove the coil mounting bolt (B)

6.5 Twist the coil, then lift it straight out

Sunroof initialization and anti-pinch feature check

27 Turn the ignition to the On position.

28 Operate the sunroof switch in the tilt up position; hold it there until the sunroof has tilted up completely.

29 Hold the switch in the tilt up position again. The sunroof should back up after a pause; release the switch.

30 Within five seconds, push the switch to the tilt up position again and hold it there; the sunroof should move from the tilt up position to the fully open position, then back to the fully closed position. Release the switch.

31 Open the sunroof completely, then place a piece of wood or other object near the front of the sunroof opening. **Warning:** *Do not use any part of your body for this check.*

32 Operate the sunroof switch with the auto-close function and verify that the sunroof automatically reverses direction as soon as it contacts the object.

4   Battery - removal and installation

Refer to illustration 4.2

1 Install a memory saver device to avoid having to reprogram several of the vehicle's systems (see Section 3). **Warning:** *If you're working near any airbag system component, DO NOT use a memory saver.*

2 Disconnect the negative battery cable, then the positive battery cable, from the battery **(see illustration)**. **Warning:** *Always disconnect the negative cable first and hook it up last or the battery may be shorted by the tool being used to loosen the cable clamps.*

3 Locate the battery hold-down clamp straddling the top of the battery. Remove the nuts and the hold-down clamp.

4 Lift out the battery. Special battery lift-

ing straps that attach to the battery posts are available at auto parts stores; lifting and moving the battery is much easier if you use one.

5 Installation is the reverse of removal. Connect the positive cable first, then the negative cable. Refer to Section 3 and perform the necessary re-learn procedures.

5   Battery cables - replacement

1 When removing the cables, always disconnect the cable from the negative battery terminal first and hook it up last, or you might accidentally short out the battery with the tool you're using to loosen the cable clamps. Even if you're only replacing the cable for the positive terminal, be sure to disconnect the negative cable from the battery first.

2 Disconnect the old cables from the battery, then trace each of them to their opposite ends and disconnect them. Be sure to note the routing of each cable before disconnecting it to ensure correct installation.

3 If you are replacing any of the old cables, take them with you when buying new cables. It is vitally important that you replace the cables with identical parts.

4 Clean the threads of the solenoid or ground connection with a wire brush to remove rust and corrosion. Apply a light coat of battery terminal corrosion inhibitor or petroleum jelly to the threads to prevent future corrosion.

5 Attach the cable to the solenoid or ground connection and tighten the mounting nut/bolt securely.

6 Before connecting a new cable to the battery, make sure that it reaches the battery post without having to be stretched.

7 Connect the cable to the positive battery terminal first, *then* connect the ground cable to the negative battery terminal.

6   Ignition coil(s) - replacement

Refer to illustrations 6.4 and 6.5

1 Remove the engine cover.

2 Remove the air inlet duct and the air filter housing (see Chapter 4).

3 If you're removing the coils from the right (rear) cylinder bank, remove the intake manifold collector (upper intake manifold) (see Chapter 2A).

4 Disconnect the electrical connector from the coil(s) **(see illustration)**.

5 Remove the coil mounting bolt, then pull the coil straight out **(see illustration)**.

6 Installation is the reverse of the removal procedure. Before installing the ignition coils, coat the interior of the boots with silicone dielectric compound.

7   Alternator - removal and installation

Refer to illustration 7.11

Warning: *The engine must be completely cool before beginning this procedure.*

1 Have the air conditioning system evacuated by a shop with the proper equipment.

2 Disconnect the cable from the negative terminal of the battery (see Section 3).

3 Remove the engine cover.

4 Loosen the lug nuts of the right front wheel. Raise the vehicle and support it securely on jackstands, then remove the wheel.

5 Remove the access cover from the right front wheel well.

6 Remove the air filter housing and inlet duct (see Chapter 4).

7 Remove the drivebelt (see Chapter 1).

8 Remove the air conditioning compressor (see Chapter 3). **Warning:** *Don't disconnect the refrigerant lines; just position the compressor aside and secure it with rope or wire.*

7.11 Alternator lower mounting nut/bolt (upper bolt not visible in this photo; it's accessed from the other side of the alternator)

8.4 Starter motor mounting details

A   S terminal electrical connector
B   B+ terminal
C   Lower mounting bolt (upper bolt not shown)

9   Remove the drivebelt idler pulley.
10   Disconnect the wiring from the oil pressure switch and the alternator.
11   Remove the alternator mounting fasteners, then remove the alternator **(see illustration)**.
12   Installation is the reverse of removal. Refer to Section 3 and perform the re-learn procedures if necessary.

---

8   Starter motor - removal and installation

Refer to illustration 8.4

1   Remove the battery (see Section 4).
2   Remove the air filter housing and the air ducts (see Chapter 4).
3   Disconnect the wiring from the engine control module (ECM), the transaxle control module (TCM) and the fuse box/power center, then remove the battery tray.
4   Disconnect the wiring from the starter **(see illustration)**.
5   Remove the two mounting bolts and remove the starter.
6   Installation is the reverse of removal.
7   Reconnect the battery and perform the necessary re-learn procedures (see Section 3).

Chapter 6
Emissions and engine control systems

Contents

1   General information

To prevent pollution of the atmosphere from incompletely burned and evaporating gases, and to maintain good driveability and fuel economy, a number of emission control systems are incorporated. They include the:

Catalytic converter

A catalytic converter is an emission control device in the exhaust system that reduces certain pollutants in the exhaust gas stream. There are two types of converters: oxidation converters and reduction converters.

Oxidation converters contain a monolithic substrate (a ceramic honeycomb) coated with the semi-precious metals platinum and palla-dium. An oxidation catalyst reduces unburned hydrocarbons (HC) and carbon monoxide (CO) by adding oxygen to the exhaust stream as it passes through the substrate, which, in the presence of high temperature and the catalyst materials, converts the HC and CO to water vapor (H_2O) and carbon dioxide (CO_2).

Reduction converters contain a monolithic substrate coated with platinum and rhodium. A reduction catalyst reduces oxides of nitrogen (NOx) by removing oxygen, which in the presence of high temperature and the catalyst material produces nitrogen (N) and carbon dioxide (CO_2).

Catalytic converters that combine both types of catalysts in one assembly are known as "three-way catalysts" or TWCs. A TWC can reduce all three pollutants.

Evaporative Emissions Control (EVAP) system

The Evaporative Emissions Control (EVAP) system prevents fuel system vapors (which contain unburned hydrocarbons) from escaping into the atmosphere. On warm days, vapors trapped inside the fuel tank expand until the pressure reaches a certain threshold. Then the fuel vapors are routed from the fuel tank through the fuel vapor vent valve and the fuel vapor control valve to the EVAP canister, where they're stored temporarily until the next time the vehicle is operated. When the conditions are right (engine warmed up, vehicle up to speed, moderate or heavy load on the engine, etc.) the PCM opens the canister purge valve, which allows fuel vapors to be drawn from the canister into the intake manifold. Once in the intake manifold, the fuel vapors mix with incoming air before being drawn through the intake ports into the combustion chambers where they're burned up with the rest of the air/fuel mixture. The EVAP system is complex and virtually impossible to troubleshoot without the right tools and training.

Powertrain Control Module (PCM)

The Powertrain Control Module (PCM) is the brain of the engine management system.

It also controls a wide variety of other vehicle systems. In order to program the new PCM, the dealer needs the vehicle as well as the new PCM. If you're planning to replace the PCM with a new one, there is no point in trying to do so at home because you won't be able to program it yourself.

Positive Crankcase Ventilation (PCV) system

The Positive Crankcase Ventilation (PCV) system reduces hydrocarbon emissions by scavenging crankcase vapors, which are rich

in unburned hydrocarbons. A PCV valve or orifice regulates the flow of gases into the intake manifold in proportion to the amount of intake vacuum available.

The PCV system generally consists of the fresh air inlet hose, the PCV valve or orifice and the crankcase ventilation hose (or PCV hose). The fresh air inlet hose connects the air intake duct to a pipe on the valve cover. The crankcase ventilation hose (or PCV hose) connects the PCV valve or orifice in the valve cover to the intake manifold.

Emissions and engine control system components

1	Intake valve timing control solenoids (rear solenoid hidden)	4	Camshaft position sensor (CMP) (other CMP valve hidden at rear valve cover)	5	Engine coolant temperature (ECT) sensor
2	Power valve system solenoid valves			6	Transmission range (TR) sensor (hidden)
3	EVAP purge control valve				

Information Sensors

Accelerator Pedal Position (APP) sensor - as you press the accelerator pedal, the APP sensor alters its voltage signal to the PCM in proportion to the angle of the pedal, and the PCM commands a motor inside the throttle body to open or close the throttle plate accordingly

Camshaft Position (CMP) sensor - produces a signal that the PCM uses to identify the number 1 cylinder and to time the firing sequence of the fuel injectors

Crankshaft Position (CKP) sensor - produces a signal that the PCM uses to calculate engine speed and crankshaft position, which enables it to synchronize ignition timing with fuel injector timing, and to detect misfires

Engine Coolant Temperature (ECT) sensor - a thermistor (temperature-sensitive variable resistor) that sends a voltage signal to the PCM, which uses this data to determine the temperature of the engine coolant

Fuel tank pressure sensor - measures the fuel tank pressure and controls fuel tank pressure by signaling the EVAP system to purge the fuel tank vapors when the pressure becomes excessive

Intake Air Temperature (IAT) sensor - monitors the temperature of the air entering the engine and sends a signal to the PCM to determine injector pulse-width (the duration of each injector's on-time) and to adjust spark timing (to prevent spark knock)

Knock sensor - a piezoelectric crystal that oscillates in proportion to engine vibration which produces a voltage output that is monitored by the PCM. This retards the ignition timing when the oscillation exceeds a certain threshold

Manifold Absolute Pressure (MAP) sensor - monitors the pressure or vacuum inside the intake manifold. The PCM uses this data to determine engine load so that it can alter the ignition advance and fuel enrichment

Mass Air Flow (MAF) sensor - measures the amount of intake air drawn into the engine. It uses a hot-wire sensing element to measure the amount of air entering the engine

Oxygen sensors - generates a small variable voltage signal in proportion to the difference between the oxygen content in the exhaust stream and the oxygen content in the ambient air. The PCM uses this information to maintain the proper air/fuel ratio. A second oxygen sensor monitors the efficiency of the catalytic converter

Throttle Position (TP) sensor - a potentiometer that generates a voltage signal that varies in relation to the opening angle of the throttle plate inside the throttle body. Works with the PCM and other sensors to calculate injector pulse width (the duration of each injector's on-time)

Photos courtesy of Wells Manufacturing, except APP and MAF sensors.

2.4a Simple code readers are an economical way to extract trouble codes when the CHECK ENGINE light comes on

2.4b Hand-held scan tools like these can extract computer codes and also perform diagnostics

3.1 The Data Link Connector (DLC) is located under the lower edge of the dash, to the left of the steering column

2 On Board Diagnosis (OBD) system

General description

1   All models are equipped with the second generation OBD-II system. This system consists of an on-board computer known as the Powertrain Control Module (PCM), and information sensors, which monitor various functions of the engine and send data to the PCM. This system incorporates a series of diagnostic monitors that detect and identify fuel injection and emissions control system faults and store the information in the computer memory. This system also tests sensors and output actuators, diagnoses drive cycles, freezes data and clears codes.

2   The PCM is the brain of the electronically controlled fuel and emissions system. It receives data from a number of sensors and other electronic components (switches, relays, etc.). Based on the information it receives, the PCM generates output signals to control various relays, solenoids (fuel injectors) and other actuators. The PCM is specifically calibrated to optimize the emissions, fuel economy and driveability of the vehicle.

3   It isn't a good idea to attempt diagnosis or replacement of the PCM or emission control components at home while the vehicle is under warranty. Because of a federally-mandated warranty which covers the emissions system components and because any owner-induced damage to the PCM, the sensors and/or the control devices may void this warranty, take the vehicle to a dealer service department if the PCM or a system component malfunctions.

Scan tool information

Refer to illustrations 2.4a and 2.4b

4   Because extracting the Diagnostic Trouble Codes (DTCs) from an engine management system is now the first step in troubleshooting many computer-controlled systems and components, a code reader, at the very least, will be required (see illustration). More powerful scan tools can also perform many of the diagnostics once associated with expensive factory scan tools (see illustration). If you're planning to obtain a generic scan tool for your vehicle, make sure that it's compatible with OBD-II systems. If you don't plan to purchase a code reader or scan tool and don't have access to one, you can have the codes extracted by a dealer service department or an independent repair shop. **Note:** *Some auto parts stores even provide this service.*

3 Obtaining and clearing Diagnostic Trouble Codes (DTCs)

All models covered by this manual are equipped with on-board diagnostics. When the PCM recognizes a malfunction in a monitored emission or engine control system, component or circuit, it turns on the Malfunction Indicator Light (MIL) on the dash. The PCM will continue to display the MIL until the problem is fixed and the Diagnostic Trouble Code (DTC) is cleared from the PCM's memory. You'll need a scan tool to access any DTCs stored in the PCM.

Before outputting any DTCs stored in the PCM, thoroughly inspect ALL electrical connectors and hoses. Make sure that all electrical connections are tight, clean and free of corrosion. And make sure that all hoses are correctly connected, fit tightly and are in good condition (no cracks or tears).

Accessing the DTCs

Refer to illustration 3.1

1   The Diagnostic Trouble Codes (DTCs) can only be accessed with a code reader or scan tool. Professional scan tools are expensive, but relatively inexpensive generic code readers or scan tools (see illustrations 2.4a and 2.4b) are available at most auto parts stores. Simply plug the connector of the scan tool into the diagnostic connector (see illustration). Then follow the instructions included with the scan tool to extract the DTCs.

2   Once you have outputted all of the stored DTCs, look them up on the accompanying DTC chart.

3   After troubleshooting the source of each DTC, make any necessary repairs or replace the defective component(s).

Clearing the DTCs

4   Clear the DTCs with the code reader or scan tool in accordance with the instructions provided by the tool's manufacturer.

Diagnostic Trouble Codes

5   The accompanying tables are a list of the Diagnostic Trouble Codes (DTCs) that can be accessed by a do-it-yourselfer working at home (there are many, many more DTCs available to professional mechanics with proprietary scan tools and software, but those codes cannot be accessed by a generic scan tool). If, after you have checked and repaired the connectors, wire harness and vacuum hoses (if applicable) for an emission-related system, component or circuit, the problem persists, have the vehicle checked by a dealer service department or other qualified repair shop.

OBD-II trouble codes

Code	Code identification
P0011	Intake valve timing control solenoid performance
P0021	Intake camshaft position timing - over-advanced (bank 2)
P0031	Upstream oxygen sensor heater control circuit low voltage signal (Bank 1)
P0032	Upstream oxygen sensor heater control circuit high voltage signal (Bank 1)
P0037	Downstream oxygen sensor heater control circuit low voltage signal (Bank 1)
P0038	Downstream oxygen sensor heater control circuit high voltage signal (Bank 1)
P0051	Upstream oxygen sensor heater control circuit low voltage signal (Bank 2)
P0052	Upstream oxygen sensor heater control circuit high voltage signal (Bank 2)
P0057	Downstream oxygen sensor heater control circuit low voltage signal (Bank 2)
P0058	Downstream oxygen sensor heater control circuit high voltage signal (Bank 2)
P0075	Intake valve timing control solenoid circuit (Bank 1)
P0081	Intake valve timing control solenoid circuit (Bank 2)
P0101	Mass Air Flow sensor circuit range or performance fault
P0102	Mass Air Flow sensor circuit low input
P0103	Mass Air Flow sensor circuit high input
P0112	Intake Air Temperature sensor circuit low input
P0113	Intake Air Temperature sensor circuit high input
P0117	Engine Coolant Temperature sensor circuit low input
P0116	Engine coolant temperature circuit range/performance problem
P0117	Engine coolant temperature circuit, low input
P0118	Engine Coolant Temperature sensor circuit high input
P0122	Throttle Position Sensor circuit low input
P0123	Throttle Position Sensor circuit high input
P0125	Engine Coolant Temperature sensor or circuit fault
P0127	Intake Air Temperature too high
P0128	Thermostat function - engine coolant does not reach correct temperature after warm-up
P0130	Upstream oxygen sensor or circuit fault (Bank 1)
P0131	Upstream oxygen sensor lean shift monitor fault (Bank 1)
P0132	Upstream oxygen sensor rich shift monitor fault (Bank 1)

Code	Code identification
P0133	O_2 sensor circuit, slow response (bank 1, sensor 1)
P0137	Downstream oxygen sensor minimum voltage monitor fault
P0138	Downstream oxygen sensor maximum voltage monitor fault
P0139	Downstream oxygen sensor circuit slow response fault
P014C	Oxygen sensor 1 problem
P014D	Oxygen sensor 1 problem
P0143	O_2 sensor circuit, low voltage (bank 1, sensor 3)
P0144	O_2 sensor circuit, high voltage (bank 1, sensor 3)
P0145	O_2 sensor circuit, slow response (bank 1, sensor 3)
P0146	O_2 sensor circuit - no activity detected (bank 1, sensor 3)
P0150	Upstream oxygen sensor or circuit fault (Bank 2)
P0151	Upstream oxygen sensor lean shift monitor fault (Bank 2)
P0152	Upstream oxygen sensor rich shift monitor fault (Bank 2)
P0153	Upstream oxygen sensor circuit slow response fault (Bank 2)
P0154	Upstream oxygen sensor circuit high voltage fault (Bank 2)
P0157	Downstream oxygen sensor minimum voltage monitor fault
P0158	Downstream oxygen sensor maximum voltage monitor fault
P0159	Downstream oxygen sensor circuit slow response fault
P0171	Fuel injection system lean (Bank 1)
P0172	Fuel injection system rich (Bank 1)
P0174	System too lean (bank 2)
P0175	System too rich (bank 2)
P0181	Fuel Tank Temperature sensor circuit range or performance
P0182	Fuel Tank Temperature sensor circuit low input
P0183	Fuel Tank Temperature sensor circuit high input
P0196	Fuel rail pressure sensor circuit, range or performance problem
P0197	Fuel rail pressure sensor circuit, low input
P0198	Fuel rail pressure sensor circuit, high input
P0222	Throttle Position Sensor circuit low input
P0223	Throttle Position Sensor circuit high input

OBD-II trouble codes (continued)

Code	Code identification
P0300	Multiple cylinder misfire detected
P0301	Cylinder no. 1 misfire detected
P0302	Cylinder no. 2 misfire detected
P0303	Cylinder no. 3 misfire detected
P0304	Cylinder no. 4 misfire detected
P0305	Cylinder no. 5 misfire detected
P0306	Cylinder no. 6 misfire detected
P0327	Knock Sensor circuit low input
P0328	Knock Sensor circuit high input
P0322	Crankshaft Position (CKP) sensor/engine speed (RPM) sensor - no signal
P0323	Crankshaft Position (CKP) sensor/engine speed (RPM) sensor - circuit intermittent
P0332	Knock sensor no. 2 circuit, low input (bank 2)
P0333	Knock sensor no. 2 circuit, high input (bank 2)
P0335	Crankshaft Position sensor (CKP) or circuit fault
P0340	Camshaft Position sensor or circuit fault (Bank 1)
P0345	Camshaft Position sensor or circuit fault (Bank 2)
P0420	Catalyst system defective (Bank 1)
P0430	Catalyst system defective (Bank 2)
P0441	EVAP control system incorrect purge flow
P0442	EVAP system small leak (negative pressure check)
P0443	EVAP canister purge control valve circuit fault
P0444	EVAP canister purge control valve circuit open
P0445	EVAP canister purge control valve circuit shorted
P0447	EVAP canister vent control valve circuit open
P0448	EVAP canister vent control valve remains closed under certain driving conditions
P0451	EVAP system pressure sensor or circuit fault
P0452	EVAP system pressure sensor low input voltage signal
P0453	EVAP system pressure sensor high input
P0455	EVAP system gross leak

Code	Code identification
P0456	EVAP system very small leak (negative pressure check)
P0460	Fuel level sensor or circuit fault
P0461	Fuel level sensor or circuit fault
P0462	Fuel level sensor circuit low input
P0463	Fuel level sensor circuit high input
P0500	Vehicle Speed Sensor or circuit fault
P0506	Idle Air Control system signal low
P0507	Idle Air Control system signal high
P0550	Power steering pressure sensor range
P0603	PCM back-up RAM does not function properly
P0605	PCM or EEPROM fault
P0607	Control module performance
P0643	PCM detects sensor power supply low or high voltage
P0850	Park/Neutral position switch circuit fault in Drive and Park
P1148	Closed loop control fault
P1168	Oxygen sensors or circuit, bank 2, closed-loop function not available
P1212	Traction control system communication line fault
P1217	Engine overheating
P1225	Closed throttle position learning value low
P1226	Closed throttle position learning performance fault
P1421	Cold start control system problem
P1550	Battery current sensor problem
P1551	Battery current sensor problem
P1552	Battery current sensor problem
P1553	Battery current sensor problem
P1554	Battery current sensor problem
P1564	ASCD steering switch problem
P1572	ASCD brake switch or circuit fault
P1574	ASCD speed sensor signal performance fault
P1700	Automatic transmission control system problem

OBD-II trouble codes (continued)

Code	Code identification
P1715	Input speed sensor problem
P1720	Vehicle speed sensor problem
P1800	VIAS control solenoid valve circuit performance fault
P1805	Brake switch or circuit fault
P2A00	Oxygen sensor 1
P2A03	Oxygen sensor 1
P2100	Throttle Control motor voltage signal is open or low voltage
P2103	Throttle Control motor relay voltage signal is shorted (ON)
P2101	Electric throttle control function problem
P2118	Throttle Control motor performance fault in circuit and/or throttle control motor
P2119	Throttle Control motor defective or stuck in position
P2122	Accelerator Pedal Position sensor 1 circuit low
P2123	Accelerator Pedal Position sensor 1 circuit high
P2127	Accelerator Pedal Position sensor 2 circuit low
P2128	Accelerator Pedal Position sensor 2 circuit high
P2135	Throttle Position Sensor circuit range or performance
P2138	Accelerator Pedal Position sensor or circuit range or performance

4.2 The Accelerator Pedal Position (APP) sensor is part of the pedal assembly

5.1 The Camshaft Position (CMP) sensors are located at the left end of each valve cover

4   Accelerator Pedal Position (APP) sensor - replacement

Refer to illustration 4.2

1   Disconnect the cable from the negative terminal of the battery (see Chapter 5).
2   Disconnect the wiring from the sensor/pedal assembly **(see illustration)**.
3   Remove the pedal fasteners and remove the pedal.
4   Installation is the reverse of removal.
5   Reconnect the battery and perform the necessary re-learn procedures (see Chapter 5).

5   Camshaft Position (CMP) sensor - replacement

Refer to illustration 5.1

1   There are two CMP sensors, located at the driver's end of each valve cover **(see illustration)**. If you're removing the sensor from the rear cylinder bank, remove the upper intake manifold (see Chapter 2B).
2   Disconnect the electrical connector from the sensor.
3   Remove the mounting bolt and pull the sensor out.
4   Installation is the reverse of removal.

6   Intake Valve Timing (IVT) control solenoid(s) - replacement

Refer to illustration 6.1

1   The IVT solenoids are installed in the IVT covers, which are on the upper part of the timing chain cover **(see illustration)**. These solenoid valves direct oil to the intake camshaft actuators in order to vary the timing of the intake camshafts. They receive commands from the PCM.

2   Disconnect the electrical connector from the solenoid.
3   Remove the mounting bolt from the IVT solenoid, then remove the solenoid from the cover.
4   Installation is the reverse of removal. Replace the O-ring with a new one.

7   Crankshaft Position (CKP) sensor - replacement

Refer to illustration 7.1

1   The CKP sensor is accessed from under the vehicle **(see illustration)**.
2   Raise the vehicle and support it securely on jackstands.
3   Remove the under-vehicle splash shield.
4   Remove the sensor mounting bolt, then remove the sensor.
5   Installation is the reverse of removal.

6.1 There are two intake valve timing control solenoids installed in the timing chain cover at the passenger's side of the engine - this view is from beneath

7.1 The Crankshaft Position (CKP) sensor is mounted in the oil pan on the front side of the engine, near the transaxle - this view is from under the vehicle

8.1 The Engine Coolant Temperature (ECT) sensor is located in the water outlet at the left (driver's side) end of the engine

8   Engine Coolant Temperature (ECT) sensor - replacement

Refer to illustration 8.1

Warning: *Wait until the engine has completely cooled before beginning this procedure.*

1   The ECT sensor is mounted in the water outlet at the left end of the engine **(see illustration)**.

2   Remove the engine cover and the air intake duct (see Chapter 4).

3   Drain some engine coolant (see Chapter 1) to minimize coolant spillage.

4   Disconnect the electrical connector from the ECT sensor.

5   Unscrew the sensor from the engine and discard the sealing washer (a new one should be used).

6   Installation is the reverse of removal. Refill the cooling system (see Chapter 1).

9   Mass Air Flow/Intake Air Temperature (MAF/IAT) sensor - replacement

Refer to illustration 9.1

1   The MAF/IAT sensor is mounted on the air filter housing **(see illustration)**.

2   Disconnect the electrical connector from the MAF/IAT sensor.

3   Remove the screws and remove the sensor from the air filter housing.

4   Installation is the reverse of removal.

10   Knock sensor - replacement

1   The knock sensor(s) is/are mounted in the engine valley between the cylinder heads (2007 and earlier models have one sensor, 2009 and later models have two).

9.1 The Mass Air Flow/Intake Air Temperature (MAF/IAT) sensor is installed in the air filter housing cover

2   Remove the upper intake manifold (see Chapter 2A).

3   Disconnect the knock sensor electrical connector.

4   Remove the sensor mounting bolt, then remove the sensor.

5   Installation is the reverse of removal. Tighten the mounting bolt to 16 ft-lbs.

11   Oxygen sensors - replacement

Note: *Because it is installed in the exhaust system, which contracts when cool, an oxygen sensor can be very difficult to loosen when the engine is cold. Rather than risking damage to the sensor or its mounting threads, run the engine for a minute or two, then shut it off. Be careful to avoid burns during this procedure.*

1   Be very careful when servicing an oxygen sensor:

11.2a Upstream oxygen sensor on the front cylinder bank

a) *The oxygen sensor has a permanently attached pigtail and electrical connector which should not be removed from the sensor. Damage or removal of the pigtail or electrical connector can adversely affect operation of the sensor.*

b) *Grease, dirt and other contaminants should be kept away from the electrical connector and the louvered end of the sensor.*

c) *Do not use cleaning solvents of any kind on the oxygen sensor.*

d) *Do not drop or roughly handle the sensor.*

e) *The silicone boot must be installed in the correct position to prevent the boot from being melted and to allow the sensor to operate properly.*

Replacement

Upstream oxygen sensors

Refer to illustration 11.2a and 11.2b

2   Locate the upstream oxygen sensor electrical connector and disconnect it **(see illustrations)**. Detach the sensor wiring harness from any clips.

3   Unscrew the sensor with an oxygen sensor socket if one is available. You may have to raise the vehicle and support it securely on jackstands to reach it.

4   If you're going to install the old sensor, apply anti-seize compound to the threads to ease future removal. If you're installing a new sensor, the threads will already have anti-seize on them.

5   Installation is the reverse of removal. Tighten the sensor securely.

Downstream oxygen sensors

Refer to illustration 11.7

6   Raise the vehicle and support it securely on jackstands. The downstream oxygen sensors are accessible only from underneath.

7   Disconnect the wiring harness from the pigtail of the sensor **(see illustration)**.

8   Unscrew the sensor, using an oxygen sensor socket if one is available.

11.2b Upstream oxygen sensor for the rear cylinder bank

11.7 Typical downstream oxygen sensor (A), installed in the exhaust pipe after the catalytic converter, and its electrical connector (B)

12.1 Transmission Range (TR) switch details

1	Manual lever nut	3	Electrical connector
2	Shift cable nut		

9   If you're going to install the old sensor, apply anti-seize compound to the threads to ease future removal. If you're installing a new sensor, the threads will already have anti-seize on them.

10   Installation is the reverse of removal. Tighten the sensor securely.

12   Transmission range switch - replacement and adjustment

Replacement

Refer to illustration 12.1

1   The transmission range switch is mounted on top of the automatic transaxle **(see illustration)**.

2   Remove the air filter housing and the air ducts (see Chapter 4). Remove the nut, then remove the manual lever from the range switch assembly.

3   Disconnect the electrical connector from the switch.

4   Remove the mounting bolts and remove the range switch.

5   Installation is the reverse of removal. Align the range switch to its original position.

6   Verify that the engine will start only in Park or Neutral. Verify that the back-up lights come on only in Reverse. Adjust the range switch as necessary to ensure that these conditions are met.

Adjustment

7   Set the parking brake.

8   Loosen the nut on the end of the shift cable.

9   Make sure the shift lever inside the vehicle and the manual lever on the transaxle are in Park.

10   Tighten the nut while making sure the manual lever stays in Park.

11   Check for proper operation (see Step 6).

13   Transmission speed sensors - replacement

Refer to illustrations 13.1a and 13.1b

1   The transmission speed sensors are mounted on top of the transaxle **(see illustrations)**. The primary speed sensor senses the speed of the primary pulley and the secondary speed sensor senses the speed of the output shaft.

2   Disconnect the electrical connector from the sensor.

3   Remove the mounting bolt and remove the sensor. Discard the O-ring.

4   Apply some transmission fluid to the new O-ring and install it on the sensor.

5   Installation is the reverse of removal.

13.1a Location of the primary transmission speed sensor

13.1b Location of the secondary transmission speed sensor

16.1a Location of the EVAP purge control solenoid valve

16.1b Schematic of the EVAP system

14   Powertrain Control Module (PCM) - replacement

The Powertrain Control Module (PCM) cannot be replaced at home because the new unit must be programmed with the Vehicle Identification Number (VIN) and other data. Doing so is impossible without a factory scan tool. Do not disconnect or remove the PCM.

15   Catalytic converter - replacement

Because the catalytic converters are part of the exhaust system, converter replacement requires replacement of the exhaust manifold (see Chapter 2A) or front exhaust pipe assembly (an expensive part), or cutting out and welding in a new converter (take the vehicle to a dealer service department or a muffler shop if you lack the necessary skill and equipment to do this).

16   Evaporative Emissions Control (EVAP) system - component replacement

EVAP purge control solenoid valve

Refer to illustration 16.1a and 16.1b

1   The solenoid valve is mounted at the top of the engine **(see illustration)**. Detach the two hoses from the solenoid valve.
2   Disconnect the electrical connector from the solenoid valve.
3   Remove the mounting bolts, then remove the valve.
4   Installation is the reverse of removal.

EVAP canister

Refer to illustration 16.6

5   Raise the vehicle and support it securely on jackstands.
6   Remove the mounting nut, then detach the canister **(see illustration)**.

16.6 EVAP canister mounting fastener

7   Disconnect the hoses from the canister.
8   Remove the EVAP control system pressure sensor from the canister by pulling it out. Replace the O-ring before replacing the sensor.
9   Remove the EVAP canister vent control valve by twisting it counterclockwise. Replace the O-ring before replacing the valve.
10   Installation is the reverse of removal.

17   Positive Crankcase Ventilation (PCV) valve - replacement

Refer to Chapter 1, Section 28 for information on the PCV system.

18   Variable Induction Air System (VIAS) solenoid valves and actuators - replacement

Refer to illustration 18.1

1   This system consists of two solenoid valves which control vacuum to the power valve actuators **(see illustration)**. The actuators move internal components of the intake manifold to change the lengths of the inlet passages for improved performance. The control solenoids are controlled electrically by the PCM.
2   The control solenoids are mounted at the front of the intake manifold. There is one actuator at each end of the upper intake manifold.

Vacuum solenoid valves

3   Disconnect the electrical connector from the solenoid valve.
4   Disconnect the vacuum hoses from the valve.
5   Remove the mounting bolts and remove the control solenoid valve.
6   Installation is the reverse of removal.

Actuators

7   Disconnect the vacuum hose from the actuator.
8   Remove the mounting bolts and remove the actuator. Discard the gasket.
9   Installation is the reverse of removal. Replace the gasket with a new one.

19 Throttle Position (TP) sensor - replacement

The Throttle Position sensor on these vehicles is an integral part of the throttle body and is not serviceable separately. Refer to Chapter 4 for the throttle body replacement procedure.

18.1 The power valve solenoids and actuators are mounted on top of the engine

1   *Power valve actuator No. 1*
2   *Power valve actuator No. 2*
3   *VIAS control solenoid No. 1*
4   *VIAS control solenoid No. 2*

Notes

Chapter 7
Automatic transaxle

Contents

Specifications

Torque specifications

	Ft-lbs
Driveplate-to-torque converter bolts	38
Transaxle mounting bolts	
Four lower bolts	37
Five upper bolts	55

1 General information

All models covered by this manual are equipped with a CVT (continuously variable transmission) automatic transaxle.

Because of the complexity of the automatic transaxle and the specialized equipment needed to service it, this Chapter contains only those procedures related to general diagnosis, routine maintenance, adjustment, and removal and installation.

If the transaxle requires major repair work, it should be taken to a dealer service department or an automotive or transmission repair shop. You can, however, save money by removing and installing the transaxle yourself, even if the repair work is done by a shop.

2 Diagnosis - general

Note: *Automatic transaxle malfunctions may be caused by five general conditions: poor engine performance, improper adjustments,* hydraulic malfunctions, mechanical malfunctions or malfunctions in the computer or its signal network. Diagnosis of these problems should always begin with a check of the easily repaired items: fluid level and condition (see Chapter 1) and shift cable adjustment. Next, perform a road test to determine if the problem has been corrected or if more diagnosis is necessary. If the problem persists after the preliminary tests and corrections are completed, additional diagnosis should be done by a dealer service department or transmission repair shop. Refer to the "Troubleshooting" Section at the front of this manual for information on symptoms of transaxle problems.

Preliminary checks

1 Drive the vehicle to warm the transaxle to normal operating temperature.

2 Check the fluid level as described in Chapter 1:

a) If the fluid level is unusually low, add enough fluid to bring the level within the designated area of the dipstick, then check for external leaks (see below).

b) If the fluid level is abnormally high, drain off the excess, then check the drained fluid for contamination by coolant. The presence of engine coolant in the automatic transmission fluid indicates that a failure has occurred in the internal radiator walls that separate the coolant from the transmission fluid (see Chapter 3).

c) If the fluid is foaming, drain it and refill the transaxle, then check for coolant in the fluid, or a high fluid level.

3 Check for the presence of any stored diagnostic trouble codes (see Chapter 6). There are many potential transaxle-specific trouble codes that could be set, but certain engine-related problems can also affect transaxle operation.

4 Inspect the shift cable (see Section 4). Make sure that it's properly adjusted and operates smoothly.

Fluid leak diagnosis

5 Most fluid leaks are easy to locate visually. Repair usually consists of replacing a seal or gasket. If a leak is difficult to find, the

following procedure may help.

6   Identify the fluid. Make sure it's transmission fluid and not engine oil or brake fluid (automatic transmission fluid is a deep red color).

7   Try to pinpoint the source of the leak. Drive the vehicle several miles, then park it over a large sheet of cardboard. After a minute or two, you should be able to locate the leak by determining the source of the fluid dripping onto the cardboard.

8   Make a careful visual inspection of the suspected component and the area immediately around it. Pay particular attention to gasket mating surfaces. A mirror is often helpful for finding leaks in areas that are hard to see.

9   If the leak still cannot be found, clean the suspected area thoroughly with a degreaser or solvent, then dry it.

10   Drive the vehicle for several miles at normal operating temperature and varying speeds. After driving the vehicle, visually inspect the suspected component again.

11   Once the leak has been located, the

3.3 Pull out this clip to detach the cable from the shifter bracket

cause must be determined before it can be properly repaired. If a gasket is replaced but the sealing flange is bent, the new gasket will not stop the leak. The bent flange must be straightened.

12   Before attempting to repair a leak, check to make sure that the following conditions are corrected or they may cause another leak. **Note:** *Some of the following conditions cannot be fixed without highly specialized tools and expertise. Such problems must be referred to a transmission shop or a dealer service department.*

Gasket leaks

13   Check the pan periodically. Make sure the bolts are tight, no bolts are missing, the gasket is in good condition and the pan is flat (dents in the pan may indicate damage to the valve body inside).

14   If the pan gasket is leaking, the fluid level or the fluid pressure may be too high, the vent may be plugged, the pan bolts may be too tight, the pan sealing flange may be warped, the sealing surface of the transaxle housing may be damaged, the gasket may be damaged or the transaxle casting may be cracked or porous. If sealant instead of gasket material has been used to form a seal between the pan and the transaxle housing, it may be the wrong sealant.

Seal leaks

15   If a transaxle seal is leaking, the fluid level or pressure may be too high, the vent may be plugged, the seal bore may be damaged, the seal itself may be damaged or improperly installed, the surface of the shaft protruding through the seal may be damaged or a loose bearing may be causing excessive shaft movement.

16   Make sure the dipstick tube seal is in good condition and the tube is properly seated. Periodically check the area around the speedometer gear or sensor for leak-

age. If transmission fluid is evident, check the O-ring for damage.

Case leaks

17   If the case itself appears to be leaking, the casting is porous and will have to be repaired or replaced.

18   Make sure the oil cooler hose fittings are tight and in good condition.

Fluid comes out vent pipe or fill tube

19   If this condition occurs, the transaxle is overfilled, there is coolant in the fluid, the case is porous, the dipstick is incorrect, the vent is plugged or the drain-back holes are plugged.

---

3   Shifter assembly - removal and installation

Refer to illustrations 3.3, 3.5a and 3.5b

Warning: *The models covered by this manual are equipped with Supplemental Restraint Systems (SRS), more commonly known as airbags. Always disable the airbag system before working in the vicinity of any airbag system components to avoid the possibility of accidental deployment of the airbags, which could cause personal injury (see Chapter 12).*

1   Remove the center console (see Chapter 11).

2   Shift into Park, then remove the nut from the end of the cable. Lift the cable end from the stud.

3   Pull out the retaining clip and remove the cable from the shifter **(see illustration)**.

4   Disconnect the wiring harness from the shifter using a flat-blade screwdriver.

5   Remove the shifter assembly mounting nuts, then remove the shifter **(see illustrations)**.

6   Slide a flat-blade screwdriver under the

3.5a Shift cable details at the shifter

A   Cable end retaining nut
B   Cable-to-bracket clip
C   Front mounting bolts

D   Serration on cable end (must face up)

3.5b Shifter mounting nuts (A) and shift lock wiring harness connector (B)

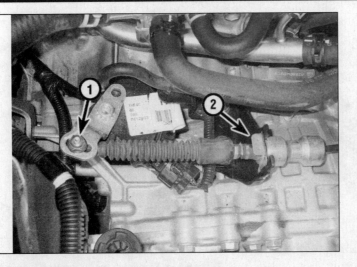

4.3 Shift cable details at the transaxle

1   *Cable-to-manual lever locknut*
2   *Cable retaining clip*

shift lock wiring connector to detach it from the shifter. Remove the shift lock unit from the bottom of the shifter.

7   Installation is the reverse of removal. Adjust the shift cable (see Section 4).

4   Shift cable - adjustment and replacement

Adjustment

Refer to illustration 4.3

1   Remove the air filter housing (see Chapter 4).
2   Place the shift lever in the "P" position.
3   Loosen the shift cable-to-manual lever locknut **(see illustration)** and place the transaxle manual shift lever fully in the Park position.
4   Holding the manual lever in position, tighten the locknut.
5   Move the shift lever from "P" to "1." Make sure that it moves smoothly.

Replacement

Warning: *The models covered by this manual are equipped with Supplemental Restraint Systems (SRS), more commonly known as airbags. Always disable the airbag system before working in the vicinity of any airbag system components to avoid the possibility of accidental deployment of the airbags, which could cause personal injury (see Chapter 12).*

6   Place the shifter in Park.
7   Remove the air intake duct and the air filter housing (see Chapter 4).
8   Remove the battery and the battery bracket (see Chapter 5).
9   Remove the cable-to-manual lever locknut **(see illustration 4.3)**.
10   Remove the cable retaining clip and detach the cable from the transaxle bracket.
11   Remove the center console (see Chapter 11).
12   Detach the cable end from the shifter (see Section 3).
13   Remove the right front lower heater air duct, then remove the cable from the vehicle.
14   Installation is the reverse of removal.

Make sure that the cable is snapped securely onto the console-mounted shifter and that the ribbed surface of the cable end is up. Be sure to adjust the cable.

5   Driveaxle oil seal - replacement

Refer to illustrations 5.5 and 5.6

1   Oil leaks can occur as a result of worn seals or O-rings. Replacement of these seals or O-rings is relatively easy, since the repairs can usually be performed without removing the transaxle from the vehicle.
2   The driveaxle oil seals are located on the sides of the transaxle or transfer case, where the inner ends of the driveaxles are splined into the differential side gears. If you suspect that a driveaxle oil seal is leaking, raise the vehicle and support it securely on jackstands. If the seal is leaking, you'll see lubricant on the side of the transaxle or transfer case, below the seal.
3   AWD models have an additional seal between the transfer case and the transaxle. If there is lubricant leaking from this seal, the transfer case must be removed in order to replace it. See Chapter 8 for more information.
4   Remove the driveaxle (see Chapter 8).
5   Using a screwdriver or seal removal tool, carefully pry the seal out of the transaxle bore **(see illustration)**.
6   Using a seal driver or a large deep socket as a drift, install the new oil seal. Drive it into the bore squarely and make sure it's properly seated **(see illustration)**. **Note:** *Lubricate the lip of the new seal with multi-purpose grease.*
7   Install the driveaxle (or driveaxle and extension shaft). Be careful not to damage the lip(s) of the new seal(s). Check the transaxle lubricant level and add some, if necessary, to bring it up to the required level (see Chapter 1).

5.5 Use care to avoid scratching the housing when prying out the driveaxle oil seals

5.6 Drive the new driveaxle oil seal in until it's flush

6.2 Mark the position of the torque converter to the driveplate, then remove the torque converter bolts by turning the crankshaft to bring each bolt into the opening

6.13a Transaxle mounting bolt length chart - 2007 and earlier models

| 1 | 2.05 inches | 3 | 4.13 inches |
| 2 | 1.42 inches | 4 | 1.38 inches |

6.13b Transaxle mounting bolt length chart

1	2.17 inches
2	1.54 inches
3	4.25 inches
4	1.77 inches

6   Automatic transaxle - removal and installation

Removal

Refer to illustration 6.2

1   Remove the engine and transaxle assembly from the vehicle (see Chapter 2B).

2   Paint match marks on the torque converter and driveplate so they can be assembled in the same position **(see illustration)**. Remove the torque converter bolts.

3   Disconnect the wiring from the transaxle components and remove the wiring harness.

4   Remove the dipstick tube. Detach the transaxle mounts from the subframe.

5   Remove the engine-to-transaxle bolts. Keep them organized so they can be installed in the same positions.

6   Separate the transaxle from the engine and slide it away, then remove the transaxle cooler hose. Remove the torque converter and seal the open end to prevent contamination.

Installation

Refer to illustrations 6.13a and 6.13b

7   Flush the transaxle cooler and the cooler hoses and lines with solvent whenever the transaxle is removed from the vehicle. Flush the lines and fluid cooler thoroughly and make sure no solvent remains in the lines or cooler after flushing. It's a good idea to repeat the flushing procedure with clean automatic transmission fluid to ensure that no solvent remains in the lines or cooler.

8   Prior to installation, make sure that the torque converter hub is securely engaged in the pump. The front face of the torque converter must be at least 1/2-inch behind the front edge of the transaxle housing to be fully seated.

9   Maneuver the transaxle to the rear of the engine.

10   Turn the torque converter to line it up with the driveplate. The marks you made on the torque converter and the driveplate must line up.

11   Move the transaxle forward carefully until the dowel pins and the torque converter are engaged.

12   Install the transaxle mounting bolts. Make sure the bolts are installed in the proper locations. **Caution:** *Don't use the bolts to force the transaxle and engine together. If the transaxle doesn't slide easily up against the engine, find out why before you tighten the bolts.*

13   Install the transaxle-to-engine bolts in their proper locations (they're different lengths) **(see illustrations)**. Tighten the bolts to the torque values listed in this Chapter's Specifications.

14   Install the torque converter bolts and tighten them to the Specifications listed in this Chapter.

15   The remainder of installation is the reverse of removal.

16   Refill the transaxle with fluid to the specified level (see Chapter 1). Note that the transaxle may require more fluid than in a normal fluid and filter change, since the torque converter may be empty (the converter is not drained during a fluid change).

17   Start the engine, set the parking brake and shift the transaxle through all gears three times. Make sure the shift cable is working properly (see Section 4).

18   Allow the engine to reach its proper operating temperature with the transaxle in Park or Neutral, then turn it off and check the fluid level.

19   Road test the vehicle and check for fluid leaks.

Chapter 8
Driveline

Contents

Specifications

Driveaxles

Driveaxle boot length

Front driveaxles
- 2003 models
  - Outer joint .... 4.84 inches
  - Inner joint .... 3.80 inches
- 2004 models
  - Outer joint .... 5.05 inches
  - Inner joint .... 4.02 inches
- 2005 models
  - Outer joint .... 4.75 inches
  - Inner joint .... 6.75 inches
- 2006 and 2007 models
  - Outer joint .... 6.70 inches
  - Inner joint
    - 2WD models .... 6.78 inches
    - AWD models .... 6.75 inches
- 2009 and later models
  - 2WD models
    - Outer joint .... 6.25 inches
    - Inner joint .... 6.45 inches
  - AWD models
    - Outer joint .... 6.25 inches
    - Inner joint
      - Left side .... 6.45 inches
      - Right side .... 6.28 inches

Rear driveaxles
- 2007 and earlier models
  - Outer joint .... 2.67 inches
  - Inner joint .... 3.13 inches
- 2009 and later models
  - Outer joint .... 3.59 inches
  - Inner joint .... 5.00 inches

Torque specifications

Ft-lbs

Note: *One foot-pound (ft-lb) of torque is equivalent to 12 inch-pounds (in-lbs) of torque. Torque values below approximately 15 ft-lbs are expressed in inch-pounds, since most foot-pound torque wrenches are not accurate at these smaller values.*

Driveaxle/hub nut	
2007 and earlier models..	92
2009 and later models...	129
Driveaxle (right front) support bearing retainer bolts	132 in-lbs
Driveaxle (right front) support bearing bracket-to-engine block bolts......	22
Driveshaft flange nuts and bolts	
Models built up to 9/30/07	44
Models built after 10/1/07	37
Driveshaft center support bearing mounting nuts....................................	33
Rear differential	
Differential-to-mounting bracket bolts/nuts...	53
Mounting bracket-to-subframe bolts/nuts	
2006 and earlier models	46
2007 models	
17 mm nut	46
18 mm nut	54
2009 and later models..	54
Differential-to-subframe rear mounting nut	57
Transfer case-to-bracket bolts..	26
Transfer case-to-transaxle bolts	
2006 and earlier models..	25
2007 models	
14 mm bolt head	25
15 mm bolt head	32
2009 and later models..	32

1 General information

The information in this Chapter deals with the components from the rear of the engine to the front wheels, except for the transaxle, which is dealt with in Chapter 7.

Since nearly all the procedures covered in this Chapter involve working under the vehicle, make sure it's securely supported on sturdy jackstands or a hoist where the vehicle can be easily raised and lowered.

2 Driveaxles - general information

1   Power is transmitted from the transaxle (and rear differential on AWD models) to the wheels through a pair of driveaxles. The inner end of each driveaxle is splined into the differential side gears. The outer ends of the driveaxles are splined to the axle hubs and locked in place by a large nut.

2   The inner ends of the driveaxles are equipped with tripod-type constant velocity joints which are capable of both angular and axial motion.

3   The outer CV joints are the ball and cage type.

4   The boots should be inspected periodically for damage and leaking lubricant. Torn CV joint boots must be replaced as soon as possible or the joints can be damaged. Boot replacement involves removal of the driveaxle (see Section 3). The most common symptom of worn or damaged CV joints, besides lubricant leaks, is a clicking noise in turns, a clunk when accelerating after coasting and vibration at highway speeds. To check for wear in the CV joints and driveaxle shafts, grasp each axle (one at a time) and rotate it in both directions while holding the CV joint housings, feeling for play indicating worn splines or sloppy CV joints.

3 Driveaxles - removal and installation

Front driveaxles

Removal

Refer to illustrations 3.2, 3.9 and 3.10

1   Loosen the front wheel lug nuts, raise the vehicle and support it securely on jackstands. Remove the wheel.

2   Remove the cotter pin and remove the driveaxle/hub nut **(see illustration)**.

3   Remove the wheel speed sensor from the steering knuckle.

4   Disconnect the brake hose from the suspension strut.

5   Remove the brake caliper and the disc (see Chapter 9). Hang the caliper out of the way on a length of wire; don't let it hang by the hose.

6   Remove the lower strut mounting bolts and disconnect the strut from the steering knuckle.

7   Push the driveaxle out of the hub. If the driveaxle splines are frozen, free them by tapping the end of the driveaxle with a soft-faced hammer or a hammer and a brass punch, or use a puller to push the driveaxle from the hub.

8   Remove the under-vehicle splash shield. Place a drain pan underneath the transaxle to catch the lubricant that may spill out when the driveaxles are removed.

9   If you're removing the left driveaxle, carefully pry the inner CV joint out of the transaxle **(see illustration)**.

10   If you're working on the right driveaxle of a 2WD vehicle, remove the bearing housing mounting bolts, then remove the driveaxle from the transaxle **(see illustration)**. Do not try to separate the bearing from the inner CV joint until you have the entire assembly on the bench (see Section 4).

11   On AWD models, remove the right driveaxle from the link shaft. **Note:** *It may be necessary to use a slide hammer to detach the driveaxle from the link shaft.* Do not try to separate the bearing from the inner CV joint until you have the entire assembly on the bench (see Section 4).

12   Install a new driveaxle oil seal in the transaxle or transfer case (see Chapter 7).

Installation

13   Installation is the reverse of removal, noting the following points:

a) *When installing the left driveaxle, push the driveaxle in sharply to seat the retaining ring on the inner CV joint in its groove in the differential side gear. To ease insertion and seating of the retaining ring, position the gap in the ring at the bottom.*

b) *When installing the right driveaxle, tighten the retainer bolts to the torque listed in this Chapter's Specifications.*

c) *Tighten the strut-to-steering knuckle fasteners to the torque listed in the Chapter 10 Specifications.*

d) *Tighten the driveaxle/hub nut to the torque listed in this Chapter's Specifications, then install a new cotter pin.*

e) *Tighten the brake caliper mounting bolts to the torque listed in the Chapter 9 Specifications.*

f) *Install the wheel and lug nuts, lower the vehicle and tighten the lug nuts to the torque listed in the Chapter 1 Specifications.*

g) *Check the transaxle lubricant and add, if necessary, to bring it to the proper level (see Chapter 1).*

3.2 Place a prybar between two wheel studs while you loosen the driveaxle nut

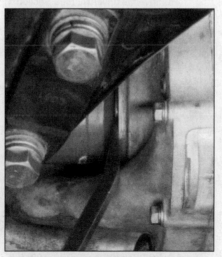

3.9 If you're removing the left driveaxle, carefully pry the inner CV joint out of the transaxle

3.10 Remove these bolts to take off the inner bearing retainer of the right driveaxle

4.2a Pry up the retaining tabs on the boot clamps . . .

4.2b . . . then open the clamps and remove them from the boot

4.3 Pull the boot back, then pry the retaining ring from its groove

Rear driveaxles (AWD models)

14   Loosen the rear wheel lug nuts, raise the vehicle and support it securely on jackstands. Remove the wheel.

15   Remove the cotter pin from the rear driveaxle/hub nut, then use a breaker bar and socket to remove the nut **(see illustration 3.2)**.

16   Remove the rear wheel speed sensor.

17   Remove the brake caliper and the disc (see Chapter 9). Hang the caliper out of the way on a length of wire; don't let it hang by the hose.

18   Push the driveaxle out of the hub. If the driveaxle splines are frozen, free them by tapping the end of the driveaxle with a soft-faced hammer or a hammer and a brass punch, or use a puller to push the driveaxle from the hub.

19   Remove the rear wheel hub and bearing assembly.

20   Pry the driveaxle from the rear differential, then remove the driveaxle from the vehicle.

21   Installation is the reverse of removal. Take care to avoid damaging the differential oil seal. Tighten the driveaxle/hub nut to the torque value listed in this Chapter's Specifications. Tighten the hub and bearing assembly to the torque listed in the Chapter 10 Specifications. Tighten the caliper mounting bolts to the torque listed in the Chapter 9 Specifications. Tighten the wheel lug nuts to the torque listed in the Chapter 1 Specifications.

---

4   Driveaxle boot - replacement

Note: *If the CV joints must be overhauled (usually due to torn boots), explore all options before beginning the job. Complete rebuilt driveaxles are available on an exchange basis, which eliminates much time and work. Whichever route you choose to take, check on the cost and availability of parts before disassembling the vehicle.*

Inner CV joint
Disassembly

Refer to illustrations 4.2a, 4.2b, 4.3, 4.4, 4.5 and 4.6

1   Remove the driveaxle (see Section 3).

2   Remove the boot clamps **(see illustrations)**.

3   Pull the boot back from the inner CV joint, remove the retaining ring, then slide off the joint housing **(see illustration)**.

4   Use a center punch to mark the tripod and axleshaft to ensure that they are reassembled properly **(see illustration)**.

5   Remove the snap-ring from the end of the axleshaft with a pair of snap-ring pliers **(see illustration)**.

6   Use a hammer and a brass punch to drive the tripod joint from the driveaxle **(see illustration)**. Some driveaxles are equipped with a rubber dynamic balancer that is retained by clamps. If it is necessary to remove the balancer, be sure to first mark the location of the balancer and clamps (or measure the distance from the end of the shaft to the balancer) so they can be reinstalled in the same location.

Check

7   Clean all components with solvent to remove the grease, and check for cracks, pitting, scoring and other signs of wear.

4.4 Use a center punch to place marks on the tripod and the driveaxle to ensure that they're properly reassembled

4.5 Remove the snap-ring from the groove in the end of the axleshaft

4.6 Drive the tripod joint from the axleshaft with a hammer and brass punch - make sure you don't damage the bearing surfaces or the splines on the shaft

Reassembly

Refer to illustrations 4.8a, 4.8b, 4.11a, 4.11b, 4.11c and 4.11d

8   Slide the clamps and boot onto the axle-shaft. It's a good idea to wrap the axleshaft splines with tape to prevent damaging the boot **(see illustration)**. Place the tripod on the shaft **(see illustration)** and install the snap-ring. Apply grease to the tripod assembly, the inside of the joint housing and the inside of the boot.

9   Install the housing on the joint, then install the retaining ring, making sure it seats in its groove in the housing.

10   Slide the boot into place, making sure both ends seat in their grooves.

11   Adjust the length of the joint **(see illustration)**, equalize the pressure in the boot **(see illustration)**, then tighten and secure the boot clamps **(see illustrations)**.

12   Install a new snap-ring on the inner CV joint stub axle.

13   Install the driveaxle (see Section 3).

Front outer CV joint

Refer to illustrations 4.15a through 4.15k

14   Remove the driveaxle (see Section 3), then remove the boot clamps **(see illustrations 4.2a and 4.2b)**.

15   Refer to the accompanying illustrations and perform the outer CV joint boot replacement procedure **(see illustrations)**.

4.8a Wrap the splined area of the axleshaft with tape to prevent damage to the boots when installing them

4.8b Install the tripod with the chamfered (tapered) ends of the splines facing toward the axleshaft

4.11a Adjust the joint to the length indicated in this Chapter's Specifications, making sure the boot isn't distorted

4.11b Equalize the pressure inside the boot by inserting a small, DULL screwdriver between the boot and the CV joint housing

4.11c To install the new clamps, bend the tang down . . .

4.11d . . . and tap the tabs down to hold it in place

4.15a Outer CV joints can be removed with a slide hammer; you'll need an adapter and a slide hammer setup such as the one shown here

4.15b With the axleshaft firmly clamped down in a bench vise and the adapter gripping the driveaxle/ hub nut, carefully extract the outer CV joint from the axleshaft. If it won't come off after five or six attempts, replace the driveaxle assembly

4.15c After the old grease has been rinsed away, move the inner race through its full range of motion and inspect the bearing surfaces for wear or damage

4.15d Apply CV joint grease through the splined hole, then insert a wooden dowel (slightly smaller in diameter than the hole) into the hole and push down - the dowel will force the grease into the joint. Repeat this until the joint is packed

4.15e Wrap the splined area of the axleshaft with tape to prevent damage to the boot when installing it

4.15f Install the small clamp and the boot on the driveaxle and apply grease to the inside of the axle boot . . .

4.15g . . . until the level is up to the end of the axle

4.15h Install a new snap-ring into the groove at the end of the driveaxle. Position the CV joint assembly on the driveaxle, aligning the splines . . .

4.15i . . . then use a hammer and brass punch to carefully drive the joint onto the driveaxle

72016-8-10.11a HAYNES

4.15j Seat the boot in its grooves and adjust the joint to the length listed in this Chapter's Specifications

4.15k Equalize the pressure inside the boot by inserting a small, dull screwdriver between the boot and the outer race, then tighten the clamps (see illustrations 4.11c and 4.11d)

Rear outer CV joint

16   Remove the driveaxle (see Section 3).

17   Clamp the main section of the driveaxle in a vise. **Note:** *Use soft inserts in the vise jaws to avoid damaging the driveaxle.*

18   Remove the boot clamp from the outer CV joint.

19   Use a slide hammer with an adapter to pull the CV joint from the end of the driveaxle **(see illustrations 4.15a and 4.15b)**. If the joint is stuck, you'll have to replace the entire axle assembly.

20   Remove the retaining ring from the axle shaft, slide the boot off, then clean all old grease from the CV joint.

21   Wrap tape around the shaft splines **(see illustration 4.15e)**, then slide the new boot on. Remove the tape.

22   Place a new retaining ring into the shaft groove.

23   Align the CV joint and the axle, then use a soft-face hammer to drive the two together. Verify that they are properly engaged.

24   Apply new CV joint grease into the boot, then clean grease from the boot sealing groove areas. Seat the boot on its sealing grooves.

25   Adjust the boot length by referring to the Specification in this Chapter **(see illustration 4.15j)**. Equalize the air pressure in the boot **(see illustration 4.15k)** and install the boot clamps.

26   Install the driveaxle assembly (see Section 3).

5   Driveshaft and universal joints (AWD models) - general information and inspection

General information

1   The driveshaft used on these vehicles is a pair of tubes that transmit power between the transfer case and the rear differential. There are universal joints at each end of the driveshaft and a constant velocity joint in the center, supported by a bearing.

2   The driveshaft assembly requires very little service. The universal joints are lubricated for life; if any part of the driveshaft develops a problem, the manufacturer states that the entire driveshaft must be replaced. Some driveline specialty shops are capable of rebuilding these assemblies, though. It's a good idea to call around to see if this is a viable option before purchasing a new driveshaft.

3   Since the driveshaft is a balanced unit, it's important that no undercoating or mud be allowed to stay on it. When the vehicle is raised for service, it's a good idea to clean the driveshaft and inspect it for obvious damage. Make sure that the small weights welded on to balance the driveshaft haven't been knocked off. Whenever it's removed, the driveshaft must be installed in the same position relative to the flanges on the transfer case and the differential in order to maintain the balance.

4   Problems with the driveshaft are usually indicated by a noise or vibration. A road test should verify if the problem is the driveshaft or another component. Refer to the *Troubleshooting* Section at the front of this manual.

Inspection

5   Raise the vehicle and support it securely on jackstands. Block the wheels at the opposite end to keep it from rolling off the stands. Release the parking brake and place the transaxle in Neutral.

6   Visually inspect the driveshaft as you turn it by hand. Look for dents and cracks. If any are found, replace the driveshaft.

7   Check for leakage at the front and rear. Oil leakage here means a defective transfer case or differential seal. Also check for looseness of the joints of the rear driveaxles. Grease leakage at the CV joint boots indicates a damaged rubber boot.

8   Rotate the driveshaft and make sure the universal joints are operating properly with no binding, noise or looseness. Listen for noise from the center bearing; this indicates wear or damage.

9   Grip each joint and try to twist it and wiggle it up and down. Any movement at all in the joint is a sign of considerable wear.

10   Check the driveshaft mounting bolts and nuts at each end to be sure they're tight. Finally, check the center bearing for looseness or rubber deterioration and be sure that the bearing bracket isn't bent.

6   Driveshaft (AWD models) - removal and installation

Refer to illustrations 6.3 and 6.5

1   Raise the rear of the vehicle and support it securely on jackstands. Block the front wheels to prevent the vehicle from rolling. **Note:** *If you're concerned about a possibly bent driveshaft causing a vibration, mount a dial indicator to the floor of the vehicle and check the driveshaft runout in the middle of the front and rear sections.*

2   Turn the key On, then shift the transaxle into Neutral. Turn the key Off. Release the parking brake.

3   Mark the relationship of the driveshaft flanges to the differential and transfer case flanges **(see illustration)**.

4   Loosen (but don't remove) the nuts of the center bearing brackets.

5   Remove the flange bolts from each end of the driveshaft **(see illustration)**. You'll have to insert a tool into the assembly to keep it from turning as you break the nuts and bolts loose.

6   Remove the center support bearing nuts and remove the driveshaft.

7   Remove the center bearing bracket from the driveshaft.

8   Installation is the reverse of removal. Attach the center bearing bracket so that the arrow on it is facing forward. Align the match marks you made previously as you attach each end of the driveshaft. Tighten the nuts and bolts to the torques listed in this Chapter's Specifications.

6.3 Mark the relationship of the driveshaft to the differential and transfer case flanges

6.5 Immobilize the driveshaft by placing a large screwdriver into the U-joint while loosening the bolts

7   Rear differential (AWD models) - removal and installation

1   Disconnect the driveshaft from the differential (see Section 6). Use wire to hang the rear of the driveshaft out of the way. **Note:** *Mark the flange alignment with paint before disconnecting the driveshaft.*
2   Remove the rear stabilizer bar (see Chapter 10).
3   Remove the EVAP canister (see Chapter 6).
4   Remove the rear driveaxles (see Section 3).
5   Note the routing of the wiring, then disconnect the wiring from the differential. Note the routing of the breather hoses, then detach them.
6   Place a floor jack under the differential and adjust it so it supports the weight of the differential.
7   Remove the differential mounting nut from the rear of the subframe.
8   Make sure that the jack is properly seated under the differential, then remove the differential mounting bracket-to-subframe nuts and bolts.
9   Carefully lower the differential with the jack until it can be slid from under the vehicle. Remove the vibration damper weights if necessary (2009 and later models).
10   Installation is the reverse of removal. Route the vent hoses and wiring as they were originally and align the driveshaft flange mark with the mark on the differential flange.
11   Tighten the mounting fasteners to the torques listed in this Chapter's Specifications. Check the lubricant level and add some if necessary (see Chapter 1).

8   Transfer case (AWD models) - removal and installation

2006 and earlier models
1   Remove the engine/transaxle assembly (see Chapter 2B).
2   Perform Steps 25, 26, 29 and 30 to remove the transfer case.

2007 and later models
Warning: *This is a complex and potentially dangerous procedure that requires working under the front of the vehicle with the suspension subframe partially unbolted from the vehicle and supported by floor jacks. So, before you decide whether to tackle this job yourself, read the following procedure carefully and decide whether this is something within the range of your skills.*
3   Remove the front wiper arms (see Chapter 12, Section 20), then remove the left and right cowl trim covers (see Chapter 11). Remove the wiper motor (see Chapter 12), then remove the cowl upper bracket (the metal base on which the wiper motor assembly is mounted).
4   Trace the electrical lead from the upstream oxygen sensor, which is screwed into the rear exhaust manifold, and disconnect the sensor electrical connector.
5   Remove the heat shield from the rear exhaust manifold/catalyst.
6   Loosen the front wheel lug nuts. Raise the vehicle and place it securely on jackstands. Remove the front wheels. Remove the engine under-cover and both inner fender splash shields.
7   Remove the left and right driveaxles (see Section 3). **Note:** *Instead of detaching the struts from the steering knuckle as described in Section 3, separate the control arms from the steering knuckle.*
8   Remove the driveshaft (see Section 6).
9   Remove the front exhaust pipe assembly **(see illustration 9.2 in Chapter 2A).**
10   Remove the heat shield from the front suspension crossmember.
11   Remove the catalyst support bracket bolts and remove the support bracket from the lower end of the rear catalyst.
12   Trace the electrical lead from the downstream oxygen sensor, which is screwed into the lower end of the rear catalyst, and disconnect the sensor electrical connector.
13   Remove the rear catalyst mounting fasteners and remove the rear catalyst from the rear exhaust manifold.
14   Remove the rear exhaust manifold fasteners and remove the rear exhaust manifold (see Chapter 2A). Remove and discard the old exhaust manifold gasket.
15   Disconnect the steering gear tie-rod ends from the steering knuckles. Detach all power steering gear lines and hoses from the subframe, then unbolt the steering gear assembly and hang it out of the way with wire (see Chapter 10). **Note:** *Do not disconnect the power steering lines from the steering gear.*
16   Support the transaxle with a floor jack. Place a piece of wood between the jack head and the transaxle to protect the aluminum housing. **Caution:** *Make sure that the jack doesn't contact the drain plug.* Place a piece of wood between the jack head and the subframe to protect the subframe from dents and scratches.
17   Support the subframe with a couple of floor jacks (one placed on each side, near the rear).
18   Remove the upper bolt from the front engine mounting bracket.
19   Remove the bolts from the left engine mounting bracket (transaxle side).
20   Remove the lower bolts from the rear engine mounting bracket.
21   Disconnect the electrical harness connectors located at and near the front and rear mounting brackets. Detach the clips for these harnesses and set the harnesses aside.
22   Disconnect the stabilizer bar links from the stabilizer bar (see Chapter 10).
23   Disconnect and remove the subframe support bracket bolts and remove the support brackets (the small brackets at the rear corners of the subframe). Loosen the subframe front mounting bolts a few turns (don't remove them), then remove the subframe rear mounting bolts.
24   Carefully lower the rear of the subframe enough to remove the transfer case.
25   Unbolt the support bearing bracket and remove the right driveaxle assembly (see Section 3).
26   Unbolt and remove the two transfer case support brackets.
27   Remove the transfer case mounting bolts from the transfer side.
28   Remove the power steering gear bracket from the rear engine mounting bracket.
29   Remove the upper bolts from the rear engine mounting bracket.
30   Move the rear engine mounting bracket aside and remove the transfer case mounting bolts from the transaxle side of the transfer unit.
31   Remove the transfer case.
32   Installation is the reverse of removal.

Chapter 9   Brakes

Contents

Specifications

General
Brake fluid type.. See Chapter 1

Disc brakes
Minimum pad thickness.. See Chapter 1
Brake disc minimum thickness*
    Front .... 1.024 inches
    Rear .... 0.551 inch
Maximum disc runout
    Front .... 0.0016 inch
    Rear .... 0.0020 inch
Maximum disc thickness variation..
*If different specifications are cast into the disc, they supersede information printed here

Brake booster
Pushrod length from booster canister to center of clevis hole
    2007 and earlier .... 4.92 inches
    2009 and later .... 5.00 inches

Brake pedal dimensions
Free height from steel floor to top of pedal
    2007 and earlier .... 7.85 to 8.25 inches
    2009 and later .... 7.76 to 8.15 inches

Parking brake
Parking brake adjustment clicks
    2007 and earlier .... 3 to 4 clicks
    2009 and later .... 5 to 6 clicks
Minimum lining thickness.. 0.059 inch

Brake light and cruise control cancel switches

Clearance between rubber bumper and threaded part of switch
  2007 and earlier .... 0.029 to 0.077 inch
  2009 and later .... 0.008 to 0.077 inch

Torque specifications   **Ft-lbs** (unless otherwise indicated)

Note: *One foot-pound (ft-lb) of torque is equivalent to 12 inch-pounds (in-lbs) of torque. Torque values below approximately 15 foot-pounds are expressed in inch-pounds, because most foot-pound torque wrenches are not accurate at these smaller values.*

Brake caliper
  Caliper mounting bolts
    Front 20
    Rear 32
  Caliper mounting bracket bolts
    Front 122
    Rear 62
  Brake hose-to-caliper banjo bolt .... 156 in-lbs
  Master cylinder-to-brake booster retaining nuts .... 120 in-lbs
  Power brake booster-to-body mounting nuts .... 120 to 132 in-lbs

1   General information

General

The vehicles covered by this manual are equipped with hydraulically operated front and rear brake systems. Both front and rear brakes are disc-type and are self-adjusting.

Hydraulic system

The hydraulic system consists of two separate circuits. The master cylinder has separate reservoirs for the two circuits, and, in the event of a leak or failure in one hydraulic circuit, the other circuit will remain operative and a warning indicator will light up on the instrument panel when a substantial amount of brake fluid is lost, showing that a failure has occurred.

Power brake booster

The power brake booster uses engine manifold vacuum to provide assistance to the brakes. It is mounted on the firewall in the engine compartment, directly behind the master cylinder.

Parking brake

Control cables are routed to the rear axle, where they operate small drum brake shoes that apply pressure to the inner diameter of the rear brake discs.

Service

After completing any operation involving disassembly of any part of the brake system, always test drive the vehicle to check for proper braking performance before resuming normal driving. When testing the brakes, perform the tests on a clean, dry, flat surface. Conditions other than these can lead to inaccurate test results.

Test the brakes at various speeds with both light and heavy pedal pressure. The vehicle should stop evenly without pulling to one side or the other. Under hard braking, the ABS system may engage, resulting in brake pedal pulsation. This is considered normal operation.

Tires, vehicle load and wheel alignment are factors which also affect braking performance.

Precautions

There are some general cautions and warnings involving the brake system on this vehicle:

a) *Use only brake fluid conforming to DOT 3 specifications.*

b) *The brake pads and linings contain fibers which are hazardous to your health if inhaled. Whenever you work on brake system components, clean all parts with brake system cleaner. Do not allow the fine dust to become airborne. Also, wear an approved filtering mask.*

c) *Safety should be paramount whenever any servicing of the brake components is performed. Do not use parts or fasteners which are not in perfect condition, and be sure that all clearances and torque specifications are adhered to. If you are at all unsure about a certain procedure, seek professional advice. Upon completion of any brake system work, test the brakes carefully in a controlled area before putting the vehicle into normal service. If a problem is suspected in the brake system, don't drive the vehicle until it's fixed.*

d) *Used brake fluid is considered a hazardous waste and it must be disposed of in accordance with federal, state and local laws. **DO NOT pour it down the sink, into septic tanks or storm drains, or on the ground.***

e) *Clean up any spilled brake fluid immediately and then wash the area with large amounts of water. This is especially true for any finished or painted surfaces.*

2 Troubleshooting

PROBABLE CAUSE	CORRECTIVE ACTION

No brakes - pedal travels to floor

1 Low fluid level 2 Air in system	1 and 2 Low fluid level and air in the system are symptoms of another problem - a leak somewhere in the hydraulic system. Locate and repair the leak
3 Defective seals in master cylinder	3 Replace master cylinder
4 Fluid overheated and vaporized due to heavy braking	4 Bleed hydraulic system (temporary fix). Replace brake fluid (proper fix)

Brake pedal slowly travels to floor under braking or at a stop

1 Defective seals in master cylinder	1 Replace master cylinder
2 Leak in a hose, line, caliper or wheel cylinder	2 Locate and repair leak
3 Air in hydraulic system	3 Bleed the system, inspect system for a leak

Brake pedal feels spongy when depressed

1 Air in hydraulic system	1 Bleed the system, inspect system for a leak
2 Master cylinder or power booster loose	2 Tighten fasteners
3 Brake fluid overheated (beginning to boil)	3 Bleed the system (temporary fix). Replace the brake fluid (proper fix)
4 Deteriorated brake hoses (ballooning under pressure)	4 Inspect hoses, replace as necessary (it's a good idea to replace all of them if one hose shows signs of deterioration)

Brake pedal feels hard when depressed and/or excessive effort required to stop vehicle

1 Power booster faulty	1 Replace booster
2 Engine not producing sufficient vacuum, or hose to booster clogged, collapsed or cracked	2 Check vacuum to booster with a vacuum gauge. Replace hose if cracked or clogged, repair engine if vacuum is extremely low
3 Brake linings contaminated by grease or brake fluid	3 Locate and repair source of contamination, replace brake pads or shoes
4 Brake linings glazed	4 Replace brake pads or shoes, check discs and drums for glazing, service as necessary
5 Caliper piston(s) or wheel cylinder(s) binding or frozen	5 Replace calipers or wheel cylinders
6 Brakes wet	6 Apply pedal to boil-off water (this should only be a momentary problem)
7 Kinked, clogged or internally split brake hose or line	7 Inspect lines and hoses, replace as necessary

Excessive brake pedal travel (but will pump up)

1 Drum brakes out of adjustment	1 Adjust brakes
2 Air in hydraulic system	2 Bleed system, inspect system for a leak

Excessive brake pedal travel (but will not pump up)

1 Master cylinder pushrod misadjusted	1 Adjust pushrod
2 Master cylinder seals defective	2 Replace master cylinder
3 Brake linings worn out	3 Inspect brakes, replace pads and/or shoes
4 Hydraulic system leak	4 Locate and repair leak

Brake pedal doesn't return

1 Brake pedal binding	1 Inspect pivot bushing and pushrod, repair or lubricate
2 Defective master cylinder	2 Replace master cylinder

Troubleshooting (continued)

PROBABLE CAUSE	CORRECTIVE ACTION

Brake pedal pulsates during brake application

PROBABLE CAUSE	CORRECTIVE ACTION
1 Brake drums out-of-round	1 Have drums machined by an automotive machine shop
2 Excessive brake disc runout or disc surfaces out-of-parallel	2 Have discs machined by an automotive machine shop
3 Loose or worn wheel bearings	3 Adjust or replace wheel bearings
4 Loose lug nuts	4 Tighten lug nuts

Brakes slow to release

PROBABLE CAUSE	CORRECTIVE ACTION
1 Malfunctioning power booster	1 Replace booster
2 Pedal linkage binding	2 Inspect pedal pivot bushing and pushrod, repair/lubricate
3 Malfunctioning proportioning valve	3 Replace proportioning valve
4 Sticking caliper or wheel cylinder	4 Repair or replace calipers or wheel cylinders
5 Kinked or internally split brake hose	5 Locate and replace faulty brake hose

Brakes grab (one or more wheels)

PROBABLE CAUSE	CORRECTIVE ACTION
1 Grease or brake fluid on brake lining	1 Locate and repair cause of contamination, replace lining
2 Brake lining glazed	2 Replace lining, deglaze disc or drum

Vehicle pulls to one side during braking

PROBABLE CAUSE	CORRECTIVE ACTION
1 Grease or brake fluid on brake lining	1 Locate and repair cause of contamination, replace lining
2 Brake lining glazed	2 Deglaze or replace lining, deglaze disc or drum
3 Restricted brake line or hose	3 Repair line or replace hose
4 Tire pressures incorrect	4 Adjust tire pressures
5 Caliper or wheel cylinder sticking	5 Repair or replace calipers or wheel cylinders
6 Wheels out of alignment	6 Have wheels aligned
7 Weak suspension spring	7 Replace springs
8 Weak or broken shock absorber	8 Replace shock absorbers

Brakes drag (indicated by sluggish engine performance or wheels being very hot after driving)

PROBABLE CAUSE	CORRECTIVE ACTION
1 Brake pedal pushrod incorrectly adjusted	1 Adjust pushrod
2 Master cylinder pushrod (between booster and master cylinder) incorrectly adjusted	2 Adjust pushrod
3 Obstructed compensating port in master cylinder	3 Replace master cylinder
4 Master cylinder piston seized in bore	4 Replace master cylinder
5 Contaminated fluid causing swollen seals throughout system	5 Flush system, replace all hydraulic components
6 Clogged brake lines or internally split brake hose(s)	6 Flush hydraulic system, replace defective hose(s)
7 Sticking caliper(s) or wheel cylinder(s)	7 Replace calipers or wheel cylinders
8 Parking brake not releasing	8 Inspect parking brake linkage and parking brake mechanism, repair as required
9 Improper shoe-to-drum clearance	9 Adjust brake shoes
10 Faulty proportioning valve	10 Replace proportioning valve

PROBABLE CAUSE

CORRECTIVE ACTION

Brakes fade (due to excessive heat)

PROBABLE CAUSE	CORRECTIVE ACTION
1 Brake linings excessively worn or glazed	1 Deglaze or replace brake pads and/or shoes
2 Excessive use of brakes	2 Downshift into a lower gear, maintain a constant slower speed (going down hills)
3 Vehicle overloaded	3 Reduce load
4 Brake drums or discs worn too thin	4 Measure drum diameter and disc thickness, replace drums or discs as required
5 Contaminated brake fluid	5 Flush system, replace fluid
6 Brakes drag	6 Repair cause of dragging brakes
7 Driver resting left foot on brake pedal	7 Don't ride the brakes

Brakes noisy (high-pitched squeal)

PROBABLE CAUSE	CORRECTIVE ACTION
1 Glazed lining	1 Deglaze or replace lining
2 Contaminated lining (brake fluid, grease, etc.)	2 Repair source of contamination, replace linings
3 Weak or broken brake shoe hold-down or return spring	3 Replace springs
4 Rivets securing lining to shoe or backing plate loose	4 Replace shoes or pads
5 Excessive dust buildup on brake linings	5 Wash brakes off with brake system cleaner
6 Brake drums worn too thin	6 Measure diameter of drums, replace if necessary
7 Wear indicator on disc brake pads contacting disc	7 Replace brake pads
8 Anti-squeal shims missing or installed improperly	8 Install shims correctly

Note: *Other remedies for quieting squealing brakes include the application of an anti-squeal compound to the backing plates of the brake pads, and lightly chamfering the edges of the brake pads with a file. The latter method should only be performed with the brake pads thoroughly wetted with brake system cleaner, so as not to allow any brake dust to become airborne.*

Brakes noisy (scraping sound)

PROBABLE CAUSE	CORRECTIVE ACTION
1 Brake pads or shoes worn out; rivets, backing plate or brake shoe metal contacting disc or drum	1 Replace linings, have discs and/or drums machined (or replace)

Brakes chatter

PROBABLE CAUSE	CORRECTIVE ACTION
1 Worn brake lining	1 Inspect brakes, replace shoes or pads as necessary
2 Glazed or scored discs or drums	2 Deglaze discs or drums with sandpaper (if glazing is severe, machining will be required)
3 Drums or discs heat checked	3 Check discs and/or drums for hard spots, heat checking, etc. Have discs/drums machined or replace them
4 Disc runout or drum out-of-round excessive	4 Measure disc runout and/or drum out-of-round, have discs or drums machined or replace them
5 Loose or worn wheel bearings	5 Adjust or replace wheel bearings
6 Loose or bent brake backing plate (drum brakes)	6 Tighten or replace backing plate
7 Grooves worn in discs or drums	7 Have discs or drums machined, if within limits (if not, replace them)
8 Brake linings contaminated (brake fluid, grease, etc.)	8 Locate and repair source of contamination, replace pads or shoes
9 Excessive dust buildup on linings	9 Wash brakes with brake system cleaner
10 Surface finish on discs or drums too rough after machining (especially on vehicles with sliding calipers)	10 Have discs or drums properly machined
11 Brake pads or shoes glazed	11 Deglaze or replace brake pads or shoes

Troubleshooting (continued)

PROBABLE CAUSE	CORRECTIVE ACTION

Brake pads or shoes click

PROBABLE CAUSE	CORRECTIVE ACTION
1 Shoe support pads on brake backing plate grooved or excessively worn	1 Replace brake backing plate
2 Brake pads loose in caliper	2 Loose pad retainers or anti-rattle clips
3 Also see items listed under Brakes chatter	

Brakes make groaning noise at end of stop

PROBABLE CAUSE	CORRECTIVE ACTION
1 Brake pads and/or shoes worn out	1 Replace pads and/or shoes
2 Brake linings contaminated (brake fluid, grease, etc.)	2 Locate and repair cause of contamination, replace brake pads or shoes
3 Brake linings glazed	3 Deglaze or replace brake pads or shoes
4 Excessive dust buildup on linings	4 Wash brakes with brake system cleaner
5 Scored or heat-checked discs or drums	5 Inspect discs/drums, have machined if within limits (if not, replace discs or drums)
6 Broken or missing brake shoe attaching hardware	6 Inspect drum brakes, replace missing hardware

Rear brakes lock up under light brake application

PROBABLE CAUSE	CORRECTIVE ACTION
1 Tire pressures too high	1 Adjust tire pressures
2 Tires excessively worn	2 Replace tires
3 Defective proportioning valve	3 Replace proportioning valve

Brake warning light on instrument panel comes on (or stays on)

PROBABLE CAUSE	CORRECTIVE ACTION
1 Low fluid level in master cylinder reservoir (reservoirs with fluid level sensor)	1 Add fluid, inspect system for leak, check the thickness of the brake pads and shoes
2 Failure in one half of the hydraulic system	2 Inspect hydraulic system for a leak
3 Piston in pressure differential warning valve not centered	3 Center piston by bleeding one circuit or the other (close bleeder valve as soon as the light goes out)
4 Defective pressure differential valve or warning switch	4 Replace valve or switch
5 Air in the hydraulic system	5 Bleed the system, check for leaks
6 Brake pads worn out (vehicles with electric wear sensors - small probes that fit into the brake pads and ground out on the disc when the pads get thin)	6 Replace brake pads (and sensors)

Brakes do not self adjust

Disc brakes

PROBABLE CAUSE	CORRECTIVE ACTION
1 Defective caliper piston seals	1 Replace calipers. Also, possible contaminated fluid causing soft or swollen seals (flush system and fill with new fluid if in doubt)
2 Corroded caliper piston(s)	2 Same as above

Drum brakes

PROBABLE CAUSE	CORRECTIVE ACTION
1 Adjuster screw frozen	1 Remove adjuster, disassemble, clean and lubricate with high-temperature grease
2 Adjuster lever does not contact star wheel or is binding	2 Inspect drum brakes, assemble correctly or clean or replace parts as required
3 Adjusters mixed up (installed on wrong wheels after brake job)	3 Reassemble correctly
4 Adjuster cable broken or installed incorrectly (cable-type adjusters)	4 Install new cable or assemble correctly

Rapid brake lining wear

PROBABLE CAUSE	CORRECTIVE ACTION
1 Driver resting left foot on brake pedal	1 Don't ride the brakes
2 Surface finish on discs or drums too rough	2 Have discs or drums properly machined
3 Also see Brakes drag	

3.2 The ABS actuator is mounted at the passenger side of the firewall - components have been removed here for clarity

3.9a Front wheel speed sensor

3.9b Rear wheel speed sensor

3 Anti-lock Brake System (ABS) - general information

1   The Anti-lock Brake System (ABS) is designed to maintain vehicle steerability, directional stability and optimum deceleration under severe braking conditions and on most road surfaces. It does so by monitoring the rotational speed of each wheel and controlling the brake line pressure to each wheel during braking. This prevents the wheels from locking up.

Actuator assembly

Refer to illustration 3.2

2   The actuator assembly consists of an electric hydraulic pump and a pair of solenoid valves for each wheel. The electric pump provides hydraulic pressure to charge the reservoirs in the actuator, which supplies pressure to the braking system during ABS operation. The solenoid valves modulate brake line pressure during ABS operation. The body contains four valves - one for each wheel. The pump, the reservoirs and the solenoid valves are all housed in the actuator assembly **(see illustration)**.

Speed sensors

3   The speed sensors, which are located at each wheel, generate a sine wave current when the sensor rotors are turning. This analog voltage signal is monitored by the ABS control unit, which converts it to a digital signal from which it can determine wheel rotational speed.

4.5 Use a C-clamp to depress the piston into the caliper before removing the caliper and pads

ABS computer

4   The ABS control unit is the brain of the ABS system. The function of the control unit is to monitor and process information received from the wheel speed sensors to control the hydraulic line pressure, avoiding wheel lock up. The control unit also monitors the system for malfunctions, even when the ABS system is inactive during normal driving conditions.

5   Each time you start the engine, the system turns on the ABS warning light on the instrument cluster for about a second. As soon as the engine is running, the light should go off. The system then performs a self-test the first time the vehicle speed exceeds four mph. You may hear a mechanical noise during the test; this is normal. If the system detects a problem, the ABS light will come on and remain on. A diagnostic code will also be stored in the control unit, which indicates the problem area or component.

Wheel speed sensor - removal and installation

Refer to illustrations 3.9a and 3.9b

6   Loosen the wheel lug nuts, raise the vehicle and support it securely on jackstands. Remove the wheel.

7   Make sure the ignition key is turned to the "OFF" position.

8   Trace the wiring back from the sensor, detaching all brackets and clips while noting

4.6a Before disassembling the brake, wash it thoroughly with brake system cleaner and allow it to dry - position a drain pan under the brake to catch the residue - DO NOT use compressed air to blow off brake dust!

its correct routing, then disconnect the electrical connector.

9   Remove the mounting bolt and carefully pull the sensor out from the knuckle **(see illustrations)**.

10   Installation is the reverse of removal. Tighten the mounting fastener securely.

11   Install the wheel and lug nuts, tightening them securely. Lower the vehicle and tighten the bolts to the torque listed in the Chapter 1 Specifications.

4 Disc brake pads - replacement

Refer to illustrations 4.5 and 4.6a through 4.6o

Warning: *Disc brake pads must be replaced on both front wheels at the same time - never replace the pads on only one wheel. Also, the dust created by the brake system is harmful to your health. Never blow it out with compressed air and don't inhale any of it. An approved filtering mask should be worn when working on the brakes. Do not, under any circumstances, use petroleum-based solvents to clean brake parts. Use brake system cleaner only!*

1   Remove the cap from the brake fluid reservoir.

2   Loosen the front or rear wheel lug nuts, raise the front or rear of the vehicle and support it securely on jackstands. Block the wheels at the opposite end.

3   Remove the wheels. Work on one brake assembly at a time, using the assembled brake for reference if necessary.

4   Inspect the brake disc carefully (see Section 6). If machining is necessary, remove the disc (see Section 6).

5   Using a C-clamp, push the piston back into its bore to provide room for the new brake pads **(see illustration)**. As the piston is depressed to the bottom of the caliper bore, the fluid in the master cylinder will rise. Make sure that it doesn't overflow. If necessary, remove some of the fluid.

Warning: *Brake fluid is poisonous - never siphon it by mouth. Use a suction gun or old poultry baster. If a baster is used, never again use it for the preparation of food.* **Caution:** *Brake fluid will damage paint. If any fluid is spilled, wash it off immediately with plenty of clean, cold water.*

6   Follow the accompanying photos **(see illustrations 4.6a through 4.6o)** for the front

4.6b If you're working on a front brake, remove the caliper lower mounting bolt. If you're working on a rear brake, remove the upper mounting bolt . . .

4.6c . . . and swing it away from the caliper mounting bracket; the brake hose banjo bolt shouldn't be removed unless the caliper or hose requires service

4.6d Support the caliper with a piece of wire

4.6e Remove the inner brake pad

4.6f Remove the outer brake pad

4.6g Remove the upper and lower pad retainers

or rear pad replacement procedure. Be sure to stay in order and read the caption under each illustration. **Note:** *The illustrations show a front brake job, but the rear is almost identical.*

7   When reinstalling the caliper, be sure to tighten the mounting bolts to the torque listed in this Chapter's Specifications. Tighten the wheel lug nuts to the torque listed in the Chapter 1 Specifications. **Warning:** *After the job has been completed, firmly depress the brake pedal a few times to bring the pads into contact with the disc. You may not have any* braking at first if this is not done.

8   Check the level of the brake fluid, adding some if necessary. Check the operation of the brakes carefully before placing the vehicle into normal service.

4.6h Thoroughly clean both slide pins, inspect them for corrosion and replace them if necessary; lubricate the lower . . .

4.6i . . . and the upper pins with high-temperature brake grease

4.6j Clean the shims, then apply anti-squeal compound to the backs of the pads (let the compound set up for a few minutes before installing the pads)

4.6k Assemble the shims to the pads in the same order in which they were originally installed

4.6l Inspect the rubber boots and replace them if necessary; reinstall the pad retainers into the caliper bracket

4.6m Install the outer pad

4.6n Install the inner pad

4.6o Swing the caliper over the pads and install the caliper mounting bolt, tightening it to the torque listed in this Chapter's Specifications. Note: *If the caliper won't fit over the pads, use a C-clamp to push the piston into the caliper a little farther*

5 Disc brake caliper - removal and installation

Warning: *The dust created by the brake system is harmful to your health. Never blow it out with compressed air and don't inhale any of it. An approved filtering mask should be worn when working on the brakes. Do not, under any circumstances, use petroleum-based solvents to clean brake parts. Use brake system cleaner only!*

Note: *If replacement is indicated (usually because of fluid leakage), it is recommended that the calipers be replaced, not overhauled. New and factory rebuilt units are available on an exchange basis, which makes this job quite easy. Always replace the calipers in pairs - never replace just one of them.*

Removal

Refer to illustrations 5.2a and 5.2b

1   Loosen the front or rear wheel lug nuts, raise the front or rear of the vehicle and place it securely on jackstands. Block the wheels at the opposite end. Remove the front or rear wheel.

2   Remove the brake hose banjo bolt **(see**

illustration). Disconnect the brake hose from the caliper and discard the sealing washers (new ones should be used on installation). Plug the brake hose to keep contaminants out of the brake system and to prevent losing any more brake fluid than is necessary **(see illustration)**. **Note:**

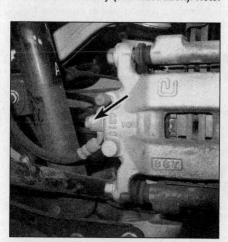

5.2a Remove the brake hose banjo bolt

If you're only removing the caliper for access to other components, don't detach the hose.

3   Remove the caliper mounting bolts and lift the caliper from its bracket. **Note:** *See Section 4 for additional information (it's part of brake pad replacement).*

5.2b Plug the brake line with a piece of rubber hose with the same outside diameter as the inside diameter of the banjo fitting

6.3 The brake pads on this vehicle were obviously neglected, as they wore down completely and cut deep grooves into the disc - wear this severe means the disc must be replaced

6.4a To check disc runout, mount a dial indicator as shown and rotate the disc

6.4b Using a swirling motion, remove the glaze from the disc surface with sandpaper or emery cloth

Installation

4   Installation is the reverse of removal, tightening the caliper mounting bolt to the torque listed in this Chapter's Specifications and the wheel lug nuts to the torque in the Chapter 1 Specifications. Don't forget to use new sealing washers for the brake hose-to-caliper banjo bolt.

5   Bleed the brake system (see Section 9). Make sure there are no leaks from the hose connections. Test the brakes carefully before returning the vehicle to normal service.

6   Brake disc - inspection, removal and installation

Inspection

Refer to illustrations 6.3, 6.4a, 6.4b and 6.5

1   Loosen the wheel lug nuts, raise the vehicle and support it securely on jackstands. Remove the wheel and install the lug nuts to hold the disc in place. **Note:** *If the lug nuts*

don't contact the disc when screwed on all the way, install washers under them.

2   Remove the brake caliper (see Section 5). It isn't necessary to disconnect the brake hose. After removing the caliper bolts, suspend the caliper out of the way with a piece of wire.

3   Visually inspect the disc surface for score marks and other damage. Light scratches and shallow grooves are normal after use and may not always be detrimental to brake operation, but deep scoring requires disc removal and refinishing by an automotive machine shop. Be sure to check both sides of the disc **(see illustration)**. If pulsating occurs during application of the brakes, suspect disc runout.

4   To check disc runout, place a dial indicator at a point about 1/2-inch from the outer edge of the disc **(see illustration)**. Set the indicator to zero and turn the disc. The indicator reading should not exceed the specified allowable runout limit. If it does, the disc should be refinished by an automotive machine shop. **Note:** *When replacing the brake pads, it's a good idea to resurface the discs regardless of the dial indicator reading,*

because it will produce a smooth finish and ensure a perfectly flat surface, eliminating any brake pedal pulsation or other undesirable symptoms related to questionable discs. If you decide not to resurface the discs, at least remove the glaze from the surface with emery cloth using a swirling motion **(see illustration)**.

5   The minimum wear (or discard) thickness is cast into the disc. The disc thickness can be checked with a micrometer **(see illustration)**. **Warning:** *The disc must not be machined to a thickness less than the specified minimum allowable disc refinish thickness.*

Removal

Refer to illustrations 6.6a and 6.6b

6   Remove the two caliper mounting bracket bolts **(see illustrations)** and detach the caliper mounting bracket. On rear discs, fully release the parking brake.

7   Remove the lug nuts that you installed to hold the disc in place and remove the disc from the hub. **Note:** *If a rear disc won't come off, remove the rubber plug from the parking*

6.5 Use a micrometer to measure disc thickness

6.6a Front caliper mounting bracket bolts

6.6b Rear caliper mounting bracket bolts

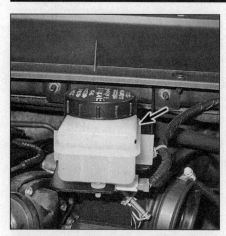

7.4 Unscrew the cap on the main brake fluid reservoir and withdraw as much fluid as you can with a syringe

brake adjuster hole. Use a small screwdriver to turn the star wheel and retract the parking brake shoes (see illustration 12.4a).

Installation

8   Place the disc in position over the threaded studs.

9   Install the caliper mounting bracket over the disc and tighten the bolts to the torque listed in this Chapter's Specifications.

10   Install the caliper and tighten the bolts to the torque listed in this Chapter's Specifications.

11   Install the wheel, then lower the vehicle to the ground. Tighten the lug nuts to the torque listed in the Chapter 1 Specifications. Depress the brake pedal a few times to bring the brake pads into contact with the disc. Bleeding won't be necessary unless the brake hose was disconnected from the caliper. Check the operation of the brakes carefully before driving the vehicle.

7   Master cylinder - removal and installation

Removal

Refer to illustrations 7.4 and 7.5

1   Disconnect the cable from the negative terminal of the battery (see Chapter 5).

2   Remove the air filter housing and the air intake duct (see Chapter 4).

3   Remove the cowl trim covers (see Chapter 11).

4   Remove as much fluid as possible from the main reservoir **(see illustration)** with a syringe. **Caution:** *All models use a remote brake fluid reservoir that's connected to the reservoir on the master cylinder by a hose. The remote reservoir must be drained before removing the master cylinder, or brake fluid will be spilled into the engine compartment when the hydraulic line fittings are disconnected from the reservoir.*

5   Disconnect the hose that connects the remote reservoir to the master cylinder reservoir. Loosen the hose clamp and disconnect the hose from the top of the master cylinder reservoir **(see illustration)**; immediately plug the hose to prevent any residual brake fluid inside the hose from dripping into the engine compartment.

6   Place rags under the brake fluid hydraulic line fittings and have caps, plugs or plastic bags to cover the ends of the lines as soon as they're disconnected. Disconnect the two brake fluid hydraulic line fittings from the master cylinder with a flare nut wrench. **Caution:** *Brake fluid will damage paint. If any fluid is spilled, wash it off immediately with plenty of clean, cold water.*

7   Pull the brake lines away from the master cylinder and plug the ends to prevent contamination.

8   Remove the nuts attaching the master cyl-

inder to the power booster. Pull the master cylinder off the studs to remove it. Again, be careful not to spill any remaining fluid as this is done.

Installation

Refer to illustrations 7.10 and 7.18

9   Bench bleed the new master cylinder before installing it. Mount the master cylinder in a vise, with the jaws of the vise clamping on the mounting flange.

10   Attach a pair of master cylinder bleeder tubes to the outlet ports of the master cylinder **(see illustration)**.

11   Fill the reservoir with brake fluid of the recommended type (see Chapter 1).

12   Slowly push the pistons into the master cylinder (a large Phillips screwdriver can be used for this) - air will be expelled from the pressure chambers and into the reservoir. Because the tubes are submerged in fluid, air can't be drawn back into the master cylinder when you release the pistons. Repeat the procedure until no more air bubbles are present.

13   Remove the bleed tubes, one at a time, and install plugs in the open ports to prevent fluid leakage and air from entering. Install the reservoir cap.

14   Install a new O-ring seal in the groove on the end of the master cylinder and coat it with silicone grease. Also coat the bore of the power brake booster.

15   Install the master cylinder over the studs on the power brake booster and tighten the nuts only finger-tight at this time.

16   Thread the brake line fittings into the master cylinder. Since the master cylinder is still a bit loose, it can be moved slightly so the fittings thread in easily. Don't strip the threads as the fittings are tightened.

17   Tighten the mounting nuts to the torque listed in this Chapter's Specifications. Tighten the brake line fittings securely.

18   Fill the master cylinder reservoir with fluid,

7.5 Master cylinder details (2009 model shown, other models similar):

1	Hose from remote reservoir	3 Master cylinder
2	Brake line fittings	mounting nuts

7.10 The best way to bleed the master cylinder before installing it is with a pair of bleeder tubes

7.18 Have an assistant depress the brake pedal and hold it down, then loosen the fitting nut, allowing the air and fluid to escape; repeat this procedure on both fittings until the fluid is clear of air bubbles

8.3 Loosen the threaded fitting on the brake line; use a flare-nut wrench to protect the corners of the nut

8.4 Pull off the U-clip with a pair of pliers

bleed the lines at the master cylinder again, then bleed the remainder of the brake system (see Section 9). To bleed the lines at the master cylinder, have an assistant depress the brake pedal and hold it down. Loosen the fitting to allow air and fluid to escape **(see illustration)**. Tighten the fitting, then allow your assistant to return the pedal to its rest position. Repeat this procedure on both fittings until the fluid is free of air bubbles, then bleed the rest of the system. Check the operation of the brake system carefully before driving the vehicle. **Warning:** *If you do not have a firm brake pedal at the end of the bleeding procedure, or have any doubts as to the effectiveness of the brake system, DO NOT drive the vehicle. Have it towed to a dealer service department or other qualified repair shop for diagnosis.*

19   Reconnect the battery and perform the necessary re-learn procedures (see Chapter 5).

8   Brake hoses and lines - inspection and replacement

Inspection

1   About every six months, with the vehicle raised and supported securely on jackstands, the flexible hoses which connect the steel brake lines with the front and rear brake assemblies should be inspected for cracks, chafing of the outer cover, leaks, blisters and other damage. These are important and vulnerable parts of the brake system and inspection should be complete. A light and mirror will be helpful for a thorough check. If a hose exhibits any of the above conditions, replace it with a new one.

Replacement

Brake hoses

Refer to illustrations 8.3 and 8.4

2   Loosen the wheel lug nuts, raise the

vehicle and support it securely on jackstands. Remove the wheel.

3   At the bracket, unscrew the brake line fitting from the hose **(see illustration)**. Use a flare-nut wrench to prevent rounding off the corners.

4   Remove the U-clip from the female fitting at the bracket with a pair of pliers **(see illustration)**, then pass the hose through the bracket.

5   At the caliper end of the hose, remove the banjo bolt, then separate the hose from the caliper. Note that there are two sealing washers on either side of the banjo fitting - they should be replaced with new ones during installation.

6   If you're replacing a front brake hose, remove the U-clip from the strut bracket, then detach the hose from the bracket.

7   To install the hose, pass the caliper fitting end through the strut bracket (front hose only), then connect the fitting to the caliper with the banjo bolt and new sealing washers.

8   Make sure the hose isn't twisted between the caliper and the strut bracket (or the chassis on rear brake hoses).

9   Route the hose into the frame bracket, again making sure it isn't twisted, then connect the brake line fitting, starting the threads by hand. Install the U-clip, then tighten the fitting securely.

10   Bleed the caliper (see Section 9).

11   Install the wheel and lug nuts, lower the vehicle and tighten the lug nuts to the torque listed in the Chapter 1 Specifications.

Metal brake lines

12   When replacing brake lines, be sure to use the correct parts. Don't use copper tubing for any brake system components. Purchase steel brake lines from a dealer or auto parts store.

13   Prefabricated brake line, with the tube ends already flared and fittings installed, is available at auto parts stores and dealer parts departments.

14   When installing the new line, make sure it's securely supported in the brackets and has plenty of clearance between moving or

hot components.

15   After installation, check the master cylinder fluid level and add fluid as necessary. Bleed the brake system (see Section 9) and test the brakes carefully before driving the vehicle in traffic.

9   Brake hydraulic system - bleeding

Refer to illustration 9.8

Warning: *Wear eye protection when bleeding the brake system. If the fluid comes in contact with your eyes, immediately rinse them with water and seek medical attention.*

Note: *Bleeding the hydraulic system is necessary to remove any air that manages to find its way into the system when it's been opened during removal and installation of a hose, line, caliper or master cylinder.*

1   You'll probably have to bleed the system at all four brakes if air has entered it due to low fluid level, or if the brake lines have been disconnected at the master cylinder.

2   If a brake line was disconnected only at a wheel, then only that caliper or wheel cylinder must be bled.

3   If a brake line is disconnected at a fitting located between the master cylinder and any of the brakes, that part of the system served by the disconnected line must be bled.

4   Remove any residual vacuum from the brake power booster by applying the brake several times with the engine off.

5   Remove the master cylinder reservoir cover and fill the reservoir with brake fluid. Reinstall the cover. Check the fluid level often during the bleeding operation and add fluid as necessary to prevent the fluid level from falling low enough to allow air bubbles into the master cylinder. **Caution:** *Turn the ignition switch off and disconnect the electrical connectors for the ABS actuator or detach the battery ground cable.*

6   Have an assistant on hand, as well as a supply of new brake fluid, a clear plastic con-

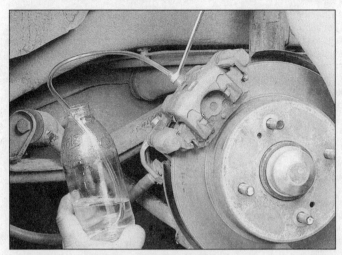

9.8 When bleeding the brakes, a hose is connected to the bleed screw at the caliper or wheel cylinder and then submerged in brake fluid - air will be seen as bubbles in the tube and container (all air must be expelled before moving to the next wheel)

10.7 Brake booster mounting details

1 Clevis pin retaining clip
2 Clevis lock nut (loosen to adjust input rod length)
3 Left mounting nuts (two right mounting nuts not visible in this photo)

tainer partially filled with clean brake fluid, a length of 3/16-inch plastic, rubber or vinyl tubing to fit over the bleeder valve and a wrench to open and close the bleeder valve.

7 Beginning at the right rear wheel, loosen the bleeder valve slightly, then tighten it to a point where it's snug but can still be loosened quickly and easily.

8 Place one end of the tubing over the bleeder valve and submerge the other end in brake fluid in the container **(see illustration)**.

9 Have the assistant pump the brakes slowly a few times to get pressure in the system, then hold the pedal down firmly.

10 While the pedal is held down, open the bleeder valve just enough to allow a flow of fluid to leave the valve. Watch for air bubbles to exit the submerged end of the tube. When the fluid flow slows after a couple of seconds, close the valve and have your assistant release the pedal.

11 Repeat Steps 9 and 10 until no more air is seen leaving the tube, then tighten the bleeder valve and proceed to the left front wheel, the left rear wheel and the right front wheel, in that order, and perform the same procedure. Be sure to check the fluid in the master cylinder reservoir frequently.

12 Never use old brake fluid. It contains moisture which will deteriorate the brake system components and could cause the fluid to boil, which could render the brake system inoperative.

13 Refill the master cylinder with fluid at the end of the operation. If you're working on a model with ABS, be sure to reconnect the electrical connectors to the ABS actuator or reconnect the battery.

14 Check the operation of the brakes. The pedal should feel solid when depressed, with no sponginess. If necessary, repeat the entire process. **Warning:** *Do not operate the vehicle if you're in doubt about the effectiveness of the brake system.*

10 Power brake booster - check, replacement and adjustment

Check
Operating check
1 Depress the brake pedal several times with the engine off and make sure there's no change in the pedal reserve distance.
2 Depress the pedal and start the engine. If the pedal goes down slightly, operation is normal.

Airtightness check
3 Start the engine and turn it off after one or two minutes. Depress the brake pedal slowly several times. If the pedal depresses less each time, the booster is airtight.
4 Depress the brake pedal while the engine is running, then stop the engine with the pedal depressed. If there's no change in the pedal reserve travel after holding the pedal for 30 seconds, the booster is airtight.

Replacement
Refer to illustration 10.7
Note: *Power brake booster units shouldn't be disassembled. They require special tools not normally found in most automotive repair stations or shops. They're fairly complex and, because of their critical relationship to brake performance, should be replaced with a new or rebuilt one.*
5 Remove the master cylinder (see Section 7).
6 Disconnect the vacuum hose from the booster.
7 Pull out the safety clip, then remove the pin from the clevis to detach the pushrod from the brake pedal **(see illustration)**.
8 Remove the four mounting nuts securing the booster to the firewall, then remove the booster from the engine compartment.

9 Before installing the new booster, measure the booster input rod length and adjust it if necessary (see Step 11).
10 Installation is the reverse of removal. Be sure to use a new gasket between the booster and the firewall.

Adjustment
Refer to illustration 10.11
11 Measure the distance between the power brake booster and the hole in the input rod clevis **(see illustration)** and compare it to the dimension listed in this Chapter's Specifications. If necessary, loosen the adjusting nut and turn the clevis in or out to the specified length, then install the booster, connect the clevis to the brake pedal, tighten the nut securely.

10.11 Measure the distance between the power brake booster and the hole in the clevis and compare your measurement to the dimension listed in this Chapter's Specifications; if necessary, adjust the clevis before installing the power brake booster

11.4 Parking brake cable adjusting nut

11   Parking brake - check and adjustment

Check

1   The parking brake pedal, when properly adjusted, should travel the correct number of clicks when a 45 pound force is applied. See the Specifications in this Chapter.

2   If the parking brake pedal travels less than the specified minimum number of clicks, it might not be releasing completely and the shoes could even be dragging against the drum. If it moves more than the specified maximum number of clicks, the parking brake may not hold adequately on an incline, allowing the car to roll.

Adjustment

Refer to illustration 11.4

3   Loosen the rear wheel lug nuts. Raise the vehicle and support it securely on jackstands. Remove the rear wheels.

4   Remove the fuse access cover above the parking brake pedal. Loosen the cable adjusting nut at the upper end of the parking brake pedal, then release the parking brake **(see illustration)**.

5   Install three lug nuts snugly to each rear disc to support it against the hub flange.

6   Remove the rubber adjuster hole plugs from the discs **(see illustration 12.4a)**.

7   Turn the star wheel downward until it locks the disc, then back it off five or six notches.

8   Turn the disc and make sure there is no drag. Readjust it if necessary to obtain a close adjust-ment with zero drag. Replace the hole plugs.

9   Tighten the adjusting nut (see Step 4) so you get the specified number of clicks (see this Chapter's Specifications) when you apply the parking brake pedal.

10   Release the parking brake and turn the rear discs again to verify that there is no drag. If drag exists, go over the adjustment procedure until it's correct.

11   Reinstall the wheels, lower the vehicle and tighten the lug nuts to the torque listed in Chapter 1.

12   Parking brake shoes - replacement

Refer to illustrations 12.4a through 12.4r

Warning: *The dust created by the brake system is harmful to your health. Never blow it out with compressed air and don't inhale any of it. An approved filtering mask should be worn when working on the brakes. Do not, under any circumstances, use petroleum-based solvents to clean brake parts. Use brake system cleaner only!*

1   Loosen the rear wheel lug nuts. Raise the vehicle and support it securely on jackstands.

12.4a If the disc can't be removed when the parking brake is fully released, you'll have to remove this rubber plug and use a screwdriver to turn the star wheel to retract the parking brake shoes

12.4b Wash the assembly with brake system cleaner; DO NOT blow off the brake dust with compressed air

12.4c Remove the upper spring . . .

12.4d . . . then take out the adjuster

12.4e Use pliers to remove the lower spring

12.4f Turn the shoe hold-down springs to release them . . .

Remove the rear wheels.
2   Release the parking brake. Remove the discs (see Section 6).
3   Inspect the parking brake surfaces of each disc for wear or damage. Replace the discs if necessary.

4   Follow the accompanying photos **(see illustrations 12.4a through 12.4r)** for the actual parking brake shoe replacement procedure. Be sure to stay in order and read the caption under each illustration. Work on only one side at a time to avoid confusion.

5   Adjust the shoes (see Section 11).
6   When reinstalling the calipers, be sure to tighten the mounting bolts to the torque listed in this Chapter's Specifications.
7   The rest of the replacement procedure is the reverse of removal.

12.4g . . . then lift the shoe off

12.4h Do the same to the remaining shoe

12.4i After cleaning the backing plates, apply brake grease to the raised contact surfaces around the perimeter

12.4j Check the actuator assembly for wear or damage

12.4k Set the actuator assembly into place

12.4l Install the new parking brake shoes . . .

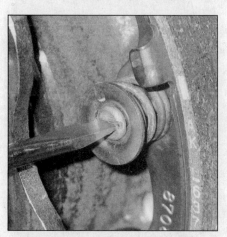
12.4m . . . and secure them with their hold-down springs

12.4n Disassemble the adjuster, clean it and lightly lubricate the threads with high-temperature brake grease

12.4o   Place the adjuster between the shoes

12.4p   Install the top spring . . .

12.4q   . . . so that it engages the star wheel

12.4r   Attach the lower spring, then reinstall the disc and adjust the shoes as described in Section 11

8   Working through the hole in the center of the brake disc **(see illustration 12.4a)**, turn the adjuster star wheel with a screwdriver until the disc is locked.

9   Turn the adjuster star wheel the other way 5 or 6 clicks. Turn the disc to verify that the parking brake shoes don't drag.

10   Install the rubber plug in the adjuster hole.

11   The parking brake pedal or lever may need adjustment in a few weeks after the parking brake shoes become seated.

---

13   Brake pedal - adjustment

---

1   With the brake pedal fully released, measure the distance from the top of the pad to the floor with the carpet and padding pulled back. Measure at a right angle to the floor.

2   If the height is not as listed in this Chapter's Specifications, it must be adjusted.

3   Release the brake light and cruise control cancel switches by turning them counterclockwise 45 degrees.

4   Loosen the lock nut just in front of the power brake booster clevis **(see illustration 10.11)**.

5   Turn the booster input rod until the pedal height is correct.

6   Tighten the lock nut.

7   With the threaded portion of the brake light and cruise control cancel switches contacting the bracket, turn the switches 45 degrees clockwise to lock them in place.

8   Adjust the brake light and cruise control switches if necessary (see Section 14).

---

14   Brake light and cruise control cancel switches - adjustment and replacement

---

Note: *The cruise control cancel switch is also know as the ASCD (Automatic Speed Control Device) switch.*

Adjustment

Refer to illustration 14.6

1   The brake light and cruise control cancel switches are located on a bracket near the top of the brake pedal. The switches activate the brake lights at the rear of the vehicle and cancel the cruise control operation when the pedal is depressed.

2   To check the brake light switch, simply note whether the brake lights come on when the pedal is depressed and go off when the pedal is released.

3   If the brake lights don't come on or the cruise control doesn't cancel when the brake pedal is depressed, make sure the brake pedal is correctly adjusted (see Section 13), then try adjusting the switch as follows.

4   Release the switch by turning it counterclockwise 45-degrees.

5   Pull the brake pedal back and hold it there, then push the switch into its bracket until the body of the switch (threaded portion) touches its stop.

6   Turn the switch 45-degrees clockwise to lock it in place. The distance from the pedal and the threaded part of the switch should be as listed in this Chapter's Specifications **(see illustration)**.

Replacement

7   Unplug the electrical connector from the switch.

8   Turn the switch 45-degrees counterclockwise, pull the switch to the rear and remove it.

9   Installation is the reverse of removal.

10   Adjust the brake pedal height (see Section 13), then adjust the switch (see Steps 4 through 6).

14.6   The clearance between the threaded body of the switch and the pedal bracket must be as shown in the Specifications

Notes

Notes

Torque specifications (continued)

Ft-lbs (unless otherwise indicated)

Note: *One foot-pound (ft-lb) of torque is equivalent to 12 inch-pounds (in-lbs) of torque. Torque values below approximately 15-ft-lbs. are expressed in inch-pounds, since most foot-pound torque wrenches are not accurate at these smaller values.*

2009 and later models

Control arm pivot bolts/nuts	114
Control arm balljoint-to-steering knuckle pinch bolt/nut	46
Hub and bearing-to-knuckle bolts	65
Stabilizer bar	
Bushing clamp bolts	37
Link nuts	58
Strut/coil spring assembly	
Strut-to-knuckle bolts/nuts	101
Strut upper mounting bolts	22
Piston rod nut	54
Subframe	
Subframe mounting bolts	114
Subframe brace bolts	41
Wheel lug nuts	See Chapter 1

Rear suspension

2007 and earlier models

Hub and bearing-to-knuckle bolts	44
Radius rod-to-subframe bolt	77
Radius rod-to-knuckle bolt/nut	77
Suspension arms	
Upper suspension arm pivot bolt nuts	77
Upper suspension arm-to-rear knuckle nut	92
Lower rear suspension arm-to-subframe pivot bolt nut	77
Lower rear suspension arm-to-knuckle pivot bolt nut	66
Lower front suspension arm-to-knuckle pivot bolt nut	77
Lower front suspension arm-to-subframe nut/bolt	77
Shock absorber	
Shock absorber mount-to-body nuts	
2005 and earlier	17
2006 and 2007	44
Shock absorber-to-knuckle bolt/nut	81
Shock absorber piston rod-to-mount nut	55
Stabilizer bar	
Bushing clamp nuts	41
Link nuts	32
Subframe	
Subframe mounting bolts	91
Subframe brace bolts	37
Wheel lug nuts	See Chapter 1

2009 and later models

Hub and bearing-to-knuckle bolts	65
Radius rod-to-subframe bolt	77
Radius rod-to-knuckle bolt/nut	77
Suspension arms	
Upper suspension arm pivot bolt nuts	77
Upper suspension arm-to-rear knuckle nut	115
Lower rear suspension arm-to-subframe nut	77
Lower rear suspension arm-to-knuckle bolt/nut	66
Lower front suspension arm-to-knuckle nut/bolt	77
Lower front suspension arm-to-subframe nut/bolt	77
Shock absorber	
Shock absorber mount-to-body nuts	17
Shock absorber-to-knuckle bolt/nut	81
Shock absorber piston rod-to-mount nut	41
Stabilizer bar	
Bushing clamp nuts	41
Link nuts	32
Subframe	
Subframe mounting bolts	91
Subframe brace bolts	37
Wheel lug nuts	See Chapter 1

Chapter 10
Suspension and steering systems

Contents

Specifications

Torque specifications
Ft-lbs (unless otherwise indicated)

Note: *One foot-pound (ft-lb) of torque is equivalent to 12 inch-pounds (in-lbs) of torque. Torque values below approximately 15-ft-lbs. are expressed in inch-pounds, since most foot-pound torque wrenches are not accurate at these smaller values.*

Front suspension

2007 and earlier models

Control arm	
Front pivot bolt	110
Rear bushing bracket bolts	91
Control arm balljoint-to-steering knuckle pinch bolt/nut	46
Hub and bearing-to-knuckle bolts	44
Stabilizer bar	
Bushing clamp bolts	37
Link nuts	66
Strut/coil spring assembly	
Strut-to-knuckle bolts/nuts	117
Strut upper mounting nuts	35
Piston rod nut	54
Subframe	
Subframe mounting nuts	91
Subframe brace bolts	156 in-lbs
Wheel lug nuts	See Chapter 1

Torque specifications

Ft-lbs (unless otherwise indicated)

Note: *One foot-pound (ft-lb) of torque is equivalent to 12 inch-pounds (in-lbs) of torque. Torque values below approximately 15-ft-lbs. are expressed in inch-pounds, since most foot-pound torque wrenches are not accurate at these smaller values.*

Steering

Airbag module bolts	82 in-lbs
Power steering pump pressure line banjo bolt	43
Steering gear mounting bolts/nuts	
2007 and earlier	100
2009 and later	114
Steering wheel nut	25
Steering shaft upper pinch bolt	33
Steering shaft lower pinch bolt	20
Steering column mounting nuts	12
Tie-rod end-to-steering knuckle nut	33
Wheel lug nuts	See Chapter 1

1.1a Front suspension and steering components

1	Strut/coil spring assembly	3	Tie-rod end	5	Steering knuckle
2	Balljoint	4	Control arm		

1   General information

Refer to illustrations 1.1a, 1.1b, 1.2a, 1.2b and 1.2c

The front suspension system **(see illustrations)** is a strut/coil spring design. The upper end of each strut is attached to the vehicle body. The lower end of the strut is connected to the upper end of the steering knuckle. The steering knuckle is attached to a balljoint mounted on the outer end of the control arm. The balljoint is an integral part of the control arm; if the balljoint is worn, the control arm must be replaced. A stabilizer bar is used on all models. The bar is attached to the subframe with a pair of clamps and to the struts with link rods.

1.1b Front suspension components - side view

1	Strut/coil spring assembly	
2	Stabilizer bar link	
3	Stabilizer bar	

4	Steering gear boot
5	Subframe
6	Control arm

7	Tie-rod end
8	Balljoint
9	Knuckle

1.2a Rear suspension components

1	Stabilizer bar	3	Front lower link	5	Coil spring
2	Subframe	4	Knuckle	6	Rear lower link and coil spring seat

The rear suspension system (see illustrations) uses separate shock absorbers and coil springs, an upper suspension arm and two lower suspension arms (front and rear) and a radius rod at each side. The upper ends of the shocks are attached to the vehicle body and their lower ends are attached to the upper ends of the rear knuckles. The coil springs are positioned between the lower rear suspension arm and the vehicle body. The lower ends of the knuckles are attached to the outer ends of the suspension arms. A stabilizer bar is attached to the subframe by a pair of brackets and to the upper suspension arms by link rods.

The rack-and-pinion steering gear is bolted to the rear part of the subframe. The steering gear actuates the tie-rods, which are attached to the steering knuckles. The inner ends of the tie-rods are protected by rubber boots which should be inspected periodically for secure attachment, tears and leaking lubricant (which would indicate failed rack seals).

The power assist system consists of a belt-driven pump and associated lines and hoses. The fluid level in the power steering pump reservoir should be checked periodically (see Chapter 1).

The steering wheel operates the steering shaft, which actuates the steering gear through universal joints. Looseness in the steering can be caused by wear in the steering shaft universal joints, the steering gear, the tie-rod ends and loose retaining bolts.

Frequently, when working on the suspension or steering system components, you may come across fasteners which seem impossible to loosen. These fasteners on the underside of the vehicle are continually subjected to water, road grime, mud, etc., and can become rusted or frozen, making them extremely difficult to remove. In order to unscrew these stubborn fasteners without damaging them (or other components), be sure to use lots of penetrating oil and allow it to soak in for a while. Using a wire brush to clean exposed threads will also ease removal of the nut or bolt and prevent damage to the threads. Sometimes a sharp blow with a hammer and punch will break the bond between a nut and bolt threads, but care must be taken to prevent the punch from slipping off the fastener and ruining the threads. Heating the stuck fastener and surrounding area with a torch sometimes helps too, but isn't recommended because of the obvious dangers associated with fire.

Long breaker bars and extension, or cheater, pipes will increase leverage, but never use an extension pipe on a ratchet - the ratcheting mechanism could be damaged. Sometimes tightening the nut or bolt first will help to break it loose. Fasteners that require drastic measures to remove should always be replaced with new ones.

Since most of the procedures dealt with in this Chapter involve jacking up the vehicle and working underneath it, a good pair of jackstands will be needed. A hydraulic floor jack is the preferred type of jack to lift the vehicle, and it can also be used to support certain components during various operations. **Warning:** *Never, under any circumstances, rely on a jack to support the vehicle while working on it. Whenever any of the suspension or steering fasteners are loosened or removed they must be inspected and, if necessary, replaced with new ones of the same part number or of original equipment quality and design. Torque specifications must be followed for proper reassembly and component retention. Never attempt to heat or straighten any suspension or steering components. Instead, replace any bent or damaged part with a new one.*

1.2b Rear suspension components - front view

1   Radius rod   2   Shock absorber

1.2c Rear suspension components - rear view

1   Upper control arm   3   Rear lower suspension arm
2   Coil spring   4   Front lower syspension arm

2.2 Strut lower mounting details

1   *ABS wheel speed sensor harness brackets*
2   *Brake hose retaining clip*
3   *Strut-to-steering knuckle nuts/bolts*

2.4 Stabilizer bar link-to-strut nut

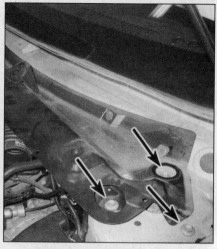

2.8 Strut upper mounting bolts

2   Strut/coil spring assembly (front) - removal, inspection and installation

Removal

Refer to illustrations 2.2, 2.4 and 2.8

1   Loosen the front wheel lug nuts, raise the front of the vehicle and support it securely on jackstands. Remove the wheels.

2   Remove the wheel speed sensor **(see illustration)**.

3   Detach the brake hose from the bracket on the strut.

4   Disconnect the stabilizer bar link from the strut **(see illustration)**.

5   Remove the strut-to-knuckle nuts and knock the bolts out with a hammer and punch.

6   Separate the strut from the steering knuckle. Be careful not to overextend the inner CV joint and don't let the knuckle fall outward, as this could damage the brake hose and the ABS speed sensor wiring (if equipped).

7   Remove the cowl cover for access to the top of the struts (see Chapter 11).

8   Support the strut and spring assembly with one hand and remove the three strut upper mounting bolts **(see illustration)**. Remove the assembly out from the fenderwell.

Inspection

9   Check the strut body for leaking fluid, dents, cracks and other obvious damage which would warrant repair or replacement.

10   Check the coil spring for chips or cracks in the spring coating (this will cause premature spring failure due to corrosion). Inspect the spring seat for cuts, hardness and general deterioration.

11   If any undesirable conditions exist, proceed to the strut disassembly procedure (see Section 3).

Installation

12   Guide the strut assembly up into the fenderwell and install the upper mounting bolts, tightening them to the torque listed in this Chapter's Specifications. This is most easily accomplished with the help of an assistant, as the strut is quite heavy and awkward. **Note:** *There is a protruding tab on the top insulator that must point outward.*

13   Slide the steering knuckle into the strut flange and insert the bolts. Install the nuts and tighten them to the torque listed in this Chapter's Specifications.

14   The remainder of installation is the reverse of removal. Tighten the stabilizer bar link nut to the torque listed in this Chapter's Specifications. Tighten the wheel lug nuts to the torque listed in the Chapter 1 Specifications.

15   Have the front end alignment checked and, if necessary, adjusted.

3   Strut/coil spring assembly (front) - replacement

1   If the struts or coil springs exhibit the telltale signs of wear (leaking fluid, loss of damping capability, chipped, sagging or cracked coil springs) explore all options before beginning any work. Strut assemblies complete with springs may be available on an exchange basis, which eliminates much time and work. Whichever route you choose to take, check on the cost and availability of parts before disassembling your vehicle. **Warning:** *Disassembling a strut is a potentially dangerous undertaking and utmost attention must be directed to the job, or serious injury may result. Use only a high-quality spring compressor and carefully follow the* manufacturer's instructions furnished with the tool. After removing the coil spring from the strut assembly, set it aside in a safe, isolated area.

Disassembly

Refer to illustrations 3.3, 3.4, 3.5 and 3.7

2   Remove the strut and spring assembly (see Section 2). Mount the strut assembly in a vise. Line the vise jaws with wood or rags to prevent damage to the unit and don't tighten the vise excessively.

3   Following the tool manufacturer's instructions, install the spring compressor (which can be obtained at most auto parts stores or equipment yards on a daily rental basis) on the spring and compress it sufficiently to relieve all pressure from the upper spring seat **(see illustration)**. This can be verified by wiggling the spring.

4   Remove the piston rod nut **(see illustration)**.

5   Remove the upper suspension support **(see illustration)**. Inspect the bearing in the suspension support for smooth operation. If it does not turn smoothly, replace the suspension support. Check the rubber portion of the suspension support for cracking and general deterioration. If there is any separation of the rubber, replace it.

6   Lift the spring seat and upper insulator from the piston rod. Check the rubber spring seat for cracking and hardness, replacing it if necessary.

7   Carefully lift the compressed spring from the assembly **(see illustration)** and set it in a safe place. **Warning:** *Carry the spring carefully and never place any part of your body near the end of the spring!*

8   Slide the dust boot off the piston rod.

9   Check the lower insulator (if equipped) for wear, cracking and hardness and replace it if necessary.

3.3 Install the spring compressor according to the tool manufacturer's instructions and compress the spring until all pressure is relieved from the upper spring seat

3.4 Remove the piston rod nut

Reassembly

Refer to illustration 3.11

10   If the lower insulator is being replaced, set it into position with the dropped portion seated in the lowest part of the seat. Extend the damper rod to its full length and install the dust boot.

11   Place the coil spring onto the lower insulator, with the end of the spring resting in the lowest part of the insulator **(see illustration)**.

12   Install the upper insulator and the spring seat. Make sure the marks or arrow on the spring seat and mount insulator are facing out (away from the vehicle), in line with the strut-to-knuckle flange.

13   Install the dust seal and suspension support to the piston rod.

14   Install the nut and tighten it to the torque listed in this Chapter's Specifications.

15   Install the strut/shock absorber and coil spring assembly (see Section 2).

4   Stabilizer bar (front) - removal and installation

Refer to illustration 4.13

1   Support the engine from above with an engine support fixture.

2   Loosen the front wheel lug nuts, raise the front of the vehicle and support it securely on jackstands, then remove the wheels.

3   Remove the front section of exhaust pipe (see Chapter 2A, **illustration 9.2**).

4   On AWD models, remove the driveshaft (see Chapter 8).

5   Separate the control arm balljoint from the steering knuckle (see Section 5).

6   Detach the tie-rod ends from the steering knuckles (see Section 17).

7   Detach the links from the ends of the stabilizer bar.

8   Disconnect the electrical connector from the power steering pressure switch.

9   Remove the pinch bolt from the lower steering column **(see illustration 19.5)**, then separate the shaft from the steering gear. Keep the steering wheel pointed straight ahead and keep the steering gear centered in its travel. **Caution:** *Don't allow the steering wheel to turn after the shaft has been disconnected; the airbag spiral cable could become damaged.*

10   Remove the front engine mount upper mounting nut and the rear engine mount through-bolt (this will allow the subframe to be lowered.

11   Free any hoses from clips securing them to the subframe.

12   Mark the position of the subframe to the chassis. Support the subframe with two floor jacks (one positioned on each side). Remove the subframe rear mounting fasteners and loosen the front mounting fasteners a few turns. Slowly and carefully lower the rear of the subframe.

3.5 Remove the upper suspension support mount and spring seat

3.7 Remove the compressed spring assembly. Warning: *Keep the ends of the spring pointed away from your body*

3.11 When installing the spring, make sure the end fits into the recessed portion of the lower seat

4.13 Stabilizer bar front clamp bolt

**5.2 Remove the nut and balljoint
pinch bolt**

13   Remove the bolts from the stabilizer bar clamps **(see illustration)** and remove the stabilizer bar.
14   Inspect the clamp bushings and the link bushings. If they're cracked or torn, replace them. **Note:** *The slit in the bushing should face the front of the vehicle. Also, be sure to install the clamps in the original positions, with the notched hole facing the front of the vehicle.*
15   Installation is the reverse of removal. Be sure to tighten all suspension and steering fasteners to the torque values listed in this Chapter's Specifications. **Note:** *The manufacturer recommends replacing the subframe fasteners and stabilizer bar clamp bolts with new ones.* Tighten the wheel lug nuts to the torque listed in the Chapter 1 Specifications.

---

5   Control arm (front) - removal, inspection and installation

Removal

Refer to illustrations 5.2, 5.3 and 5.5

1   Loosen the wheel lug nuts, raise the front of the vehicle, support it securely on jackstands and remove the wheel.
2   Remove the balljoint pinch bolt **(see illustration).**
3   Use a prybar to separate the balljoint stud from the steering knuckle **(see illustration).**
4   On 2007 and earlier models, remove the front pivot bolt and the two rear bushing bracket bolts, then remove the control arm.
5   On 2009 and later models, remove the control arm bushing nuts and bolts **(see illustration).** Remove the control arm.

Inspection

6   Inspect the front and rear bushings for cracks and tears. If either bushing is damaged or worn, replace the control arm; the bushings are not replaceable.
7   Inspect the control arm for straightness. If it's bent, replace it. Do not attempt to straighten a bent control arm.

Installation

8   Installation is the reverse of removal. Tighten all of the fasteners to the torque listed in this Chapter's Specifications.

9   Install the wheel and lug nuts, lower the vehicle and tighten the lug nuts to the torque listed in the Chapter 1 Specifications.

---

6   Balljoints - replacement

The balljoint is an integral part of the control arm. If it's worn or damaged, the control arm must be replaced (see Section 5).

---

7   Steering knuckle - removal and installation

Warning: *Dust created by the brake system is harmful to your health. Never blow it out with compressed air and don't inhale any of it. Do not, under any circumstances, use petroleum-based solvents to clean brake parts. Use brake system cleaner only.*

Removal

1   Loosen the wheel lug nuts, raise the vehicle and support it securely on jackstands. Remove the wheel.
2   Remove the cotter pin, then remove the driveaxle/hub nut (see Chapter 8).
3   Remove the brake disc (see Chapter 9).
4   Remove the wheel speed sensor from the knuckle.
5   Separate the tie-rod end from the steering knuckle (see Section 17).
6   Remove the strut-to-steering knuckle nuts, but don't remove the bolts yet (see Section 2).
7   Separate the control arm balljoint from the steering knuckle (see Section 5).
8   Separate the driveaxle from the steering knuckle (see Chapter 8). Support the end of the driveaxle with a length of wire so the CV joints aren't overextended.
9   Remove the strut-to-knuckle bolts and separate the knuckle from the strut.
10   Remove the hub-to-steering knuckle bolts (see Section 8), then detach the two components and remove the brake disc splash shield.

**5.3 Pry the balljoint out of the steering knuckle, taking care to
avoid damaging the rubber boot**

5.5 Control arm bushing bolts - 2009 and later models

8.4 Front hub and bearing mounting bolts (fourth bolt not visible in this photo)

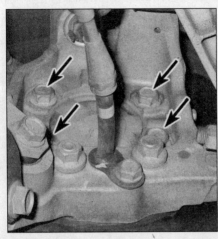

8.10 Rear hub and bearing mounting bolts

9.2 Rear stabilizer bar link nuts

Installation

11   Assemble the hub, knuckle and splash shield. Tighten the bolts to the torque listed in this Chapter's Specifications.

12   Lubricate the splines of the driveaxle with multi-purpose grease. Guide the knuckle and hub assembly into position, inserting the driveaxle into the hub.

13   Push the knuckle into the strut flange and install the bolts and nuts, but don't tighten them yet.

14   Attach the control arm balljoint to the steering knuckle (see Section 5).

15   Attach the tie-rod end to the steering knuckle arm (see Section 17). Tighten the tie-rod end nut and the strut-to-knuckle nuts to the torque listed in this Chapter's Specifications. Install a new cotter pin through the tie-rod end ballstud.

16   Place the brake disc on the hub and install the caliper (see Chapter 9).

17   Install the driveaxle/hub nut and tighten it to the torque listed in the Chapter 8 Specifications.

18   Install the wheel and lug nuts. Lower the vehicle and tighten the lug nuts to the torque listed in the Chapter 1 Specifications.

8   Hub and bearing assembly - removal and installation

Front

Refer to illustration 8.4

1   Loosen the wheel lug nuts, raise the front of the vehicle and support it securely on jackstands. Remove the wheel.

2   Loosen the driveaxle/hub nut (see Chapter 8).

3   Remove the brake disc (see Chapter 9). Detach the wheel speed sensor from the steering knuckle.

4   Remove the hub/bearing assembly mounting bolts from the rear of the steering knuckle **(see illustration)**.

5   Remove the hub/bearing assembly from the steering knuckle. **Note:** *If the driveaxle splines stick in the hub, push the driveaxle out of the hub with a two-jaw puller. Once the driveaxle has been freed from the hub, support it with a length of wire to prevent over-extension of the inner CV joint.*

6   Installation is the reverse of removal. Be sure to tighten all fasteners to the proper torque values.

Rear

Refer to illustration 8.10

7   Loosen the wheel lug nuts, raise the rear of the vehicle and support it securely on jackstands. Remove the wheel.

8   If you're working on an AWD model, loosen the driveaxle/hub nut (see Chapter 8).

9   Remove the brake disc (see Chapter 9). Detach the wheel speed sensor from the rear knuckle (see Chapter 9).

10   Remove the hub and bearing assembly mounting bolts **(see illustration)**.

11   Remove the hub and bearing assembly.

Note: *On AWD models, if the driveaxle splines stick in the hub, push the driveaxle out of the hub with a two-jaw puller. Once the driveaxle has been freed from the hub, support it with a length of wire to prevent over-extension of the inner CV joint.*

12   Installation is the reverse of removal. Be sure to tighten all fasteners to the proper torque values.

9   Stabilizer bar (rear) - removal and installation

Refer to illustrations 9.2 and 9.3

1   Raise the vehicle and support it securely on jackstands.

2   Remove the nuts from the link rods at the stabilizer bar ends **(see illustration)**.

3   Remove the bushing clamp nuts **(see**

9.3 Rear stabilizer bar clamp bolts

illustration), then remove the stabilizer bar.

4   Inspect all clamp bushings. If they're cracked or torn, replace them.

5   Installation is the reverse of removal. Be sure to tighten all fasteners to the torques listed in this Chapter's Specifications.

10   Knuckle (rear) - removal and installation

Refer to illustrations 10.5, 10.7 and 10.8

1   Loosen the rear wheel lug nuts. Raise the rear of the vehicle and support it securely on jackstands. Block the front wheels to prevent the vehicle from rolling. Remove the wheel.

2   Remove the caliper and disc (see Chapter 9).

3   Remove the hub and bearing assembly (see Section 8).

4   Remove the anchor block and the brake backing plate.

10.5 Support the rear lower control arm with a floor jack positioned under the spring pocket

10.7 With the rear lower arm supported by a floor jack, remove these fasteners and detach both lower control arms from the knuckle

5   Support the lower control arm with a floor jack positioned under the coil spring pocket **(see illustration). Warning:** *The jack must remain in this position throughout the entire procedure.*

6   Detach the radius rod from the knuckle (see Section 14).

7   Disconnect the front and rear lower suspension arms from the knuckle **(see illustration).**

8   Disconnect the upper suspension arm from the knuckle (see Section 13) **(see illustration).**

9   Disconnect the lower shock mounting bolt and nut from the knuckle (see Section 12).

10   Remove the knuckle from the vehicle.

11   Installation is the reverse of removal. Be sure to tighten all fasteners to the torque listed in this Chapter's Specifications. **Note:** *Before tightening the radius arm fasteners, the lower arm-to-knuckle fasteners and the shock absorber lower mounting fasteners, raise the rear lower arm with the floor jack to simulate normal ride height.*

11   Coil springs (rear) - removal and installation

Refer to illustrations 11.4 and 11.7

1   Loosen the rear wheel lug nuts, raise the rear of the vehicle, support it securely on jackstands and remove the wheels.

2   Disconnect the stabilizer bar link from the stabilizer bar (see Section 9).

3   Position a floor jack under the lower rear suspension arm and raise the suspension arm slightly **(see illustration 10.5).**

4   Mark the relationship of the adjusting cam to the subframe **(see illustration),** then loosen the bolt for the rear lower suspension arm at the subframe.

5   Remove the bolt and nut for the lower rear suspension arm at the knuckle **(see illustration 10.7).**

6   Carefully lower the suspension arm using the floor jack until the coil spring is fully extended.

7   Remove the coil spring, the rubber mount and the rubber seal **(see illustration).**

8   Installation is the reverse of removal, noting the following points:

a)   *Raise the lower suspension arm with a floor jack until it is at normal ride height, then tighten the suspension arm bolt/ nuts to the torque listed in this Chapter's Specifications. Be sure to align the marks on the adjusting cam and the subframe before tightening the fasteners.*

b)   *Tighten the wheel lug nuts to the torque listed in the Chapter 1 Specifications.*

12   Shock absorbers (rear) - removal and installation

Refer to illustrations 12.4 and 12.5

Warning: *Always replace the shock absorbers in pairs - never replace just one of them.*

1   Loosen the rear wheel lug nuts. Raise the rear of the vehicle and support it securely on jackstands. Block the front wheels to prevent the vehicle from rolling. Remove the wheel.

2   Support the lower rear suspension arm with a floor jack placed under the coil spring pocket. **Warning:** *The jack must remain in this position until the shock absorber is reinstalled.*

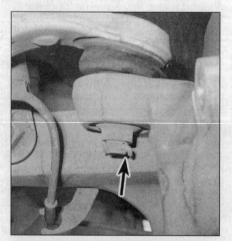

10.8 Remove the cotter pin, then use a balljoint separator to release the upper arm balljoint stud from the knuckle

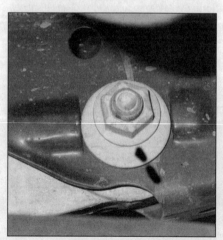

11.4 Mark the position of the cam to the subframe before loosening the bolt - set it in the same position when you assemble it

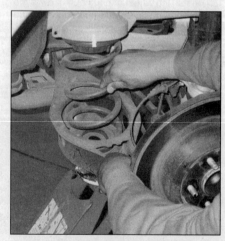

11.7 Slowly lower the lower rear suspension arm until the spring is no longer compressed

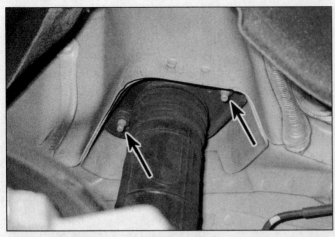
12.4 Remove these nuts from the top of the rear shock absorber

12.5 Rear shock absorber lower mounting bolt

13.3 Remove the arm-to-knuckle bolt to remove the coil spring, then remove the arm-to-frame bolt to remove the arm from the vehicle. Warning: *The arm must be supported with a floor jack before removing the bolts*

13.7a Mark the position of this adjusting cam before you remove the bolt - it must be installed in its original position and the marks must line up

3　Disconnect the stabilizer bar link from the stabilizer bar (see Section 9).
4　Remove the shock absorber upper mounting nuts **(see illustration)**.
5　Remove the shock absorber lower mounting bolt and remove the shock absorber **(see illustration)**.
6　Installation is the reverse of removal, noting the following points:

a) *Raise the lower suspension arm with the jack to simulate normal ride height, then tighten the mounting fasteners to the torque listed in this Chapter's Specifications*

b) *Install the wheel and lug nuts. Lower the vehicle and tighten the lug nuts to the torque listed in the Chapter 1 Specifications.*

13　Rear suspension arms and rear subframe - removal and installation

1　Loosen the rear wheel lug nuts. Raise the rear of the vehicle and support it securely on jackstands. Remove the wheel.

Rear lower suspension arm
Refer to illustration 13.3

2　Remove the coil spring (see Section 11).
3　Remove the lower arm-to-frame mounting bolt/nut **(see illustration)**.
4　Remove the lower rear suspension arm from the vehicle.
5　Installation is the reverse of removal, noting the following points:

a) *Raise the lower suspension arm with a floor jack until it is at normal ride height, then tighten the suspension arm bolt/nuts to the torque listed in this Chapter's Specifications. Be sure to align the marks on the adjusting cam and the subframe before tightening the bolt/nut.*

b) *Tighten the wheel lug nuts to the torque listed in the Chapter 1 Specifications.*

Front lower suspension arm
Refer to illustrations 13.7a and 13.7b

6　Support the rear lower suspension arm with a floor jack placed under the coil spring pocket. **Warning:** *The jack must remain in this position until the arm is reinstalled.*
7　Mark the relationship of the adjust-

ing cam to the subframe **(see illustration)**. Remove the lower front suspension arm-to-subframe mounting bolt/nut and the lower front suspension arm-to-knuckle mounting bolt/nut **(see illustration)**.

13.7b Lower front suspension arm pivot bolts and nuts

13.13 Upper suspension arm pivot bolts

14.2 Rear radius rod pivot bolts and nut

8   Remove the arm from the vehicle.
9   Installation is the reverse of removal, noting the following points:

a) *Raise the rear lower suspension arm with a floor jack until it is at normal ride height, then tighten the front lower suspension arm bolt/nuts to the torque listed in this Chapter's Specifications. Be sure to align the marks on the adjusting cam and the subframe before tightening the bolt/nut.*

b) *Tighten the wheel lug nuts to the torque listed in the Chapter 1 Specifications.*

Upper suspension arm

2WD models

Refer to illustration 13.13

10   Detach the wheel speed sensor wiring harness from the arm.
11   Detach the stabilizer bar link from the bracket on the arm (see Section 9).
12   Separate the balljoint from the knuckle using a balljoint separator (see Section 5). **Caution:** *Don't allow the knuckle to swing outward, as this could strain the wheel speed sensor harness.*
13   Remove the suspension arm pivot bolts, then remove the arm **(see illustration)**.
14   Installation is the reverse of removal. Tighten all fasteners to the torques listed in this Chapter's Specifications.

AWD models

15   The upper suspension arm must be removed along with the rear suspension subframe (see Steps 16 through 28).

Rear suspension subframe

16   Remove the brake calipers without disconnecting the hoses, then hang them out of the way with a piece of wire so the brake hoses aren't stressed.
17   Remove the rear portion of the exhaust system.
18   Remove the rear wheel speed sensors and the wiring harnesses.

19   Remove the rear stabilizer bar (see Section 9).
20   On AWD models, remove the rear differential (see Chapter 8).
21   Disconnect the parking brake cables from the rear subframe.
22   Remove the rear lower suspension arms and the coil springs (see Steps 2 through 4).
23   Unbolt the lower ends of the shock absorbers from the front lower suspension arms **(see illustration 12.5)**.
24   Support the rear suspension subframe with two floor jacks (one on each side).
25   Remove the subframe front corner braces.
26   Remove the remaining subframe-to-chassis braces. Carefully lower the jack until the subframe and the attached suspension components are clear of the body.
27   The suspension arms can now be removed if necessary.
28   Installation is the reverse of removal, noting the following points:

a) *Tighten the balljoint stud nut to the torque listed in this Chapter's Specifications, then install a new cotter pin.*

b) *With the rear suspension supported by jackstands, raise the lower suspension arm with a floor jack until it is at normal ride height, then tighten the pivot bolt nuts to the torque listed in this Chapter's Specifications.*

c) *Tighten all other fasteners to the torques listed in this Chapter's Specifications. Tighten the brake fasteners to the torque values listed in the Chapter 9 Specifications. Tighten the wheel lug nuts to the torque listed in the Chapter 1 Specifications.*

14 Radius rod (rear) - removal and installation

Refer to illustration 14.2

1   Loosen the rear wheel lug nuts. Raise the rear of the vehicle and support it securely

on jackstands. Block the front wheels to prevent the vehicle from rolling. Remove the wheel.
2   Remove the radius rod-to-subframe mounting bolt and the radius rod-to-knuckle mounting bolt/nut **(see illustration)**.
3   Remove the radius rod from the vehicle.
4   Installation is the reverse of removal, noting the following points:

a) *Raise the rear lower suspension arm with a floor jack until it is at normal ride height, then tighten the radius rod fasteners to the torque listed in this Chapter's Specifications.*

b) *Tighten the wheel lug nuts to the torque listed in the Chapter 1 Specifications.*

15 Subframe (front) - removal and installation

Refer to illustration 15.11

Note: *The subframe can be removed with other components still attached. Parts such as the control arms and the stabilizer bar can be left attached to the subframe if they are first detached from the rest of the vehicle.*
1   Disconnect the cable from the negative terminal of the battery (see Chapter 5).
2   Loosen the front wheel lug nuts. Raise the vehicle and support it securely on jackstands. Be sure that it's low enough to get an engine hoist over the engine compartment yet high enough to work comfortably under the vehicle. Remove the front wheels. **Note:** *The jackstands must be placed away from the subframe and the suspension components to allow the subframe to be lowered.*
3   Attach an engine support fixture to the engine or attach an engine hoist to support the engine and transaxle (see Chapter 2B).
4   Remove the air duct and any lower engine splash shields from the bottom of the engine.
5   Raise the engine slightly with the hoist to take weight from the mounts, then disconnect the engine mounts from the subframe.

15.11 Front subframe mounting bolts and rear braces

6   Disconnect the steering shaft from the steering gear (see Section 19). Don't turn the steering wheel or the steering components, or the steering wheel and steering gear will have to be centered.
7   Remove the front portion of the exhaust system.
8   Disconnect the fluid lines from the power steering gear.
9   Detach the stabilizer bar links from the stabilizer bar (see Section 4).
10   Unbolt the lower control arms from the

subframe (see Section 5).
11   Remove the two rear corner subframe braces **(see illustration)**.
12   Verify that all necessary components are disconnected from the subframe. Make sure that the subframe isn't supporting the weight of the engine or any other components.
13   Place two jacks under the subframe to support it. Remove the subframe mounting bolts, then carefully lower the subframe to the ground.
14   Installation is the reverse of removal.

15   Reconnect the battery and perform the necessary re-learn procedures (see Chapter 5).
16   Have the front wheel alignment checked and, if necessary, adjusted.

16 Steering wheel - removal and installation

Warning: *The models covered by this manual are equipped with Supplemental Restraint Systems (SRS), more commonly known as airbags. Always disarm the airbag system before working in the vicinity of any airbag system component to avoid the possibility of accidental deployment of the airbag, which could cause personal injury (see Chapter 12). Do not use a memory saving device to preserve the PCM's memory when working on or near airbag system components.*

Removal

Refer to illustrations 16.2a, 16.2b, 16.3, 16.5 and 16.6

1   Disconnect the cable from the negative terminal of the battery (see Chapter 5).
2   Pry off the steering wheel side covers, then remove the airbag bolts **(see illustrations)**. **Warning:** *The manufacturer recommends replacing these bolts with new ones*

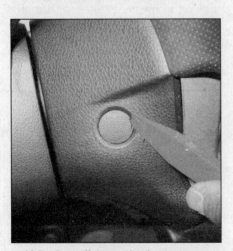

16.2a Pop off these plastic covers ...

16.2b ... then unscrew the airbag bolts

16.3 Pry up the locking clip (A), then detach the electrical connector (B) from each terminal

16.5 If your vehicle doesn't have steering wheel alignment marks like these, make your own

16.6 Use a steering wheel puller to break it loose from the steering shaft. Caution: *Do not hammer on the steering wheel or shaft to break it loose*

(of original part number) whenever they are removed.

3   Remove the airbag module and disconnect the electrical connectors **(see illustration). Note:** *Use a small screwdriver to lift the lock button on each connector before trying to disconnect them.*

4   Set the airbag module out of the way. **Warning:** *Handle the airbag module with care, carry the module with the trim cover side facing away from your body and store it in a safe location with the trim side facing up. See the precautions in Chapter 12.*

5   Remove the steering wheel retaining nut, then mark the relationship of the steering wheel to the steering shaft (if there are no factory alignment marks) **(see illustration)**.

6   Use a steering wheel puller to separate the steering wheel from the steering shaft **(see illustration)**. When removing the wheel, make sure the electrical leads for the airbag module and the cruise control system don't

snag on the wheel. **Warning:** *Do not turn the steering shaft while the steering wheel is removed.*

Installation

Refer to illustration 16.7

7   Verify that the front wheels are pointing straight ahead. If the spiral cable for the airbag has been removed and/or its center position lost, turn the spiral cable clockwise by hand until it becomes hard to turn (don't apply too much force), then rotate it about two turns counterclockwise until the marks align and the location pin is straight up at the 12 o'clock position **(see illustration)**.

8   Pull the electrical leads for the airbag module and the cruise control system through the steering wheel and install the wheel, aligning the marks as you do so. Make sure the spiral cable pin is properly engaged with the corresponding hole in the back of the steering wheel.

9   Install the steering wheel retaining nut and tighten it to the torque listed in this Chapter's Specifications.

10   Install the airbag module, tightening the bolts to the torque listed in this Chapter's Specifications. Install the covers.

11   Reconnect the battery and perform the necessary re-learn procedures (see Chapter 5).

12   Verify that the airbag circuit is operational by turning the ignition key to the On or Start position. The "AIR BAG" warning light should illuminate for a few seconds, then turn off.

17   Tie-rod ends - removal and installation

Removal

Refer to illustrations 17.2, 17.3 and 17.4

1   Loosen the wheel lug nuts. Raise the front of the vehicle, support it securely on

jackstands, then remove the front wheel.

2   Loosen the jam nut enough to mark the position of the tie-rod end in relation to the threads **(see illustration)**.

3   Remove the cotter pin and loosen, but don't remove, the nut on the tie-rod end stud **(see illustration)**.

4   Disconnect the tie-rod end from the steering knuckle arm with a puller **(see illustration)**. Remove the nut and separate the tie-rod.

5   Unscrew the tie-rod end from the steering rod.

Installation

6   Thread the tie-rod end on to the marked position and insert the tie-rod stud into the steering knuckle arm. Tighten the jam nut securely.

7   Install the nut on the ballstud and tighten it to the torque listed in this Chapter's Specifications. Install a new cotter pin.

8   Install the wheel and lug nuts. Lower the vehicle and tighten the lug nuts to the torque listed in the Chapter 1 Specifications.

9   Have the wheel alignment checked by a dealer service department or an alignment shop.

18   Steering gear boots - replacement

Refer to illustration 18.3

1   Loosen the lug nuts, raise the vehicle and support it securely on jackstands. Remove the wheel.

2   Remove the tie-rod end and jam nut (see Section 17).

3   Remove the outer steering gear boot clamp with a pair of pliers **(see illustration)**. Cut off the inner boot clamp with a pair of diagonal cutters. Slide the boot off.

4   Before installing the new boot, wrap the threads on the end of the steering rod with

16.7 These two arrows (A) on the spiral cable housing will be aligned when it's centered; the white locating pin (B) must be at the top

17.2 Loosen the jam nut, then mark the position of the tie-rod end on the threaded part of the tie-rod

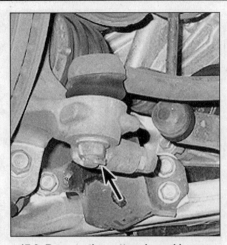

17.3 Remove the cotter pin and loosen (but don't remove) the tie-rod end nut

17.4 Install a small puller to separate the tie-rod end from the steering knuckle

18.3 The outer end of the boot is secured by a spring clamp that can be slid off by pinching the ends together; the inner end of the boot is retained by a clamp that must be cut off and discarded

19.3 Disconnect the high pressure line (A) and the return hose (B) - (C) is the left mounting bolt and nut

tape so the small end of the new boot isn't damaged.

5   Slide the new boot into position on the steering gear until it seats in the groove in the steering rod and install new clamps.

6   Remove the tape and install the tie-rod end (see Section 17).

7   Install the wheel and lug nuts. Lower the vehicle and tighten the lug nuts to the torque listed in the Chapter 1 Specifications.

8   Have the wheel alignment checked by a dealer service department or an alignment shop.

19 Steering gear - removal and installation

Warning: *The models covered by this manual are equipped with Supplemental Restraint Systems (SRS), more commonly known as airbags. Always disarm the airbag system before working in the vicinity of any airbag system component to avoid the possibility of accidental deployment of the airbag, which could cause personal injury (see Chapter 12). Do not use a memory saving device to preserve the PCM's memory when working on or near airbag system components.*

Removal

Refer to illustrations 19.3, 19.4 and 19.5

1   Loosen the front wheel lug nuts, raise the front of the vehicle and support it securely on jackstands. Make sure the wheels are pointed straight ahead, then use the seat belt or some rope to tie the steering wheel in this position. Apply the parking brake and remove the wheels. Remove the access panels from the wheel wells.

2   Separate the tie-rod ends from the steering knuckle arms (see Section 17).

3   Place a drain pan under the steering gear, then disconnect the fluid lines **(see illustration)**. Plug the ends to prevent contamination.

4   Remove the tubing support bracket. Disconnect the steering gear wiring harness **(see illustration)**.

19.4 Steering gear wiring harness connector

19.5 Remove the pinch bolt from the lower steering shaft U-joint

20.4 Power steering pressure line (A), feed hose (B), and upper mounting bolt (C)

5   Mark the relationship of the steering shaft to the steering gear. Remove the pinch bolt from the lower steering shaft **(see illustration)**, then separate the shaft from the steering gear. Keep the steering wheel pointed straight ahead. **Warning:** *Do not turn the steering wheel while the steering gear is removed. If the steering wheel is inadvertently turned, remove the steering wheel and center the spiral cable (see Section 16). To prevent the steering wheel from turning, loop the seat belt through the steering wheel and fasten it into its latch.*
6   Remove the stabilizer bar (see Section 4).
7   Remove the steering gear mounting bolts and maneuver the steering gear out from the left-side wheelwell.

Installation
Note: *Make sure the steering gear is centered from side to side before installing it.*
8   Installation is the reverse of removal.
9   Install the bolts and tighten them to the torque listed in this Chapter's Specifications.
10   Connect the tie-rod ends to the steering

20.7 Power steering pump lower mounting bolt

knuckle arms (see Section 17).
11   Install the steering column pinch bolt and tighten it to the torque listed in this Chapter's Specifications.
12   Connect the power steering pressure and return hoses to the steering gear and fill the power steering pump reservoir with the recommended fluid (see Chapter 1).
13   Install the wheels and lug nuts, then lower the vehicle and tighten the lug nuts to the torque listed in the Chapter 1 Specifications. Bleed the steering system (see Section 21).
14   Have the wheel alignment checked by a dealer service department or an alignment shop.

20   Power steering pump - removal and installation

Removal
Refer to illustrations 20.4 and 20.7
1   Disconnect the cable from the negative terminal of the battery (see Chapter 5).
2   Loosen the right front wheel lug nuts. Raise the vehicle and support it securely on jackstands, then remove the wheel. Remove the engine lower splash shield and the right inner fender access panel (see Chapter 11).
3   Using a large syringe or suction gun, suck as much fluid out of the power steering fluid reservoir as possible. Place a drain pan under the vehicle to catch any fluid that spills out when the hoses are disconnected.
4   Loosen the clamp and disconnect the fluid feed hose from the pump **(see illustration)**.
5   Remove the pressure line-to-pump banjo bolt, then detach the line from the pump **(see illustration 20.4)**. Remove and discard the sealing washers. They should be replaced when installing the pump.
6   Remove the drivebelt from the pump (see Chapter 1).
7   Remove the pump mounting bolts **(see**

accompanying illustration and illustration 20.4), then remove the pump from the vehicle.

Installation
8   Installation is the reverse of removal. Be sure to use new sealing washers and tighten the banjo bolt to the torque listed in this Chapter's Specifications. Reconnect the battery and perform the necessary re-learn procedures (see Chapter 5).
9   Top up the fluid level in the reservoir (see Chapter 1) and bleed the system (see Section 21).

21   Power steering system - bleeding

1   Following any operation in which the power steering fluid lines have been disconnected, the power steering system must be bled to remove all air and obtain proper steering performance.
2   With the front wheels in the straight ahead position, check the power steering fluid level and, if low, add fluid until it reaches the Cold mark.
3   Turn the steering wheel from lock to lock several times with the engine Off.
4   Start the engine, then hold the steering wheel against each lock for no more than three seconds. Repeat this until air has been removed from the system and bubbles stop appearing in the reservoir.
5   Recheck the fluid level and add more if necessary to reach the Cold mark on the reservoir.
6   When the air is worked out of the system, return the wheels to the straight ahead position and leave the vehicle running for several more minutes before shutting it off.
7   Road test the vehicle to be sure the steering system is functioning normally and quietly.
8   Recheck the fluid level to be sure it is up to the Hot mark while the engine is at normal operating temperature. Add fluid if necessary (see Chapter 1).

22 Wheels and tires - general information

Refer to illustration 22.1

1   All vehicles covered by this manual are equipped with metric-sized steel belted radial tires **(see illustration)**. Use of other size or type of tires may affect the ride and handling of the vehicle. Don't mix different types of tires, such as radials and bias belted, on the same vehicle as handling may be seriously affected. It's recommended that tires be replaced in pairs on the same axle, but if only one tire is being replaced, be sure it's the same size, structure and tread design as the other.

2   Because tire pressure has a substantial effect on handling and wear, the pressure on all tires should be checked at least once a month or before any extended trips (see Chapter 1).

3   Wheels must be replaced if they are bent, dented, leak air, have elongated bolt holes, are heavily rusted, out of vertical symmetry or if the lug nuts won't stay tight. Wheel repairs that use welding or peening are not recommended.

4   Tire and wheel balance is important in the overall handling, braking and performance of the vehicle. Unbalanced wheels can adversely affect handling and ride characteristics as well as tire life. Whenever a tire is installed on a wheel, the tire and wheel should be balanced by a shop with the proper equipment.

23 Wheel alignment - general information

Refer to illustration 23.1

A wheel alignment refers to the adjustments made to the wheels so they are in proper angular relationship to the suspension and the ground. Wheels that are out of proper alignment not only affect vehicle control, but also increase tire wear. The front end angles normally measured are camber, caster and toe-in **(see illustration)**. Camber and caster are preset at the factory on the vehicles covered by this manual; toe-in is the only adjustable angle on these vehicles (however, camber and caster are usually measured to check for bent or worn suspension parts). Toe-in and camber are both adjustable at the rear.

Getting the proper wheel alignment is an exacting process, one in which complicated and expensive machines are necessary to perform the job properly. Because of this, you should have a technician with the proper equipment perform these tasks. We will, however, use this space to give you a basic idea of what is involved with a wheel alignment so you can better understand the process and deal intelligently with the shop that does the work.

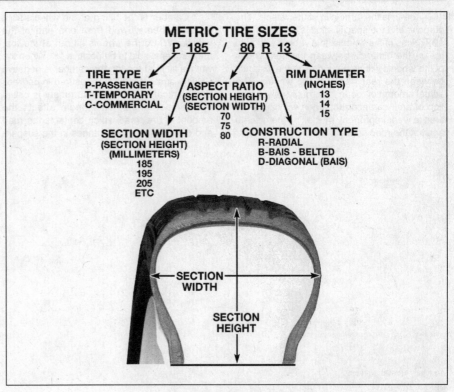

22.1 Metric tire size code

23.1 Camber, caster and toe-in angles

Toe-in is the turning in of the wheels. The purpose of a toe specification is to ensure parallel rolling of the wheels. In a vehicle with zero toe-in, the distance between the front edges of the wheels will be the same as the distance between the rear edges of the wheels. The actual amount of toe-in is normally only a fraction of an inch. Incorrect toe-in will cause the tires to wear improperly by making them scrub against the road surface.

Camber is the tilting of the wheels from vertical when viewed from one end of the vehicle. When the wheels tilt out at the top, the camber is said to be positive (+). When the wheels tilt in at the top the camber is negative (-). The amount of tilt is measured in degrees from vertical and this measurement is called the camber angle. This angle affects the amount of tire tread which contacts the road and compensates for changes in the suspension geometry when the vehicle is cornering or traveling over an undulating surface.

Caster is the tilting of the front steering axis from the vertical. A tilt toward the rear is positive caster and a tilt toward the front is negative caster.

Chapter 11 Body

Contents

1 General information

Warning: *The models covered by this manual are equipped with Supplemental Restraint Systems (SRS), more commonly known as airbags. Always disable the airbag system before working in the vicinity of any airbag system components to avoid the possibility of accidental deployment of the airbags, which could cause personal injury (see Chapter 12).*

Certain body components are particularly vulnerable to accident damage and can be unbolted and repaired or replaced. Among these parts are the hood, doors, tailgate, liftgate, bumpers and front fenders.

Only general body maintenance practices and body panel repair procedures within the scope of the do-it-yourselfer are included in this Chapter.

Make sure the damaged area is perfectly clean and rust free. If the touch-up kit has a wire brush, use it to clean the scratch or chip. Or use fine steel wool wrapped around the end of a pencil. Clean the scratched or chipped surface only, not the good paint surrounding it. Rinse the area with water and allow it to dry thoroughly

Thoroughly mix the paint, then apply a small amount with the touch-up kit brush or a very fine artist's brush. Brush in one direction as you fill the scratch area. Do not build up the paint higher than the surrounding paint

2   Repair minor paint scratches

No matter how hard you try to keep your vehicle looking like new, it will inevitably be scratched, chipped or dented at some point. If the metal is actually dented, seek the advice of a professional. But you can fix minor scratches and chips yourself. Buy a touch-up paint kit from a dealer parts department or an auto parts store. To ensure that you get the right color, you'll need to have the specific make, model and year of your vehicle and, ideally, the paint code, which is located on a special metal plate under the hood or in the door jamb.

3   Body repair - minor damage

Plastic body panels

The following repair procedures are for minor scratches and gouges. Repair of more serious damage should be left to a dealer service department or qualified auto body shop. Below is a list of the equipment and materials necessary to perform the following repair procedures on plastic body panels.

Wax, grease and silicone removing solvent
Cloth-backed body tape
Sanding discs
Drill motor with three-inch disc holder
Hand sanding block
Rubber squeegees
Sandpaper
Non-porous mixing palette
Wood paddle or putty knife
Curved-tooth body file
Flexible parts repair material

Flexible panels (bumper trim)

1   Remove the damaged panel, if necessary or desirable. In most cases, repairs can be car-

If the vehicle has a two-coat finish, apply the clear coat after the color coat has dried

ried out with the panel installed.
2   Clean the area(s) to be repaired with a wax, grease and silicone removing solvent applied with a water-dampened cloth.
3   If the damage is structural, that is, if it extends through the panel, clean the backside of the panel area to be repaired as well. Wipe dry.
4   Sand the rear surface about 1-1/2 inches beyond the break.
5   Cut two pieces of fiberglass cloth large enough to overlap the break by about 1-1/2 inches. Cut only to the required length.
6   Mix the adhesive from the repair kit according to the instructions included with the kit, and apply a layer of the mixture approximately 1/8-inch thick on the backside of the panel. Overlap the break by at least 1-1/2 inches.
7   Apply one piece of fiberglass cloth to the adhesive and cover the cloth with additional adhesive. Apply a second piece of fiberglass

Wait a few days for the paint to dry thoroughly, then rub out the repainted area with a polishing compound to blend the new paint with the surrounding area. When you're happy with your work, wash and polish the area

cloth to the adhesive and immediately cover the cloth with additional adhesive in sufficient quantity to fill the weave.
8   Allow the repair to cure for 20 to 30 minutes at 60-degrees to 80-degrees F.
9   If necessary, trim the excess repair material at the edge.
10   Remove all of the paint film over and around the area(s) to be repaired. The repair material should not overlap the painted surface.
11   With a drill motor and a sanding disc (or a rotary file), cut a "V" along the break line approximately 1/2-inch wide. Remove all dust and loose particles from the repair area.
12   Mix and apply the repair material. Apply a light coat first over the damaged area; then continue applying material until it reaches a level

slightly higher than the surrounding finish.

13   Cure the mixture for 20 to 30 minutes at 60-degrees to 80-degrees F.

14   Roughly establish the contour of the area being repaired with a body file. If low areas or pits remain, mix and apply additional adhesive.

15   Block sand the damaged area with sandpaper to establish the actual contour of the surrounding surface.

16   If desired, the repaired area can be temporarily protected with several light coats of primer. Because of the special paints and techniques required for flexible body panels, it is recommended that the vehicle be taken to a paint shop for completion of the body repair.

Steel body panels

See photo sequence

Repair of dents

17   When repairing dents, the first job is to pull the dent out until the affected area is as close as possible to its original shape. There is no point in trying to restore the original shape completely as the metal in the damaged area will have stretched on impact and cannot be restored to its original contours. It is better to bring the level of the dent up to a point that is about 1/8-inch below the level of the surrounding metal. In cases where the dent is very shallow, it is not worth trying to pull it out at all.

18   If the backside of the dent is accessible, it can be hammered out gently from behind using a soft-face hammer. While doing this, hold a block of wood firmly against the opposite side of the metal to absorb the hammer blows and prevent the metal from being stretched.

19   If the dent is in a section of the body which has double layers, or some other factor makes it inaccessible from behind, a different technique is required. Drill several small holes through the metal inside the damaged area, particularly in the deeper sections. Screw long, self-tapping screws into the holes just enough for them to get a good grip in the metal. Now pulling on the protruding heads of the screws with locking pliers can pull out the dent.

20   The next stage of repair is the removal of paint from the damaged area and from an inch or so of the surrounding metal. This is easily done with a wire brush or sanding disk in a drill motor, although it can be done just as effectively by hand with sandpaper. To complete the preparation for filling, score the surface of the bare metal with a screwdriver or the tang of a file or drill small holes in the affected area. This will provide a good grip for the filler material. To complete the repair, see the Section on filling and painting.

Repair of rust holes or gashes

21   Remove all paint from the affected area and from an inch or so of the surrounding metal using a sanding disk or wire brush mounted in a drill motor. If these are not available, a few sheets of sandpaper will do the job just as effectively.

22   With the paint removed, you will be able to determine the severity of the corrosion and

decide whether to replace the whole panel, if possible, or repair the affected area. New body panels are not as expensive as most people think and it is often quicker to install a new panel than to repair large areas of rust.

23   Remove all trim pieces from the affected area except those which will act as a guide to the original shape of the damaged body, such as headlight shells, etc. Using metal snips or a hacksaw blade, remove all loose metal and any other metal that is badly affected by rust. Hammer the edges of the hole in to create a slight depression for the filler material.

24   Wire-brush the affected area to remove the powdery rust from the surface of the metal. If the back of the rusted area is accessible, treat it with rust inhibiting paint.

25   Before filling is done, block the hole in some way. This can be done with sheet metal riveted or screwed into place, or by stuffing the hole with wire mesh.

26   Once the hole is blocked off, the affected area can be filled and painted. See the following subsection on filling and painting.

Filling and painting

27   Many types of body fillers are available, but generally speaking, body repair kits which contain filler paste and a tube of resin hardener are best for this type of repair work. A wide, flexible plastic or nylon applicator will be necessary for imparting a smooth and contoured finish to the surface of the filler material. Mix up a small amount of filler on a clean piece of wood or cardboard (use the hardener sparingly). Follow the manufacturer's instructions on the package, otherwise the filler will set incorrectly.

28   Using the applicator, apply the filler paste to the prepared area. Draw the applicator across the surface of the filler to achieve the desired contour and to level the filler surface. As soon as a contour that approximates the original one is achieved, stop working the paste. If you continue, the paste will begin to stick to the applicator. Continue to add thin layers of paste at 20-minute intervals until the level of the filler is just above the surrounding metal.

29   Once the filler has hardened, the excess can be removed with a body file. From then on, progressively finer grades of sandpaper should be used, starting with a 180-grit paper and finishing with 600-grit wet-or-dry paper. Always wrap the sandpaper around a flat rubber or wooden block, otherwise the surface of the filler will not be completely flat. During the sanding of the filler surface, the wet-or-dry paper should be periodically rinsed in water. This will ensure that a very smooth finish is produced in the final stage.

30   At this point, the repair area should be surrounded by a ring of bare metal, which in turn should be encircled by the finely feathered edge of good paint. Rinse the repair area with clean water until all of the dust produced by the sanding operation is gone.

31   Spray the entire area with a light coat of primer. This will reveal any imperfections in the surface of the filler. Repair the imperfections with

fresh filler paste or glaze filler and once more smooth the surface with sandpaper. Repeat this spray-and-repair procedure until you are satisfied that the surface of the filler and the feathered edge of the paint are perfect. Rinse the area with clean water and allow it to dry completely.

32   The repair area is now ready for painting. Spray painting must be carried out in a warm, dry, windless and dust free atmosphere. These conditions can be created if you have access to a large indoor work area, but if you are forced to work in the open, you will have to pick the day very carefully. If you are working indoors, dousing the floor in the work area with water will help settle the dust that would otherwise be in the air. If the repair area is confined to one body panel, mask off the surrounding panels. This will help minimize the effects of a slight mismatch in paint color. Trim pieces such as chrome strips, door handles, etc., will also need to be masked off or removed. Use masking tape and several thickness of newspaper for the masking operations.

33   Before spraying, shake the paint can thoroughly, then spray a test area until the spray painting technique is mastered. Cover the repair area with a thick coat of primer. The thickness should be built up using several thin layers of primer rather than one thick one. Using 600-grit wet-or-dry sandpaper, rub down the surface of the primer until it is very smooth. While doing this, the work area should be thoroughly rinsed with water and the wet-or-dry sandpaper periodically rinsed as well. Allow the primer to dry before spraying additional coats.

34   Spray on the top coat, again building up the thickness by using several thin layers of paint. Begin spraying in the center of the repair area and then, using a circular motion, work out until the whole repair area and about two inches of the surrounding original paint is covered. Remove all masking material 10 to 15 minutes after spraying on the final coat of paint. Allow the new paint at least two weeks to harden, then use a very fine rubbing compound to blend the edges of the new paint into the existing paint. Finally, apply a coat of wax

4   Body repair - major damage

1   Major damage must be repaired by an auto body shop specifically equipped to perform body and frame repairs. These shops have the specialized equipment required to do the job properly.

2   If the damage is extensive, the frame must be checked for proper alignment or the vehicle's handling characteristics may be adversely affected and other components may wear at an accelerated rate.

3   Due to the fact that all of the major body components (hood, fenders, etc.) are separate and replaceable units, any seriously damaged components should be replaced rather than repaired. Sometimes the components can be found in a wrecking yard that specializes in used vehicle components, often at considerable savings over the cost of new parts.

These photos illustrate a method of repairing simple dents. They are intended to supplement *Body repair - minor damage* in this Chapter and should not be used as the sole instructions for body repair on these vehicles.

1 If you can't access the backside of the body panel to hammer out the dent, pull it out with a slide-hammer-type dent puller. Tap with a hammer near the edge of the dent to help 'pop' the metal back to its original shape, about 1/8-inch below the surface of the surrounding metal

2 Using coarse-grit sandpaper, remove the paint down to the bare metal. Clean the repair area with wax/silicone remover.

3 Following label instructions, mix up a batch of plastic filler and hardener, then quickly press it into the metal with a plastic applicator. Work the filler until it matches the original contour and is slightly above the surrounding metal

4 Let the filler harden until you can just dent it with your fingernail. File, then sand the filler down until it's smooth and even. Work down to finer grits of sandpaper - always using a board or block - ending up with 360 or 400 grit

5 When the area is smooth to the touch, clean the area and mask around it. Apply several layers of primer to the area. A professional-type spray gun is being used here, but aerosol spray primer works fine

6 Fill imperfections or scratches with glazing compound. Sand with 360 or 400-grit and re-spray. Finish sand the primer with 600 grit, clean thoroughly, then apply the finish coat. Don't attempt to rub out or wax the repair area until the paint has dried completely (at least two weeks)

5 Upholstery, carpets and vinyl trim - maintenance

Upholstery and carpets

1 Every three months remove the floor-mats and clean the interior of the vehicle (more frequently if necessary). Use a stiff whiskbroom to brush the carpeting and loosen dirt and dust, then vacuum the upholstery and carpets thoroughly, especially along seams and crevices.

2 Dirt and stains can be removed from carpeting with basic household or automotive carpet shampoos available in spray cans. Follow the directions and vacuum again, then use a stiff brush to bring back the "nap" of the carpet.

3 Most interiors have cloth or vinyl upholstery, either of which can be cleaned and maintained with a number of material-specific cleaners or shampoos available in auto supply stores. Follow the directions on the product for usage, and always spot-test any upholstery cleaner on an inconspicuous area (bottom edge of a backseat cushion) to ensure that it doesn't cause a color shift in the material.

4 After cleaning, vinyl upholstery should be treated with a protectant. **Note:** *Make sure the protectant container indicates the product can be used on seats - some products may make a seat too slippery.* **Caution:** *Do not use protectant on vinyl-covered steering wheels.*

5 Leather upholstery requires special care. It should be cleaned regularly with saddle-soap or leather cleaner. Never use alcohol, gasoline, nail polish remover or thinner to clean leather upholstery.

6 After cleaning, regularly treat leather upholstery with a leather conditioner, rubbed in with a soft cotton cloth. Never use car wax on leather upholstery.

7 In areas where the interior of the vehicle is subject to bright sunlight, cover leather seating areas of the seats with a sheet if the vehicle is to be left out for any length of time.

Vinyl trim

8 Don't clean vinyl trim with detergents, caustic soap or petroleum-based cleaners. Plain soap and water works just fine, with a soft brush to clean dirt that may be ingrained. Wash the vinyl as frequently as the rest of the vehicle.

9 After cleaning, application of a high-qual-ity rubber and vinyl protectant will help prevent oxidation and cracks. The protectant can also be applied to weather-stripping, vacuum lines and rubber hoses, which often fail as a result of chemical degradation, and to the tires.

6 Fastener and trim removal

Refer to illustration 6.4

1 There is a variety of plastic fasteners used to hold trim panels, splash shields and other parts in place in addition to typical screws, nuts and bolts. Once you are familiar with them, they can usually be removed without too much difficulty.

2 The proper tools and approach can prevent added time and expense to a project by minimizing the number of broken fasteners and/or parts.

3 The following illustration shows various types of fasteners that are typically used on most vehicles and how to remove and install them **(see illustration)**. Replacement fasteners are commonly found at most auto parts stores, if necessary.

Fasteners

This tool is designed to remove special fasteners. A small pry tool used for removing nails will also work well in place of this tool

A Phillips head screwdriver can be used to release the center portion, but light pressure must be used because the plastic is easily damaged. Once the center is up, the fastener can easily be pried from its hole

Here is a view with the center portion fully released. Install the fastener as shown, then press the center in to set it

This fastener is used for exterior panels and shields. The center portion must be pried up to release the fastener. Install the fastener with the center up, then press the center in to set it

This type of fastener is used commonly for interior panels. Use a small blunt tool to press the small pin at the center in to release it . . .

. . . the pin will stay with the fastener in the released position

Reset the fastener for installation by moving the pin out. Install the fastener, then press the pin flush with the fastener to set it

This fastener is used for exterior and interior panels. It has no moving parts. Simply pry the fastener from its hole like the claw of a hammer removes a nail. Without a tool that can get under the top of the fastener, it can be very difficult to remove

4   Trim panels are typically made of plastic and their flexibility can help during removal. The key to their removal is to use a tool to pry the panel near its retainers to release it without damaging surrounding areas or breaking-off any retainers. The retainers will usually snap out of their designated slot or hole after force is applied to them. Stiff plastic tools designed for prying on trim panels are available at most auto parts stores **(see illustration)**. Tools that are tapered and wrapped in protective tape, such as a screwdriver or small pry tool, are also very effective when used with care.

6.4 These small plastic pry tools are ideal for prying off trim panels

7   Hinges and locks - maintenance

Once every 3000 miles, or every three months, the hinges and latch assemblies on the doors, hood and trunk should be given a few drops of light oil or lock lubricant. The door latch strikers should also be lubricated with a thin coat of grease to reduce wear and ensure free movement. Lubricate the door and trunk locks with spray-on graphite lubricant.

8   Windshield and fixed glass - replacement

Replacement of the windshield and fixed glass requires the use of special fast-setting adhesive/caulk materials and some specialized tools. It is recommended that these operations be left to a dealer or a shop specializing in glass work.

9   Hood - removal, installation and adjustment

Note: *The hood is heavy and somewhat awkward to remove and install - at least two people should perform this procedure.*

Removal and installation

Refer to illustrations 9.2 and 9.5

1   Use blankets or pads to cover the cowl area of the body and fenders. This will protect the body and paint as the hood is lifted off.
2   Make marks or scribe a line around the hood hinge to ensure proper alignment during installation **(see illustration)**.
3   Disconnect any cables or wires that will interfere with removal.
4   Place a prop under the hood to hold it open after the support strut is detached.
5   Use a small flat-blade screwdriver to pry off the steel retainer clip that secures the upper end of the support strut to the hood **(see illustration)**. Detach the strut from the hood and allow it to rest against the fender.
6   With an assistant supporting the hood, remove the hood mounting nuts from the hinges.
7   Lift off the hood. **Caution:** *Do NOT try to remove the hood by yourself; it's heavy, and you could injure yourself and/or scratch or damage something.*
8   Installation is the reverse of removal.

Adjustment

Refer to illustration 9.13

9   Adjust the hood fore-and-aft and side-to-

side by moving the hinge plate slot after loosening the bolts or nuts.
10   Scribe a line around the entire hinge plate so you can determine the amount of movement **(see illustration 9.2)**.
11   Loosen the bolts or nuts and move the hood into correct alignment. Move it only a little at a time. Tighten the hinge bolts and carefully lower the hood to check the position.
12   If necessary after installation, the entire hood latch assembly can be adjusted up-and-down as well as from side-to-side on the radiator support so the hood closes securely and flush with the fenders. To make the adjustment, scribe a line or mark around the hood latch mounting bolts to provide a reference point, then loosen them and reposition the latch assembly, as necessary (see Section 10). Following adjustment, retighten the mounting bolts.
13   Finally, adjust the hood bumpers on the radiator support so the hood, when closed, is flush with the fenders **(see illustration)**.
14   Periodically, lubricate the hood latch assembly, as well as the hinges, with white, lithium-base grease to prevent binding and wear.

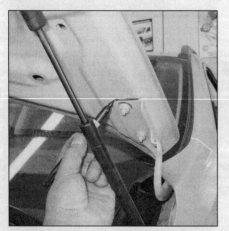

9.2 Before removing the hood, draw a mark around the hinge plate

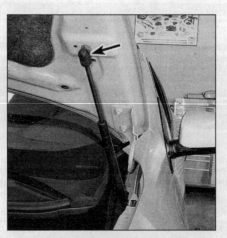

9.5 Use a small screwdriver to pry off the clip

9.13 Adjust the hood closing height by turning the hood bumpers in or out

10 Hood release latch and cable - removal and installation

Latch

Refer to illustration 10.2

1   Remove the radiator grille (see Section 11).
2   Scribe a line around the latch to aid alignment when installing. Remove the latch retaining bolts **(see illustration)** and remove the latch.
3   Flip the hood latch assembly over and disengage the hood release cable from the latch.
4   Installation is the reverse of removal.
Note: *Adjust the latch so the hood engages securely when closed and the hood bumpers are slightly compressed.*

Cable

Refer to illustrations 10.7 and 10.8

5   Unbolt the hood release latch and disconnect the hood release cable from the latch (see Steps 1 through 3).
6   Remove the left inner fender well liner (see Section 19).
7   Detach the cable from the clips along its length **(see illustration)**.
8   Disconnect the cable from the release handle **(see illustration)**.
9   Pull the cable grommet into the passenger compartment, then pull the cable through the hole.
10 Installation is the reverse of removal.
Note: *Push on the grommet with your fingers from the passenger compartment to seat the grommet snugly in the firewall.*

11 Radiator grille - removal and installation

Refer to illustrations 11.1, 11.2, 11.3, 11.4a and 11.4b
Warning: *The models covered by this manual*

10.2 Scribe a line around the hood latch before removing the three mounting bolts

10.7 The hood release cable is secured along its length with clips

10.8 Under-dash hood release cable details:

1   *Pull down the ferrule where the cable enters the hood release lever assembly*
2   *Swing the cable down through the guide in the hood release lever until it's aligned with the removal slot for the cable end plug*
3   *Push the cable end plug out of its mounting hole in the release lever*

are equipped with a Supplemental Restraint System (SRS), more commonly known as airbags. Always disarm the airbag system before working in the vicinity of any airbag system component to avoid the possibility of accidental deployment of the airbag, which could cause personal injury (see Chapter 12). Do not use a memory saving device to pre-

serve the PCM's memory when working on or near airbag system components.
1   Open the hood, remove the fasteners **(see illustration)** from the upper radiator covers and remove the covers.
2   Remove the upper grille mounting fasteners **(see illustration)**.
3   Use pliers to disengage the mounting

11.1 The radiator covers are secured with these fasteners

11.2 Six fasteners retain the top of the grille

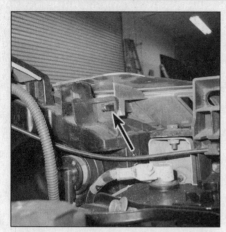

11.3 Pinch these retainers to release them

11.4a To detach the lower part of the grille, carefully pry loose the grille retaining clips

11.4b Location of the four lower clips

tabs from the inside of the grille at each end near the headlights **(see illustration)**.

4   Carefully pry loose the four lower grille clips **(see illustrations)**, then remove the grille.

5   Installation is the reverse of removal.

---

12   Liftgate - removal, installation and adjustment

Note: *The rear liftgate is heavy and somewhat awkward to remove and install - at least two people should perform this procedure.*

Removal and installation

Refer to illustrations 12.5, 12.6a and 12.6b

1   Open the liftgate and cover the edges of the open rear compartment with pads or cloths to protect the painted surfaces when the liftgate is removed.

2   Remove the trim panels from the liftgate (see Section 14).

3   Working through the access hole in the upper part of the liftgate, disconnect the electrical connectors for all harnesses routed between the liftgate and the vehicle body. Disconnect the washer line, then pull the harnesses and the washer line out of the liftgate.

4   Support the liftgate securely with a hood prop or with and broom handle; whatever you use must be strong enough to support the considerable weight of the liftgate when the support struts are removed.

5   Use a small flat-blade screwdriver to release the steel clip at the liftgate end of each support strut **(see illustration)**. Detach the struts from the liftgate and allow it to rest against the prop.

6   Remove the small trim cover from each hinge **(see illustration)**. Outline the exact positions of the liftgate hinges on the liftgate prior to removal. Have an assistant help you as you carefully remove the liftgate mounting nuts **(see illustration)** from the hinges. **Note:** *When reinstalling the liftgate, align the lid-to-hinge bolts with the marks made during removal.*

7   Installation is the reverse of removal.

Adjustment

8   Fore-and-aft and side-to-side adjustments of the liftgate are accomplished by moving the liftgate in relation to the hinge after loosening the bolts or nuts.

9   Scribe a line around the entire hinge plate so you can determine the amount of movement.

10   Loosen the bolts or nuts and move the liftgate into correct alignment. Move it only a little at a time. Tighten the hinge bolts or nuts and carefully lower the liftgate to check the alignment.

11   If necessary after installation, the entire liftgate striker assembly can be adjusted up and down as well as from side to side on the liftgate, so the lid closes securely and is flush with the quarter panels. To do this, scribe a line around the liftgate striker assembly to provide a reference point. Loosen the bolts and reposition the striker as necessary. Following adjustment, retighten the mounting bolts.

12   The liftgate latch assembly, as well as the hinges, should be periodically lubricated with white lithium-base grease to prevent sticking and wear.

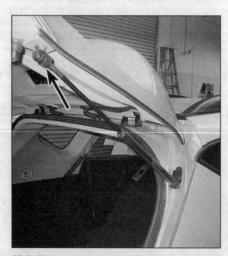

12.5 Make sure that the liftgate is securely supported before you pry out the retainers and detach the struts from the liftgate

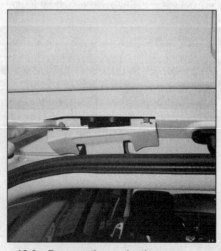

12.6a Remove these plastic covers . . .

12.6b . . . for access to the liftgate hinge fasteners

13.1 Pull off the latch trim cover

13   Liftgate latch - removal and installation

Refer to illustrations 13.1 and 13.5

1   Remove the liftgate inner trim panel (see Section 14). Pull the cover from the latch **(see illustration)**.

13.5 Liftgate latch mounting bolts

2   Detach the cables from the inner and outer door handles.
3   Scribe a line around the latch assembly for a reference point to aid the installation procedure.
4   Disconnect the electrical connectors.
5   Remove the mounting bolts and remove the latch **(see illustration)**.
6   Installation is the reverse of removal.

14   Door trim panels - removal and installation

Side doors

Refer to illustrations 14.2, 14.3, 14.4, 14.5a, 14.5b, 14.6, 14.7 and 14.9

1   Open the window all the way.
2   Carefully pry off the inside handle trim cover **(see illustration)**, then remove the mounting fastener under the trim.
3   Carefully pry up the power window switch trim panel, disengaging the clips as you go **(see illustration)**. Pull out the switch, flip it over, disconnect the electrical connectors and remove the switch panel.
4   Remove the bolt under the power window switch panel **(see illustration)**.
5   Carefully pry up the arm rest pad, then remove the mounting fastener under it **(see illustrations)**.
6   Carefully pry off the door lamp lens **(see illustration)**, then disconnect the electrical connector. Also remove the seat control switches.
7   Starting at the bottom of the door trim panel, carefully pry loose the panel retaining

14.2 Carefully pry off the handle cover, then remove the mounting fastener under it

14.3 Carefully pry up the switch panel, starting at the rear - release each clip

14.4 Remove the trim panel mounting fastener from the armrest area

14.5a Pry up the armrest, carefully releasing each clip . . .

14.5b . . . then remove the hidden bolt

14.6 Pry off the door lamp lens

14.7 Start at the bottom when prying loose the door trim panel clips, then work your way all the way around the rear, lower and front edges of the trim panel

14.9 Disengage the latch and lock cables from the inside door handle

14.11 Carefully pry off the inside grips

clips **(see illustration)**. Work around the edge until the panel is loose. **Caution:** *Pry next to the clips only. Prying between the clips can damage the door panel.*

8   When all the clips are disengaged, lift the panel UP to disengage the channel along the upper edge of the trim panel from the ridge running along the top of the door window opening.

9   Once the trim panel is free, disconnect the two cables from the inside door handle **(see illustration)**.

10   Installation is the reverse of removal.

Liftgate

Refer to illustrations 14.11, 14.12, 14.13 and 14.17

11   Open the liftgate and carefully pry off the handle grip panel **(see illustration)**.

12   Release the push-pin clips **(see illustration)**.

13   Pry off the lenses of the cargo area lights **(see illustration)**, disconnect the electrical connectors and remove the lights.

14   Pry off the other trim panel access panels.

15   Release the steel clips at each upper corner of the trim panel.

16   Insert the trim removal tool between the upper edge of the trim panel and the glass, then pull down to release the clips along the top edge.

17   Work the tool along the other three edges of the trim panel, releasing the clips as you go, then remove the liftgate trim panel **(see illustration)**.

18   Use the same tool to remove the liftgate center plate and the hinge covers.

19   Installation is the reverse of removal.

15   Door - removal, installation and adjustment

Note: *The doors are heavy and somewhat awkward to remove and install - at least two people should perform this procedure.*

Removal and installation

Refer to illustrations 15.5, 15.7a and 15.7b

1   Lower the window completely in the door. Disconnect the cable from the negative terminal of the battery (see Chapter 5).

2   Open the door all the way and support it on jacks or blocks covered with rags to prevent damaging the paint.

3   It's easiest to remove the door trim panel and watershield at this time (see Section 14).

4   Pull the grommet and wiring harness out of the front door jamb until the connectors are exposed, then disconnect the electrical connectors.

5   Unbolt the door stop **(see illustration)**.

6   Mark around the door hinges with a pen or a scribe to facilitate realignment during reassembly.

7   With an assistant holding the door, remove the hinge-to-door nuts **(see illustrations)** and lift the door off.

8   Installation is the reverse of removal. Reconnect the battery and perform the necessary re-learn procedures (see Chapter 5).

14.12 Push-pin clip locations

14.13 Pry out the lights, then disconnect the wiring and remove them

14.17 Pry off the liftgate trim panel starting at the top, then working around the glass; be careful to avoid damaging the clips

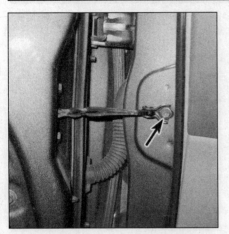

15.5 Unbolt the door check strut

15.7a The lower front door hinge . . .

15.7b . . . and the upper hinge - unbolt the lower hinge first and allow the door to rest on its support while removing the upper bolts

Adjustment

Refer to illustration 15.12

9   Having proper door-to-body alignment is a critical part of a well-functioning door assembly. Check the door hinge pins for excessive play. Fully open the door and lift up and down on the door without lifting the body. If a door has 1/16-inch or more excessive play, the hinges should be replaced.

10   Door-to-body alignment adjustments are made by loosening the hinge-to-body bolts or hinge-to-door bolts and moving the door. Proper body alignment is achieved when the top of the doors are parallel with the roof section, the front door is flush with the fender, the rear door is flush with the rear quarter panel and the bottom of the doors are aligned with the lower rocker panel. If these goals can't be reached by adjusting the hinge-to-body or hinge-to-door bolts, body alignment shims may have to be purchased and inserted behind the hinges to achieve correct alignment.

11   To adjust the door closed position, scribe a line or mark around the striker plate to provide a reference point, then check that the door latch is contacting the center of the latch striker. If not, adjust the up and down position first.

12   Finally, adjust the latch striker sideways position, so that the door panel is flush with

the center pillar or rear quarter panel and provides positive engagement with the latch mechanism **(see illustration)**.

16   Door latch, key lock cylinder and handles - removal and installation

Inside door handle

Refer to illustration 16.1

1   Remove the door trim panel (see Section 14), disconnect the actuator cable from the handle **(see illustration 14.9)**, then unscrew the handle from the backside of the door trim panel **(see illustration)**.

2   Installation is the reverse of removal.

Key lock cylinder and outside door handle

Refer to illustrations 16.5, 16.6, 16.7, 16.8, 16.9a and 16.9b

3   Remove the door trim panel (see Section 14).

4   Remove the door window glass and the door module assembly (see Section 17).

5   Remove the rubber plug from the rear

15.12 Adjust the door lock striker by loosening the mounting screws and gently tapping the striker in the desired direction

edge of the door **(see illustration)**, then loosen the Torx bolt that secures the door lock cylinder (driver's door) or the handle trim (passenger's door). **Caution:** *Don't try to remove the Torx bolt completely; just back it out until it stops.*

16.1 Access the inside door handle retaining screws on the backside of the door trim panel

16.5 Remove this plug from the rear edge of the door to access the Torx bolt that secures the key lock cylinder

16.6 To disconnect either end of the actuator rod (A), pop off the slotted part of the clip that wraps around the rod, then push the end of the rod out of the clip

16.9a To remove the outside door handle mounting bracket (A), slide it to the rear. (B) is the actuator cable

16.9b To disengage the actuator cable, push the cable ferrule (A) out of its slot, then align the cable with the slot (B) and slide out the cable end plug

16.7 Pull the door handle out and remove the lock cylinder assembly

6   Disconnect the actuator rod that connects the key lock cylinder to the door latch assembly **(see illustration)**. If you're removing the outside door handle, disconnect the upper end of the rod; if you're removing the latch assembly, disconnect the lower end of the rod. The rod is secured to the actuator arms on both the key lock cylinder and the latch by small nylon clips. To disconnect either end of the rod, pop the part of the clip that wraps around the rod free of the rod, then push the end of the rod out of the nylon clip.

7   Pull the outside door handle, then remove the lock cylinder assembly **(see illustration)** (driver's side) or the outside handle trim cap (passenger's side).

8   Pull out the lock cylinder end of the outside handle and slide it to the rear to remove it **(see illustration)**.

9   To remove the outside door handle mounting bracket, slide it toward the rear of the vehicle **(see illustration)** and pull it out of the door. Then flip it over and disconnect the actuator cable **(see illustration)**.

10   Installation is the reverse of removal.

16.13 To detach the latch from the door, remove these three Torx bolts

16.8 To remove the outside handle, pull it out, then slide it to the rear

Door latch

Refer to illustrations 16.13 and 16.14

11   Remove the door trim panel (see Section 14).

12   Remove the door window glass and the door module assembly (see Section 17).

13   Remove the Torx bolts from the rear edge of the door **(see illustration)** and pull the latch assembly out of the door.

14   Disconnect the electrical connector and the actuator cable from the door latch **(see illustration)** and remove the latch assembly.

15   Installation is the reverse of removal.

---

17   Door window glass - removal and installation

Removal and installation

Refer to illustrations 17.2 and 17.3

1   Remove the door trim panel (see Section 14).

2   Remove the two round rubber access

16.14 Disconnect the electrical connector (A), disengage the actuator cable ferrule (B) from its bracket and disconnect the cable end plug (C) from the latch actuator arm

17.2 Peel off these two rubber protective covers to access the door window glass bolts

17.3 Door window glass bolts

hole covers **(see illustration)** from the door module assembly.

3 Temporarily connect the power window switch, then move the window to align the glass mounting bolts with the access holes **(see illustration)**.

4 Remove the glass mounting bolts.

5 Pry off the trim cover for the outside mirror **(see illustration 21.2)**.

6 Carefully pry up and remove the inner seal that runs along the bottom of the window opening.

7 Pull the rear of the glass up and tilt it to the outside of the door as you remove it.

8 Installation is the reverse of removal. Check the alignment of the glass and adjust the regulator or guide rails if necessary.

9 Initialize the system (see Steps 10 through 15).

System initialization

Note: *This procedure must be done whenever any window component has been removed or when an electrical component of the system has been removed or disconnected. These parts include the battery, switches, glass, regulator, etc.*

10 Disconnect the battery (see Chapter 5), wait for one minute, then reconnect the battery.

11 Turn the ignition switch to ON.

12 Open the window completely.

13 Select AUTO UP and close the window, then hold the switch for at least four more seconds with the window fully closed.

14 Check the anti-pinch system by opening the window fully. Put a piece of plastic or wood such as a hammer handle into the opening.

15 Raise the window using the AUTO UP button. Make sure that the window reverses itself after it contacts the object.

18 Door window glass regulator - removal and installation

Refer to illustrations 18.2, 18.4 and 18.5

1 Remove the door trim panel (see Section 14).

2 Remove the window glass assembly (see Section 17). **Note:** *The glass need not be removed completely. It can be held in the top position and out of the way with tape* **(see illustration).**

3 Disconnect the electrical connector from the window regulator motor.

4 Remove the fasteners securing the door module panel **(see illustration)**, then remove the door module panel. Detach the wiring harness from the rear of the panel.

18.2 Secure the glass in its fully raised position to avoid having to remove it when servicing the door module and window regulator

5 Remove the bolts securing the regulator to the door module **(see illustrations 18.4 and 18.5)**. Remove the regulator from the door module.

6 Installation is the reverse of removal. Apply light grease to all moving parts.

7 See Section 17 for the initialization procedure.

18.4 Door module details:

1 *Door module mounting bolts*

2 *Window regulator bolts (do not remove these bolts until the module has been removed from the door)*

18.5 Window regulator bolt locations

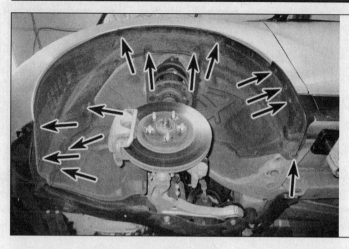

19.2 Inner fender splash shield fasteners (some fasteners - behind the brake rotor and suspension assembly and behind the mudguard - not visible in this photo)

19.3a Open the front door and remove the bolt (not shown) at the rear of the fender, then remove this insulator

19 Fenders - removal and installation

Refer to illustrations 19.2, 19.3a, 19.3b, 19.3c. 19.3d, 19.3e, 19.6a, 19.6b, 19.8a, 19.8b and 19.8c

Note: *This procedure applies to either fender.*

1 Loosen the front wheel lug nuts. Raise the vehicle and support it securely on jackstands. Remove the front wheel.
2 Remove the inner fender splash shield **(see illustration)**.
3 Remove the inner fender noise insulator and the two upper fender trim pieces **(see illustrations)**.

4 Remove the radiator grille (see Section 11).
5 Remove the front bumper cover (see Section 20) and the headlight housing (see Chapter 12).
6 Carefully pry the upper rear part of the small triangular fender trim panel, then remove the upper rear fender bolt **(see illustrations)**.

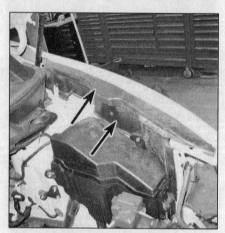

19.3b These two plastic panels must be removed for access to the upper fender bolts

19.3c Pull back the upper panel to reach the push-pin clips under it . . .

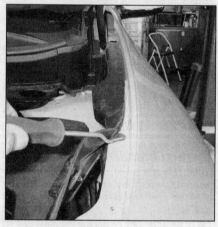

19.3d . . . then pry out the clips . . .

19.3e . . . and remove the panels

19.6a Pry off this trim panel . . .

19.6b . . . and remove the upper rear fender bolt

19.8a Remove this lower rear fender bolt, then open the door to reach the bolt directly above it

19.8b Front fender mounting bolt locations

19.8c Upper fender mounting bolt locations

7   Detach the windshield molding from the fender.

8   Remove the fender mounting bolts (see illustrations) and remove the fender. Caution: The fender is glued to the body with foam. The foam can be peeled off a little at a time until it's removed. Use care when sepa-rating the fender from the body to avoid bend-ing the fender.

9   Installation is the reverse of removal.

20   Bumper covers - removal and installation

Warning: The models covered by this manual are equipped with a Supplemental Restraint System (SRS), more commonly known as airbags. Always disarm the airbag system before working in the vicinity of any airbag system component to avoid the pos-sibility of accidental deployment of the air-bag, which could cause personal injury (see Chapter 12). Do not use a memory saving device to preserve the PCM's memory when working on or near airbag system compo-nents.

Front bumper cover

Refer to illustrations 20.3, 20.4, 20.6a, 20.6b, 20.7, 20.8 and 20.10

1   Apply the parking brake, raise the front of the vehicle and support it securely on jackstands.

2   Remove the radiator grille (see Sec-tion 11).

3   Remove the trim panels above the head-lights (see illustration).

4   Remove the fasteners from the upper edge of the bumper cover (see illustration).

5   Remove the fasteners from each front lower edge of the inner fender splash shields (see illustration 19.2).

6   Remove all three splash shields from the lower rear part of the bumper cover (see illustrations).

20.3 Remove the single retaining bolt (already removed), pull the trim panel forward to disengage the mounting clips, and remove the trim panel

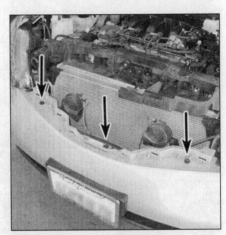

20.4 There are three clips under the grille

20.6a Center lower splash shield fastener locations

20.6b Left lower splash shield fasteners (right lower splash shield the same)

20.7 Bumper cover lower fasteners

20.8 This screw secures the upper rear part of the bumper cover

20.10 Release the bumper ends from the fenders, then carefully pull it away (get help if you need it)

7   Remove the lower bolts from the bumper cover (see illustration).

8   Working inside the bumper cover, remove the screws from the upper rear corners of the bumper cover where it's attached to the fenders (see illustration).

9   Disconnect the electrical connectors from the fog lights.

10   Grasp each end of the bumper cover and pull it outward to separate its clips from the fenders (see illustration), then remove it. Note: You might need an assistant to help with this Step.

11   Installation is the reverse of removal.

Rear bumper cover

Refer to illustrations 20.14, 20.15, 20.16 and 20.17

12   Apply the parking brake, raise the rear of the vehicle and support it securely on jackstands. Open the rear liftgate.

13   Remove the taillight assemblies (see Chapter 12).

14   Remove the bumper cover clip and screw under each taillight (see illustration).

15   Remove the rear mudguards from both rear wheel wells (see illustration).

16   Remove the clips from the lower edge of

the bumper cover (see illustration).

17   Remove the two rear fasteners from the inner fender splash shield (see illustration 20.15) and peel back the splash shield. Remove the screw from each upper corner of the bumper cover's ends (see illustration).

18   Pull the bumper cover carefully to release the clips at the side brackets, then remove it.

19   Installation is the reverse of removal.

20.14 Remove the clip (A) and screw (B) located in each taillight housing area

20.15 To remove each rear mudguard, remove these three screws (A). To detach the rear part of the inner fender splash shield, remove these fasteners (B)

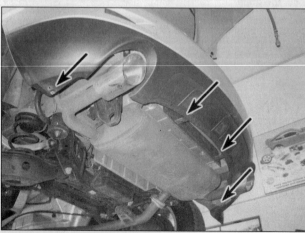

20.16 Lower rear bumper clip locations

20.17 Remove the clips from the inner fender splash shield, then remove this screw (arrow)

21 Outside mirrors - removal and installation

Refer to illustrations 21.2 and 21.4

1   Remove the door trim panel (see Section 14).
2   Pry off the outside mirror trim panel **(see illustration)**.
3   Disconnect the mirror electrical connector.
4   Remove the mirror mounting nuts **(see illustration)** and remove the mirror from the door.
5   Installation is the reverse of removal.

22 Center console - removal and installation

Refer to illustrations 22.2a, 22.2b, 22.3, 22.5a, 22.5b, 22.6, 22.7, 22.8 and 22.9

Warning: *The models covered by this manual are equipped with a Supplemental Restraint System (SRS), more commonly known as airbags. Always disarm the airbag system before working in the vicinity of any airbag system component to avoid the possibility of accidental deployment of the airbag, which could cause personal injury (see Chapter 12).*

21.2 Carefully pry off the mirror trim panel

Do not use a memory saving device to preserve the PCM's memory when working on or near airbag system components.

1   Place the shifter in Drive.
2   Slide the cover under the shift knob down, then pry back and remove the knob retaining clip with a small screwdriver or an awl **(see illustrations)**. Remove the knob.
3   Open the console lid, then use a plastic trim removal tool or a screwdriver wrapped with tape to carefully pry up around the edges of the shift lever trim panel, releasing the clips as

21.4 Disconnect the electrical connector from the mirror before removing the mounting fasteners (arrows)

you go **(see illustration)**. There are two plastic claws at the rear that must be disengaged also.
4   Lift the trim panel up, disconnect the electrical connectors from the underside and remove it.
5   Remove the screw that secures the trim panel in front of the shift lever, then use a trim removal tool to release the clips on the sides of the panel **(see illustrations)**. Remove the panel and disconnect the wiring as you remove it.

22.2a Pull down the shift knob trim ring . . .

22.2b . . . then pull out the retaining clip to remove the knob

22.3 Use care when prying up the sides, then release the rear of the trim panel

22.5a Remove this screw . . .

22.5b . . . then lift off the front panel

22.6 To remove this compartment, pull it out, then reach your hand under the indicated area and release the retainer

22.7 Remove these two trim covers and remove the two screws

22.8 Noting the locations of the clips, pry off the console rear cover

22.9 Rear console screw locations

6   Open the compartment at the rear of the console and release the retainer at the top **(see illustration)** to remove the compartment.
7   Remove the small trim covers from the upper corners of the rear compartment **(see illustration)** and remove the screws.
8   Carefully pry off the console rear cover **(see illustration)**. Disconnect the wiring as you remove it.
9   Remove the console mounting screws **(see illustration)**. Pull up the rear, then slide it rearward to remove the console. Carefully lift it out of the vehicle.
10   Installation is the reverse of removal.

23   Steering column covers - removal and installation

Refer to illustrations 23.2 and 23.3
Warning: *The models covered by this manual are equipped with a Supplemental Restraint System (SRS), more commonly known as airbags. Always disarm the airbag system before working in the vicinity of any*

airbag system component to avoid the possibility of accidental deployment of the airbag, which could cause personal injury (see Chapter 12). Do not use a memory saving device to preserve the PCM's memory when working on or near airbag system components.
1   Disconnect the cable from the negative terminal of the battery (see Chapter 5).
2   Remove the three steering column cover screws. There is one screw in the lower cover and there are two in the upper cover, behind the steering wheel. To access each of the upper screws, turn the steering wheel slightly to expose each screw **(see illustration)**.
3   The upper and lower covers are secured by four mounting tabs located in the upper half of the cover (two on each side). Grasp the upper and lower column cover halves firmly and pull them apart **(see illustration)**.
4   Carefully work the two parts of the steering column cover off the steering column. Make sure that you don't scratch or damage anything.
5   Installation is the reverse of removal. Reconnect the battery and perform the necessary re-learn procedures (see Chapter 5).

24   Dashboard trim panels - removal and installation

Warning: *The models covered by this manual are equipped with a Supplemental Restraint System (SRS), more commonly known as airbags. Always disarm the airbag system before working in the vicinity of any airbag system component to avoid the possibility of accidental deployment of the airbag, which could cause personal injury (see Chapter 12). Do not use a memory saving device to preserve the PCM's memory when working on or near airbag system components.*
Caution: *Use plastic trim removal tools on all procedures in this Section to avoid damage to the soft plastic dashboard trim panels (see Section 6).*

Instrument panel end caps
Refer to illustration 24.1
Note: *The accompanying photo depicts the removal of the right end cap, but this procedure applies to either end cap.*
1   Use a plastic trim tool or a screwdriver wrapped with tape to pry out either end cap **(see illustration)**.
2   To install an end cap, align the clips with their corresponding holes in the dash and push the cap firmly onto the dash until the clips snap into place.

23.2 Access the upper screws by turning the steering wheel slightly as shown

23.3 To separate the upper and lower halves of the steering column cover, grasp them firmly and pull them apart as shown

24.1 Pry off the instrument panel end caps with a plastic trim tool

24.4 Hood release lever assembly mounting bolts

Knee bolster trim panel

Refer to illustrations 24.4 and 24.5

3   Remove the left instrument panel end cap (see Step 1).
4   Remove the hood release handle mounting bolts **(see illustration)**.
5   Noting the location of the clips **(see illustration)** that secure the knee bolster trim panel, grasp the panel firmly and pull it off. Detach the data link connector and all wiring and ducting attached to the backside of the panel, and remove the panel.
6   Installation is the reverse of removal.

Instrument cluster trim bezel

Refer to illustration 24.9

7   Remove the knee bolster trim panel (see Steps 3 through 5).
8   Remove the steering column covers (see Section 23).
9   Carefully pry off the instrument cluster bezel **(see illustration)**. Detach any wiring harnesses attached to the backside of the bezel and remove it.
10   Installation is the reverse of removal.

A-pillar (windshield pillar) trim

Refer to illustration 24.12

11   Pull the rubber weatherstrip loose in the area of the A-pillar trim.
12   Use a plastic trim tool or a screwdriver

24.5 Location of the clips on knee bolster trim panel

wrapped with tape, carefully pry loose the two mounting clips under the trim **(see illustration)**.
13   Pull the trim up to disengage the two locator tabs at the lower end of the trim from the instrument panel, then remove it.
14   To install the A-pillar trim, align the two locator tabs on the lower end of the trim with their corresponding slots in the instrument panel. Push the trim down against the instrument panel until it seats, then push the trim against the A-pillar until the two clips snap into place.

24.9 Carefully pry off the instrument cluster trim bezel

Dashboard speaker covers

Refer to illustrations 24.16a and 24.16b

15   If you're removing one of the tweeter covers (at the left and right corners of the dash, next to the A-pillars), remove the A-pillar trim (see Steps 11 through 13).
16   Carefully pry off the left, right or center speaker cover **(see illustrations)**.
17   When installing a speaker cover, make sure that it snaps into place.
18   If you installed a tweeter cover, install the A-pillar trim (see Step 14).

Lower center trim panel

Refer to illustration 24.19

19   Carefully pry the panel down to disengage the two mounting clips and four mounting tabs **(see illustration)**.
20   Lower the panel, disconnect any wiring harnesses, and remove the panel.
21   Installation is the reverse of removal.

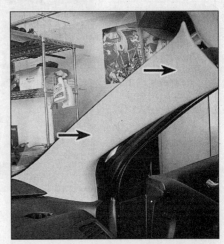

24.12 Disengage the two clips that secure the A-pillar trim to the A-pillar (arrows indicate approximate locations of the two clips)

24.19 Center lower trim panel mounting clip (A) and mounting tab (B) locations (two mounting tabs on the sides of the panel not visible in this photo)

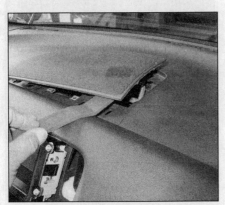

24.16a Carefully pry off the center speaker cover . . .

24.16b . . . or one of the tweeter covers (right cover shown, left cover same)

24.23 Remove the screw from the lower end of each center trim panel

24.24 Use a plastic trim removal tool to disengage the clips (A) and mounting tabs (B) (arrows indicate approximate locations; two additional mounting tabs are in the same area)

24.27 These two screws secure the center vent unit. Arrows indicate the approximate locations of the clips (A) and mounting tabs (B)

Center vent unit

Refer to illustration 24.27

26   Remove the left and right center trim panels (see Steps 22 through 24) and the heater and air conditioning control unit (see Chapter 3).

27   Remove the screws from the bottom of the vent unit **(see illustration)**.

28   Pull the vent unit rearward to release it from its clips **(see illustration 23.27)**.

29   When installing the center vent unit, make sure that it snaps firmly into place, then install the retaining screws.

30   Installation is otherwise the reverse of removal.

Glove box

Refer to illustrations 24.31, 24.32 and 24.33

31   Remove the screws from the bottom of the glove box **(see illustration)**.

32   Open the glove box, then remove the screws from the top edge and interior of the glove box **(see illustration)**.

33   Remove the glove box and disconnect the wiring harness **(see illustration)**.

34   Installation is the reverse of removal. Reconnect the battery and perform the necessary re-learn procedures (see Chapter 5).

Left and right center trim panels

Refer to illustrations 24.23 and 24.24

Note: *The accompanying photos depict the removal of the left center trim panel, but this procedure applies to both trim panels.*

22   Remove the center lower trim panel (see Steps 19 through 21).

23   Remove the screw from the lower end of each panel **(see illustration)**.

24   Use a plastic trim tool or a screwdriver wrapped with tape to pry the panels loose, releasing the clips as you work your way around them **(see illustration)**. Pull the panels back up to remove them.

25   Installation is the reverse of removal.

24.31 Glove box outer screws

24.32 Remove the glove box mounting screws

24.33 Pull out the glove box and disconnect the wiring harness (arrow)

25 Instrument panel - removal and installation

Refer to illustrations 25.12a through 25.12f

Warning: *The models covered by this manual are equipped with a Supplemental Restraint System (SRS), more commonly known as airbags. Always disarm the airbag system before working in the vicinity of any airbag system component to avoid the possibility of accidental deployment of the airbag, which could cause personal injury (see Chapter 12). Do not use a memory saving device to preserve the PCM's memory when working on or near airbag system components.*

Caution: *This is definitely a two-man job. Even stripped of all its components, the instrument panel, or dashboard, is fairly heavy. Do NOT attempt to lift it out of the vehicle by yourself.*

1 Disconnect the cable from the negative terminal of the battery (see Chapter 5).

2 Move the front seats as far back as they will go. Removing the seats will give you more working room (see Section 27)

3 Remove the center console (see Section 22).

4 Remove the steering wheel (see Chapter 10), the steering column covers (see Section 23) and all of the dashboard trim panels (see Section 24).

5 Remove all dashboard-mounted speakers (see Chapter 12).

6 Remove the instrument cluster (see Chapter 12).

7 Remove the heater and air conditioning control unit (see Chapter 3).

8 Remove the audio unit (see Chapter 12).

9 Remove the display screen from behind the center vent unit (see Chapter 12).

10 Disconnect the wiring from the passenger's airbag module, then remove the module's mounting bolt. **Note:** *All electrical connectors for airbag harnesses are bright yellow.*

11 Clearly label, then disconnect, all electrical connectors in the dashboard area and detach all wiring harnesses from the dash. **Note:** *You might not be able to reach every harness clip; keep this in mind while pulling out the dash.*

12 Remove all eight instrument panel mounting screws **(see illustrations)**.

13 With the help of an assistant, lift the instrument panel back just far enough to access and disconnect any remaining wiring harnesses or other components.

14 Carefully remove the instrument panel through the passenger's door opening.

15 Installation is the reverse of removal. Reconnect the battery and perform the necessary re-learn procedures (see Chapter 5).

26 Cowl cover - removal and installation

Refer to illustrations 26.2, 26.3, 26.4, 26.5a and 26.5b

1 Pry off the plastic trim caps on the windshield wiper arms. Remove the wiper arm retaining nuts and wiggle the wiper arms up and down to remove them (see Chapter 12, Section 20).

2 Disconnect the windshield washer line

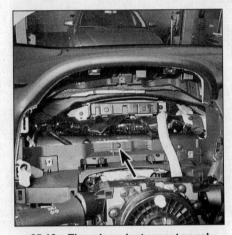

25.12a There is an instrument panel mounting screw behind the instrument cluster . . .

25.12b . . . two screws at the right end of the instrument panel and one at the left end (not shown) . . .

25.12c . . . one screw at the right corner of the glove box . . .

25.12d . . . one screw at the lower left of the instrument panel . . .

25.12e . . . one on the left side of the tunnel . . .

25.12f . . . and one on the right side of the tunnel

26.2 Disconnect the washer hose at one of its fittings

26.3 Remove the clip (A) from each windshield corner trim piece (B) (right trim piece shown, left trim piece identical)

then remove the cowl **(see illustrations)**.
6   Installation is the reverse of removal.

---

27 Seats - removal and installation

Warning: *The models covered by this manual are equipped with a Supplemental Restraint System (SRS), more commonly known as airbags. Always disarm the airbag system before working in the vicinity of any airbag system component to avoid the possibility of accidental deployment of the airbag, which could cause personal injury (see Chapter 12). Do not use a memory saving device to preserve the PCM's memory when working on or near airbag system components.*

Front seat

Refer to illustration 27.3

1   Disconnect the cable from the negative terminal of the battery (see Chapter 5).
2   Position the seat in the middle of its travel to access all of the seat mounting bolts.

at the splice connector in the engine compartment **(see illustration)**.
3   Remove the fasteners from the plastic trim pieces from the left and right lower corners of the windshield **(see illustration)**, then

remove the trim pieces.
4   Remove the upper cowl fasteners, then pull the cowl forward to remove it **(see illustration)**.
5   Remove the lower cowl mounting bolts,

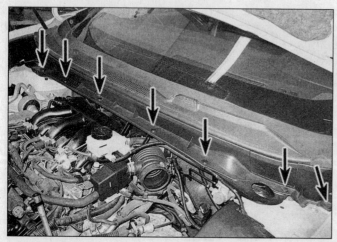

26.4 Remove all of the plastic clips from the upper section of the cowl (not all fasteners visible)

26.5a Lower cowl mounting bolts

26.5b Remove the lower cowl carefully to avoid scratching the paint

27.3 Slide off these plastic trim covers to access the front seat mounting bolts

27.6 After removing the cargo floor carpet, remove this nut and bolt underneath the left and right parts of the rear seat

27.9 Remove the bolt trim covers (A), then remove the mounting bolts (B) from the lower front edge of the rear seat

3   Remove the trim covers from the seat bolts **(see illustration)**.

4   Remove the mounting bolts, then tilt the seat fully upward. Disconnect the airbag wiring harness and any other wiring attached to the seat. Detach the wiring harness clips, then carefully lift the seat out.

5   Installation is the reverse of removal. Reconnect the battery and perform the necessary re-learn procedures (see Chapter 5).

Rear seat

Refer to illustrations 27.6 and 27.9

6   Pull up the rear floor panel for access to the rear of the seat, then remove the seat mounting nuts and bolts **(see illustration)**.

7   Disconnect any wiring from the seat (wiring depends on installed accessories and options).

8   Remove the plastic cover from the recliner device. Detach the seat back cable from the recliner, then remove the seat mounting bolt.

9   Remove the hinge covers from the front of the seat cushion **(see illustration)**. Remove the bolts under the covers.

10   Raise the seat cushion and remove the seat mounting bolt under it.

11   Open the liftgate and remove the seat assembly through the opening.

12   Installation is the reverse of removal.

Notes

Chapter 12
Chassis electrical system

Contents

1 General information

The electrical system is a 12-volt, negative ground type. Power for the lights and all electrical accessories is supplied by a lead/acid-type battery that is charged by the alternator.

This Chapter covers repair and service procedures for the various electrical components not associated with the engine. Information on the battery, alternator, ignition system and starter motor can be found in Chapter 5.

It should be noted that when portions of the electrical system are serviced, the negative cable should be disconnected from the battery to prevent electrical shorts and/or fires.

2 Electrical troubleshooting - general information

Refer to illustrations 2.5a, 2.5b, 2.6 and 2.9

A typical electrical circuit consists of an electrical component, any switches, relays, motors, fuses, fusible links or circuit breakers related to that component and the wiring and connectors that link the component to both the battery and the chassis. To help you pinpoint an electrical circuit problem, wiring diagrams are included at the end of this Chapter.

Before tackling any troublesome electrical circuit, first study the appropriate wiring diagrams to get a complete understanding of what makes up that individual circuit. Trouble spots, for instance, can often be narrowed down by noting if other components related to the circuit are operating properly. If several components or circuits fail at one time, chances are the problem is in a fuse or ground connection, because several circuits are often routed through the same fuse and ground connections.

Electrical problems usually stem from simple causes, such as loose or corroded connections, a blown fuse, a melted fusible link or a failed relay. Visually inspect the condition of all fuses, wires and connections in a problem circuit before troubleshooting the circuit.

If test equipment and instruments are going to be utilized, use the diagrams to plan ahead of time where you will make the necessary connections in order to accurately pinpoint the trouble spot.

The basic tools needed for electrical troubleshooting include a circuit tester or voltmeter (a 12-volt bulb with a set of test leads can also be used), a continuity tester, which includes a bulb, battery and set of test leads, and a jumper wire, preferably with a circuit breaker incorporated, which can be used to bypass electrical components (see illustrations). Before attempting to locate a problem with test instruments, use the wiring diagram(s) to decide where to make the connections.

Voltage checks

Voltage checks should be performed if a circuit is not functioning properly. Connect one lead of a circuit tester to either the negative battery terminal or a known good ground. Connect the other lead to a connector in the circuit being tested, preferably nearest to the battery or fuse (see illustration). If the bulb of the tester lights, voltage is present, which means that the part of the circuit between the connector and the battery is problem free. Continue checking the rest of the circuit in the same fashion. When you reach a point at which no voltage is present, the problem lies between that point and the last test point with voltage. Most of the time the problem can be traced to a loose connection. **Note:** *Keep in mind that some circuits receive voltage only when the ignition key is in the Accessory or Run position.*

Finding a short

One method of finding shorts in a circuit is to remove the fuse and connect a test light or voltmeter in place of the fuse terminals. There should be no voltage present in the circuit. Move the wiring harness from side-to-side while watching the test light. If the bulb goes on, there is a short to ground somewhere in that area, probably where the insulation has rubbed through. The same test can be performed on each component in the circuit, even a switch.

2.5a The most useful tool for electrical troubleshooting is a digital multimeter that can check volts, amps, and test continuity

Ground check

Perform a ground test to check whether a component is properly grounded. Disconnect the battery and connect one lead of a continuity tester or multimeter (set to the ohms scale), to a known good ground. Connect the other lead to the wire or ground connection being tested. If the resistance is low (less than 5 ohms), the ground is good. If the bulb on a self-powered test light does not go on, the ground is not good.

Continuity check

A continuity check is done to determine if there are any breaks in a circuit - if it is passing electricity properly. With the circuit off (no power in the circuit), a self-powered continuity tester or multimeter can be used to check the circuit. Connect the test leads to both ends of the circuit (or to the power end and a good ground), and if the test light comes on the circuit is passing current properly (see illustration). If the resistance is low (less than 5

2.5b A test light is a very handy tool for checking voltage

ohms), there is continuity; if the reading is 10,000 ohms or higher, there is a break somewhere in the circuit. The same procedure can be used to test a switch, by connecting the continuity tester to the switch terminals. With the switch turned On, the test light should come on (or low resistance should be indicated on a meter).

Finding an open circuit

When diagnosing for possible open circuits, it is often difficult to locate them by sight because the connectors hide oxidation or terminal misalignment. Merely wiggling a connector on a sensor or in the wiring harness may correct the open circuit condition. Remember this when an open circuit is indicated when troubleshooting a circuit. Intermittent problems may also be caused by oxidized or loose connections.

Electrical troubleshooting is simple if you keep in mind that all electrical circuits are basically electricity running from the battery, through the wires, switches, relays, fuses

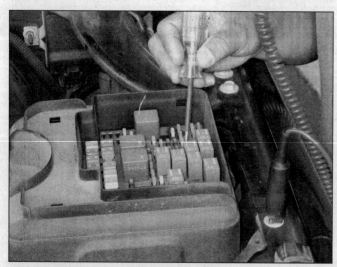

2.6 In use, a basic test light's lead is clipped to a known good ground, then the pointed probe can test connectors, wires or electrical sockets - if the bulb lights, the part being tested has battery voltage

2.9 With a multimeter set to the ohms scale, resistance can be checked across two terminals - when checking for continuity, a low reading indicates continuity, a high reading indicates lack of continuity

3.1a The engine compartment fuse/relay box is located along the left side of the engine compartment. To release the cover, depress the tab at the rear and lift up

3.1b The interior fuse box is located at the left side of the instrument panel, behind the fuse panel cover

3.3 When a fuse blows, the element between the terminals melts - the fuse on the left is blown, the fuse on the right is good

and fusible links to each electrical component (light bulb, motor, etc.) and to ground, from which it is passed back to the battery. Any electrical problem is an interruption in the flow of electricity to and from the battery.

3 Fuses and fusible links - general information

Fuses

Refer to illustrations 3.1a, 3.1b and 3.3

The electrical circuits of the vehicle are protected by a combination of fuses, circuit breakers and fusible links. The main fuse/relay panel is in the engine compartment **(see illustration)**, while the interior fuse/relay panel is located inside the passenger compartment **(see illustration)**. Each of the fuses is designed to protect a specific circuit, and the various circuits are identified on the fuse panel itself.

Several sizes of fuses are employed in the fuse blocks. There are small, medium and large sizes of the same design, all with the same blade terminal design. The medium and large fuses can be removed with your fingers, but the small fuses require the use of pliers or the small plastic fuse-puller tool found in most fuse boxes.

If an electrical component fails, always check the fuse first. The best way to check the fuses is with a test light. Check for power at the exposed terminal tips of each fuse. If power is present at one side of the fuse but not the other, the fuse is blown. A blown fuse can also be identified by visually inspecting it **(see illustration)**.

Be sure to replace blown fuses with the correct type. Fuses (of the same physical size) of different ratings may be physically interchangeable, but only fuses of the proper rating should be used. Replacing a fuse with one of a higher or lower value than specified is not recommended. Each electrical circuit

needs a specific amount of protection. The amperage value of each fuse is molded into the top of the fuse body.

If the replacement fuse immediately fails, don't replace it again until the cause of the problem is isolated and corrected. In most cases, this will be a short circuit in the wiring caused by a broken or deteriorated wire.

Fusible links

Refer to illustration 3.7

Some circuits are protected by fusible links. The links are used in circuits which are not ordinarily fused, or which carry high current, such as the circuit between the alternator and the starter motor. Cartridge-type fusible links are located in the engine compartment fuse/relay box and are similar to a large fuse **(see illustration)**. After disconnecting the negative battery cable, simply unplug the fusible link and replace it with a fusible link of the same amperage. If you have to replace a blown fusible link, make sure that you replace it with one of the same rating. If the replacement fusible link blows in the same circuit, make sure that you troubleshoot the circuit in which the fusible link melted BEFORE installing another fusible link.

4 Circuit breakers - general information

Circuit breakers protect certain circuits, such as the power windows or heated seats. Depending on the vehicle's accessories, there may be one or two circuit breakers, located in the fuse/relay box in the engine compartment.

Because the circuit breakers reset automatically, an electrical overload in a circuit breaker-protected system will cause the circuit to fail momentarily, then come back on. If the circuit does not come back on, check it immediately.

For a basic check, pull the circuit breaker

3.7 Location of the fusible links in the underhood fuse/relay box

up out of its socket on the fuse panel, but just far enough to probe with a voltmeter. The breaker should still contact the sockets. With the voltmeter negative lead on a good chassis ground, touch each end prong of the circuit breaker with the positive meter probe. There should be battery voltage at each end. If there is battery voltage only at one end, the circuit breaker must be replaced.

Some circuit breakers must be reset manually.

5 Relays - general information

Several electrical accessories in the vehicle, such as the fuel injection system, horns, starter, and fog lamps use relays to transmit the electrical signal to the component. Relays use a low-current circuit (the control circuit) to open and close a high-current circuit (the power circuit). If the relay is defective, that component will not operate properly. Most relays are mounted in the engine compartment and interior fuse/relay boxes **(see illustrations 3.1a and 3.1b)**.

6   Electrical connectors - general information

Most electrical connections on these vehicles are made with multiwire plastic connectors. The mating halves of many connectors are secured with locking clips molded into the plastic connector shells. The mating halves of some large connectors, such as some of those under the instrument panel, are held together by a bolt through the center of the connector.

To separate a connector with locking clips, use a small screwdriver to pry the clips apart carefully, then separate the connector halves. Pull only on the shell, never

pull on the wiring harness as you may damage the individual wires and terminals inside the connectors. Look at the connector closely before trying to separate the halves. Often the locking clips are engaged in a way that is not immediately clear. Additionally, many connectors have more than one set of clips.

Each pair of connector terminals has a male half and a female half. When you look at the end view of a connector in a diagram, be sure to understand whether the view shows the harness side or the component side of the connector. Connector halves are mirror images of each other, and a terminal shown on the right side end-view of one half will be

on the left side end-view of the other half.

It is often necessary to take circuit voltage measurements with a connector connected. Whenever possible, carefully insert a small straight pin (not your meter probe) into the rear of the connector shell to contact the terminal inside, then clip your meter lead to the pin. This kind of connection is called "back-probing." When inserting a test probe into a terminal, be careful not to distort the terminal opening. Doing so can lead to a poor connection and corrosion at that terminal later. Using the small straight pin instead of a meter probe results in less chance of deforming the terminal connector.

Electrical connectors

Most electrical connectors have a single release tab that you depress to release the connector

Some electrical connectors have a retaining tab which must be pried up to free the connector

Some connectors have two release tabs that you must squeeze to release the connector

Some connectors use wire retainers that you squeeze to release the connector

Critical connectors often employ a sliding lock (1) that you must pull out before you can depress the release tab (2)

Here's another sliding-lock style connector, with the lock (1) and the release tab (2) on the side of the connector

On some connectors the lock (1) must be pulled out to the side and removed before you can lift the release tab (2)

Some critical connectors, like the multi-pin connectors at the Powertrain Control Module employ pivoting locks that must be flipped open

7.1 Remove the key and pry the remote keyless fob apart . . .

7.2 . . . then carefully remove the battery without touching any other components

7 Remote keyless entry fob - battery replacement

Refer to illustrations 7.1, 7.2 and 7.3

1   Remove the key from the fob, then carefully pry open the keyless entry fob by inserting a small screwdriver into the notch in the body of the transmitter **(see illustration)**.

2   Carefully pry out the old battery with a small screwdriver **(see illustration)**. **Caution:** *Do not touch the circuit board or battery terminal contacts inside the key fob.*

3   Install the new battery, making sure the positive (+) terminal faces the bottom of the case, then reassemble the two halves **(see illustration)**. **Caution:** *Handle the battery by its edges only; holding it like a coin (touching both sides) can reduce the battery's life by partially discharging it.*

8 Body Control Module (BCM) - general information

Refer to illustration 8.2

The Body Control Module (BCM) receives inputs from various switches and sensors and sends commands, some in the form of multiplex voltage signals, to corresponding components to operate them. Some circuits are controlled by the BCM in conjunction with the IPDM (see Section 26) and/or the Powertrain Control Module (PCM) (see Chapter 6). The circuits under BCM control include the:

Combination switch system
Signal buffer system
Power consumption control system
Auto light system
Turn signal and hazard warning
  light system
Headlight system
Fog light system
Daytime running lights system
Interior illumination system
Interior illumination battery saver system

Windshield wiper/washer system
Warning chime system
Power door lock system
Power window system
Air conditioning compressor clutch
Nissan Anti-Theft System (NATS)
Vehicle security system
Rear window defogger system
Remote keyless entry system
Intelligent Key system
Ignition push switch system
Electronic steering column lock
Tire pressure monitor system
Retained accessory power (RAP) system

The BCM is located at the driver's side of the instrument panel **(see illustration)**. Removal and installation of the BCM is not covered in this manual because special equipment is required to diagnose it and the systems it controls. Additionally, if the BCM requires replacement, it must be programmed with the same special equipment before it will work. So, diagnosis and replacement of the BCM must be performed at a dealer service department or other qualified repair shop equipped with the necessary tool.

7.3 To assemble the halves, engage the lip of the back half of the cover (A) into the end of the other half of the fob, then swing the other end down and snap it into place (B)

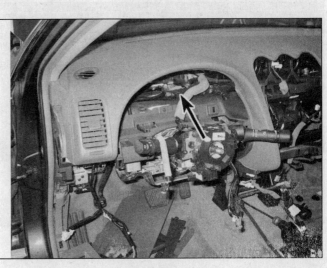

8.2 The Body Control Module is mounted behind the instrument cluster

9.3a The combination switch can be removed without having to first remove the steering wheel (it has been removed for clarity); the left mounting screw . . .

9.3b . . . and the right mounting screw can be reached by turning the steering wheel

9 Steering column switches - replacement

Refer to illustrations 9.3a and 9.3b

Warning: *The models covered by this manual are equipped with Supplemental Restraint Systems (SRS), more commonly known as airbags. Always disable the airbag system before working in the vicinity of any airbag system components to avoid the possibility of accidental deployment of the airbags, which could cause personal injury (see Section 25).*

1   Disconnect the cable from the negative terminal of the battery (see Chapter 5).
2   Remove the steering column covers (see Chapter 11).
3   Rotate the steering wheel for access to the two switch mounting screws **(see illustrations)**.
4   Disconnect the wiring harnesses, then remove the switch by sliding it upward.
5   Installation is the reverse of removal. Reconnect the battery and perform the necessary re-learn procedures (see Chapter 5).

10 Dashboard switches - replacement

Warning: *The models covered by this manual are equipped with Supplemental Restraint Systems (SRS), more commonly known as airbags. Always disable the airbag system before working in the vicinity of any airbag system components to avoid the possibility of accidental deployment of the airbags, which could cause personal injury (see Section 25).*

1   Disconnect the cable from the negative terminal of the battery (see Chapter 5).
2   On lower driver's side switches, remove the driver's knee bolster (see Chapter 11).
3   There are meter control switches at each side of the instrument cluster. For access to these switches, remove the instrument cluster bezel (see Chapter 11). The switches can be unplugged after the wiring is disconnected.
4   On center dash switches, remove the center trim panel (see Chapter 11).
5   Disconnect the electrical connector from the switch being replaced.

6   Use a small screwdriver to release the clips and pull out the switch.
7   Installation is the reverse of removal. Reconnect the battery and perform the necessary re-learn procedures (see Chapter 5).

11 Instrument cluster - removal and installation

Refer to illustrations 11.5 and 11.6

Warning: *The models covered by this manual are equipped with Supplemental Restraint Systems (SRS), more commonly known as airbags. Always disable the airbag system before working in the vicinity of any airbag system components to avoid the possibility of accidental deployment of the airbags, which could cause personal injury (see Section 25).*

1   Disconnect the cable from the negative terminal of the battery (see Chapter 5).
2   Remove the trim panel cap from the left end of the instrument panel, then remove the

11.5 Remove these screws to pull back the instrument cluster . . .

11.6 . . . then disconnect the instrument cluster electrical connector(s)

12.4 Radio mounting screws

12.8 Display module mounting screws

12.12 Remove the instrument panel speaker mounting screws

driver's knee bolster panel (see Chapter 11, Section 24).

3   Lower the steering column and remove the steering column covers (see Chapter 11).

4   Carefully pry off the instrument cluster bezel.

5   Remove the mounting screws from the instrument cluster and pull out the cluster **(see illustration)**.

6   Unplug the electrical connectors and remove the cluster from the vehicle **(see illustration)**.

7   Installation is the reverse of removal. Reconnect the battery and perform the necessary re-learn procedures (see Chapter 5).

12   Radio and speakers - removal and installation

Warning: *The models covered by this manual are equipped with Supplemental Restraint Systems (SRS), more commonly known as airbags. Always disable the airbag system before working in the vicinity of any airbag system components to avoid the possibility of accidental deployment of the airbags, which could cause personal injury (see Section 25).*

12.15 Door speaker mounting screws

Radio

Refer to illustration 12.4

1   Disconnect the cable from the negative terminal of the battery (see Chapter 5).

2   Remove the small trim panel below the radio (see Chapter 11, Section 24).

3   Remove the trim panel from each side of the radio.

4   Remove the radio mounting screws **(see illustration)**. Remove the radio and disconnect the electrical connectors.

5   Remove the radio bracket screws and remove the brackets if necessary.

6   Installation is the reverse of removal. Reconnect the battery and perform the necessary re-learn procedures (see Chapter 5).

Radio and A/C display

Refer to illustration 12.8

7   Remove the center vent unit (see Chapter 11).

8   Remove the mounting screws from the display bracket, then remove the display assembly **(see illustration)**.

9   The radio display can be removed from the bracket if necessary. Installation is the reverse of removal.

Instrument panel speakers

Refer to illustration 12.12

10   Disconnect the cable from the negative terminal of the battery (see Chapter 5). Remove the windshield pillar trim panels if you're removing the end speakers (see Chapter 11, Section 24).

11   Carefully pry up the speaker grilles (see Chapter 11, Section 24).

12   Remove the speaker mounting screws, then disconnect the electrical connector and remove the speakers **(see illustration)**.

13   Installation is the reverse of removal. Reconnect the battery and perform the necessary re-learn procedures (see Chapter 5).

Door speakers

Refer to illustration 12.15

14   Remove the door trim panels (see Chapter 11).

15   Remove the speaker mounting screws, disconnect the electrical connector and remove the speakers **(see illustration)**.

16   Installation is the reverse of removal.

13   Rear window defogger - check and repair

1   The rear window defogger consists of a number of horizontal heating elements baked onto the inside surface of the glass. Power is supplied through two fuses and a relay in the IPDM relay box in the engine compartment. A defogger switch on the instrument panel controls the defogger grid.

2   Small breaks in the element can be repaired without removing the rear window.

Check

Refer to illustrations 13.5, 13.6 and 13.8

3   Turn the ignition and defogger switches to the ON position.

4   Using a voltmeter, place the positive probe against the defogger grid positive side and the negative probe against the ground side. If battery voltage is not indicated, check that the ignition switch is On and that the feed and ground wires are properly connected. Check the two fuses, defogger switch, defogger relay and related wiring. A dealer can scan the body control module if necessary. If voltage is indicated, but all or part of the defogger doesn't heat, proceed with the following tests.

5   When measuring voltage during the next two tests, wrap a piece of aluminum foil around the tip of the voltmeter positive probe and press the foil against the heating element

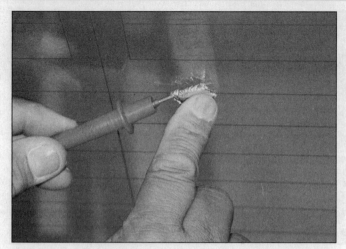

13.5 When measuring the voltage at the rear window defogger grid, wrap a piece of aluminum foil around the negative probe of the voltmeter and press the foil against the wire with your finger

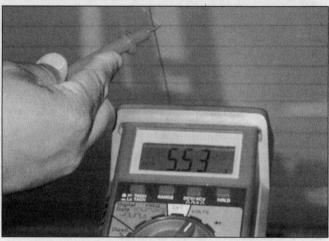

13.6 To determine if a heating element has broken, check the voltage at the center of each element - if the voltage is 6-volts, the element is unbroken

with your finger **(see illustration)**. Place the negative probe on the defogger grid ground terminal.

6   Check the voltage at the center of each heating element **(see illustration)**. If the voltage is 5 to 6 volts, the element is okay (there is no break). If the voltage is 0 volts, the element is broken between the center of the element and the positive end. If the voltage is 10 to 12 volts, the element is broken between the center of the element and the ground side. Check each heating element.

7   If none of the elements are broken, connect the negative probe to a good chassis ground. The voltage reading should stay the same; if it doesn't, the ground connection is bad.

8   To find the break, place the voltmeter negative probe against the defogger ground terminal. Place the voltmeter positive probe

with the foil strip against the heating element at the positive side and slide it toward the negative side. The point at which the voltmeter deflects from several volts to zero is the point where the heating element is broken **(see illustration)**.

Repair

Refer to illustration 13.14

9   Repair the break in the element using a repair kit specifically for this purpose, such as DuPont paste No. 4817 (or equivalent). The kit includes conductive plastic epoxy.

10   Before repairing a break, turn off the system and allow it to cool for a few minutes.

11   Lightly buff the element area with fine steel wool, then clean it thoroughly with rubbing alcohol.

12   Use masking tape to mask off the area

being repaired.

13   Thoroughly mix the epoxy, following the kit instructions.

14   Apply the epoxy material to the slit in the masking tape, overlapping the undamaged area about 3/4-inch on either end **(see illustration)**.

15   Allow the repair to cure for 24 hours before removing the tape and using the system.

---

14   Antenna - removal and installation

Antenna mast

1   Unscrew the mast from the antenna base to remove it.

2   Installation is the reverse of removal.

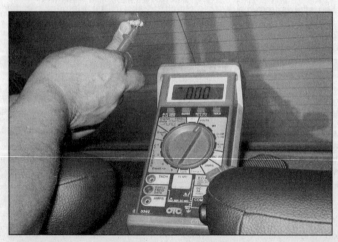

13.8 To find the break, place the voltmeter negative lead against the defogger ground terminal, place the voltmeter positive lead with the foil strip against the heat wire at the positive terminal end and slide it toward the negative terminal end. The point at which the voltmeter deflects from several volts to zero volts is the point at which the wire is broken

13.14 To use a defogger repair kit, apply masking tape to the inside of the window at the damaged area, then brush on the special conductive coating

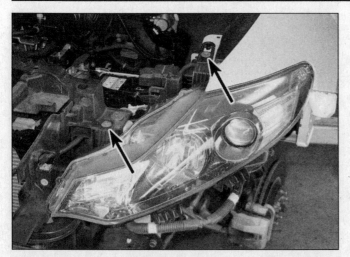

15.4a The upper . . .

15.4b . . . and lower headlight housing mounting bolts

Antenna base

3   The rear section of the headliner must be detached and carefully pulled down for access to the inside of the antenna base. It is usually best to have this done by an experienced auto upholstery shop. If you attempt it at home, refer to Chapter 11 for general information about removing plastic interior trim panels.

4   With the rear of the headliner lowered, disconnect the antenna cable from the extension cable at the right rear corner of the roof.

5   Remove the antenna base nut, then pull the antenna base and cable out from the roof of the vehicle.

6   Installation is the reverse of removal. **Note**: *Make sure to tighten the base nut to 58 in-lbs. Any more torque may dent the roof and less will result in poor radio reception.*

---

15 Headlight housing - removal and installation

Warning: *The models covered by this manual are equipped with Supplemental*

Restraint Systems (SRS), more commonly known as airbags. Always disable the airbag system before working in the vicinity of any airbag system components to avoid the possibility of accidental deployment of the airbags, which could cause personal injury (see Section 25).

Models equipped with halogen bulbs

Refer to illustrations 15.4a and 15.4b

1   Remove the grille (see Chapter 11).

2   Remove the small panel from the upper inner part of the headlight housing.

3   Remove the front bumper cover (see Chapter 11).

4   Remove the mounting bolts from the headlight housing **(see illustrations)**.

5   Detach the wiring harness clips from the assembly, then slide the headlight unit forward to remove it. Disconnect the electrical connector as you lift it out.

6   Installation is the reverse of removal.

Models equipped with xenon bulbs

Warning: *Some models use xenon bulbs (also known as High Intensity Discharge [HID] bulbs) instead of halogen bulbs. These can be identified by the high-voltage warning sticker on the headlight housing or under the hood. According to the manufacturer, the high voltages produced by this system can be fatal in the event of a shock. Also, the voltage can remain in the circuit even after the headlight switch has been turned to OFF and the ignition key has been removed. Therefore, for your safety, we don't recommend that you try to remove the headlight housing(s) on a vehicle equipped with xenon bulbs. Instead, have this service performed by a dealer service department or other qualified repair shop.*

---

16 Headlight bulb - replacement

Models equipped with halogen bulbs

Refer to illustration 16.1a, 16.1b, 16.2a and 16.2b

Warning: *Halogen gas-filled bulbs, which are under pressure, may shatter if the surface is scratched or the bulb is dropped. Wear eye protection and handle the bulbs carefully, grasping only the base whenever possible. Do not touch the surface of the bulb with your fingers because the oil from your skin could cause it to overheat and fail prematurely. If you do touch the bulb surface, clean it with rubbing alcohol.*

Note: *There are separate headlight bulbs for the high and low beams.*

1   If you're working on a low beam bulb, first remove the rubber fender shield from the engine compartment **(see illustrations)**. This isn't necessary for high beam bulb replacement.

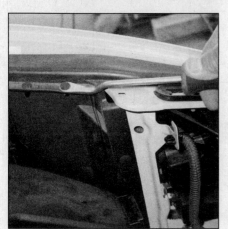

16.1a Remove this cover . . .

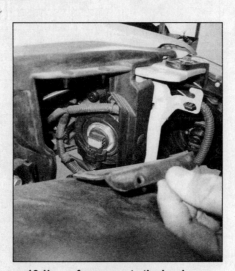

16.1b . . . for access to the low beam headlight bulb

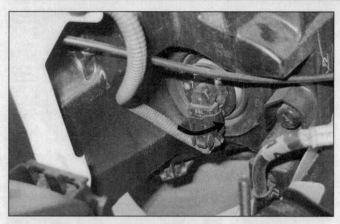

16.2a Both headlight bulbs are removed by turning counterclockwise . . .

16.2b . . . then pulling straight out - pull the bulb from the socket, but don't handle the replacement with bare fingers

2   Twist the bulb holder counterclockwise and pull it out **(see illustrations)**.
3   Unplug the electrical connector from the bulb holder.
4   Installation is the reverse of removal.

Models equipped with xenon bulbs

Warning: *Some models use xenon bulbs (also known as High Intensity Discharge [HID] bulbs) instead of halogen bulbs. These can be identified by the high-voltage warning sticker on the headlight housing or under the hood. According to the manufacturer, the high voltages produced by this system can be fatal in the event of a shock. Also, the voltage can remain in the circuit even after the headlight switch has been turned to OFF and the ignition key has been removed. Therefore, for your safety, we don't recommend that you try to replace one of these bulbs yourself. Instead, have this service performed by a dealer service department or other qualified repair shop.*

17   Headlights - adjustment

Refer to illustrations 17.2 and 17.7
Note: *It is important that the headlights are aimed correctly. If adjusted incorrectly they could blind the driver of an oncoming vehicle*

17.2 Headlight housing adjustment screw

and cause a serious accident or seriously reduce your ability to see the road. The headlights should be checked for proper aim every 12 months and any time a new headlight is installed or front end body work is performed. It should be emphasized that the following procedure is only an interim step that will provide temporary adjustment until the headlights can be adjusted by a properly equipped shop.
1   Adjustment should be made with the vehicle sitting level, the gas tank half-full and no unusually heavy load in the vehicle.
2   All models are equipped with one adjustment screw in each headlight housing **(see illustration)**. The headlights are only adjustable vertically.
3   If headlight housing has been replaced or the vehicle has suffered front end damage refer to following procedure.

4   This method requires a blank wall, masking tape and a level floor.
5   Position masking tape vertically on the wall in reference to the vehicle centerline and the centerlines of both headlights.
6   Position a horizontal tape line in reference to the centerline of all the headlights. **Note:** *It may be easier to position the tape on the wall with the vehicle parked only a few inches away.*
7   Adjustment should be made with the vehicle parked 25 feet from the wall, sitting level, the gas tank half-full and no unusually heavy load in the vehicle **(see illustration)**.
8   Starting with the low beam adjustment, position the high intensity zone so it is two inches below the horizontal line and two inches to the side of the headlight vertical line away from oncoming traffic.
9   With the high beams on, the high inten-

17.7 Headlight adjustment details

18.2a There are four bulbs in the headlight assembly - left housing removed for clarity

A Front side marker light
B Low beam headlight
C High beam headlight
D Turn signal and parking light

18.2b Most bulb holders are removed by twisting them counterclockwise - the bulb can be removed by pulling it straight out of the bulb holder

sity zone should be vertically centered with the exact center just below the horizontal line. **Note:** *It may not be possible to position the headlight aim exactly for both high and low beams. If a compromise must be made, keep in mind that the low beams are the most used and have the greatest effect on safety.*

10   Have the headlights adjusted by a dealer service department or service station at the earliest opportunity.

18   Bulb replacement

Warning: *Wear eye protection and handle the bulbs carefully, grasping only the base whenever possible. Do not touch the surface of the bulb with your fingers because the oil from your skin could cause it to overheat and fail prematurely. If you do touch the bulb surface, clean it with rubbing alcohol.*

Front parking and turn signal lights

Refer to illustrations 18.2a and 18.2b

1   Remove the grille (see Chapter 11).
2   Turn the bulb socket counterclockwise and pull it out of the housing **(see illustrations)**.
3   Remove the bulb from the bulb holder (see *"Bulb removal"*).
4   Installation is the reverse of removal.

Bulb removal

To remove many modern exterior bulbs from their holders, simply pull them out

On bulbs with a cylindrical base ("bayonet" bulbs), the socket is spring-loaded; a pair of small posts on the side of the base hold the bulb in place against spring pressure. To remove this type of bulb, push it into the holder, rotate it 1/4-turn counterclockwise, then pull it out

If a bayonet bulb has dual filaments, the posts are staggered, so the bulb can only be installed one way

To remove most overhead interior light bulbs, simply unclip them

18.9a Pry this trim panel off . . .

18.9b . . . then remove the taillight mounting screws

18.10a Pull the taillight housing off to reach the bulbs

18.10b Turn signal bulb (A) and rear side marker light (B); the larger access cover is for the LED lights

Front side marker lights

5   Remove the rubber fender shield from the engine compartment **(see illustration 16.1a)**

6   Turn the bulb socket counterclockwise and pull it out of the housing.
7   Remove the bulb from the bulb holder (see *"Bulb removal"*).
8   Installation is the reverse of removal.

Rear turn signal and side marker lights

Refer to illustrations 18.9a, 18.9b, 18.10a and 18.10b

9   Open the liftgate and remove the taillight trim panel **(see illustrations)**.
10   Remove the taillight assembly **(see illustrations)**.
11   Twist the bulb holder counterclockwise and pull it from the housing. Remove the bulb from the bulb holder (see *"Bulb removal"*).
12   Installation is the reverse of removal.

Fog lights

13   Detach the plastic inner fender liner at the front edge, then pull the liner back to access the bulb (see Chapter 11).
14   Disconnect the electrical connector from the bulb holder.

15   Turn the bulb holder counterclockwise and pull it out of the housing. Remove the bulb from the bulb holder (see *"Bulb removal"*).
16   Installation is the reverse of removal.

License plate light

17   Remove the liftgate trim panel (see Chapter 11).
18   Twist the bulb socket counterclockwise and pull it out of the license plate light housing.
19   Remove the bulb from the bulb holder (see *"Bulb removal"*).
20   Installation is the reverse of removal.

High-mounted stop light

Refer to illustrations 18.22a and 18.22b

21   This light uses LEDs instead of bulbs. If it doesn't light, the entire unit must be replaced.
22   To replace the unit, pry off the interior access panel, then disconnect the wiring and remove the mounting nuts **(see illustrations)**.
23   Installation is the reverse of removal.

18.22a Carefully pry off the high-mounted stop light access cover

18.22b Disconnect the wiring (A), then remove the mounting nuts (B)

18.26 You must remove the liftgate interior trim panel to access the back-up light housing nuts and remove it - with the housing removed you can replace the bulb

18.29 Use a small screwdriver to carefully pry off the lenses of the interior lights - the bulbs can then be pulled out of the housing

Back-up lights

Refer to illustration 18.26

24   Remove the lifgate trim panel (see Chapter 11).
25   Remove the mounting nuts and the clip from the back-up light.
26   Pull the back-up light housing out of the hatch **(see illustration)**
27   Turn the bulb holder counterclockwise and pull it out of the housing. Remove the bulb from the bulb holder (see *"Bulb removal"*).
28   Installation is the reverse of removal.

Interior lights

Refer to illustration 18.29

29   All interior light bulbs are replaced in the same general way. Use a small screwdriver or trim tool to carefully pry off the lens **(see illustration)**.
30   Pull the bulb straight out of its socket to remove it.
31   Replace the bulb, then snap the lens

back in place.
32   To replace the trunk light bulb, release the tab on the side of the lens, then pivot the lens open. The bulb can then be replaced as above.

Instrument cluster illumination

33   Instrument cluster illumination is contained within the cluster. Replace the cluster (see Section 11) as a complete unit if there is a problem with any of its individual components.

19   Horn - replacement

Refer to illustration 19.2

1   Remove the grille (see Chapter 11).
2   To replace the horn(s), disconnect the electrical connector and remove the bracket bolt **(see illustration)**.
3   Installation is the reverse of removal.

20   Wiper motor - replacement

Refer to illustrations 20.3, 20.7a, 20.7b and 20.8

1   Turn the wiper ON then OFF, making sure that the blades are at the proper park position.
2   Mark the positions of the blades on the windshield with tape so they can be installed in the same alignment.
3   Pry off the wiper arm pivot caps, then remove the nuts **(see illustration)**.
4   Remove the wiper arms from the drive studs. Wiggle the ends of the arms up and down to release them.
5   If you're working on a windshield wiper, remove the upper cowl cover (see Chapter 11). For the liftgate window wiper, remove the interior hatch trim panel (see Chapter 11).
6   Disconnect the electrical connector from the wiper motor.
7   Remove the mounting bolts, then lift the

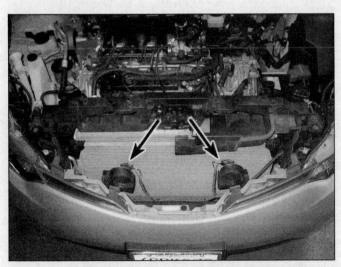

19.2 Disconnect the electrical connectors

20.3 Pry up the wiper arm covers, then remove the nuts - front wiper is shown, the rear is similar

20.7a Windshield wiper module mounting bolts

20.7b Liftgate window wiper mounting bolts

20.8 This nut secures the wiper linkage
to the motor

wiper assembly out **(see illustrations)**.
8   Remove the linkage arm from the windshield wiper motor, taking care to avoid damaging the plastic parts of the joints **(see illustration)**. Unbolt the motor from the frame and
remove it.
9   When installing the wiper motor assembly, connect the electrical connector to the
motor, then turn it ON and then OFF to place
the unit in the PARK position before attaching the wiper arms. Make sure the pivot seal
in the rear glass is in good condition before
inserting the wiper shaft through it.

21   Cruise control system -
description and check

All models have an electronically-con-
trolled throttle body - there is no accelerator
cable (or cruise control cable). When you
select the speed that you want to maintain,
the PCM controls vehicle speed by opening
and closing the throttle plate by means of a
computer-controlled solenoid (motor) inside
the throttle body.

The diagnostic procedures for troubleshooting the cruise control system are beyond
the scope of this manual, but if the system
can't be set, or the set speed doesn't cancel
when the brake pedal is depressed, check the
fuses. Start with the fuses in the engine compartment fuse and relay box, then check the
fuses in the under-dash fuse and relay box. If
the set speed doesn't cancel when the CAN-
CEL button is depressed, check the fuse for
that circuit.

Other than checking fuses, the diagnostic procedures for troubleshooting the cruise
control system on these models are beyond
the scope of this manual. A dealer service
department should handle any further testing.

22   Power window system - general
information

The power window system operates
electric motors, mounted on the doors, which
lower and raise the windows. The system
consists of the control switches, the motors,
regulators, glass mechanisms, the Body Control Module (BCM) and associated wiring.

The power windows can be lowered and
raised from the master control switch by the
driver or by the switch located at the passenger window. Each window has a separate motor that is reversible. The position of
the control switch determines the polarity and
therefore the direction of operation.

The circuit is protected by fuses and a
circuit breaker. Check the fuses in the fuse
panel. Each motor is equipped with an internal circuit breaker; this prevents one stuck
window from disabling the whole system.
Refer to the wiring diagrams at the end of
this Chapter. Problems within this system can
only be diagnosed with a factory scan tool. If
you have eliminated the obvious causes of a
problem, have the vehicle checked at a dealership service department or other properly
equipped repair shop.

23   Power door lock system - general
information

1   The power door lock system operates the
power door motors, which are integral components of the door latch units in each door.
The system consists of a fuse (in the engine
compartment fuse and relay box), the Body
Control Module (BCM), the control switches
(in each of the front doors), the power door
motors and the electrical wiring harnesses
connecting all of these components.
2   The lock mechanisms in the door latch
units are actuated by a reversible electric
motor in each door. When you push the door
lock switch to LOCK, the motor operates one
way and locks the latch mechanism. When
you push the door lock switch the other way,
to the UNLOCK position, the motor operates
in the other direction, unlocking the latch
mechanism. Because the motors and lock
mechanisms are an integral part of the door
latch units, they cannot be repaired. If a door
lock motor or lock mechanism fails, replace
the door latch unit (see Chapter 11).
3   Some vehicles have an optional Intelligent Key system that allows you to lock and
unlock the doors from outside the vehicle.
The intelligent key system consists of the
transmitter (the electronic push-button "key")
and a remote keyless entry receiver mounted
behind the glove box.
4   Some features of the door lock system
on these vehicles rely on resources that they
share with other electronic modules through
the Programmable Communications Inter-
face (PCI) data bus network. Professional
diagnosis of these modules and the PCI data
bus network requires the use of a CONSULT-
III (proprietary factory) scan tool and factory
diagnostic information. At-home repairs are
therefore limited to inspecting the wiring for
bad connections and for minor faults that can
be easily repaired. If you are unable to locate
the trouble using the following general steps,
consult your dealer service department.

25.3 The front crash zone sensor is mounted to the rear of the radiator support panel

5   Always check the circuit fuses first. Refer to the wiring diagrams at the end of this Chapter. Problems within this system can only be diagnosed with a factory scan tool. If you have eliminated the obvious causes of a problem, have the vehicle checked at a dealership service department or other properly equipped repair shop. **Note:** *It is not uncommon for wires to break in the harness between the body and the door because repeatedly opening and closing the door fatigues and eventually breaks the wires.*

24 Sunroof - general information

1   The sunroof is powered by a single motor located in the roof.
2   The sunroof switch (tilt and slide) sends an operation signal to the sunroof motor CPU encoder when the switches are pressed. Power is supplied to the motor from the Body Control Module (BCM) located under the instrument panel. The front door switch detects the open/close condition and sends an operating signal to the BCM. The sunroof will retain power for 45 seconds after the key has been turned off to operate the system. The retained power can be cancelled by opening the front door, turning the ignition switch to ON again or allowing the 45 seconds to elapse.
3   With the ignition On but the engine Off, operate the sunroof control switch through the tilt and slide functions.
4   Listen carefully for the sound of the sunroof motor running in the roof.
5   If the motor can be heard but the sunroof glass doesn't move, there's probably a problem with the drive mechanism.
6   If the sunroof does not operate and no sound comes from the motor, check the fuses (in the interior fuse panel *and* in the engine compartment power distribution center).
7   If there's voltage at the switch, disconnect it. Check the switch for continuity in all its operating positions. If the switch does not have

continuity, replace it. If you have eliminated the obvious causes of a problem, have the vehicle checked at a dealership service department or other properly equipped repair shop.

25 Airbag system - general information

1   These models are equipped with a Supplemental Restraint System (SRS), more commonly known as airbags, designed to protect the driver and the passenger from serious injury in the event of a head-on collision. Some models are also equipped with side impact airbags in the front seats and along the roof rail. All models have a diagnostic control unit, located on the floor under the center console. **Warning:** *If your vehicle is ever involved in a flood, or the interior carpeting is soaked for any reason, disconnect the battery and do not start the vehicle until the airbag system can be checked by a dealer service department or other repair facility equipped with the proper tool. If the SRS system is subjected to flooding, the airbags could go off upon starting the vehicle, even without an accident taking place.*

Airbag modules

2   The airbag modules consist of a housing incorporating the cushion (airbag) and inflator unit. The inflator assembly is mounted on the back of the housing over a hole through which gas is expelled, inflating the bag almost instantaneously when an electrical signal is sent from the system. The specially wound wire on the driver's side that carries this signal to the module is called a spiral cable. The spiral cable is a flat, ribbon-like electrically conductive tape that is wound many times so that it can transmit an electrical signal regardless of steering wheel position. Airbag modules are located in the steering wheel, on the passenger side above the glove box and, on some models, side-impact airbags located in the seat backs and head-

level airbags located along the roof rails (side curtain airbags).

Control unit and sensors

Refer to illustration 25.3

3   The diagnosis/sensor unit contains an on-board microprocessor which monitors the operation of the system, and also contains a crash sensor. It checks this system every time the vehicle is started, causing the "AIRBAG" light to go on then off, if the system is operating properly. If there is a fault in the system, the light will go on and stay on and the unit will store fault codes indicating the nature of the fault. If the AIRBAG light goes on and stays on, the vehicle should be taken to your dealer immediately for service. The diagnosis/sensor unit is located under the center console. The crash zone sensor is located on the radiator support **(see illustration)** and the side airbags sensor (satellite crash sensor) is in each door "B" pillar.

Operation

4   For the airbag(s) to deploy, the impact sensor(s) must be activated. When this condition occurs, the circuit to the airbag inflator is closed and the airbag inflates.

Self-diagnosis system

5   A self-diagnosis circuit in the SRS unit displays a light on the instrument panel when the ignition switch is turned to the On position. If the system is operating normally, the light should go out after about five seconds. If the light doesn't come on, or doesn't go out after a short time, or if it comes on while you're driving the vehicle, or if it blinks at any time, there's a malfunction in the SRS system. Have it inspected and repaired as soon as possible. Do not attempt to troubleshoot or service the SRS system yourself. Even a small mistake could cause the SRS system to malfunction when you need it.

Servicing components near the SRS system

6   Nevertheless, there are times when you need to remove the steering wheel, radio or service other components on or near the dashboard. At these times, you'll be working around components and wire harnesses for the SRS system. **Warning:** *Do not use electrical test equipment on airbag system wires; it could cause the airbag(s) to deploy.* **ALWAYS DISABLE THE SRS SYSTEM BEFORE WORKING NEAR THE SRS SYSTEM COMPONENTS OR RELATED WIRING.**

Disabling the SRS system

Warning: *Any time you are working in the vicinity of airbag wiring or components, DISABLE THE SRS SYSTEM.*
Warning: *An auxiliary voltage input device (memory saver) must not be used when working near airbag system components.*
7   To disable the airbag system, perform

the following steps:

a) *Turn the steering wheel to the straight-ahead position and turn the ignition switch to the Lock position, then remove the key.*

b) *Disconnect the battery negative and positive cables, then wait ten minutes before proceeding with any work.*

c) *Before touching any airbag system component, ground yourself to a metal part of the vehicle to discharge any static electricity built up in your body.*

Enabling the system

8   After you've disabled the airbag and performed the necessary service, reconnect the two-pin airbag connector into the two-pin spiral cable connector (driver's side), the SRS main harness (passenger's side) or the side-impact airbag. Reinstall the lid to the underside of the steering wheel or reinstall the glove box/trim panel or upper trim panels.

9   To enable the airbag system, perform the following steps:

a) *Turn the ignition switch to the On position.*

b) *Make sure nobody is inside the vehicle.*

c) *Connect the battery cables.*

d) *Turn the ignition to the Off position, then with your body out of the path of the airbag, turn the ignition switch to the On position. Confirm that the airbag warning light is functioning properly.*

e) *Perform the necessary re-learn procedures (see Chapter 5).*

f) *Take the vehicle to a dealer service department or other qualified repair facility and have the airbag system checked and the warning light canceled if it remains lit.*

Removal and installation

Warning: *The bolts used throughout the airbag system to mount the airbag modules, diagnosis sensor unit, crash zone sensor and satellite sensors have a special coating. These bolts are designed to be used once. Replace them with new factory bolts, and never use a substitute fastener.*

Driver's side airbag and spiral cable

10   Refer to Chapter 10, Section 16, for removal and installation of the driver's side airbag and steering wheel (which will give you access to the spiral cable). **Warning:** *When installing the spiral cable, be sure to follow the centering instructions carefully.*

Passenger side airbag and other airbag modules

11   Even if you have to remove the instrument panel, it's not necessary to remove the passenger airbag module to do so; it can simply remain installed in the instrument panel. We don't recommend removing any of the other airbag modules either. These jobs are best left to a professional.

Impact seat belt retractors

12   All models are equipped with pyrotechnic (explosive) units in the front seat belt retracting mechanisms for both the lap and shoulder belts. During an impact that would trigger the airbag system, the airbag control unit also triggers the seat belt retractors. When the pyrotechnic charges go off, they accelerate the retractors to instantly take up any slack in the seat belt system to more fully prepare the driver and front seat passenger for impact. The airbag system should be disabled any time work is done to or around the seats. **Warning:** *Never strike the pillars or floor pan with a hammer or use an impact-driver tool in these areas unless the system is disabled.*

---

26   Intelligent Power Distribution Module (IPDM) - description, check and replacement

Description

1   The Intelligent Power Distribution Module (IPDM) is a solid state device that controls various relays and circuits when commands are received from the Powertrain Control Module (PCM) and/or the Body Control Module (BCM). The circuits under its control are:

Headlights
Parking and side marker lights
Tail lights/license plate lights
Fog lights
Windshield wipers
Electronic steering column lock
Air conditioning compressor clutch
Starter relay
Fuel pump relay
Cooling fan relay
Horn relay
Rear window defogger relay

Check

2   Although the IPDM is usually very reliable, it must always be factored in to any diagnosis of the circuits under its control. Thorough testing of the unit requires a proprietary Nissan scan tool, but a simple test, called the Auto Active Test, can help you determine the possible source of a problem with some of the circuits under its control. The circuits checked in this test include the:

Front windshield wiper circuit
Tail/parking/license plate/side marker light circuits
Fog light circuit
Headlight circuit
Air conditioning compressor clutch circuit
Engine cooling fan circuit
Oil pressure warning light

3   Lift the windshield wipers from the windshield and close the right front door. **Note:** *If you must keep the hood open during the test, leave the wipers down and spray some water on the glass to prevent scratching.* Make sure

the ignition switch is in the Off position.

4   To initiate the Auto Active Test, turn the ignition switch to the On position and depress the left front door switch 10 times within 20 seconds, then turn the ignition switch to the Off position.

5   Within 10 seconds, turn the ignition switch back to the On position. The horn should beep once, signifying the start of the test.

6   When the test begins, the following sequence of events should happen (and the sequence of events should repeat three times):

The oil pressure light should blink continuously for the duration of the test.

The windshield wiper should operate on low speed for 5 seconds, then high speed for 5 seconds

The parking lights/taillights/license plate lights/fog lights should come on for 10 seconds

The headlights should turn on and switch from low-beam to high-beam five times

The air conditioning compressor clutch should engage (click on and off) 5 times

The engine cooling fan should come on for 10 seconds (low for 5 seconds, medium for 3 seconds and high for 2 seconds)

Diagnosis

Wipers, parking lights/daytime running lights (if equipped)/tail lights/license plate lights/fog lights

7   If any of these systems do not operate during the Auto Active Test, the problem could be caused by:

a) *Wiper motor or the circuit between IPDM and wiper motor faulty*

b) *Wiper motor ground problem*

c) *Light bulb or the circuit between IPDM and light faulty*

d) *Light bulb/housing ground problem*

e) *Faulty IPDM*

8   If the system in question *does* operate during the Auto Active Test but doesn't operate under normal conditions, the problem could be a faulty switch, a faulty Body Control Module (BCM), or the circuit between the two.

Air conditioning compressor clutch

9   If the compressor clutch doesn't operate during the Auto Active Test, the problem could be caused by:

a) *Compressor clutch or the circuit between IPDM and compressor clutch faulty*

b) *Faulty IPDM*

10   If the compressor clutch *does* operate during the Auto Active Test but doesn't operate under normal conditions, the problem could be a faulty switch, a faulty Body Control Module (BCM), a faulty PCM, a fault in the circuit between the PCM and the BCM, or a fault in the circuit between the PCM and the IPDM.

Electric engine cooling fan

11   If the engine cooling fan doesn't operate

26.17 Intelligent Power Distribution Module (IPDM) details

1   *Electrical connectors*
2   *Release tabs*
3   *IPDM*

Replacement

Refer to illustration 26.17

Note: *The IPDM is located in the left rear corner of the engine compartment.*

15   Disconnect the cable from the negative terminal of the battery (see Chapter 5).
16   Remove the cover from the IPDM.
17   Disconnect the electrical connector, push back the two retainers at the rear end of the IPDM **(see illustration)**, pull the IPDM up and remove it from the vehicle.
18   Installation is the reverse of removal.

27   Wiring diagrams - general information

during the Auto Active Test, the problem could be caused by:

   a) *Cooling fan motor or the circuit between cooling fan motor and IPDM faulty*
   b) *Faulty IPDM*

12   If the engine cooling fan *does* operate during the Auto Active Test but doesn't operate under normal conditions, the problem could be a faulty PCM, a faulty coolant temperature sensor, the circuit between the coolant temperature sensor and the PCM, or the circuit between the PCM and the IPDM.

Oil pressure warning light

13   If the oil pressure warning light doesn't blink during the Auto Active Test, the problem could be caused by:

   a) *Problem in the CAN communication circuit between the BCM and the IPDM*
   b) *Problem in the CAN communication circuit between the BCM and the instrument cluster*
   c) *Faulty instrument cluster*

14   If the oil pressure warning light *does* blink during the Auto Active Test but doesn't operate when it should (during the bulb check when the ignition is turned On), the problem could be a faulty oil pressure sending unit, a faulty IPDM, or the circuit between the two.

Since it isn't possible to include all wiring diagrams for every year and model covered by this manual, the following diagrams are those that are typical and most commonly needed.

Prior to troubleshooting any circuits, check the fuses and circuit breakers (if equipped) to make sure they are in good condition. Make sure the battery is properly charged and has clean, tight cable connections (see Chapter 1).

When checking the wiring system, make sure that all electrical connectors are clean, with no broken or loose pins. When unplugging an electrical connector, do not pull on the wires, only on the connector housings themselves.

Notes

Wiring diagrams on the following pages

Air conditioning system - 2007 and earlier models (1 of 2)

Air conditioning system - 2007 and earlier models (2 of 2)

Air conditioning system - 2009 and later models (1 of 2)

Air conditioning system - 2009 and later models (2 of 2)

Audio system - 2005 and earlier models

Audio system - 2006 and 2007 models (1 of 2)

Audio system - 2006 and 2007 models (2 of 2)

Audio system - 2009 and later models

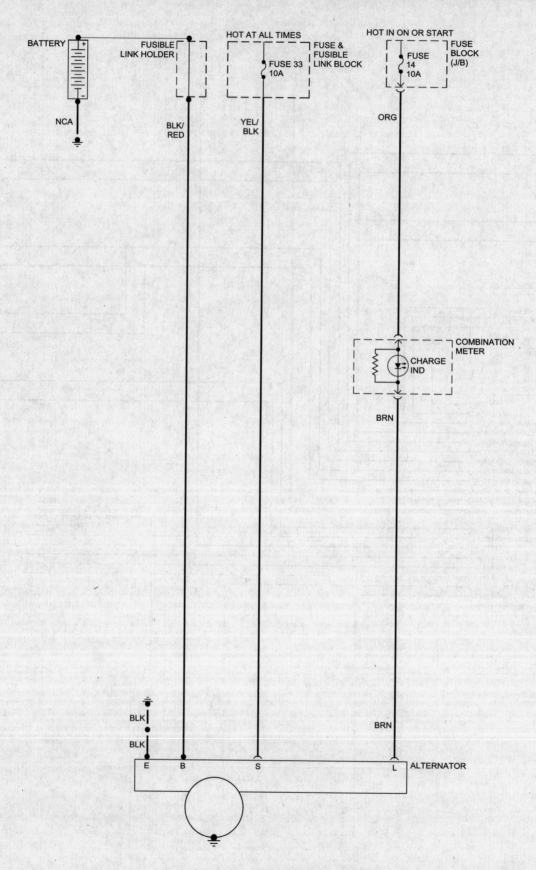

Charging system - 2007 and earlier models

Charging system - 2009 and later models

Exterior lighting system (except headlights) - 2005 and earlier models

Exterior lighting system (except headlights) - 2006 and 2007 models (1 of 2)

Exterior lighting system (except headlights) - 2006 and 2007 models (2 of 2)

Back-up lights system

Exterior lighting system (except headlights) - 2009 and later models (1 of 2)

Exterior lighting system (except headlights) - 2009 and later models (2 of 2)

Headlight system (Xenon bulbs) - 2007 and earlier models

Headlight system (Halogen bulbs) - 2007 and earlier models

Headlight system (Xenon bulbs) - 2009 and later models (1 of 2)

Headlight system (Xenon bulbs) - 2009 and later models (2 of 2)

Headlight system (Halogen bulbs) - 2009 and later models (1 of 2)

Headlight system (Halogen bulbs) - 2009 and later models (2 of 2)

Courtesy lights system - 2007 and earlier models (1 of 2)

Courtesy lights system - 2007 and earlier models (2 of 2)

Instrument panel and switch illumination - 2007 and earlier models

Courtesy lights system - 2009 and later models

Instrument panel and switch illumination - 2009 and later models (1 of 2)

Instrument panel and switch illumination - 2009 and later models (2 of 2)

Power door lock system (without Intelligent Key) - 2007 and earlier models

Power door lock system (without Intelligent Key) - 2009 models

Power door lock system (with Intelligent Key) - 2005 through 2007 models (1 of 3)

Power door lock system (with Intelligent Key) - 2005 through 2007 models (2 of 3)

Power door lock system (with Intelligent Key) - 2005 through 2007 models (3 of 3)

Power door lock system (with Intelligent Key) - 2009 and later models (1 of 3)

Power door lock system (with Intelligent Key) - 2009 and later models (2 of 3)

Power door locks system (with Intelligent Key) - 2009 and later models (3 of 3)

SHIFT POSITION	INH SW1	INH SW2	INH SW3	INH SW4	INH SW3M
P	OFF	OFF	OFF	OFF	OFF
R	ON	OFF	OFF	ON	OFF
N	ON	ON	OFF	OFF	OFF
D	ON	ON	ON	ON	ON
L	OFF	ON	ON	OFF	ON

Starting system - 2007 and earlier models

Starting system - 2008 and later models

Warning lights and gauges - 2007 and earlier models

Warning lights and gauges - 2009 and later models

Power widow system (without Intelligent Key) - 2007 and earlier models

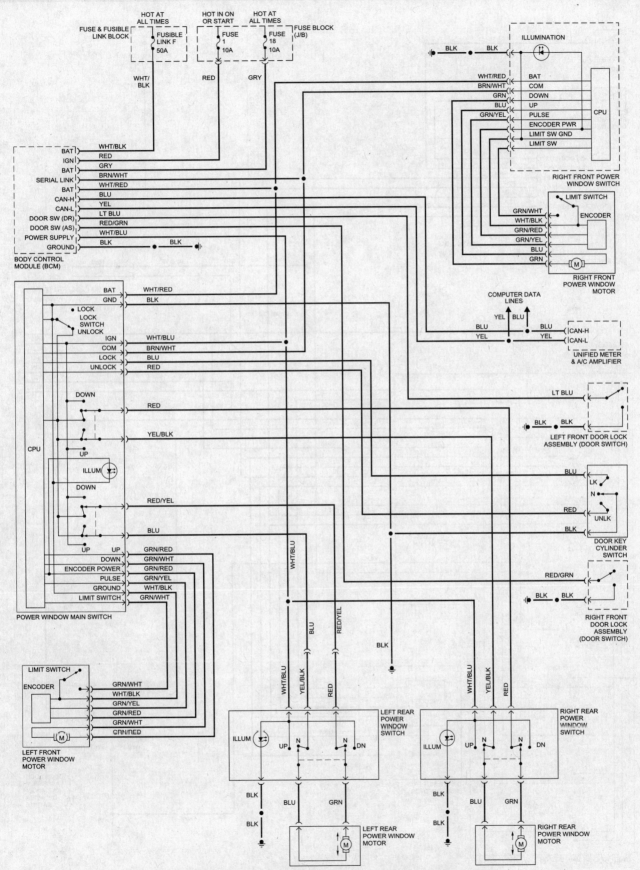

Power widow system (with Intelligent Key) - 2007 and earlier models

Power widow system - 2009 and later models (1 of 2)

Power widow system - 2009 and later models (2 of 2)

Rear wiper/washer system

Windshield wiper/washer system - 2007 and earlier models

Windshield wiper/washer system - 2009 and later models

Index

A

B

Notes

Notes

Haynes Automotive Manuals

ACURA
- **12020** **Integra** '86 thru '89 & **Legend** '86 thru '90
- **12021** **Integra** '90 thru '93 & **Legend** '91 thru '95
  Integra '94 thru '00 - *see HONDA Civic (42025)*
  MDX '01 thru '07 - *see HONDA Pilot (42037)*
- **12050** **Acura TL** all models '99 thru '08

AMC
- **Jeep CJ** - *see JEEP (50020)*
- **14020** **Mid-size models** '70 thru '83
- **14025** **(Renault) Alliance & Encore** '83 thru '87

AUDI
- **15020** **4000** all models '80 thru '87
- **15025** **5000** all models '77 thru '83
- **15026** **5000** all models '84 thru '88
  Audi A4 '96 thru '01 - *see VW Passat (96023)*
- **15030** **Audi A4** '02 thru '08

AUSTIN-HEALEY
- **Sprite** - *see MG Midget (66015)*

BMW
- **18020** **3/5 Series** '82 thru '92
- **18021** **3-Series** incl. Z3 models '92 thru '98
- **18022** **3-Series** incl. Z4 models '99 thru '05
- **18023** **3-Series** '06 thru '10
- **18025** **320i** all 4 cyl models '75 thru '83
- **18050** **1500 thru 2002** except Turbo '59 thru '77

BUICK
- **19010** **Buick Century** '97 thru '05
  Century (front-wheel drive) - *see GM (38005)*
- **19020** **Buick, Oldsmobile & Pontiac Full-size** (Front-wheel drive) '85 thru '05
  Buick Electra, LeSabre and Park Avenue; **Oldsmobile** Delta 88 Royale, and Regency; **Pontiac** Bonneville
- **19025** **Buick, Oldsmobile & Pontiac Full-size** (Rear wheel drive) '70 thru '90
  Buick Estate, Electra, LeSabre, Limited, **Oldsmobile** Custom Cruiser, Delta 88, Ninety-eight, **Pontiac** Bonneville, Catalina, Grandville, Parisienne
- **19030** **Mid-size Regal & Century** all rear-drive models with V6, V8 and Turbo '74 thru '87
  Regal - *see GENERAL MOTORS (38010)*
  Riviera - *see GENERAL MOTORS (38030)*
  Roadmaster - *see CHEVROLET (24046)*
  Skyhawk - *see GENERAL MOTORS (38015)*
  Skylark - *see GM (38020, 38025)*
  Somerset - *see GENERAL MOTORS (38025)*

CADILLAC
- **21015** **CTS & CTS-V** '03 thru '12
- **21030** **Cadillac Rear Wheel Drive** '70 thru '93
  Cimarron - *see GENERAL MOTORS (38015)*
  DeVille - *see GM (38031 & 38032)*
  Eldorado - *see GM (38030 & 38031)*
  Fleetwood - *see GM (38031)*
  Seville - *see GM (38030, 38031 & 38032)*

CHEVROLET
- **10305** **Chevrolet Engine Overhaul Manual**
- **24010** **Astro & GMC Safari Mini-vans** '85 thru '05
- **24015** **Camaro V8** all models '70 thru '81
- **24016** **Camaro** all models '82 thru '92
- **24017** **Camaro & Firebird** '93 thru '02
  Cavalier - *see GENERAL MOTORS (38016)*
  Celebrity - *see GENERAL MOTORS (38005)*
- **24020** **Chevelle, Malibu & El Camino** '69 thru '87
- **24024** **Chevette & Pontiac T1000** '76 thru '87
  Citation - *see GENERAL MOTORS (38020)*
- **24027** **Colorado & GMC Canyon** '04 thru '10
- **24032** **Corsica/Beretta** all models '87 thru '96
- **24040** **Corvette** all V8 models '68 thru '82
- **24041** **Corvette** all models '84 thru '96
- **24045** **Full-size Sedans** Caprice, Impala, Biscayne, Bel Air & Wagons '69 thru '90
- **24046** **Impala SS & Caprice and Buick Roadmaster** '91 thru '96
  Impala '00 thru '05 - *see LUMINA (24048)*
- **24047** **Impala & Monte Carlo** all models '06 thru '11
  Lumina '90 thru '94 - *see GM (38010)*
- **24048** **Lumina & Monte Carlo** '95 thru '05
  Lumina APV - *see GM (38035)*
- **24050** **Luv Pick-up** all 2WD & 4WD '72 thru '82
  Malibu '97 thru '00 - *see GM (38026)*
- **24055** **Monte Carlo** all models '70 thru '88
  Monte Carlo '95 thru '01 - *see LUMINA (24048)*
- **24059** **Nova** all V8 models '69 thru '79
- **24060** **Nova and Geo Prizm** '85 thru '92
- **24064** **Pick-ups** '67 thru '87 - Chevrolet & GMC
- **24065** **Pick-ups** '88 thru '98 - Chevrolet & GMC
- **24066** **Pick-ups** '99 thru '06 - Chevrolet & GMC
- **24067** **Chevrolet Silverado & GMC Sierra** '07 thru '12
- **24070** **S-10 & S-15 Pick-ups** '82 thru '93, **Blazer & Jimmy** '83 thru '94,
- **24071** **S-10 & Sonoma Pick-ups** '94 thru '04, including Blazer, Jimmy & Hombre
- **24072** **Chevrolet TrailBlazer, GMC Envoy & Oldsmobile Bravada** '02 thru '09
- **24075** **Sprint** '85 thru '88 & **Geo Metro** '89 thru '01
- **24080** **Vans** - Chevrolet & GMC '68 thru '96
- **24081** **Chevrolet Express & GMC Savana** Full-size Vans '96 thru '10

CHRYSLER
- **10310** **Chrysler Engine Overhaul Manual**
- **25015** **Chrysler Cirrus, Dodge Stratus, Plymouth Breeze** '95 thru '00
- **25020** **Full-size Front-Wheel Drive** '88 thru '93
  K-Cars - *see DODGE Aries (30008)*
  Laser - *see DODGE Daytona (30030)*
- **25025** **Chrysler LHS, Concorde, New Yorker, Dodge** Intrepid, **Eagle** Vision, '93 thru '97
- **25026** **Chrysler LHS, Concorde, 300M, Dodge** Intrepid, '98 thru '04
- **25027** **Chrysler 300, Dodge Charger & Magnum** '05 thru '09
- **25030** **Chrysler & Plymouth Mid-size** front wheel drive '82 thru '95
  Rear-wheel Drive - *see Dodge (30050)*
- **25035** **PT Cruiser** all models '01 thru '10
- **25040** **Chrysler** Sebring '95 thru '06, **Dodge** Stratus '01 thru '06, **Dodge** Avenger '95 thru '00

DATSUN
- **28005** **200SX** all models '80 thru '83
- **28007** **B-210** all models '73 thru '78
- **28009** **210** all models '79 thru '82
- **28012** **240Z, 260Z & 280Z** Coupe '70 thru '78
- **28014** **280ZX** Coupe & 2+2 '79 thru '83
  300ZX - *see NISSAN (72010)*
- **28018** **510 & PL521 Pick-up** '68 thru '73
- **28020** **510** all models '78 thru '81
- **28022** **620 Series Pick-up** all models '73 thru '79
  720 Series Pick-up - *see NISSAN (72030)*
- **28025** **810/Maxima** all gasoline models '77 thru '84

DODGE
- **400 & 600** - *see CHRYSLER (25030)*
- **30008** **Aries & Plymouth Reliant** '81 thru '89
- **30010** **Caravan & Plymouth Voyager** '84 thru '95
- **30011** **Caravan & Plymouth Voyager** '96 thru '02
- **30012** **Challenger/Plymouth Saporro** '78 thru '83
- **30013** **Caravan, Chrysler Voyager, Town & Country** '03 thru '07
- **30016** **Colt & Plymouth Champ** '78 thru '87
- **30020** **Dakota Pick-ups** all models '87 thru '96
- **30021** **Durango** '98 & '99, **Dakota** '97 thru '99
- **30022** **Durango** '00 thru '03 **Dakota** '00 thru '04
- **30023** **Durango** '04 thru '09, **Dakota** '05 thru '11
- **30025** **Dart, Demon, Plymouth Barracuda, Duster & Valiant** 6 cyl models '67 thru '76
- **30030** **Daytona & Chrysler Laser** '84 thru '89
  Intrepid - *see CHRYSLER (25025, 25026)*
- **30034** **Neon** all models '95 thru '99
- **30035** **Omni & Plymouth Horizon** '78 thru '90
- **30036** **Dodge and Plymouth Neon** '00 thru '05
- **30040** **Pick-ups** all full-size models '74 thru '93
- **30041** **Pick-ups** all full-size models '94 thru '01
- **30042** **Pick-ups** full-size models '02 thru '08
- **30045** **Ram 50/D50 Pick-ups & Raider and Plymouth Arrow Pick-ups** '79 thru '93
- **30050** **Dodge/Plymouth/Chrysler RWD** '71 thru '89
- **30055** **Shadow & Plymouth Sundance** '87 thru '94
- **30060** **Spirit & Plymouth Acclaim** '89 thru '95
- **30065** **Vans** - Dodge & Plymouth '71 thru '03

EAGLE
- **Talon** - *see MITSUBISHI (68030, 68031)*
- **Vision** - *see CHRYSLER (25025)*

FIAT
- **34010** **124 Sport Coupe & Spider** '68 thru '78
- **34025** **X1/9** all models '74 thru '80

FORD
- **10320** **Ford Engine Overhaul Manual**
- **10355** **Ford Automatic Transmission Overhaul**
- **11500** **Mustang** '64-1/2 thru '70 Restoration Guide
- **36004** **Aerostar Mini-vans** all models '86 thru '97
- **36006** **Contour & Mercury Mystique** '95 thru '00
- **36008** **Courier Pick-up** all models '72 thru '82
- **36012** **Crown Victoria & Mercury Grand Marquis** '88 thru '10
- **36016** **Escort/Mercury Lynx** all models '81 thru '90
- **36020** **Escort/Mercury Tracer** '91 thru '02
- **36022** **Escape & Mazda Tribute** '01 thru '11
- **36024** **Explorer & Mazda Navajo** '91 thru '01
- **36025** **Explorer/Mercury Mountaineer** '02 thru '10
- **36028** **Fairmont & Mercury Zephyr** '78 thru '83
- **36030** **Festiva & Aspire** '88 thru '97
- **36032** **Fiesta** all models '77 thru '80
- **36034** **Focus** all models '00 thru '11
- **36036** **Ford & Mercury Full-size** '75 thru '87
- **36044** **Ford & Mercury Mid-size** '75 thru '86
- **36045** **Fusion & Mercury Milan** '06 thru '10
- **36048** **Mustang V8** all models '64-1/2 thru '73
- **36049** **Mustang II** 4 cyl, V6 & V8 models '74 thru '78
- **36050** **Mustang & Mercury Capri** '79 thru '93
- **36051** **Mustang** all models '94 thru '04
- **36052** **Mustang** '05 thru '10
- **36054** **Pick-ups & Bronco** '73 thru '79
- **36058** **Pick-ups & Bronco** '80 thru '96
- **36059** **F-150 & Expedition** '97 thru '09, **F-250** '97 thru '99 & **Lincoln Navigator** '98 thru '09
- **36060** **Super Duty Pick-ups, Excursion** '99 thru '10
- **36061** **F-150** full-size '04 thru '10
- **36062** **Pinto & Mercury Bobcat** '75 thru '80
- **36066** **Probe** all models '89 thru '92
  Probe '93 thru '97 - *see MAZDA 626 (61042)*
- **36070** **Ranger/Bronco II** gasoline models '83 thru '92
- **36071** **Ranger** '93 thru '10 & **Mazda Pick-ups** '94 thru '09
- **36074** **Taurus & Mercury Sable** '86 thru '95
- **36075** **Taurus & Mercury Sable** '96 thru '05
- **36078** **Tempo & Mercury Topaz** '84 thru '94
- **36082** **Thunderbird/Mercury Cougar** '83 thru '88
- **36086** **Thunderbird/Mercury Cougar** '89 thru '97
- **36090** **Vans** all V8 Econoline models '69 thru '91
- **36094** **Vans** full size '92 thru '10
- **36097** **Windstar Mini-van** '95 thru '07

GENERAL MOTORS
- **10360** **GM Automatic Transmission Overhaul**
- **38005** **Buick Century, Chevrolet Celebrity, Oldsmobile Cutlass Ciera & Pontiac 6000** all models '82 thru '96
- **38010** **Buick Regal, Chevrolet Lumina, Oldsmobile Cutlass Supreme & Pontiac Grand Prix** (FWD) '88 thru '07
- **38015** **Buick Skyhawk, Cadillac Cimarron, Chevrolet Cavalier, Oldsmobile Firenza & Pontiac J-2000 & Sunbird** '82 thru '94
- **38016** **Chevrolet Cavalier & Pontiac Sunfire** '95 thru '05
- **38017** **Chevrolet Cobalt & Pontiac G5** '05 thru '11
- **38020** **Buick Skylark, Chevrolet Citation, Olds Omega, Pontiac Phoenix** '80 thru '85
- **38025** **Buick Skylark & Somerset, Oldsmobile Achieva & Calais and Pontiac Grand Am** all models '85 thru '98
- **38026** **Chevrolet Malibu, Olds Alero & Cutlass, Pontiac Grand Am** '97 thru '03
- **38027** **Chevrolet Malibu** '04 thru '10
- **38030** **Cadillac Eldorado, Seville, Oldsmobile Toronado, Buick Riviera** '71 thru '85
- **38031** **Cadillac Eldorado & Seville, DeVille, Fleetwood & Olds Toronado, Buick Riviera** '86 thru '93
- **38032** **Cadillac DeVille** '94 thru '05 & **Seville** '92 thru '04 **Cadillac DTS** '06 thru '10
- **38035** **Chevrolet Lumina APV, Olds Silhouette & Pontiac Trans Sport** all models '90 thru '96
- **38036** **Chevrolet Venture, Olds Silhouette, Pontiac Trans Sport & Montana** '97 thru '05
  General Motors Full-size Rear-wheel Drive - *see BUICK (19025)*
- **38040** **Chevrolet Equinox** '05 thru '09 **Pontiac Torrent** '06 thru '09
- **38070** **Chevrolet HHR** '06 thru '11

GEO
- **Metro** - *see CHEVROLET Sprint (24075)*
- **Prizm** - '85 thru '92 see CHEVY (24060), '93 thru '02 see TOYOTA Corolla (92036)
- **40030** **Storm** all models '90 thru '93
  Tracker - *see SUZUKI Samurai (90010)*

GMC
- **Vans & Pick-ups** - *see CHEVROLET*

HONDA
- **42010** **Accord CVCC** all models '76 thru '83
- **42011** **Accord** all models '84 thru '89
- **42012** **Accord** all models '90 thru '93
- **42013** **Accord** all models '94 thru '97
- **42014** **Accord** all models '98 thru '02
- **42015** **Accord** '03 thru '07
- **42020** **Civic 1200** all models '73 thru '79
- **42021** **Civic 1300 & 1500 CVCC** '80 thru '83
- **42022** **Civic 1500 CVCC** all models '75 thru '79

(Continued on other side)

Haynes North America, Inc., 861 Lawrence Drive, Newbury Park, CA 91320-1514 • (805) 498-6703 • http://www.haynes.com

Haynes Automotive Manuals (continued)

NOTE: If you do not see a listing for your vehicle, consult your local Haynes dealer for the latest product information.

42023 **Civic** all models '84 thru '91
42024 **Civic & del Sol** '92 thru '95
42025 **Civic** '96 thru '00, **CR-V** '97 thru '01, **Acura Integra** '94 thru '00
42026 **Civic** '01 thru '10, **CR-V** '02 thru '09
42035 **Odyssey** all models '99 thru '10
  Passport - see ISUZU Rodeo (47017)
42037 **Honda Pilot** '03 thru '07, **Acura MDX** '01 thru '07
42040 **Prelude CVCC** all models '79 thru '89

HYUNDAI
43010 **Elantra** all models '96 thru '10
43015 **Excel & Accent** all models '86 thru '09
43050 **Santa Fe** all models '01 thru '06
43055 **Sonata** all models '99 thru '08

INFINITI
G35 '03 thru '08 - see NISSAN 350Z (72011)

ISUZU
Hombre - see CHEVROLET S-10 (24071)
47017 **Rodeo, Amigo & Honda Passport** '89 thru '02
47020 **Trooper & Pick-up** '81 thru '93

JAGUAR
49010 **XJ6** all 6 cyl models '68 thru '86
49011 **XJ6** all models '88 thru '94
49015 **XJ12 & XJS** all 12 cyl models '72 thru '85

JEEP
50010 **Cherokee, Comanche & Wagoneer Limited** all models '84 thru '01
50020 **CJ** all models '49 thru '86
50025 **Grand Cherokee** all models '93 thru '04
50026 **Grand Cherokee** '05 thru '09
50029 **Grand Wagoneer & Pick-up** '72 thru '91
  Grand Wagoneer '84 thru '91, **Cherokee & Wagoneer** '72 thru '83, **Pick-up** '72 thru '88
50030 **Wrangler** all models '87 thru '11
50035 **Liberty** '02 thru '07

KIA
54050 **Optima** '01 thru '10
54070 **Sephia** '94 thru '01, **Spectra** '00 thru '09, **Sportage** '05 thru '10

LEXUS
ES 300/330 - see TOYOTA Camry (92007) (92008)
RX 330 - see TOYOTA Highlander (92095)

LINCOLN
Navigator - see FORD Pick-up (36059)
59010 **Rear-Wheel Drive** all models '70 thru '10

MAZDA
61010 **GLC Hatchback** (rear-wheel drive) '77 thru '83
61011 **GLC** (front-wheel drive) '81 thru '85
61012 **Mazda3** '04 thru '11
61015 **323 & Protegé** '90 thru '03
61016 **MX-5 Miata** '90 thru '09
61020 **MPV** all models '89 thru '98
  Navajo - see Ford Explorer (36024)
61030 **Pick-ups** '72 thru '93
  Pick-ups '94 thru '00 - see Ford Ranger (36071)
61035 **RX-7** all models '79 thru '85
61036 **RX-7** all models '86 thru '91
61040 **626** (rear-wheel drive) all models '79 thru '82
61041 **626/MX-6** (front-wheel drive) '83 thru '92
61042 **626, MX-6/Ford Probe** '93 thru '02
61043 **Mazda6** '03 thru '11

MERCEDES-BENZ
63012 **123 Series Diesel** '76 thru '85
63015 **190 Series** four-cyl gas models, '84 thru '88
63020 **230/250/280** 6 cyl sohc models '68 thru '72
63025 **280** 123 Series gasoline models '77 thru '81
63030 **350 & 450** all models '71 thru '80
63040 **C-Class:** C230/C240/C280/C320/C350 '01 thru '07

MERCURY
64200 **Villager & Nissan Quest** '93 thru '01
  All other titles, see FORD Listing.

MG
66010 **MGB** Roadster & GT Coupe '62 thru '80
66015 **MG Midget, Austin Healey Sprite** '58 thru '80

MINI
67020 **Mini** '02 thru '11

MITSUBISHI
68020 **Cordia, Tredia, Galant, Precis & Mirage** '83 thru '93
68030 **Eclipse, Eagle Talon & Ply. Laser** '90 thru '94
68031 **Eclipse** '95 thru '05, **Eagle Talon** '95 thru '98
68035 **Galant** '94 thru '10
68040 **Pick-up** '83 thru '96 & **Montero** '83 thru '93

NISSAN
72010 **300ZX** all models including Turbo '84 thru '89
72011 **350Z & Infiniti G35** all models '03 thru '08
72015 **Altima** all models '93 thru '06
72016 **Altima** '07 thru '10
72020 **Maxima** all models '85 thru '92
72021 **Maxima** all models '93 thru '04
72025 **Murano** '03 thru '10
72030 **Pick-ups** '80 thru '97 **Pathfinder** '87 thru '95
72031 **Frontier Pick-up, Xterra, Pathfinder** '96 thru '04
72032 **Frontier & Xterra** '05 thru '11
72040 **Pulsar** all models '83 thru '86
  Quest - see MERCURY Villager (64200)
72050 **Sentra** all models '82 thru '94
72051 **Sentra & 200SX** all models '95 thru '06
72060 **Stanza** all models '82 thru '90
72070 **Titan pick-ups** '04 thru '10 **Armada** '05 thru '10

OLDSMOBILE
73015 **Cutlass** V6 & V8 gas models '74 thru '88
  For other OLDSMOBILE titles, see BUICK, CHEVROLET or GENERAL MOTORS listing.

PLYMOUTH
  For PLYMOUTH titles, see DODGE listing.

PONTIAC
79008 **Fiero** all models '84 thru '88
79018 **Firebird** V8 models except Turbo '70 thru '81
79019 **Firebird** all models '82 thru '92
79025 **G6** all models '05 thru '09
79040 **Mid-size Rear-wheel Drive** '70 thru '87
  Vibe '03 thru '11 - see TOYOTA Matrix (92060)
  For other PONTIAC titles, see BUICK, CHEVROLET or GENERAL MOTORS listing.

PORSCHE
80020 **911** except Turbo & Carrera 4 '65 thru '89
80025 **914** all 4 cyl models '69 thru '76
80030 **924** all models including Turbo '76 thru '82
80035 **944** all models including Turbo '83 thru '89

RENAULT
  Alliance & Encore - see AMC (14020)

SAAB
84010 **900** all models including Turbo '79 thru '88

SATURN
87010 **Saturn** all S-series models '91 thru '02
87011 **Saturn Ion** '03 thru '07
87020 **Saturn** all L-series models '00 thru '04
87040 **Saturn VUE** '02 thru '07

SUBARU
89002 **1100, 1300, 1400 & 1600** '71 thru '79
89003 **1600 & 1800** 2WD & 4WD '80 thru '94
89100 **Legacy** all models '90 thru '99
89101 **Legacy & Forester** '00 thru '06

SUZUKI
90010 **Samurai/Sidekick & Geo Tracker** '86 thru '01

TOYOTA
92005 **Camry** all models '83 thru '91
92006 **Camry** all models '92 thru '96
92007 **Camry, Avalon, Solara, Lexus ES 300** '97 thru '01
92008 **Toyota Camry, Avalon and Solara and Lexus ES 300/330** all models '02 thru '06
92009 **Camry** '07 thru '11
92015 **Celica Rear Wheel Drive** '71 thru '85
92020 **Celica Front Wheel Drive** '86 thru '99
92025 **Celica Supra** all models '79 thru '92
92030 **Corolla** all models '75 thru '79
92032 **Corolla** all rear wheel drive models '80 thru '87
92035 **Corolla** all front wheel drive models '84 thru '92
92036 **Corolla & Geo Prizm** '93 thru '02
92037 **Corolla** models '03 thru '11
92040 **Corolla Tercel** all models '80 thru '82
92045 **Corona** all models '74 thru '82
92050 **Cressida** all models '78 thru '82
92055 **Land Cruiser** FJ40, 43, 45, 55 '68 thru '82
92056 **Land Cruiser** FJ60, 62, 80, FZJ80 '80 thru '96
92060 **Matrix & Pontiac Vibe** '03 thru '11
92065 **MR2** all models '85 thru '87
92070 **Pick-up** all models '69 thru '78
92075 **Pick-up** all models '79 thru '95
92076 **Tacoma, 4Runner, & T100** '93 thru '04
92077 **Tacoma** all models '05 thru '09
92078 **Tundra** '00 thru '06 & **Sequoia** '01 thru '07
92079 **4Runner** all models '03 thru '09
92080 **Previa** all models '91 thru '95
92081 **Prius** all models '01 thru '08
92082 **RAV4** all models '96 thru '10
92085 **Tercel** all models '87 thru '94
92090 **Sienna** all models '98 thru '09
92095 **Highlander & Lexus RX-330** '99 thru '07

TRIUMPH
94007 **Spitfire** all models '62 thru '81
94010 **TR7** all models '75 thru '81

VW
96008 **Beetle & Karmann Ghia** '54 thru '79
96009 **New Beetle** '98 thru '11
96016 **Rabbit, Jetta, Scirocco & Pick-up** gas models '75 thru '92 & **Convertible** '80 thru '92
96017 **Golf, GTI & Jetta** '93 thru '98, **Cabrio** '95 thru '02
96018 **Golf, GTI, Jetta** '99 thru '05
96019 **Jetta, Rabbit, GTI & Golf** '05 thru '11
96020 **Rabbit, Jetta & Pick-up** diesel '77 thru '84
96023 **Passat** '98 thru '05, **Audi A4** '96 thru '01
96030 **Transporter 1600** all models '68 thru '79
96035 **Transporter 1700, 1800 & 2000** '72 thru '79
96040 **Type 3 1500 & 1600** all models '63 thru '73
96045 **Vanagon** all air-cooled models '80 thru '83

VOLVO
97010 **120, 130 Series & 1800 Sports** '61 thru '73
97015 **140 Series** all models '66 thru '74
97020 **240 Series** all models '76 thru '93
97040 **740 & 760 Series** all models '82 thru '88
97050 **850 Series** all models '93 thru '97

TECHBOOK MANUALS
10205 **Automotive Computer Codes**
10206 **OBD-II & Electronic Engine Management**
10210 **Automotive Emissions Control Manual**
10215 **Fuel Injection Manual** '78 thru '85
10220 **Fuel Injection Manual** '86 thru '99
10225 **Holley Carburetor Manual**
10230 **Rochester Carburetor Manual**
10240 **Weber/Zenith/Stromberg/SU Carburetors**
10305 **Chevrolet Engine Overhaul Manual**
10310 **Chrysler Engine Overhaul Manual**
10320 **Ford Engine Overhaul Manual**
10330 **GM and Ford Diesel Engine Repair Manual**
10333 **Engine Performance Manual**
10340 **Small Engine Repair Manual,** 5 HP & Less
10341 **Small Engine Repair Manual,** 5.5 - 20 HP
10345 **Suspension, Steering & Driveline Manual**
10355 **Ford Automatic Transmission Overhaul**
10360 **GM Automatic Transmission Overhaul**
10405 **Automotive Body Repair & Painting**
10410 **Automotive Brake Manual**
10411 **Automotive Anti-lock Brake (ABS) Systems**
10415 **Automotive Detailing Manual**
10420 **Automotive Electrical Manual**
10425 **Automotive Heating & Air Conditioning**
10430 **Automotive Reference Manual & Dictionary**
10435 **Automotive Tools Manual**
10440 **Used Car Buying Guide**
10445 **Welding Manual**
10450 **ATV Basics**
10452 **Scooters 50cc to 250cc**

SPANISH MANUALS
98903 **Reparación de Carrocería & Pintura**
98904 **Manual de Carburador Modelos Holley & Rochester**
98905 **Códigos Automotrices de la Computadora**
98906 **OBD-II & Sistemas de Control Electrónico del Motor**
98910 **Frenos Automotriz**
98913 **Electricidad Automotriz**
98915 **Inyección de Combustible** '86 al '99
99040 **Chevrolet & GMC Camionetas** '67 al '87
99041 **Chevrolet & GMC Camionetas** '88 al '98
99042 **Chevrolet & GMC Camionetas Cerradas** '68 al '95
99043 **Chevrolet/GMC Camionetas** '94 al '04
99048 **Chevrolet/GMC Camionetas** '99 al '06
99055 **Dodge Caravan & Plymouth Voyager** '84 al '95
99075 **Ford Camionetas y Bronco** '80 al '94
99076 **Ford F-150** '97 al '09
99077 **Ford Camionetas Cerradas** '69 al '91
99088 **Ford Modelos de Tamaño Mediano** '75 al '86
99089 **Ford Camionetas Ranger** '93 al '10
99091 **Ford Taurus & Mercury Sable** '86 al '95
99095 **GM Modelos de Tamaño Grande** '70 al '90
99100 **GM Modelos de Tamaño Mediano** '70 al '88
99106 **Jeep Cherokee, Wagoneer & Comanche** '84 al '00
99110 **Nissan Camioneta** '80 al '96, **Pathfinder** '87 al '95
99118 **Nissan Sentra** '82 al '94
99125 **Toyota Camionetas y 4Runner** '79 al '95

Over 100 Haynes motorcycle manuals also available

7-12